W9-AZL-010

BATTLEFIELDS

OF THE

CIVIL WAR

BATTLEFIELDS

OF THE

CIVIL WAR

ARNO

New York, 1979

Reprint edition, 1979 by Arno Press, Inc.

Library of Congress Cataloging in Publication Data

Main entry under title:

Battlefields of the Civil War.

Reprint of the 1961 ed. published by National
Park Service, Washington, which was issued in:
Historical handbook series.
1. United States—History—Civil War, 1861-
1865—Campaigns and battles. I. United States.
National Park Service. II. Series: United
States. National Park Service. Historical
handbook series.
E470.B3 1979   973.7'3   79-15432
ISBN 0-405-12296-9

Manufactured in the United States of America.

ONTENTS

III BATTLE OF SHILOH / 65

IV PENINSULA CAMPAIGN / 89

V SECOND BATTLE OF BULL RUN / 117

VI BATTLE OF ANTIETAM / 133

II BATTLE OF FREDERICKSBURG / 183

III BATTLE OF CHANCELLORSVILLE / 199

X BATTLE OF VICKSBURG / 211

X BATTLE OF GETTYSBURG / 265

CHAPTER I

Attack on Fort Sumter

*The housetops in Charleston during the bombardment of April
12–13, 1861.* From Harper's Weekly, May 4, 1861.

A T 4:30 A. M., APRIL 12, 1861, a mortar battery at Fort Johnson fired a shell that burst directly over Fort Sumter. This was the signal for a general bombardment by the Confederate batteries about Charleston Harbor. For 34 hours, April 12 and 13, Fort Sumter was battered with shot and shell. Then the Federal commander, Maj. Robert Anderson, agreed to evacuate; and, on April 14, he and his small garrison departed with the full honors of war. On the following day, President Abraham Lincoln issued a call for 75,000 militia. The tragedy of the American Civil War had begun.

Two years later, Fort Sumter, now a Confederate stronghold, became the scene of a stubborn defense. From April 1863 to February 1865 its garrison withstood a series of devastating bombardments and direct attacks by Federal forces from land and sea. Fort Sumter was evacuated only when Federal forces bypassed Charleston from the rear. At the end, buttressed with sand and cotton as well as its own fallen brick and masonry, it was stronger than ever militarily. And it had become a symbol of resistance and courage for the entire South.

Both the "first shot" of April 1861 and the long siege of 1863–65 are commemorated today by Fort Sumter National Monument.

Construction of Fort Sumter

". . . the character of the times particularly inculcates the lesson that, whether to prevent or repel danger, we ought not to be unprepared for it. This consideration will sufficiently recommend to Congress a liberal provision for the immediate extension and gradual completion of the works of defense, both fixed and floating, on our maritime frontier. . . ."

—President Madison to Congress,
December 5, 1815.

1

The War of 1812 had shown the gross inadequacy of the coastal defenses of the United States. The crowning indignity had been the burning of Washington. Accordingly, Congress now answered President Madison's call by setting up a military Board of Engineers for Seacoast Fortifications to devise a new system of national defense. Brig. Gen. Simon Bernard, the famed military engineer of Napoleon, was commissioned in the Corps of Engineers and assigned to the Board. Under his unofficial direction, the Board began surveying the entire coast line of the United States in 1817. The South Atlantic coast, "especially regarded as less important," was not surveyed until 1821. One fortification report, covering the Gulf coast and the Atlantic coast between Cape Hatteras and the St. Croix River, had been submitted to Congress earlier that year. Thus, not till the revised form of this report was submitted to Congress in 1826 was the possibility that the "shoal opposite [Fort Moultrie] may be occupied permanently" officially broached. This was the genesis of Fort Sumter. If the location were feasible, reported the Board, "the fortification of the harbor may be considered as an easy and simple problem." With the guns of the projected fort crossing fire with those of Fort

The rock-ring of Fort Sumter's foundation as it looked 4 years after operations were begun. Courtesy National Archives.

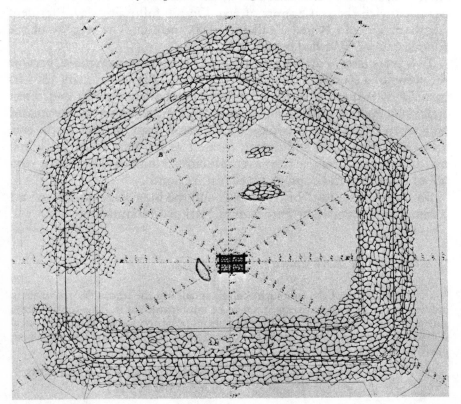

Moultrie, the commercial city of Charleston would be most effectively protected against attack.

Plans for the new fort were drawn up in 1827 and adopted on December 5, 1828. In the course of that winter Lt. Henry Brewerton, Corps of Engineers, assumed charge of the project and active operations were commenced. Progress was slow, however, and as late as 1834 the new fort was no more than a hollow pentagonal rock "mole" 2 feet above low water and open at one side to permit supply ships to pass to the interior. Meanwhile, it had been named Sumter in honor of Thomas Sumter, of South Carolina, the "Gamecock" of the Revolution.

Late in the autumn of 1834 operations were suddenly suspended. Ownership of the site was in question. In the preceding May, one William Laval, resident of Charleston, had secured from the State a conveniently vague grant to 870 acres of "land" in Charleston Harbor. In November, acting under this grant, Laval notified the representative of the United States Engineers at Fort Johnson of his claim to the site of Fort Sumter. In the meantime, the South Carolina Legislature had become curious about the operations in Charleston Harbor. Late in

First-floor plan, Fort Sumter, March 1861. The Gorge (designed for officers' quarters) is at the base of the plan. Gun casemates line the other four sides. The fort magazines were at either extremity of the Gorge in both casemate tiers. Courtesy National Archives.

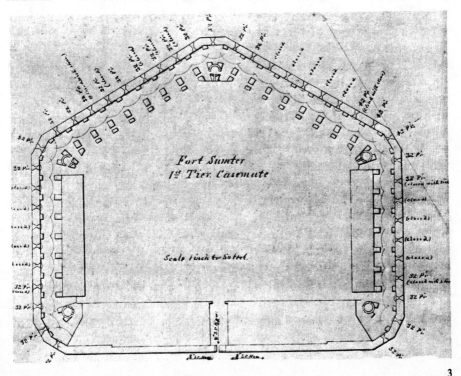

November, inquiry had been instituted as to "whether the creation of an Island on a shoal in the Channel, may not injuriously affect the navigation and commerce of [Charleston] Harbor. . . ." Reporting the following month, the Committee on Federal Relations had made the ominous pronouncement that they had not "been able to ascertain by what authority the Government have assumed to erect the works alluded to. . . ." Apparently under the impression that a formal deed of cession to "land" ordinarily covered with water had not been necessary, the Federal Government had commenced operations at the mouth of Charleston Harbor without consulting the State of South Carolina.

It was not until January 1841 that work was resumed on the site of Fort Sumter. Laval's claim was invalidated by the State attorney general under act of the South Carolina Legislature, December 20, 1837. But the harbor issue remained and was complicated still further by a memorial presented to the legislature by James C. Holmes, Charleston lawyer, on that same date. Not before November 22, 1841, was the Federal Government's title to 125 acres of harbor "land" recorded in the office of the Secretary of State of South Carolina.

Under the skilful guidance of Capt. A. H. Bowman, the work was now pushed forward. The original plans were changed in several respects. Perhaps the most important modification was with respect to the foundation. Instead of a "grillage of continuous square timbers" upon the rock mass, Bowman's idea of laying several courses of granite blocks was adopted, in the main. Bowman had feared the complete destruction of the wood by worms; and palmetto, which might have resisted such attack, had not the compactness of fiber or the necessary strength to support the weight of the superstructure.

The work was difficult. The granite of the foundation, for example, was laid between high and low watermarks, and there were periods of time when the tide permitted no work to be done at all. Yellow fever was a recurrent problem; so was the excessive heat of the Charleston summers. Much of the building material had to be brought in from the north. The magnitude of the task is indicated by the quantities involved: about 10,000 tons of granite (some of it from as far away as the Penobscot River region in Maine) and well over 60,000 tons of other rock. Bricks, shells, and sand could be obtained locally, but even here there were problems. Local brickyard capacities were small and millions of bricks were required. Similarly, hundreds of thousands of bushels of shells were needed—for concrete, for the foundation of the first-tier casemate floors, and for use in the parade fill next to the enrockment. Even the actual delivery of supplies, however local in origin, was a problem, for then, as now, Fort Sumter was a difficult spot at which to land.

Fort Sumter in December 1860 was a five-sided brick masonry fort designed for three tiers of guns. Its 5-foot-thick outer walls, towering nearly 50 feet above low water, enclosed a parade ground of roughly 1 acre. Along four of the walls extended two tiers of arched gunrooms.

Spiking the guns at Fort Moultrie, just prior to departure for Fort Sumter, December 26, 1860. From Frank Leslie's Illustrated Newspaper, January 5, 1861.

Officers' quarters lined the fifth side—the 316.7-foot gorge. This wall was to be armed only along the parapet. Three-story brick barracks for the enlisted garrison paralleled the gunrooms on each flank. At the center of the gorge was the sally port. It opened on the 25½-foot-wide stone esplanade that extended the length of that wall and on a 171-foot wharf.

Fort Sumter was unfinished when, late in December, gathering events prompted its occupation by artillery troops. Eight-foot-square openings yawned in place of gun embrasures on the second tier. Of the 135 guns planned for the gunrooms and the open terreplein above, only 15 had been mounted. Most of these were "32 pounders"; none was heavier. Various details of the interior finish of barracks, quarters, and gunrooms were incomplete. Congressional economies had had their effect, as much as difficulties of construction. As late as 1858 and 1859, work had been virtually at a standstill for lack of funds.

On December 20, 1860, South Carolina seceded from the Union. On the night of the 26th, fearing attack by the excited populace, Maj. Robert Anderson removed the small garrison he commanded at Fort Moultrie to Fort Sumter out in the harbor. Ignorant of an apparent pledge to maintain the harbor *status quo*, given by President Buchanan some weeks before, Anderson moved in accordance with instructions received December 11, which read:

". . . you are to hold possession of the forts in this harbor, and if attacked you are to defend yourself to the last extremity. The smallness of your force will not permit you, perhaps, to occupy more than one of the three forts, but an attack on or attempt to take possession of any one of them will be regarded as an act of hostility, and you may then put your command into either of them which you may deem most proper to increase its power of resistance. You are also authorized to take similar steps whenever you have tangible evidence of a design to proceed to a hostile act."

Anderson thought he had "tangible evidence" of hostile intent, both towards Fort Moultrie—an old fort most vulnerable to land attack—and towards unoccupied Fort Sumter. He moved now "to prevent the effusion of blood" and because he was certain "that if attacked my men must have been sacrificed, and the command of the harbor lost." To Anderson, a Kentuckian married to a Georgia girl, preservation of peace was of paramount importance. At the same time, a veteran soldier of "unquestioned loyalty," he had a duty to perform.

Charleston was filled with excitement and rage. Crowds collected in the streets; military organizations paraded; and "loud and violent were the expressions of feeling against Major Anderson and his action."

There was almost as much consternation in Washington as in Charleston. Senators calling at the White House found President Buchanan greatly agitated. He stood by the mantelpiece, crushing a cigar in the palm of one hand, and stammered that the move was against his policy. The cabinet was called into session, and on December 27, Secretary of War Floyd wired Major Anderson:

"Intelligence has reached here this morning that you have abandoned Fort Moultrie, . . . and gone to Fort Sumter. It is not believed, because there is no order for any such movement. Explain the meaning of this report."

South Carolina regarded Anderson's move not only as an "outrageous breach of faith," but as an act of aggression, and demanded, through commissioners, that the United States Government evacuate Charleston Harbor. President Buchanan, anxious to conciliate as well as maintain authority, wavered. Cabinet pressures were brought to bear. Meanwhile, on the 27th, South Carolina volunteers seized Castle Pinckney and Fort Moultrie. On the 28th, the President refused to accede to South Carolina's demand.

The North was exultant. Amid cheers for Major Anderson, salvos of artillery resounded in northern cities on New Year's Day, 1861. By

Maj. Robert Anderson. From Lossing, *A History of the Civil War.*

an imposing majority, the House of Representatives voted approval of Major Anderson's "bold and patriotic" act.

At Fort Sumter, Major Anderson had two companies of the First United States Artillery—about 85 officers and men in a fortification intended for as many as 650. He had only "about 4 months" supply of provisions for his command. The question of reenforcement and supply was to trouble all the remaining days of the Buchanan administration and to carry over to the succeeding administration. In it were the seeds of war.

The Star of the West

President Buchanan was persuaded to send off a relief expedition almost immediately. Initial plans called for the dispatch of the sloop of war *Brooklyn* for this purpose, but when word came which indicated that the South Carolinians had obstructed the harbor entrance by sinking several ships, it was decided to use an ordinary merchant ship. The *Brooklyn,* of heavy draft, could probably not now pass into the harbor. A merchant ship would certainly excite less suspicion and would avoid the appearance of a coercive movement. Accordingly, the *Star of the West*—a ship which regularly sailed southward from New York—was chartered. Two hundred men, small arms and ammunition, and several months' provisions were placed aboard. The men were to remain below deck on entering Charleston Harbor; the *Brooklyn* would follow, in case the *Star of the West* were fired upon and disabled.

But Charleston was forewarned. When the *Star of the West* appeared at the entrance of the harbor on January 9, 1861, Citadel cadets opened fire

The Star of the West. From *Battles and Leaders of the Civil War.*

with a gun mounted on Cummings Point; and the merchant ship, unarmed, steamed out of the harbor. Anderson had held his fire, thinking the firing unauthorized by the State authorities. Orders authorizing supporting fire on his part had failed to reach him in time. As if accidentally, civil war had been averted for the moment.

There was some Northern reaction to the incident, but further plans for Anderson's relief, once projected, were delayed. Anderson indicated no immediate need, and President Buchanan was anxious to end his term of office in peace. On January 10, the Secretary of War had ordered Major Anderson to act "strictly on the defensive." Anderson and Governor Pickens of South Carolina exchanged angry letters, and the Governor's demand for the fort's surrender (January 11) was resolved in the "mission" to Washington of the State's attorney general, I. G. Hayne. When that mission, tempered by the efforts of cooler-headed Southern Senators, met stubborn resistance on the part of President Buchanan, the situation was resolved in the formation of the Southern Confederacy, with the consequent assumption of the Fort Sumter problem by that government.

Preparations for War

Fort Sumter was now preparing for attack. Thirty-eight more guns were mounted in the first tier of casemates and along the parapet, including heavier "42 pounders" and Columbiads. Five Columbiads were mounted in the parade as mortars and three howitzers about the sally port in the gorge. By April 12, a total of 60 guns was ready. "Bombproof" shelters and "splinter-proof" traverses were constructed on the parade ground and along the parapet. Overhanging galleries were built out from the parapet at strategic points for dropping shells on an assaulting force. Special protection was given the gateway. Left unarmed, however, was the second tier of casemates; the 8-foot-square openings in the outer wall were bricked up. The small size of Major Anderson's garrison did not permit manning it.

Charleston, too, prepared. In addition to routine preparations at Castle Pinckney and Fort Moultrie, additional batteries were prepared on Sullivan's Island, at Cummings Point on Morris Island, and outside Fort Johnson. An "ironclad" Columbiad battery, constructed of inclined logs plated with iron, was mounted at Cummings Point. Meanwhile, Governor Pickens permitted Anderson to buy fresh meat and vegetables in town to supplement his garrison "issue" supply.

On February 4, 1861, delegates from six seceding States—South Carolina, Georgia, Florida, Alabama, Mississippi, and Louisiana—had met at Montgomery, Ala., to form the Confederate government. A constitution had been adopted and Jefferson Davis, of Mississippi, had been elected President and inaugurated on February 18. Texas came into the Confederacy on March 2. By this time all forts, arsenals, and navy yards in the seceding States had been seized by the Confederate government without resistance, except Fort Pickens on Pensacola Bay in Florida, two minor forts (Jefferson and Taylor) on and near the Florida coast, and Fort Sumter. Because of its association with the "hotbed of secession" and because of Major Anderson's dramatic move, Fort Sumter had assumed undeserved importance.

On March 3, Brig. Gen. P. G. T. Beauregard took command of the Confederate troops at Charleston. Like Major Anderson, Beauregard was a veteran of the Mexican War. He was a member of a Louisiana family of distinguished French lineage. Late captain in the United States Army, he had served briefly as superintendent of the United States Military Academy at West Point as recently as January. Once, years back, he had studied artillery there under Major Anderson; now, pupil confronted master.

Lincoln Orders a Relief Expedition to Fort Sumter

On March 4, Abraham Lincoln assumed office as President of the United States. In a firm, but generally conciliatory, inaugural address, he made it clear that national authority must be upheld against the threat of disunion. As to the Federal forts and property in the seceded States he said: "The power confided to me will be used to hold, occupy, and possess the property and places belonging to the Government. . . ." He did not say "repossess." Furthermore, there needed to be "no bloodshed or violence" as the result of this policy "unless it be forced upon the national authority." The President concluded:

Confederate preparations at Cummings Point, Morris Island. The inclined Ironclad Battery is at the left. From Frank Leslie's Illustrated Newspaper, March 30, 1861.

*In the face of war preparations, wives and children leave Fort
Sumter, February 3, 1861.* From Frank Leslie's Illustrated Newspaper, February 23, 1861.

"In your hands, my dissatisfied fellow-countrymen, and not in mine, is the momentous issue of civil war. The Government will not assail you. You can have no
conflict without being yourselves the aggressors. You have no oath registered in
Heaven to destroy the Government, while I shall have the most solemn one to
'preserve, protect, and defend' it."

The Sumter situation was placed squarely before Lincoln on the day
he assumed office. On the morning of Inaugural Day the outgoing Secretary of War received a dispatch from Major Anderson at Fort Sumter
indicating that the remainder of the "issue" rations brought over from
Fort Moultrie in December would last only a few more weeks. Meanwhile, in the face of local preparations, an estimated force of 20,000 men
would now be needed to reenforce and supply Fort Sumter. It was clear
that if Anderson's local "fresh food" supply were cut off, he would soon
be in a desperate state. At the same time, it seemed almost equally clear
that a relief expedition would be an impossibility. The entire Army of
the United States numbered less than 16,000 men. "Evacuation seems
almost inevitable," wrote General Scott; the majority of Lincoln's Cabinet agreed. But Lincoln investigated further. In the meantime, reassured

11

Brig. Gen. Pierre Gustave Toutant Beauregard. Courtesy National Archives.

by Secretary of State Seward as well as by others, the South came to believe Fort Sumter would be evacuated.

On April 4, President Lincoln sent word to Major Anderson that an attempt would be made to supply Fort Sumter with provisions "and, in case the effort is resisted . . . to reenforce you." Convinced from "on the spot" reports that such an expedition was feasible, and that there was no Union sentiment in South Carolina to which to appeal, Lincoln had decided upon the nearest thing to preserving the *status quo*. Merchant steamers under cover of ships of war would carry "subsistence and other supplies" to Anderson; the ships of war (with troop reenforcements) would be used only if a peaceable landing were opposed. Capt. G. V. Fox, long an advocate of a relief expedition, would command. Meanwhile, in accordance with pledge already given, the Governor of South Carolina would be carefully informed in advance.

The announcement of the expedition to supply Fort Sumter was the spark that set off the explosive forces which had been building up since 1850. The Confederate capital at Montgomery was informed. Anderson's "fresh" provision supply had already been cut off on the 7th; now, his mail was seized.

Work was pushed on the harbor fortifications. A new battery mounting two "24 pounders" and two "32 pounders" was unmasked on Sullivan's Island; another ironclad battery was put into position at its western tip. Originally designed to be "floating," this battery mounted two heavy "42 pounders" in addition to two "32 pounders." Near Mount Pleasant another (10-inch) mortar battery was installed. At Fort Moultrie, 11 guns now bore on Fort Sumter, including three 8-inch Columbiads. Additional guns were mounted to command the channels and to guard against landings by the fleet. Three thousand more troops were called, to be added to the 3,700 already on the post. The harbor seethed with activity.

"The gage is thrown down," said the Charleston *Mercury*, "and we accept the challenge. We will meet the invader, and God and Battle must decide the issue between the hirelings of Abolition hate and Northern tyranny, and the people of South Carolina defending their freedom and their homes."

Now, just in time, a small (12-pounder Blakely) rifled gun arrived from England as a gift of a Charlestonian, resident in London. It was mounted at Cummings Point, ominous forerunner of the powerful rifled guns that 2 years later would reduce Fort Sumter to ruin.

The Confederates Demand Fort Sumter's Evacuation

After cabinet debate in Montgomery, the Confederate Secretary of War ordered General Beauregard to demand the evacuation of the fort, and if that demand were refused, to "reduce it." On the afternoon of April 11, three of Beauregard's aides visited the fort under a flag of truce and presented the ultimatum. Major Anderson refused compliance, but at the

Artist's conception of the Confederate floating battery. The structure at the right was designed to be a hospital. From Frank Leslie's Illustrated Newspaper, March 30, 1861.

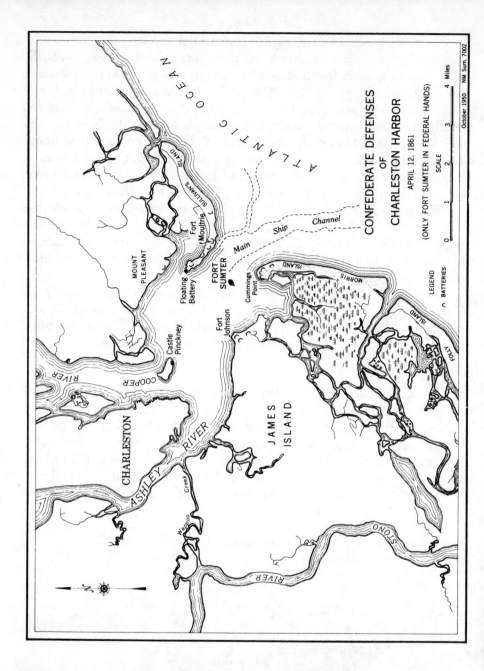

CONFEDERATE DEFENSES
OF
CHARLESTON HARBOR
APRIL 12, 1861
(ONLY FORT SUMTER IN FEDERAL HANDS)

SCALE
0   1   2   3   4 Miles

October 1950   NM Sum. 7002

LEGEND
^ BATTERIES

same time he said, "Gentlemen, if you do not batter the fort to pieces about us, we shall be starved out in a few days." Still reluctant to initiate conflict, the Montgomery government telegraphed:

"Do not desire needlessly to bombard Fort Sumter. If Major Anderson will state the time at which . . . he will evacuate, and agree that in the meantime he will not use his guns against us unless ours should be employed against Fort Sumter, you are authorized thus to avoid the effusion of blood. If this or its equivalent be refused, reduce the fort. . . ."

The atmosphere in Charleston was tense. In at least one household, dinner was the "merriest, maddest . . . yet. Men were more audaciously wise and witty. We had an unspoken foreboding it was to be our last pleasant meeting."

Shortly after midnight, four Confederate officers confronted Major Anderson again. About 3 hours later, in a carefully worded reply, the Union commander agreed to evacuate "by noon on the 15th" unless he should receive prior to that time "controlling instructions from my Government or additional supplies." But it was expected in Charleston that the Federal supply ships would arrive before the 15th. Major Anderson's reply was rejected by the Confederate officers, who proceeded at once to Fort Johnson to give the order to open fire.

The War Begins—April 12, 1861

"I count four by St. Michael's chimes, and I begin to hope. At half past four, the heavy booming of a cannon! I sprang out of bed and on my knees, prostrate, I prayed as I never prayed before."

At 4:30 a. m., a mortar at Fort Johnson fired a shell which arched across the sky and burst almost directly over Fort Sumter. This was the signal for opening the bombardment. Within a few minutes, a ring of guns and mortars about the harbor—43 in all—were firing at Sumter.

Artist's conception of the bombardment of Fort Sumter, April 12, 1861. Fort Johnson is in the foreground. From Harper's Weekly, April 27, 1861.

Major Anderson withheld fire until about 7 o'clock. Then Capt. Abner Doubleday, of latter-day baseball fame, fired a shot at the Ironclad Battery on Cummings Point. Ominously, the light shot "bounded off from the sloping roof . . . without producing any apparent effect." Not at any time during the battle did the guns of Fort Sumter do great damage to the Confederate defenses. Most of Fort Sumter's heaviest guns were on the parapet and in the parade, and, to reduce casualties in the small garrison, Major Anderson ordered these left unmanned. For a while, with the help of the 43 engineer workmen remaining at the fort, 9 or 10 of the casemate guns were manned. But by noon, the expenditure of ammunition was so much more rapid than the manufacture of new cartridge bags that the firing was restricted to 6 guns only. Meanwhile

"Showers of balls from 10-inch Columbiads and 42 pounders, and shells from [10] inch mortars poured into the fort in one incessant stream, causing great flakes of masonry to fall in all directions. When the immense mortar shells, after sailing high in the air, came down in a vertical direction, and buried themselves in the parade ground, their explosion shook the fort like an earthquake."

All Charleston watched. Business was entirely suspended. King Street was deserted. The Battery, the wharves and shipping, and "every steeple and cupalo in the city" were crowded with anxious spectators. And "never before had such crowds of ladies without attendants" visited the streets of Charleston. "The women were wild" on the housetops. In the darkness before dawn there were "Prayers from the women and imprecations from the men; and then a shell would light up the scene." As the

Preparing to fire the first shot from Fort Sumter, April 12, 1861. Contemporary artist's conception. Courtesy Charleston Library Society.

The bombardment of Fort Sumter, April 13, 1861.

day advanced, the city became rife with rumors: "Tonight, they say, the forces are to attempt to land. The *Harriet Lane* had her wheel house smashed and put back to sea. . . . We hear nothing, can listen to nothing. Boom boom goes the cannon all the time. The nervous strain is awful. . . ." Volunteers rushed to join their companies. There was "Stark Means marching under the piazza at the head of his regiment . . . ," his proud mother leaning over the balcony rail "looking with tearful eyes." Two members of the Palmetto Guards paid $50 for a boat to carry them to Morris Island.

The barracks at Fort Sumter caught fire three times that first day, but each time the fire was extinguished. One gun on the parapet was dismounted; another damaged. The wall about one embrasure was shattered to a depth of 20 inches. That was the Blakely rifle, in part, firing with "the accuracy of a duelling pistol." The quarters on the gorge were completely riddled. When night descended, dark and stormy, Fort Sumter's fire ceased entirely. With the six needles available, the work of making cartridge bags went forward; blankets, old clothing, extra hospital sheets,

Col. Louis T. Wigfall.

and even paper, were used in the emergency. In the meantime, the supply fleet, off the bar since the onset of hostilities, did no more than maintain its position. It had been crippled upon departure when Seward's meddling had caused withdrawal of the powerful warship *Powhatan*. Now, bad weather prevented even a minimum supporting operation.

On the morning of the 13th, Sumter opened "early and spitefully," and, with the increased supply of cartridges, for a while kept up a brisk fire. About midmorning hot shot set fire to the officers' quarters. The Confederate fire then increased; soon the whole extent of the quarters was in flames; the powder magazines were in danger. The blaze spread to the barracks. By noon the fort was almost uninhabitable. The men crowded to the embrasures for air or lay on the ground with handkerchiefs over their mouths. For a time the fort continued to fire; valiant efforts had saved some of the powder before the onrush of the flames forced the closing of the magazines. Meanwhile, at every shot, the Confederate troops, "carried away by their natural generous impulses," mounted the different batteries and "cheered the garrison for its pluck and gallantry and hooted the fleet lying inactive just outside the bar."

About 1:30 in the afternoon the flag was shot down. Almost accidentally, this led to surrender. By authority of General Simons, commanding

Interior of Fort Sumter after the bombardment of April 1861. The Left Flank barrack is at the left; the Left Face is at the right. From G. S. Crawford, *The Genesis of the Civil War.*

Interior of the Gorge after the April 1861 bombardment. Parade entrance to sally port is at center.

on Morris Island, Col. Louis T. Wigfall, one of General Beauregard's aides detached for duty at that spot, set out by small boat to ascertain whether Major Anderson would capitulate. Till recently, Wigfall had been United States Senator from Texas. Before he arrived at the beleaguered fort, the United States flag was again flying, but Wigfall continued on. The firing continued from the batteries across the harbor. Once through an embrasure on the Left Flank, white handkerchief on the point of his sword, Colonel Wigfall offered the Federal commander any terms he desired, only "the precise nature of which" would have to be arranged with General Beauregard. Anderson accepted on the basis of Beauregard's original terms: evacuation with his command, taking arms and all private and company property, saluting the United States flag as it was lowered, and being conveyed, if desired, to a Northern port. The white flag went up again; the firing ceased. Wigfall departed confident that Anderson had surrendered unconditionally. He and his boatman were borne ashore "in triumph."

Meanwhile, officers had arrived at the fort direct from General Beauregard's headquarters in Charleston. From these men, dispatched to offer assistance to the Federal commander, Anderson learned that Wigfall's action was unauthorized; that, indeed, the colonel had not seen the Commanding General since the start of the battle. From another party

Exterior of the Gorge after the April 1861 bombardment. The sally port is at the left.

Rear Adm. Samuel F. Du Pont. From Johnson, *The Defense of Charleston Harbor.*

of officers he learned Beauregard's exact terms of surrender. They failed to include the privilege of saluting the flag, though in all other respects they were the same as those Anderson believed he had accepted from Wigfall. Impetuously, Anderson had first declared he would run up his flag again. Then, restrained by Beauregard's aides, he waited while his request for permission to salute the flag was conveyed to the Commanding General. In the course of the afternoon, General Beauregard courteously sent over a fire engine from the city. About 7:30 that evening, Beauregard's chief of staff returned with word that Major Anderson's request would be granted and the terms offered on the 11th would be faithfully adhered to. The engagement was officially at an end. During the 34-hour bombardment, more than 3,000 shells had been hurled at the fort.

On Sunday, April 14, Major Anderson and his garrison marched out of the fort with drums beating and colors flying and boarded ship to join the Federal fleet off the bar. On the 50th round of what was to have been a 100-gun salute to the United States flag, there occurred the only fatality of the engagement. The premature discharge of a gun and the explosion of a pile of cartridges resulted in the death of Pvt. Daniel Hough. Another man, mortally wounded, died several days later. The 50th round was the last. Now, as the steamer *Isabel* went down the channel, the soldiers of the Confederate batteries on Cummings Point lined the beach, silent, heads uncovered.

The following day, April 15, 1861, Abraham Lincoln issued a call for 75,000 militia. Civil war, so long dreaded, had begun. The States of Virginia, Arkansas, Tennessee, and North Carolina now joined the Confederacy.

Charleston and the Federal Blockade—1861–63

With Fort Sumter in Confederate hands, the port of Charleston became a most irritating loophole in the Federal naval blockade of the Atlantic coast—doubly irritating because at Charleston "rebellion first lighted the flame of civil war." As late as January 1863, it was reported that "vessels ply to and from Charleston and Nassau [Bahamas] with the certainty and promptness of a regular line." In 2 months of the spring following, 21 Confederate vessels cleared Charleston and 15 came in. Into Charleston came needed war supplies; out went cotton in payment.

Capture of Port Royal Harbor on November 7, 1861, by a Federal fleet under Capt. Samuel F. Du Pont, however, had made possible land and sea operations against Charleston. In June 1862, an attempt was made by Maj. Gen. D. H. Hunter to push through to Charleston by James Island on the south. This ended in Union disaster at Secessionville. Meanwhile, the *Monitor-Merrimac* action in Hampton Roads had indicated the feasibility of a naval "ironclad" expedition against Fort Sumter, the key to the harbor. Sumter, now largely rebuilt, had become a formidable work armed with some 95 guns and garrisoned with upwards of 500 men. In May 1862, the Navy Department had determined to capture Charleston "as soon as Richmond falls." To Du Pont, who was now rear admiral, there seemed to be a "morbid appetite in the land to have Charleston." The War Department, meanwhile, far from supplying additional troops to General Hunter's command in South Carolina, withdrew units to reenforce General McClellan in Virginia.

Federal Ironclads Attack Fort Sumter

On April 5, 1863, a fleet of 9 Federal ironclads, armed with 32 guns "of the heaviest calibres ever used in war," appeared off Charleston bar. Seven were of the single-turret "cheesebox on a raft" monitor type; one was a double-turreted affair; the flagship *New Ironsides* was an ironclad frigate. With the ebb tide, on the afternoon of the 7th, the "newfangled" ironclads steamed single file up the main ship channel east of Morris Island.

Contemporary artist's conception of Ironclad attack, April 7, 1863. The flagship New Ironsides *is at left center.* From Harper's Weekly, May 2, 1863.

The weather was clear and bright; the water "as stable as of a river." By 3 o'clock, the *Weehawken*, the leading monitor, had come within range, and Fort Moultrie opened fire. The *Passaic*, second in line, responded. Fort Sumter held fire, guns trained on a buoy at the turn of the channel. When the *Weehawken* came abreast of that point, all the guns atop Sumter's right flank let loose, followed by all the guns on Sullivan's Island, at Fort Moultrie, and at Cummings Point that could be brought to bear.

It was too much for the ironclads, slow and unwieldy, possessed of limited vision, and operating in a narrow and uncertain channel. In the course of the 2½-hour fight, only one came as close as 900 yards to Fort Sumter. To the 2,209 rounds hurled against them, the ironclads were able to return only 154, of which only 34 found the target. These breached and loosened the right flank parapet for a length of 25 feet and pocked the walls elsewhere with craters up to 2½ feet deep. But it was far from enough; Fort Sumter remained strong and secure. In the meantime, five of the ironclads were seriously disabled by the accurate fire, and one, the *Keokuk*, sank the following morning in the shallow water off Morris Island. In a daring exploit sometime later, Confederate troops recovered the guns of the *Keokuk* and mounted one at Fort Sumter.

Admiral Du Pont had "attempted to take the bull by the horns but had failed." The North, so confident of victory, was stunned at a time when the general military situation gave cause for gloom. The war in the East had been bloody and indecisive till now; the news from the West was bad.

Federal authorities looked to a combined operation to seize Morris Island and from there demolish Fort Sumter. With Fort Sumter reduced, the harbor could be entered.

The Morris Island Approach to Fort Sumter

Folly Island and Cole's Island, next south of Morris Island, had been occupied by Northern troops just prior to the naval attack. In June and July, the northern end of Folly Island was fortified. In a remarkable operation, 47 guns and mortars were secretly placed "within speaking distance of the enemy's pickets." Some 11,000 men were concentrated on the island. Brig. Gen. Quincy A. Gillmore, the "breacher" of Fort Pulaski, assumed command on June 12. Rear Adm. John A. Dahlgren superseded Admiral Du Pont on July 6.

During that time the Confederates mounted guns at the southern end of Morris Island and built up the earthworks at its upper end—Battery Gregg at Cummings Point and Battery Wagner some 1,400 yards to the south. The latter work, commanding the island at its narrowest point, was made into a formidable "sand fort" mounting about 15 guns.

Fort Sumter, 1,390 yards distant from Battery Gregg, prepared for siege, too. Brick and stone masonry "counterforts," already built at each extremity of the esplanade as protection for the magazines, were now strengthened, and much of the remaining gorge exterior was sandbagged,

Col. Alfred Rhett. From Johnson, *The Defense of Charleston Harbor.*

Bvt. Maj. Gen. Quincy A. Gillmore. From Johnson, *The Defense of Charleston Harbor.*

or otherwise protected. The casemates on the right flank ("sea front") were filled with sand, and the rooms on the gorge were filled with damp cotton bales laid in sand. The upper-tier magazines were abandoned and filled with sandbags to protect the magazines below. Protective revetments and defensive devices of various sorts were introduced at various points throughout the fort. During this period the garrison was host at frequent intervals to officers on leave, citizens of Charleston, and even many ladies, who came to see the scars of the April battle, to admire the drill, or to observe the preparations. At the end of June 1863, Fort Sumter was garrisoned with 5 companies (perhaps 500 men) of the First South Carolina Artillery, under the command of Col. Alfred Rhett. Its armament, meanwhile, had been reduced to 68 guns and mortars, many of the finest pieces having been removed to strengthen other fortifications about the harbor.

On the morning of July 10, 3,000 Union infantrymen, supported by the artillery on Folly Island and the guns of 4 monitors, descended on the southern end of Morris Island. Brig. Gen. Truman Seymour, a company commander at Fort Sumter 2 years before, commanded the assault. Within 4 hours, three-fourths of Morris Island was in his hands. Hopelessly outgunned and outmanned, the Confederate forces fell back to Battery Wagner. The guns of Fort Sumter helped to cover the retreat.

A "desperate" assault upon Wagner the following morning failed, though the parapet was briefly gained. General Gillmore established counterbatteries and tried again on the 18th. From noon until nightfall that day "without cessation or intermission," Federal guns poured a "storm of shot and shell upon Fort Wagner . . . perhaps unequalled in history"; then, some 6,000 troops assaulted—in the van, the 54th Massachusetts, "the first colored regiment of the North to go to war." In a short savage struggle, Seymour's force suffered 1,500 casualties. Though one angle of the fort was gained and held for a time, the attack was repulsed.

Thwarted in his plan to secure easy possession of Morris Island as a base for breaching operations against Fort Sumter, General Gillmore now determined to attempt that fort's reduction from the ground already in his possession. Batteries Wagner and Gregg would be taken by protracted siege operations. At Fort Sumter, removal of guns and ammunition continued apace. Anticipating that Sumter was "liable to be silenced sooner or later," and fearing attack at other points about the harbor, the Confederate authorities husbanded their resources. By mid-August, Fort Sumter's armament was reduced to a safe minimum of 38 guns and 2 mortars.

At distances of 2 to 2½ miles from Fort Sumter—distances extraordinary for such operations—Gillmore set up eight batteries of heavy rifled cannon. In the marsh west of Morris Island, where the mud was "like liquid," his engineers successfully emplaced a "200 pounder" to fire on Charleston; this was to be the notorious "Swamp Angel."

The first great breech in Fort Sumter's walls. Left Face interior, August 20, 1863. From an original photograph by G. S. Cook. Courtesy Mrs. T. R. Simmons, Charleston.

The First Great Bombardment of Fort Sumter

After some experimental firing starting August 12, the bombardment of Fort Sumter began in earnest on August 17. Nearly 1,000 shells were hurled at the fort that first day; nearly 5,000 more during the week following. Even at the end of the first day it was obvious that Fort Sumter was never intended to withstand "200 pound Yankee Parrotts." Then, 3 days later, a 13-ton monster throwing 250-pound shells was added, making 18 rifled cannon in action. Because of the range involved, the fort could not reply to the land batteries, and the monitors presented themselves only fleetingly.

On the 21st, with the "Swamp Angel" in position, Gillmore demanded the evacuation of Fort Sumter and Morris Island, threatening direct fire on the city of Charleston. Gillmore's ultimatum was unsigned, and General Beauregard was absent from his headquarters; but before confirmation could be secured, Gillmore had opened fire on the city. But little damage had been done when, on the 36th round, the "Swamp Angel" burst. Meanwhile, Beauregard had delivered an indignant reply. The bombardment of Fort Sumter continued.

By the 24th, General Gillmore was able to report the "practical demolition" of the fort. On that date, only one gun remained "serviceable in action." On the morning of the 23d, against Dahlgren's ironclads, Fort Sumter had fired what were to be its last shots in action. Its brick masonry walls were shattered and undermined; a breach 8 by 10 feet yawned in the upper casemates of the left face; at points, the sloped debris of the walls already provided a practicable route for assault.

Still, the Confederate garrison, supplemented by a force of 200 to 400 Negroes, labored night and day, strengthening and repairing. The debris, accumulating above the sand- and cotton-filled rooms, itself bolstered the crumbling walls. On August 26, General Beauregard ordered Fort Sumter held "to the last extremity."

The bombardment continued sporadically during the week following. On the night of September 1–2, the ironclads moved against the fort—the first major naval operation against Fort Sumter since the preceding April. Attempts earlier in the week had been thwarted by circumstance; now, conditions were right. For 5 hours, the frigate *New Ironsides* and five monitors bombarded the fort, now without a gun with which to reply to the "sneaking sea-devils." Two hundred and forty-five shot and shell were hurled against the ruin—twice as many as were thrown in the April attack. Then, tidal conditions, as much as a "rapid and sustained" fire from Fort Moultrie, forced the monitors' withdrawal.

Maj. Stephen Elliott. From Johnson, *The Defense of Charleston Harbor.*

Shell from the monitor Weehawken *exploding on the interior of Fort Sumter, September 8, 1863.* From an original photograph by G. S. Cook, Courtesy Charleston Chapter No. 4, United Daughters of the Confederacy.

Some desultory firing on the 2d brought to a close the first sustained bombardment of Fort Sumter. Over 7,300 rounds had been hurled against the fort since the opening of fire on August 17. With the fort, to all intents, reduced to a "shapeless and harmless mass of ruins," the Federal commanders now concentrated on Battery Wagner, to which General Gillmore's sappers had come within 100 yards.

On the morning of September 5, Federal cannoneers commenced a devastating barrage against that work. For 42 hours, night and day, in a spectacle "of surpassing sublimity and grandeur," 17 mortars and 9 rifled cannon, as well as the powerful guns of the ironclads, pounded the earthwork. Calcium lights "turned night into day." On the night of September 6–7, the Confederate garrisons at Wagner and Gregg evacuated; Morris Island, after 58 days, was at last in the hands of Union troops. Just three-quarters of a mile away stood Fort Sumter.

Sumter remained defiant. When Admiral Dahlgren demanded the fort's surrender, on the morning of the 7th, General Beauregard sent word that the admiral could have it when he could "take it and hold it." On September 4 the garrison had been relieved with fresh troops—320 strong. Maj. Stephen Elliott succeeded to the command.

Admiral Dahlgren "immediately designed to put into operation a plan to capture Fort Sumter." As a preliminary, the monitor *Weehawken* was ordered to pass in around Cummings Point "to cut off all communication by that direction." Later in the day, the *New Ironsides* and the remaining ironclads were to move up "to feel, and if possible, pass" the obstructions believed to be in the channel north of Sumter. But the *Weehawken* grounded, and the monitors caught such a severe fire from Fort Moultrie and the other Confederate batteries on Sullivan's Island, that Admiral Dahlgren "deemed it best to give [his] entire attention to

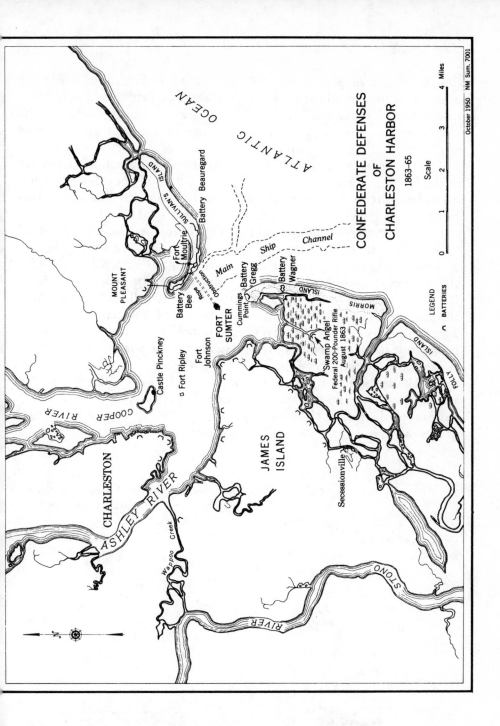

CONFEDERATE DEFENSES
OF
CHARLESTON HARBOR

1863–65

Scale

0   1   2   3   4   Miles

October 1950   NM   Sum. 7001

ATLANTIC OCEAN

SULLIVAN'S ISLAND

Battery Beauregard

Fort Moultrie

MOUNT PLEASANT

Battery Bee

Rope Obstruction

Main

Ship   Channel

Battery Gregg

Cummings Point

Battery Wagner

MORRIS ISLAND

"Swamp Angel"
Federal 200-Pounder Rifle
August 1863

FOLLY ISLAND

LEGEND

∪ BATTERIES

FORT SUMTER

Fort Johnson

Fort Ripley

Castle Pinckney

COOPER RIVER

CHARLESTON

ASHLEY RIVER

Wappoo Creek

JAMES ISLAND

Secessionville

STONO RIVER

the *Weehawken*" and withdraw. Whatever his original plan, Admiral Dahlgren now determined upon a small-boat assault. The task seemed simple; there was "nothing but a corporal's guard in the fort . . . all we have to do is go and take possession."

29

The Small-boat Assault

On the night of September 8–9, 400 sailors and marines made the attempt. A tug towed the small boats within 800 yards of the fort, then, too awkwardly, cast them loose. In the darkness and confusion, plans went awry. Without the benefit of a diversionary assault, two columns advanced simultaneously upon the right flank of the fort.

The Confederate garrison coolly held fire till the leading boats were in the act of landing, then let loose with a galling fire of musketry, hand grenades, "fire balls," grape and canister, brickbats, and masonry fragments. At a signal from the fort, the Confederate gunboat *Chicora* steamed out from the harbor and opened fire; Fort Moultrie "fired like a devil."

From the outer boats, the marines replied rapidly for a few minutes. Some of the sailors ashore fired a few times from their revolvers, but for the most part sought refuge in the embrasures or breaches of the wall. It was all over in 20 minutes. Most of the boats did not even touch shore. The Federal loss was 124 killed, wounded, and captured; 5 boats were taken. A similar expedition from Gillmore's command was detained by low tide in a creek west of Morris Island. Service rivalry had prevented active cooperation that might have meant victory.

For 19 days following the small-boat assault, Fort Sumter was free of attack; then, after a 6-day bombardment of "minor" proportions, for 23 days more. Damages sustained by the monitors in the Morris Island operation, as much as fear of channel obstructions (a menace afterwards

"The Flag of Sumter, October 20, 1863" painted by Conrad Wise Chapman, Confederate artist. Courtesy Confederate Museum, Richmond.

"Fort Sumter from Fort Moultrie, November 10, 1863" painted by Conrad Wise Chapman. Courtesy Confederate Museum, Richmond.

proved greatly exaggerated) and Fort Moultrie's evidently increased fire-power, made Admiral Dahlgren reluctant to make another move at this time. General Gillmore, engaged now in rebuilding and rearming the captured Confederate batteries on Cummings Point, thought he had accomplished his part of the operation. In his opinion, Fort Sumter was effectively reduced; its seizure and occupation would be a costly and unnecessary operation. Further offensive operations by his force had never been contemplated; and the reenforcements needed for such operations were not to be had. Indeed, with the "turn of the tide" at Vicksburg and Gettysburg, Charleston had suddenly become much less important.

Meanwhile, Fort Sumter's garrison was not idle. It was at this time that the great "central bombproof," with quarters for 100 men, was built out from the gorge interior and, in the remaining casemates of the right face, a new 3-gun battery mounted.

The Second Great Bombardment

On October 26, "on the strength of certain reports . . . that the enemy have recently been at work remounting some guns," Gillmore resumed the bombardment; at least Fort Sumter could be "kept down" while the Navy prepared. For the next 12 days, the concentration of fire was comparable to the great bombardment of the preceding August. But now, firing from the new batteries on Cummings Point, with range shortened to less than a mile, the effect was far greater. For the first time, 16 heavy mortars were in use—2 of them 8½-ton pieces (13-inch bore) throwing 200-pound projectiles. Their sharp, plunging fire was added to that of

31

12 Parrott rifles—the types already used so effectively against the fort—and 1 powerful Columbiad. In addition, 2 monitors, with guns "equal to a dozen" Parrotts, crossed fire with Gillmore's artillery.

Sumter's "sea front" (right flank), upright and relatively unscathed till then, was breached now for nearly half its length. The ramparts and arches of its upper casemates were cut down and the interior barracks demolished. The accumulated debris made ascent easy inside and out. Through the breach, the Federal guns took the channel fronts "in reverse." For the first time, these were exposed to direct fire; soon they were "cut and jagged." Still, the gorge ruin remained much the same; to Admiral Dahlgren, that "heap of rubbish" looked "invincible."

Night and day, Gillmore's batteries maintained a "slow fire" against Fort Sumter throughout November and into December. On occasion the monitors assisted. Sumter could return merely "harmless musketry"; only telescopic rifle sights made even that much possible. But, the "rebels" seemed "snug in the ruins"; and if Sumter was without guns, Confederate batteries on James and Sullivan's Islands kept up an irritating counterfire.

On November 6, the Confederate engineer at Fort Sumter reported the bombproofs (quarters) unhurt. Although the height of the mass of the fort was "diminishing visibly on the sides away from the city," still, "when it gets down to the lower casemates [he wrote] it will have become so thick from accumulated debris as to resist further battering." Two weeks later, Major Johnson found the fort stronger than ever, and

Capt. John C. Mitchel. From Johnson, *The Defense of Charleston Harbor.*

Capt. Thomas A. Huguenin. From Johnson, *The Defense of Charleston Harbor.*

casualties were "either among those carelessly exposing themselves, outside the bombproof, or obliged to do so when at work." Indeed, casualties had been surprisingly low—only 2 men had been killed in the bombardment of August and only 22 more since the start of the second great bombardment; 118 had been wounded. Major Johnson did not "apprehend being run out by the big guns"; his chief anxiety was over "exposure to assault from barges at night."

In mid-November such an attack seemed to be forthcoming. During the early hours of the 18th, the defenders of the fort had "four distinct alarms" as small boats approached within hailing distance; "all hands out each time and expecting a fight." On the following night, a force estimated at 250 men approached within 300 yards of the fort, only to be driven off by the muskets of the aroused garrison.

But General Gillmore had merely ordered a "reconnaissance . . . of the nature of a simulated attack, with a view to compel the garrison to show its strength." Nor would he make another attempt. The next move remained up to the Navy.

Admiral Dahlgren continued to make no move. In any event, he could not advance until the repairs on the monitors were finished. As late as January 1864 these still were not complete. Meanwhile, in the face of reports of greatly strengthened harbor fortifications other than Fort Sumter, and increasingly concerned over the nature of the harbor obstructions, he was reluctant now to move forward without additional monitors. Defeat was always possible, and defeat for the Union's "only ironclad squadron" might have serious consequences, not only for the blockade and Gillmore's command on Morris Island, but for future operations elsewhere along the coast. In the meantime, "substantial" advantages had already been gained; the blockade at Charleston was tighter with Morris Island in Federal hands. To all this, the Navy Department agreed. Elsewhere, however, the war gathered momentum. In November, the North won decisively at Chattanooga.

The additional monitors, always promised, never seemed to arrive. On December 5, General Gillmore stopped the bombardment of Fort Sumter begun 41 days earlier. There seemed no great advantage in continuing, and it required considerable ammunition.

Stalemate—Spring of 1864

The general had made his last sustained effort against the fort. On only four other days in December did he fire any rounds at all. During the 4 months he remained in command the firing was intermittent, never more than "minor" in character. Meanwhile, forthcoming operations in Virginia required all the troops available. On May 1, 1864, General Gillmore departed for Fort Monroe with 18,000 picked men and quantities of valuable matériel.

General Grant's operations required the services of the additional monitors awaited by Admiral Dahlgren. With the monitor force reduced to six by the foundering of the *Weehawken* in December, further offensive operations against Charleston seemed completely out of the question. In June, the ironclad frigate *New Ironsides* was withdrawn to the north.

Fort Sumter Strengthened

In the preceding December, Fort Sumter had been an "almost chaotic ruin." At night, below the "rugged outline of the ramparts," wrote one of the garrison, all was—

"dark with piles of disordered material; a chance shower of sparks blows out from smouldering fire and lights up some great rough blocks of brick work and the pools of stagnant water into which they have been violently thrown some days before. Or lanterns move about in unseen hands, some to light a way for long trains of men toiling with heavy timbers and bags of sand over the roughest footing and up steep and uncertain, tumbling slopes; some to direct the heaping of material over old damaged hiding places repaired for the twentieth time since the firing began, or to build up newer and more lasting shelters for the garrison. . . ."

With the fort practically left alone during the months immediately following, the garrison gradually restored order from chaos. The parade ground, excavated well below high-water level to provide sand-filling, was cleared, drained, and partially rebuilt. Trim ranks of gabions (wicker baskets filled with sand) bolstered the sloping debris of the walls on the interior. The three-gun battery in the lower right face was lined with logs and planks, 10 feet deep, and revetted more thoroughly in the rear. In casemates of the left flank another three-gun battery was created. Through the disordered debris of the left and right faces, the garrison tunneled a 275-foot timbered gallery connecting the two batteries and fort headquarters in the left flank. In from the rubble of the "sea front," the garrison built a loopholed timber blockhouse to cover the parade ground in the event of further assault. In May, Capt. John C. Mitchel, son of the Irish patriot, relieved Lt. Col. Stephen Elliott in command.

The Third Great Bombardment

The onset of summer, 1864, brought one more attempt to take Fort Sumter; likewise another officer of the original Fort Sumter garrison came into the operation. Maj. Gen. J. G. Foster, engineer of the fort in April 1861, succeeding to Gillmore's command on May 26, was convinced that "with proper arrangements" the fort could easily be taken "at any time." The "proper arrangements" included special light-draft steamers and 1,000-man "assaulting arks" equipped with elevated towers for sharpshooters and 51-foot scaling ladders. Though initial War Department reaction was cool, Foster went ahead with a preliminary operation to complete the demolition of the fort. "Yankee ingenuity" might succeed where routine operations had failed or been judged too costly.

On July 7, 1864, Foster's batteries opened a sustained bombardment against the ruin of Fort Sumter. During the remainder of that month, an average of 350 rounds daily was hurled at the beleagured fort. In some respects, this was the heaviest bombardment Fort Sumter had yet received. Although the gorge ruin was wasted away at one point to within 20 feet of the water, and the shattered "sea front" was still further reduced, the right face remained erect, its three-gun battery intact, likewise most of the left flank. To Admiral Dahlgren, as late as July 21, the work seemed "nearly impregnable." Debris added to debris, feverish work day and night, and thousands of bags of sand brought from the city by night actually made the fort stronger than ever. If a casemate were breached, it was speedily filled; if the slopes of the ruin invited assault, a bristling array of wooden pikes and barbed-wire entanglements were provided; and there were always the muskets of the 300-man garrison.

The fire slackened in August; Foster's supply of ammunition was dwindling. A scheme for "shaking down" the fort walls by floating down large "powder rafts" failed miserably. Mid-August brought final War Department refusal to supply light-draft steamers; the end of August, sharp disapproval for Foster's "assaulting arks." Meanwhile, Admiral Dahlgren had been unwilling to cooperate in an alternate plan of assault.

With his requisitions for more ammunition unfilled, General Foster was now called upon to ship north most of his remaining ammunition and four more regiments of troops to be used in Grant's operations against Richmond. Foster was ordered to remain strictly on the defensive.

On September 4, the bombardment begun on July 7 came to an end. In the 61 days, another 14,666 rounds had been hurled against the fort. Sixteen of the garrison had been killed, 65 wounded. On July 20, Captain Mitchel fell mortally wounded. Capt. Thomas A. Huguenin succeeded him that night.

Sherman's March Forces Sumter's Evacuation

The last great bombardment of Fort Sumter had taken place. The firing was no more than desultory after September 1864; less than a hundred rounds were hurled at the fort in the months of December and January; none at all in February. During the autumn months it was all Foster's batteries could do to make a "decent defense" of Morris Island, let alone carry on any offensive operations. Wrote one of the commanders in mid-September:

"The shelling from the enemy's mortars was severe . . . and having but little mortar powder, we were unable to reply effectually. . . . I regret that our ordnance supplies are so scanty. . . . No powder for the mortars; no suitable fuses for the fire on Charleston; no shells for the 30-pounder Parrotts, a most useful gun for silencing the enemy's fire; no material for making cartridge bags, or grease for lubricating the projectiles. . . . More ammunition for the 300-pounder, the most useful guns in these works, is also very much needed. . . ."

And Sumter itself was more than irritating:

"Within the last 2 days the work . . . has been greatly interfered with by a corps of sharpshooters . . . stationed on Fort Sumter. The bullets came in very thick when I was at the front this morning. . . ."

In February 1865, the long stalemate came to an end. In that month, General Sherman commenced his march north from Savannah through the interior of South Carolina, slicing between the remnants of Hood's army on the west and the small Confederate force remaining along the coast. On the 17th, with Sherman in Columbia, Fort Sumter and the other Confederate fortifications in Charleston harbor were quietly evacuated. At 9 o'clock on the morning of the 18th, the United States flag was once more raised over Fort Sumter. The fortunes of war had accomplished what 3,500 tons of metal, a fleet of ironclads, and thousands of men had failed to do.

Major Anderson Returns

On April 14, 1865, Robert Anderson, now a retired brigadier general, returned to Fort Sumter to raise again the flag he had pulled down 4 years before. The guns of the harbor thundered in salute. In an address before the throng of spectators brought down from New York, Henry Ward Beecher said:

"We raise our fathers' banner, that it may bring back better blessings than those of old, that it may cast out the devil of discord; that it may restore lawful government and a prosperity purer and more enduring than that which it protected before; that it may win parted friends from their alienation; that it may inspire hope and inaugurate universal liberty; . . . that it may heal all jealousies, unite all policies, inspire a new national life, compact our strength, purify our principles, ennoble our national ambitions, and make this people great and strong . . . for the peace of the world. . . ."

That night, with tragic coincidence, an assassin's bullet felled Abraham Lincoln in Washington.

Raising the original flag at Fort Sumter, April 14, 1865. Contemporary artist's sketch from French and Cary, The Trip of the Steamer Oceanus to Fort Sumter.

CHAPTER II
Battle of Manassas

*Wartime photograph of the Stone House, which still stands as
the most conspicuous landmark of both the First and Second
Battles of Manassas.* Courtesy National Archives.

On April 15, Lincoln issued his call for 75,000 volunteers, and soon troops were pouring into Washington. On May 23, Virginia voted to ratify the Ordinance of Secession, and the next day columns of Federal troops crossed the Potomac and seized Alexandria and Arlington Heights. Eight days later Richmond became the capital of the Confederacy and the chief objective of the Federal armies in the East. Stretching from the Ohio to Chesapeake Bay, Virginia constituted the wealthiest and most populous state of the Confederacy. Here were to be found rich natural resources and a heavy network of railroads and highways for military transport. These military advantages, however, were somewhat offset by the deep waters which flanked much of the state, increasing its vulnerability to Federal attack.

Straight across the path of one of the main high roads to Richmond from the north lay Manassas, a small railroad settlement, only a few miles east of the Bull Run Mountains. Here the Orange and Alexandria Railroad formed a junction with the Manassas Gap line which extended westward through the Blue Ridge to Strasburg, near Winchester. By seizure of this significant junction, located approximately 25 miles southwest of Washington, the Federal army could follow the Orange and Alexandria southwest to Gordonsville and thence proceed by the Virginia Central eastward to Richmond. This, with good supporting highways, would assure an overland approach that would avoid many of the natural barriers found in the shortest route by Aquia Creek and Fredericksburg.

The significance of Manassas was likewise apparent to the Confederates. As early as May 6, Col. St. George Cocke, commanding the Potomac Department, had received a dispatch from Gen. Robert E. Lee: "You are desired to post at Manassas Gap Junction a force sufficient to defend that point against an attack likely to be made against it by troops from Washington."

The first troops to arrive were two raw, undrilled, and ununiformed Irish regiments from Alexandria, armed with altered muskets. By May 14, Cocke was able to write Lee that he had succeeded in assembling a force of 918 men at Manassas. That he had a clear grasp of the military significance of the area is seen in his dispatch to Lee the next day: "It is obvious, sir, with a strong *corps d'armee* at Manassas, and at least a division at Winchester, these two bodies being connected by a continuous railway through Manassas Gap, there should be kept at all times upon that road ample means of transportation. These two columns— one at Manassas and one at Winchester—could readily co-operate and concentrate upon the one point or the other." Here then was a significant germ of Confederate strategy.

As a phase of this strategy, Brig. Gen. Joseph E. Johnston had been sent to take command of the Confederate force of about 12,000 men stationed in the northern end of the Shenandoah Valley at Harper's Ferry. Here was the gateway to the North through the Cumberland Valley of Maryland and here passed the great Baltimore and Ohio Railroad which connected Washington with the West. But Maj. Gen. Winfield Scott, then in command of the Army of the United States, had dispatched Maj. Gen. Robert Patterson with a force of about 18,000 men to seize this strategic position and to prevent, at all odds, the junction of Johnston's forces with the Confederate army at Manassas.

Confederates Look to Manassas Defenses

On June 1, Brig. Gen. Pierre G. T. Beauregard, the Confederate hero of Fort Sumter, arrived to take command at Manassas. Two days later he was writing President Jefferson Davis requesting reinforcements. At this early date the defenses of Manassas appeared anything but formidable to the eyes of an English lieutenant of artillery who, arriving at night, viewed them for the first time: "I could scarcely believe that this was a great military depot, there being nothing within my range of vision to indicate that such was the fact. The station itself was a low, one-storied building, about seventy-five feet in length, with bales and boxes scattered about; a house of refreshment close by was uninviting, and except one or two small cottages scattered here and there, naught was to be seen."

Brig. Gen. Pierre Gustave Toutant Beauregard in command of the Confederate Army of the Potomac. Courtesy National Archives.

By the end of June this picture had materially changed. The roads, the fields, and the town were filled with soldiers by the thousands. Around the junction massive fortifications had been erected running out in different directions from the station. Through the embrasures of these earthworks the muzzles of heavy cannon pointed menacingly toward Washington. Acres of trees had been felled to give free range to artillery, and at key positions along the front men were constantly on guard at their battle stations. Camps had sprung up like mushrooms in the open countryside, and here troops in and out of uniform could be seen almost incessantly engaged in drill.

By June 23, Beauregard was able to advise the Confederate Secretary of War that, in consequence of large reinforcements lately received, he had been able to divide his forces into six brigades commanded by Bonham, Ewell, D. R. Jones, Terrett, Cocke, and Early. Advance detachments had been stationed at key points including Centreville, Fairfax Court House, Germantown, the junction of the Old Braddock Road with the Fairfax Court House Road, and at Sangster's Crossroads. With the main body of his troops partially intrenched along Bull Run, from Union Mills to the Stone Bridge, Beauregard watched closely the Federal preparations for an advance.

As the tension mounted, alarms occurred with increasing frequency. Bootless, hatless, and coatless men often dashed to assembly sounded by the "thump, thump of the big drums." Rumors of the Federal advance "filled every breeze." In a dispatch, dated July 9, Beauregard informed President Davis: "Enemy's force increasing, and advancing daily this side of Potomac. He will soon attack with very superior numbers. No time should be lost in re-enforcing me here with at least ten thousand men—volunteers or militia."

On the 17th Beauregard telegraphed President Davis informing him of an attack on his outposts and requesting that he send reinforcements "at the earliest possible moment." Confronted with this crisis, Davis acted quickly. Advising Beauregard of the dispatch of reinforcements of Hampton's Legion, McRae's regiment, and two battalions of Mississippi and Alabama troops, he ordered Holmes' troops up from Fredericksburg. The same day, through his adjutant, he sent the following dispatch to Johnston in Winchester:

RICHMOND, *July* 17, 1861.

General J. E. JOHNSTON, *WINCHESTER, Va.:*

General Beauregard is attacked. To strike the enemy a decisive blow a junction of all your effective force will be needed. If practicable, make the movement, sending your sick and baggage to Culpeper Court-House either by railroad or by Warrenton. In all the arrangements exercise your discretion.

S. COOPER,
Adjutant and Inspector General.

Realizing that Harper's Ferry was untenable, Johnston had previously retired upon Winchester, with Patterson in cautious pursuit. Receiving Davis' dispatch at 1 a. m., July 18, Johnston determined to elude Patterson and join Beauregard as quickly as possible. By a forced march he reached Piedmont where his various brigades entrained for Manassas Junction, 35 miles away. Brig. Gen. Thomas J. Jackson's brigade was in advance, followed by those of Bee, Bartow, and Elzey.

Thus, after approximately 3 months of hurried preparation following Sumter, the stage was finally set—the drama of the opening battle was about to unfold.

The Federal Army Moves Toward Manassas

On July 16, Brig. Gen. Irvin McDowell had reluctantly put the Federal army in motion. In vain he had attempted to delay the movement until adequate training could provide him with an effective fighting force composed of the 3-year volunteers, authorized by President Lincoln on May 3, but popular clamor would not be denied. Pressure for a forward movement was heightened by the realization that the term of enlistment was rapidly expiring for a large body of the troops. Further delay would mean the loss of their services.

With excitement and high expectancy, the army, accompanied by many notables in fine carriages, took the road 35,000 strong. Seldom had the country seen such a splash of color as was presented by the brilliant

Brig. Gen. Irvin McDowell, in command of the Federal Army in the First Battle of Manassas. Courtesy National Archives.

uniforms of the various regiments and the gaily fluttering national and regimental flags. The first day's advance covered only 6 miles. Oppressive heat, dust, thirst, and the weight of heavy equipment slowed the step and caused considerable straggling.

Lagging spirits, however, caught fire with the triumphant advance of Hunter's division into Fairfax Court House. As the head of the column swung into town, Confederate units stationed there fled in such haste as to leave large quantities of forage and camp equipage behind. In an impressive show of martial splendor, the troops, four abreast with fixed bayonets, paraded through the streets to the stirring strains of the national anthem and other patriotic airs struck up by the regimental bands.

From Fairfax Court House the advance moved cautiously toward Centreville, with engineers and axmen flung forward to alert the army to "masked batteries" and to clear roadblocks of fallen timber left by the retiring Confederates. By noon of the 18th the main body of McDowell's army had assembled at Centreville and now stood poised to strike.

During the advance, little or no information had been received regarding Patterson's movements in the valley. Irked by this, Scott telegraphed Patterson as follows:

Washington, *July* 18, 1861.

Major-General Patterson, . . .

I have certainly been expecting you to beat the enemy. If not, to hear that you had felt him strongly, or, at least, had occupied him by threats and demonstrations. You have been at least his equal, and, I suppose, superior, in numbers. Has he not stolen a march and sent reenforcements toward Manassas Junction? A week is enough to win victories. . . .

WINFIELD SCOTT

Confederate fortifications at Manassas, Va. Wartime photograph. Courtesy National Archives.

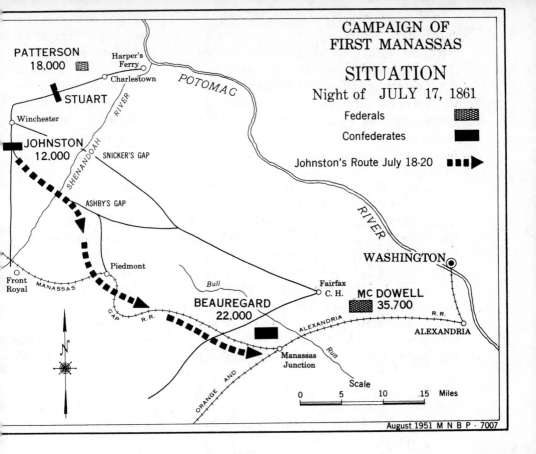

SITUATION

Night of JULY 17, 1861

Federals

Confederates

Johnston's Route July 18-20

PATTERSON
18,000

Harper's
Ferry

Charlestown

POTOMAC

STUART

Winchester

JOHNSTON
12,000

SNICKER'S GAP

ASHBY'S GAP

RIVER

WASHINGTON

Piedmont

Bull

Fairfax
C. H.

MC DOWELL
35,700

Front
Royal

MANASSAS

BEAUREGARD
22,000

ALEXANDRIA

R. R.

GAP

R. R.

Manassas
Junction

Run

ALEXANDRIA

ORANGE AND

Scale

0   5   10   15   Miles

August 1951 M N B P · 7007

To this, Patterson sent the following reply to Colonel Townsend in Scotts' headquarters:

CHARLESTOWN, VA., *July* 18th, 1861

Col. E. D. Townsend:

Telegram of to-day received. The enemy has stolen no march upon me. I have kept him actively employed, and by threats and reconnaissances in force caused him to be re-enforced. I have accomplished in this respect more than the General-in-Chief asked, or could well be expected, in face of an enemy far superior in numbers, with no line of communication to protect. . . .

R. PATTERSON, . . .

The events of the next few days more than justified Scott's suspicions.

McDowell Tests the Confederate Right

On July 18, in a feeling movement on the Confederate right, Tyler made a thrust against Beauregard's troops stationed in the vicinity of Blackburn's Ford. The affair got somewhat out of hand with the result that

45

the Federal force was smartly repulsed. The action had a depressing effect on Union morale but greatly boosted that of the Confederates. There then followed 2 days of costly delay for McDowell during which time he brought forward his supplies—a delay the Confederates were quick to capitalize upon. To the sound of the axe and the crash of falling trees, they built roadblocks along the Warrenton Pike in the vicinity of the Stone Bridge and in general strengthened their defenses. More important, the delay gave Johnston much needed time in which to reach Manassas.

Confederate reinforcements were now steadily moving in. On the 19th, Jackson arrived 2,500 strong, having covered approximately 55 miles in 25 hours. At sunrise of the 20th, more of Johnston's reinforcements had come in—the 7th and 8th Georgia regiments of Bartow's brigade numbering 1,400 men. About noon, Johnston himself arrived accompanied by Bee, the 4th Alabama, the 2d Mississippi, and two companies of the 11th Mississippi. The Confederate camp now became a scene of busy activity. While the reinforcements moved up to position in the line, Beauregard and Johnston conferred on plans for an offensive. Candles burned low in headquarters that night as Beauregard and his staff put the finishing touches to the Confederate plan of attack. At 4:30 a. m., he submitted it to Johnston, his superior, for the approval that was quickly granted. The plan involved the flanking of the Federal left, but the early movement of McDowell, the delayed arrival of expected reinforcements, and the miscarriage of orders combined to prevent its execution.

First Battle of Manassas   (SEE MAP ON PAGES 22–23.)

Sunday, July 21, dawned bright and clear. The listless stirring of the trees gave early promise that the day would be hot. Dust lay thick upon the grass, the brush, and the uniforms of the men. The Confederate camps were just beginning to stir from a restless night when, suddenly about 5:15 a. m., there was heard the thunderous roar of a big gun in the vicinity of the Stone Bridge. With this shot, fired from a 30-pounder Parrott rifle of Tyler's command, McDowell opened the first battle of the war.

Since 2:30 a. m. his troops had been in motion executing a well-conceived plan of attack. In bright moonlight, across the valley from Centreville "sparkling with the frost of steel," the Federal army had moved in a three-pronged attack. McDowell had originally planned to turn the Confederate right, but the affair of the 18th at Blackburn's Ford had shown the Confederates in considerable strength in that sector. Further informed that the Stone Bridge was mined and that the turnpike west of the bridge was blocked by a heavy abatis, he determined to turn the extreme Confederate left. By this flanking movement he hoped to

Young Confederates in Richmond who were soon to receive their baptism of fire at the First Battle of Manassas. From "Photographic History of the Civil War."

seize the Stone Bridge and destroy the Manassas Gap Railroad at or near Gainesville, thus breaking the line of communication between Johnston, supposedly at Winchester, and Beauregard at Manassas. To screen the main attack, Tyler was to make a feinting thrust at the Confederate defenses at the Stone Bridge, while Richardson was to make a diversion at Blackburn's Ford. Miles' division was to cover Centreville, while

Federal Army near Fairfax Court House en route to the First Battle of Manassas. A detachment of the 2d Ohio is shown in the foreground. From original sketch by A. R. Waud. Courtesy Library of Congress.

Runyon's division covered the road to Washington. To a large extent the success of the attack depended upon two factors—rapidity of movement and the element of surprise.

Turning to the right at Cub Run Bridge, the main Federal column, composed of Hunter's and Heintzelman's divisions, had followed a narrow dirt road to Sudley Ford which they reached, after exasperating delays, about 9:30 a. m. Here the men stopped to drink and fill their canteens. Though this loss of time was costly, success might still have been theirs if the movement had not been detected.

From Signal Hill, a high observation point within the Manassas defenses, the Confederate signal officer, E. P. Alexander, had been scanning the horizon for any evidence of a flanking movement. With glass in hand he was examining the area in the vicinity of Sudley Ford when about 8:45 a. m. his attention was arrested by the glint of the morning sun on a brass field piece. Closer observation revealed the glitter of bayonets and musket barrels. Quickly he signaled Evans at the Stone Bridge, "Look out for your left; you are turned." This message, which was to play an important part in the tactical development of the battle,

Sudley Springs Ford, Catharpin Run. Wartime photograph. Courtesy Library of Congress.

The ruins of the Stone Bridge over Bull Run, from the east.
Here opened the First Battle of Manassas. Wartime photograph.
Courtesy National Archives.

represents probably the first use under combat conditions of the "wig-wag" system of signaling.

MORNING PHASE—THE FIGHT AT MATTHEWS HILL.   Since 8 o'clock it had been apparent to Evans that Tyler's attack was simply a feint. Now warned of the approach of the flanking column, he moved rapidly to counter it. Leaving four companies of his command to guard the bridge with two pieces of artillery, he pushed northwestward about 1,700 yards to a point near the crossing of the Warrenton Turnpike and the Manassas-Sudley Road. There, about 10:15 a. m., he opened with artillery and infantry fire upon the advancing Federal column led by Burnside's brigade. Soon Col. Andrew Porter moved to Burnside's assistance. Hard-pressed after a gallant stand of about an hour, Evans sent an urgent request to Bee for help. Temporarily attached to Bee's brigade was Bartow with two Georgia regiments. With his command Bee had previously taken up a position on Henry Hill from which point Imboden's battery had played with telling effect upon the flanking column of McDowell.

Bee moved promptly forward, taking up a position on the right of Evans' line about 11 a. m. Here the combined Confederate force of approximately five regiments with six field pieces held stubbornly until about noon. The arrival of fresh Federal reinforcements of Heintzelman, and later of Sherman and Keyes, so increased the pressure on the Confederate right that its defenses gave way. Eagerly the Federal columns pushed their advantage as the now demoralized Confederates retreated across Young's Branch to the shelter of the Robinson House Hill. Following closely, Keyes moved downstream and took up a position in the shelter of the hills where he remained to take little effective part in further fighting during the day.

In a position near the Robinson House, Hampton's Legion, 600 strong, courageously attempted to cover the Confederate retreat. The Federal attack, however, finally forced them back with the disordered commands of Bee, Bartow, and Evans.

In the midst of the wild confusion that then ensued, as the fate of the battle hung in the balance, there occurred one of the dramatic moments of the war. Bee, desperately attempting to rally his men, glanced toward Henry Hill where he saw Jackson and his command standing bold and

Confederate officers rallying their troops behind the Robinson House du

resolute. Catching the inspiration of the moment, Bee leaned forward in his stirrups and with pointed sword shouted to his men, "Look! There is Jackson standing like a stone wall! Rally behind the Virginians!" Thus "Stonewall" Jackson won his famous sobriquet.

It was about this time that Johnston and Beauregard galloped upon the field. In the presence of their commanding officers the men gained new confidence. The line stiffened, formed again, and advanced to the front. Reinforcements from Cocke's and Bonham's brigades, at fords farther down Bull Run, were now fast coming up. Quickly upon their arrival they were sent into position to the right and left of Jackson. Johnston soon retired to the Lewis House ("Portici"), where he directed the movement of reinforcements from the rear, while Beauregard took immediate command of the field.

There now occurred a lull between 1 and 2 p. m. as the victorious Federal troops crossed the valley of Young's Branch and re-formed for a renewal of the attack.

AFTERNOON PHASE.   About 2 p. m., McDowell ordered forward the two splendid, regular batteries of Ricketts and Griffin, directing them to take

irst Battle of Manassas. From "Battles and Leaders of the Civil War."

up an exposed position just south of the Henry House. At a distance of not much more than 300 yards, these batteries were soon engaged in a furious duel with the artillery arrayed in Jackson's front. For about 15 minutes the din was terrific. Finally, in an effort to gain a better enfilading fire, Griffin advanced three of his guns slightly. The movement proved fatal.

At this moment J. E. B. Stuart made a dashing cavalry charge up the Manassas-Sudley Road, scattering the colorful Fire Zouaves who had been advanced to the support of Ricketts and Griffin. Almost simultaneously the 33rd Virginia regiment moved forward. Mistaken by one of the Federal officers as a battery support, it was allowed to come within 70 yards of Griffin's guns. Suddenly the regiment delivered a murderous volley, which killed most of the horses and men of both batteries. The immobilized guns were seized by the Virginians, only to be recaptured by a spirited Federal advance. In heated charges and countercharges the guns changed hands a number of times, yet neither side was able to employ them effectively. Their loss to the Federal command was irreparable.

Federal pressure now became so strong that Beauregard decided to attack. As Jackson penetrated the center of the Federal line, the Confederate right swept clear the area in the vicinity of the Robinson House. In a gallant countercharge, however, the Union brigades of Franklin, Willcox, Sherman, and Porter surged forward to reclaim the lost ground. In the attack, McDowell displayed reckless courage by climbing to the upper story of the Henry House to obtain a better view of the whole field.

The battle now raged with increasing severity as both sides fought desperately for possession of the plateau—"the key to victory." The

The Federal assault on Henry Hill in the First Battle of Manassas. From "Battles and Leaders of the Civil War."

Gen. Joseph E. Johnston in command of the Army of the Shenandoah. Courtesy National Archives.

Brig. Gen. Thomas J. "Stonewall" Jackson. Courtesy National Archives.

weight of Federal pressure upon Beauregard's left and right flanks so increased as to endanger his whole position. It was now about 3 p. m. The scorching rays of the sun beat unmercifully upon the exhausted troops as Beauregard, at this critical stage, ordered yet another general attack all along the line. Just then Fisher's 6th North Carolina regiment arrived to take position on the Confederate left. With Beauregard leading the charge, the Confederate line advanced to clear the field and regain final possession of the Henry and Robinson Houses.

Despite the loss of the plateau, McDowell's position was still strong. With his right anchored in the woods in the vicinity of the Chinn House, his line stretched in a great crescent back of the Stone House to a position near the Stone Bridge. However, the right held by Howard's brigade and Sykes' regulars had become so extended as to face almost east towards Centreville. Thus extended, it invited an attack which the Confederate command was quick to mount. Reinforcements, sent forward by Johnston, now rapidly moved up. In the lead were Kershaw's 2d and Cash's 8th South Carolina regiments followed by Kemper's battery. Quickly following these troops came Elzey's brigade, 1,700 strong. This brigade of Johnston's Army, detrained only a few hours before, had advanced to the sound of firing, led by Kirby Smith. To the weight of these numbers was added still another fresh brigade— Early's. Coming into position to the left of Elzey's brigade, Early struck the Federal right in flank and rear.

The combined attack, delivered about 3:45 p. m., proved overwhelming. The Federal line staggered and fell back, retiring across the field in some semblance of order. A brief rally north of Young's Branch was broken up by Confederate artillery fire. All other attempts to rally the men proved futile. They had had enough. Now they continued homeward by the various routes of the morning's advance. Bravely covering the retreat were Sykes' regulars and Palmer's squadron of cavalry.

As the main body of the Federal army retreated in the direction of Sudley Ford, Keyes' brigade recrossed at the Stone Bridge closely pursued by a Confederate detachment led by Kemper's battery. Riding astraddle one of the guns was the venerable "Yankee hater," Edmund Ruffin, who had fired one of the first shots at Fort Sumter. Dusty and weary he had arrived upon the field in the closing moments of the battle in time to hail Kemper's battery as it was passing. Eager to get another shot at the enemy, he held precariously to his seat as the battery went jolting past the Stone Bridge and along the pike now littered with arms, accoutrements, haversacks, knapsacks, loose articles of clothing, blankets, drums, and brass musical instruments left by the rapidly retiring troops.

After proceeding a few miles, Kemper's guns reached an advantageous rise. There they were unlimbered and quickly made ready for firing. The first shot, fired by the elderly Ruffin, hit squarely upon the suspension bridge over Cub Run upsetting a wagon that had just been driven upon it. This served to barricade the bridge to further use by other vehicles. In quick succession more shots were fired. Complete panic now seized the Federal troops as they fled in a wild rout back to Washington. Adding to the confusion were the throngs of sightseers and fugitives who crowded the narrow roads. The roar of the flight, wrote Russell, *The London Times'* correspondent, was like the rush of a great river. All

The Robinson House. From a wartime photograph in "Photographic History of the Civil War."

through the night and the rain of the next day the tide of soldiers and civilians streamed into Washington. Attempts by McDowell to rally the soldiers were in vain.

The exhausted, battle-weary Confederates made no effective pursuit. Early's brigade and Stuart's cavalry did succeed in capturing quite a number of prisoners, but the main Union force escaped. July 22 found both armies in the positions they had occupied prior to the 16th.

EFFECTS OF FIRST MANASSAS. The news of the disaster was first received in the Capital with incredulity and amazement, then with consternation. Throughout the night President Lincoln received spectators of the battle and listened in silence to their descriptions of the engagement.

"For a few days," writes Channing, "the North was dazed, stocks went down, money went up, and people sat around with their hands folded in despair. Then, almost as by magic, the scene shifted and stern resolve took the place of the hysteria of the Hundred Days since Sumter. Lincoln called for volunteers. The best blood of the North in all ranks of society, in the East, in the Ohio Valley, and on the shores of the Great Lakes responded. The new men went into the conflict with a determination and a spirit that has seldom been seen and never excelled."

In the South, the news of the victory was received with great elation. Thanksgiving sermons were preached from the pulpits while public officials commemorated the event with congratulatory proclamations. In the ill-considered opinion of many Southerners the war was over, yet seldom if ever has so complete a victory borne such meager results. An overweening confidence and a false sense of security developed in the South a paralysis of enterprise more damaging to it than was the disaster of defeat for the North.

The battle, however, as the English historian Fuller points out, was to have a profound influence on the grand strategy of the war. "First, it imbued the Southern politicians with an exaggerated idea of the prowess of their soldiers and so led them to under-estimate the fighting capacity of their enemy; secondly, it so terrified Lincoln and his Government that from now onwards until 1864, east of the Alleghanies, the defence of Washington became the pivot of Northern strategy."

Though the men of each army had fought with flashes of steadiness and exceptional courage, there was ample evidence to show the costly result of inadequate training.

	FEDERAL	CONFEDERATE
Strength, approximate	35, 000	32, 000
CASUALTIES		
Killed	460	387
Wounded	1, 124	1, 582
Captured or missing	1, 312	13
Total	2, 896	1, 982

Winter's Lull

Following the conclusion of the first Manassas campaign, the war in Virginia "languished" until the spring of 1862. The North, smarting from the humiliating defeat suffered at Bull Run, now turned with grim determination to the mobilization of its resources and to the training of the great land forces necessary to subjugate the South. Maj. Gen. George B. McClellan, fresh from victories in western Virginia, was immediately called to the command of the Federal forces around Washington. Soldierly in bearing and engaging in manner, McClellan proved a popular choice with the Nation and the army. With marked success he initiated a program of organization and training of the great Army of the Potomac. Recruits now streamed into Washington by the thousand. By December, there were 150,000 in training; by spring, over 200,000.

Meanwhile, the Confederate army under Joseph E. Johnston remained encamped at Centreville with outposts along the Potomac. Jackson, with a detachment, was stationed at Winchester. It was during this time that Johnston established a very strongly fortified position consisting of an L-shaped line of earthwork forts and batteries connected by infantry trenches that extended along the eastern and northern crests of Centreville for a distance of approximately 5 miles. Gradually, on the approach of winter, log or board huts were constructed for winter quarters for the troops. These were so located as to permit the troops easy access to the fortifications.

With the worsening condition of the roads the problem of supply became increasingly difficult. It was then that Johnston built a branch

Quaker guns at Centreville. Confederate winter quarters are shown in background. Wartime photograph. Courtesy National Archives.

railroad from his base at Manassas Junction. This was one of the first railroads ever to be used solely for military purposes.

Preliminary Operations to Second Manassas

McClellan's failure to move against Johnston resulted in a restive public and press. Richmond, rather than Centreville, now became the immediate Federal objective. Learning of an anticipated movement against Richmond via Urbanna, Johnston, on March 9, fell back from Centreville to take up a position south of the Rappahannock, with his right resting at Fredericksburg and his left at Culpeper Court House. This forced a modification of McClellan's original plan. He thereupon decided to make the movement by water to Fortress Monroe and from there advance up the Peninsula upon Richmond.

On March 17, the Federal army embarked from Alexandria. McClellan had anticipated the use of a force of about 155,000 men. The brilliant operations of "Stonewall" Jackson in the Shenandoah Valley during the next 3 months, however, so alarmed President Lincoln as to cause him to immobilize nearly 40,000 of McDowell's troops at Fredericksburg to secure the defenses of Washington. This, together with the detention of Banks' expected reinforcements in the Valley, reduced McClellan's force to approximately 100,000, thereby materially minimizing his chances of success. Seldom has so small a force as that of Jackson (approximately 16,000) so largely influenced the final outcome of a major military operation.

Johnston, in the meantime, had reinforced Magruder at Yorktown. On May 4 the town was evacuated, and the next day a successful rear-guard action was fought at Williamsburg, covering the Confederate withdrawal to Richmond. The Federal army followed by land and water to White House on the Pamunkey where, on May 16, McClellan set up his headquarters. The next day the Federal forces resumed their advance on Richmond.

Gathering a force of some 63,000 men, Johnston then determined to attack. On May 31, in the Battle of Seven Pines, followed by the Battle of Fair Oaks the next day, the Confederates were repulsed, and Johnston was severely wounded. The command of the Army of Northern Virginia now devolved upon Robert E. Lee, a command that he was not to relinquish until the end of the war. Within 2 weeks the defenses of Richmond had been strengthened and the morale of the troops greatly improved.

By June 25, Lee had assembled a force of about 90,000 men, including Jackson's victorious command from the Valley. The next day he launched his great counteroffensive. In a series of desperately contested operations, known as the Seven Days' Battles before Richmond, McClellan was forced back upon Harrison's Landing on the James. Though the cam-

Maj. Gen. John Pope, in command of the Federal Army, Second Battle of Manassas. Courtesy National Archives.

Gen. Robert E. Lee, in command of the Army of Northern Virginia. Courtesy National Archives.

paign was costly in Confederate casualties, Lee saved Richmond and cloaked his army with a sense of invincibility.

Pope Concentrates Behind the Rapidan

The failure of Fremont, Banks, and McDowell in the Shenandoah Valley convinced President Lincoln of the desirability of consolidating their armies under a single head. By order of June 26 the "Army of Virginia" was created, and Maj. Gen. John Pope, who had won recent successes in the West, was given the command. Shortly thereafter, Gen. Henry W. Halleck was recalled from the West to be made general in chief of the Federal armies.

To Pope was entrusted the responsibility for covering Washington, protecting the Shenandoah Valley, and so operating against the Confederate communications at Gordonsville and Charlottesville as to draw off heavy detachments from Richmond, thereby relieving the pressure on McClellan. On July 14, Pope ordered an advance on Gordonsville. Lee, anticipating the movement, had ordered Jackson to this point the day before.

On August 7, Jackson, having been reinforced by A. P. Hill, moved toward Culpeper in the hope of capturing the town and using it in a series of operations against Pope. Two days later he fell upon Banks at Cedar Mountain in a sharp but indecisive encounter.

Lee now learned that McClellan had been ordered to evacuate the Peninsula and reinforce Pope. Appreciating the necessity of striking Pope before he could be joined by such heavy reinforcements, Lee moved with Longstreet's corps to reinforce Jackson. Pope's force now numbered about 47,000 effectives, while Lee had approximately 55,000.

Lee's Operations Along the Rapidan and Rappahannock

Pope's center was now at Cedar Mountain, his right at Robertson's River, and his left near Raccoon Ford on the Rapidan. Thus stationed, his army was directly opposite Gordonsville where Jackson's force had recently arrived. On Clark's Mountain (a high hill opposite Pope's left) the Confederates had established a signal station. From here, stretching for miles, could be seen the white tents of the Federal encampment dotting the Culpeper tablelands. Spurs from Clark's Mountain paralleled the Rapidan to Somerville Ford, located about 2 miles from Raccoon Ford.

Lee was quick to appreciate the advantage this topography afforded him. Massing his troops behind Clark's Mountain he might move under its protecting screen, fall upon Pope's left at Somerville Ford, and cut off his retreat to Washington. The opportunity held bright possibilities of success, and August 18 was set as the date for the initiation of the movement. Unforeseen delays postponed the movement until the 20th. Worse still for the Confederates, Stuart's adjutant general was captured, bearing a copy of Lee's order.

Thus warned, Pope withdrew his army behind the Rappahannock. Lee followed closely on the 20th, crossing to the north side of the river. Pope took up an advantageous position where he stood fast during 5 days of feints and demonstrations as Lee sought eagerly for an opening on the right. In the meantime, Stuart had captured Pope's headquarters. Thus, Lee learned that 20,000 troops, composing the corps of Heintzelman and Porter and the division of Reynolds, were within 2 days' march of the front. Within 5 days other expected reinforcements would swell Pope's numbers to about 130,000 men.

The situation was so desperate as to demand a bold expedient. Quickly, Lee made his decision. Jackson, with Stuart's cavalry comprising about 24,000 men, was to be sent on a wide flanking movement of Pope's right for the purpose of destroying his communications with Washington.

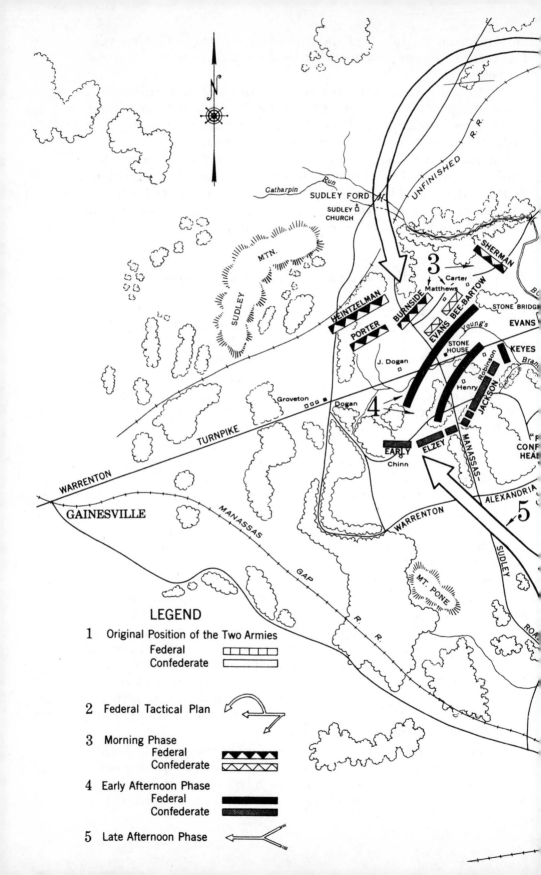

N

Catharpin Run

SUDLEY FORD

SUDLEY
CHURCH

R. R.

UNFINISHED

SUDLEY MTN.

SHERMAN

3

Carter

Matthews

STONE BRIDGE

HEINTZELMAN

PORTER

BURNSIDE

EVANS BEE-BARTOW

EVANS

Young's

STONE HOUSE

KEYES

J. Dogan

Robinson

Branch

Henry

JACKSON

Groveton

Dogan

4

EARLY

ELZEY

MANASSAS-

"P
CONF
HEAD

TURNPIKE

Chinn

WARRENTON

WARRENTON

ALEXANDRIA

5

GAINESVILLE

MANASSAS

SUDLEY

GAP

MT. PONE

R. R.

ROA

LEGEND

1 Original Position of the Two Armies
    Federal
    Confederate

2 Federal Tactical Plan

3 Morning Phase
    Federal
    Confederate

4 Early Afternoon Phase
    Federal
    Confederate

5 Late Afternoon Phase

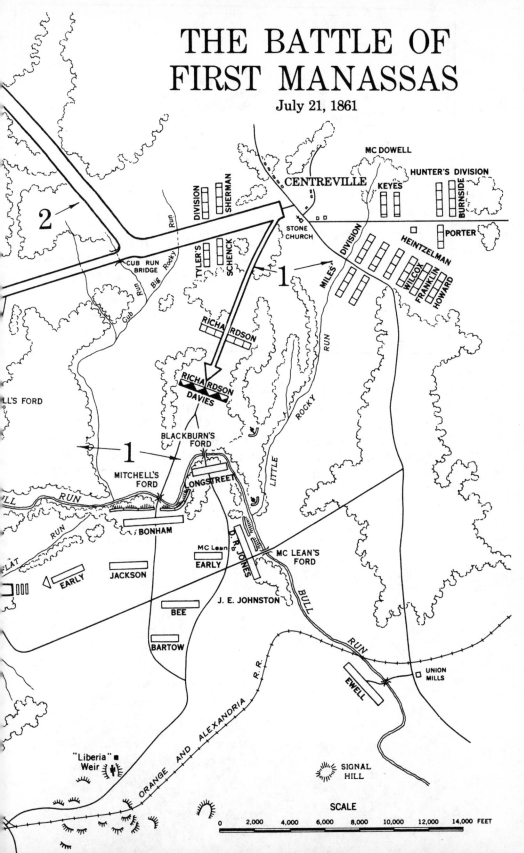

THE BATTLE OF FIRST MANASSAS

July 21, 1861

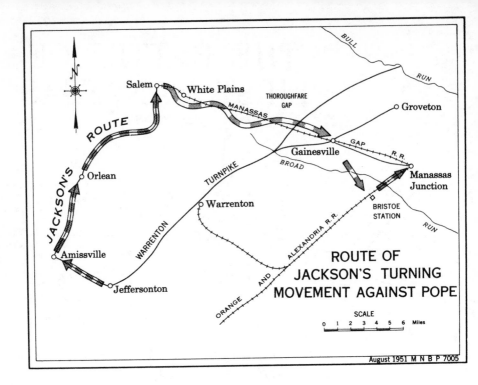

Commenting on this decision, Henderson, the English biographer of Jackson, says "we have record of few enterprises of greater daring."

With Lee and Longstreet covering the line of the Rappahannock, Jackson began his march from Jeffersonton on August 25. He moved through Amissville and Orlean to bivouac that night at Salem. The next day he pushed on past Thoroughfare Gap and Gainesville to Bris-

Jackson and his foot cavalry. From the painting by Hoffbauer in Battle Abbey, Richmond, Va. Courtesy Virginia Historical Society.

toe. Never did the "foot cavalry" better deserve its name, for in 2 days it had covered approximately 51 miles. That night Jackson sent Stuart and two regiments to Manassas Junction to capture Pope's great base of supplies. The task was accomplished with little effort.

The next day Jackson left Ewell to cover the rear at Bristoe and moved with the rest of his command to Manassas Junction. There then followed a scene of feasting and plunder the like of which has seldom been witnessed. Knapsacks, haversacks, and canteens were filled with articles of every description. Added to vast quantities of quartermaster and commissary supplies were innumerable luxuries from sutler stores, including expensive liquors and imported wines. An eyewitness writes, "To see a starving man eating lobster salad & drinking rhine wine, barefooted & in tatters was curious; the whole thing is indescribable." What could not be eaten or carried away was finally put to the torch. With the destruction of these supplies one of the chief objectives of the campaign had been accomplished.

Manassas Junction, Va., as it looked after Jackson's raid. Wartime photograph. Courtesy National Archives.

Shiloh Church, painted by Capt. A. M. Connett, 24th Indiana Volunteer Infantry, a participant in the battle.

CHAPTER III

Battle of Shiloh

SHILOH NATIONAL MILITARY PARK preserves the scene of the first great battle in the West of the War Between the States. In this 2-day battle, April 6 and 7, 1862, both the Union and Confederate Armies suffered heavy casualties, bringing home the horrors of war to the North and South alike. Nearly 24,000 were killed, wounded, or reported missing—a number equal to more than one-fifth of the combined Union and Confederate Armies engaged in the battle. By their failure to destroy the Federal Armies at Shiloh the Confederates were forced to return to Corinth, Miss., relinquishing all hold upon West Tennessee, except a few forts on the Mississippi which were soon to be wrested from them. Their failure at Shiloh foreshadowed the loss of the Memphis and Charleston Railroad, the South's vital line of communication between Chattanooga and the Mississippi. After the fall of Memphis, early in June, the Federals were in position to strike at Vicksburg, the conquest of which would give them control of the Mississippi and split the Confederacy in two.

The psychological effect on the South of the Union campaigns was probably of greater importance than the material gains or losses of the contending armies. The Confederates learned by bitter experience the error of their former opinion of the Union soldier. No longer could they boast that the fighting ability of one Confederate was equal to that of 10 Federals, now that Southern dash and chivalry had been grievously tried against Northern valor and endurance.

The near-defeat at Shiloh removed the illusion of easy victory, created by the fall of Forts Henry and Donelson, from the minds of Northerners. They now realized that the struggle was to be a long and bloody one. A few days after Donelson, one Union soldier wrote: "My opinion is that this war will be closed in less than six months from this time." Shortly after Shiloh the same soldier wrote: ". . . if my life is spared I will continue in my country's service until this rebellion is put down, should it be ten years."

Shiloh is not distinguished by outstanding generalship on either side, but it is interesting as a battle fought by raw volunteers—young men without previous experience in a major engagement and with little or no military training.

Preliminary Campaign

War activity west of the Appalachian Mountains in 1861 was confined chiefly to the States of Kentucky and Missouri. Toward the end of the year when loyalty, or at least the neutrality, of the governments of these border States seemed assured, the Federals began making plans for the invasion of the South by way of the western rivers and railroads. Each side began to maneuver for strategic positions. The Confederate General, Leonidas Polk, believing that the Southern States were about to be invaded through Kentucky, moved up quickly from his position at Union City, Tenn., and seized Columbus, Ky., the northern terminus of the Mobile and Ohio Railroad. Gen. Ulysses S. Grant, recently appointed commander of the Federal troops in and around Cairo, Ill., had made preparations to occupy that important river port and railway center on the following day. Thwarted at Columbus, Grant retaliated by taking Paducah, Ky., located at the junction of the Tennessee and Ohio Rivers.

It now became apparent to the Confederate high command in Richmond that a strong line would have to be established along the northwestern border of the Confederacy before the Union armies had time to occupy more of the strategic points. They believed that the task could be performed more effectively if all troops in that theater of operation were placed under one commander. Accordingly, Confederate President Jefferson Davis sent Gen. Albert Sidney Johnston to the West with the imposing title of "General Commanding the Western Department of the Army of the Confederate States of America."

Arriving in Nashville on September 14, 1861, General Johnston studied his difficult assignment. The line he was supposed to occupy extended from the mountains of eastern Tennessee westward across the Mississippi to the Kansas boundary. Only two points on the proposed line were then in Confederate hands: Columbus, which he considered the natural key to the Confederate defense of the Mississippi, and Cumberland Gap, Ky., which he had previously ordered Gen. Felix K. Zollicoffer to occupy.

One of Johnston's first official acts upon arriving at Nashville was to order Gen. Simon B. Buckner to secure Bowling Green, Ky., one of the most important railroad centers south of the Ohio. He also ordered garrisons to the incomplete works at Fort Henry, on the Tennessee, and Fort Donelson, on the Cumberland, hoping to prevent a Union advance up either of these natural highways. A Federal offensive up the Tennessee or the Cumberland would endanger the important railroad and industrial center of Nashville, Tenn.

Since the outbreak of the war, Nashville had been converted into a huge arsenal and depot of supplies. Large quantities of food, clothing, and munitions had been collected and stored in its warehouses. Its factories were turning out percussion caps, sabers, muskets, saddles, harness, knapsacks, cannon, and rifled pieces. Its looms were turning out thou-

Commodore Foote's gunboats ascending the Tennessee to attack Fort Henry.

sands of yards of gray cloth which were being made into uniforms for the soldiers. The loss of this city would be an irreparable blow to the Confederacy.

While General Johnston was establishing his positions, the Federals were rapidly organizing their forces preparatory to an attack upon the Confederate line. Gen. Henry W. Halleck, from headquarters in St. Louis, was strengthening his positions at Cairo, Ill., and Paducah, Ky. At the same time, he was making ready a large number of river steamers so that his troops could be moved by water to almost any point along his front. From headquarters in Louisville, Gen. Don Carlos Buell, commander of the Department of the Ohio, reinforced his line so that Johnston had to keep his main force at Bowling Green, Ky., to guard the important railroads which penetrated Middle and West Tennessee.

Various plans for an attack upon the Confederate line were considered by the Federals. General Halleck, commander of the Department of the Missouri, believed that it would take an army of not less than 60,000 men, under one commander, to break the well-established line. He, therefore, asked that General Buell's army be transferred to him, or at least placed under his command.

Before a union of the two departments could be effected, General Grant asked for, and received, permission to attack the line at Fort Henry. A combined land and naval attack by Grant's troops and the gunboat fleet of Commodore Andrew H. Foote resulted in the surrender of Fort Henry on February 6, 1862, and the capture of Fort Donelson, with about 12,000 prisoners, on the 16th. The loss of these forts broke Johnston's line at its center and compelled him to evacuate Bowling Green and Columbus, permitting western Kentucky to fall into Union hands. To prevent encirclement, he was also forced to withdraw from Nashville, abandon Middle and West Tennessee, and seek a new line on the Memphis and Charleston Railroad.

Following the fall of Forts Henry and Donelson, Grant incurred the displeasure of General Halleck by sending a division of troops into Buell's department at Clarksville. Halleck's indignation increased when he learned that Grant had gone to Nashville for consultation with Buell. Halleck directed the withdrawal of the division from Clarksville, suspended Grant from command, and ordered him to Fort Henry to await orders.

Dover Tavern, General Buckner's headquarters and scene of the surrender of Fort Donelson.

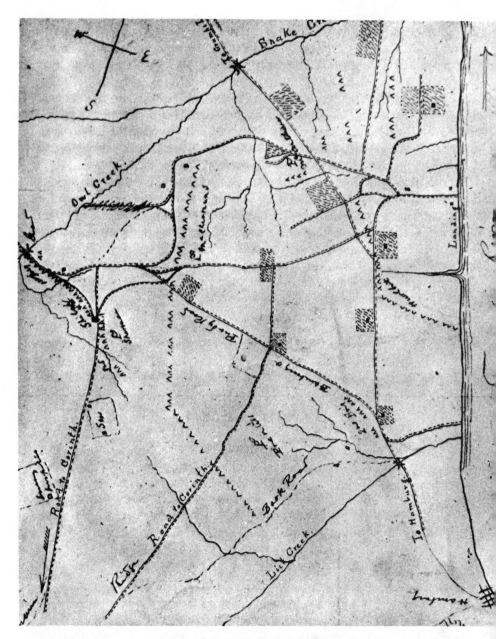

Map of the battlefield of Shiloh, made by Gen. W. T. Sherman soon after the battle.

The army under Grant's successor, Gen. Charles F. Smith, moved up the Tennessee toward the heart of the Confederacy, with the intention of rendezvousing at Savannah, Tenn., on the east side of the river. Gen. Willian T. Sherman was sent forward on the so-called Yellow Creek Expedition for the purpose of destroying railroad communications to the west of Corinth, Miss., the objective of the campaign. High water made Sherman's mission a failure, and he was compelled to return. He reported to General Smith that a more convenient place for the assembling of his army was at Pittsburg Landing, Tenn., 9 miles above Savannah, and on the west side of the river, from which direct roads led to Corinth. General Smith, therefore, instructed him to disembark his division and that of Gen. Stephen A. Hurlbut at Pittsburg Landing, in positions far enough back to afford room for the other divisions of the army to encamp near the river.

Conference of Confederate commanders the night before the battle. From left to right, Gen. P. G. T. Beauregard, Gen. Leonidas Polk (seated), Gen. John C. Breckinridge, Gen. A. S. Johnston, Gen. Braxton Bragg, and Maj. J. F. Gilmer. Gen. W. J. Hardee was not present.

Cherry Mansion, Savannah, Tenn., used as headquarters for the Union Army, March 13 to April 29, 1862. While eating breakfast in this house, General Grant heard the sounds of heavy firing which told him the battle had begun. Generals W. H. L. Wallace and C. F. Smith died here in April 1862.

In obedience to this order, Sherman encamped his division along a ridge on either side of Shiloh Church, almost 3 miles from Pittsburg Landing, with General Hurlbut's division about a mile to his rear. Within a few days, Gen. Benjamin M. Prentiss' division took position on Sherman's left, while Gen. John A. McClernand and Gen. W. H. L. Wallace formed their divisions between Sherman and the river. The 3d Division, commanded by Gen. Lew Wallace, was stationed at Crump's Landing, about 4 miles downstream from the main encampment. Thus, by April 5, 1862, there were in the five divisions of the Army of the Tennessee at Pittsburg Landing 39,830 officers and men present for duty and 7,564 at nearby Crump's Landing.

While this concentration of troops was in progress, General Smith received a leg injury which became so serious that he had to give up his command. General Grant was restored to duty and sent to Savannah with orders to concentrate troops and supplies, but to bring on no general engagement until a union could be made with Buell's army, and Halleck had arrived to assume personal command of the combined forces.

General Johnston, in the meantime, was concentrating all available forces at Corinth, Miss., on the Memphis and Charleston Railroad. After this had been accomplished, he resolved to take the offensive and attack Grant's army at Pittsburg Landing, hoping to defeat that army before it could be reinforced by General Buell. Hearing that Buell was nearing Savannah, Johnston determined to attack at once and accordingly on the 3d of April issued the order for the forward movement. He expected to give battle at daylight on April 5th, but heavy rains and bad roads made progress so slow that the last of his columns did not reach the field until late afternoon. It was then decided that the attack should be postponed until daylight the next morning. Johnston's army, 43,968 strong, went into bivouac in order of battle within less than 2 miles of the Federal camps. The Confederate forces were formed in three lines. Gen. W. J. Hardee's corps and one of Gen. Braxton Bragg's brigades were in the first line, the remainder of Bragg's corps in the second line, and Generals Leonidas Polk's and J. C. Breckinridge's corps in the third line.

During the night of April 5th the two hostile armies were encamped within a short distance of each other: the Confederates poised, ready to attack, while the unsuspecting Union army went about its normal camp routine, making no preparations for the defense of its position. On Saturday, a few hours before the battle, Sherman wrote Grant: "I have no doubt that nothing will occur to-day more than some picket firing," and that he did not "apprehend anything like an attack" on his position. The same day, after Sherman's report from the front, Grant, who was at Savannah, telegraphed Halleck: "I have scarcely the faintest idea of an attack (general one) being made upon us, but will be prepared should such a thing take place."

The First Day

The battle began about 4:55 a. m., Sunday, April 6, when a reconnoitering party of Prentiss' Union division encountered Hardee's skirmish line, under Maj. Aaron B. Hardcastle, a short distance in front of Sherman's camps. The reconnoitering party—three companies of the 25th Missouri under Maj. James E. Powell—fighting and retreating slowly toward its camps was reinforced by four companies of the 16th Wisconsin and five companies of the 21st Missouri. These troops were, in turn, reinforced at the northeast corner of Rhea Field by all of Col. Everett Peabody's brigade. Here they succeeded in holding the Confederates in check until about 8 a. m., when they fell back to Prentiss' line of camps, closely followed by the enemy.

General Sherman, hearing the picket firing in his front, immediately got his division under arms and posted a battery at Shiloh Church and another on the ridge to the south. The left of this hastily formed line

The Confederate charge upon Prentiss' camps. From "Battles and Leaders of the Civil War."

received the full impact of the Confederate onslaught at about the same time that Prentiss' camps were attacked. One of the regiments in the left brigade—the 53d Ohio—consisted of raw troops who had never been under fire. Unable to withstand the fierce Confederate attack, this regiment soon broke and fled to the rear. A short time later the other two regiments of the brigade did likewise. The commander of the brigade, Col. Jesse Hildebrand, refused to leave the field with his men. Since he had no troops of his own, he acted as aide for General McClernand the rest of the day.

General Prentiss, in the meantime, was making a gallant, but futile, stand along his line of camps. Assailed by the eager Confederates in front and on the flanks, his whole division soon broke and fell back in confusion. He succeeded in rallying about 1,000 of his men on the center of a line that W. H. L. Wallace and Hurlbut were forming with parts of their divisions in a strong position in the rear. This new line, running through a densely wooded area along an old sunken road, proved to be such a strong position that the Confederates named the place "Hornets' Nest" because of the stinging shot and shell they had to face there.

Meanwhile, General Grant at breakfast in Savannah heard the guns in the battle of Shiloh. He at once sent word to the advance of Buell's army, which had already arrived at Savannah, to march immediately to the point on the river opposite the battlefield. He then hurried up the river aboard the steamer *Tigress,* moving in close enough to the shore at Crump's Landing to instruct Gen. Lew Wallace to be prepared to execute any order he might receive. Upon arriving at the field, he dispatched reinforcements to Prentiss and formed two regiments in line near Pittsburg Landing, to arrest the tide of stragglers from the battle and organize them to return. He then rode to the front.

While the Confederate right was engaged with Prentiss, the left, supported by continuous artillery fire, was hurled against the combined forces of Sherman and McClernand who were making a stubborn stand along the ridge at Shiloh Church. This small log building, which gave its name to the battle, was considered the key position of the field, as it commanded the best road from Corinth to Pittsburg Landing. When General Grant reached the church, about 10 a. m., his troops were heavily engaged all along the line. They had resisted the relentless pounding from the Confederate artillery and the repeated infantry charges for over 2 hours. Seeing that the line could not hold much longer, Grant dispatched orders to Lew Wallace to move to the field, expecting him to reinforce the Union right. Leaving Sherman, he moved down the line to the left to confer with his other division commanders. He visited Prentiss in the Hornets' Nest and directed him to hold his position there at all hazards.

Union defenders of the Hornets' Nest repulsed 11 Confederate charges against the Sunken Road.

The Sunken Road near Bloody Pond.

Soon after Grant's departure, Sherman withdrew from Shiloh Ridge, abandoning his camps and much of his equipment. He took a new position behind the Hamburg-Purdy Road alongside McClernand who had been pushed back on line with Prentiss' Hornets' Nest position.

Grant's army was now posted on either side of Prentiss, making a line approximately 3 ½ miles long. The opposing army was charging this line with a series of frontal attacks, just as hard on the left as on the right. This was contrary to Johnston's plan of battle. He had intended to push hardest on the Union left and seize their base of supplies at the Landing. Without supplies or an avenue of escape, he hoped to drive the disorganized Federals into the swamps of Snake and Owl Creeks and destroy them.

Seeing that the enemy was being driven into its base of supplies rather than away from it, Johnston, about noon, moved to the extreme right to direct in person the activities of that wing of his army. There, he found his troops exposed to a galling fire and unable to advance. Determined to move his line forward, Johnston ordered and led a successful charge. The Union lines recoiled, and the Confederates surged forward about three-fourths of a mile. As Johnston sat on his horse, watching the lines re-form, a ball from the gun of an unknown Union soldier struck the Southern commander, severing the large artery in his right leg. No surgeon being near, he died from loss of blood at 2:30 p. m.

The death of Johnston caused a lull in the battle on the right flank for about an hour. The situation was relieved somewhat by the fact that a second in command was on the field. Gen. Pierre G. T. Beauregard was in charge of headquarters which had been established near Shiloh Church. When informed of Johnston's death, he immediately assumed command. He sent General Bragg to the right of the field and put Gen. Daniel Ruggles in command at the center.

General Ruggles, having witnessed 11 unsuccessful charges against the Hornets' Nest, decided to concentrate artillery fire upon the position. Therefore, he collected all the artillery he could find—62 pieces—and opened fire upon the Union line. Under cover of continuous fire from these guns, the Confederates attacked with renewed courage and redoubled energy. Unable to withstand the assault, the troops on both the Federal right and left withdrew toward the Landing, leaving Prentiss and W. H. L. Wallace isolated in the Hornets' Nest. As the Union forces withdrew, the left of the Confederate line swung around and joined flanks with the troops moving around from the right, thus forming a circle of fire around Wallace and Prentiss.

Wallace, seeing that the other divisions were withdrawing and that his command was being surrounded, gave the order for his troops to fall back. To execute the order, his division had to pass through a ravine which was already under the crossfire of the encircling Confederates. Wallace was mortally wounded in the attempt, but two of his regiments succeeded in passing through the valley, between the Confederate lines, which they appropriately named "Hell's Hollow." Prentiss continued the resistance until 5:30 p. m., when he was compelled to surrender with over 2,200 troops—all that remained of the two divisions.

During the afternoon, Col. Joseph D. Webster, Grant's Chief of Artillery, placed a battery of siege guns around the crest of a hill about

Johnston mortally wounded.

Gen. Ulysses S. Grant.
Courtesy National Archives.

a quarter of a mile in from the Landing. The smaller field artillery pieces were put in position on either side of them as they were moved back from the front. The two wooden gunboats, *Tyler* and *Lexington,* anchored opposite the mouth of Dill Branch, further strengthened the line. As the remnants of the shattered Union Army drifted back toward the Landing, they were rallied along this line of cannon.

After the capture of Prentiss, an attempt was made to reorganize the Confederates for an attack upon the Union position near the Landing. Before a coordinated attack could be made, Beauregard, who had received word that Buell would not arrive in time to save Grant's army, sent out the order from his headquarters at Shiloh Church to suspend the attack. Unknown to Beauregard, the advance of Buell's army had already arrived opposite Pittsburg Landing and was being rapidly ferried across the river.

During Sunday night and Monday morning, Buell moved approximately 17,000 troops into line on the Union left. Lew Wallace put al-

Gen. Don Carlos Buell.
Courtesy National Archives.

most 6,000 fresh troops—Fort Donelson veterans—in position on the right. The Confederates, receiving no reinforcements, spent a sleepless night in the captured Union camps annoyed by shells from the gunboats, which were thrown among them at 15-minute intervals throughout the night.

The battle had already raged for 13 hours. Charge after charge had been made by the Confederates, followed by Federal countercharges. Ground had been gained and lost, but the general direction of movement had always been toward the Landing. By the time the day was over and the weary soldiers had lain down to rest, the Confederates were in possession of all the field, except the Landing and a bit of adjoining territory. Many Southern soldiers, in view of the gains made during the day, believed that the victory was already theirs. An equally large number of Northerners were willing to concede defeat. When night at last closed in around the hostile armies, feelings of uncertainty prevailed among the leaders on both sides. Many of them were well aware that the battle was yet to be won or lost.

The Second Day

Monday morning, April 7, at daylight, the vanquished of the previous day renewed the struggle with increased strength and restored confidence. Anxious to take the initiative, the Union armies were put in motion almost simultaneously, with Buell on the left, Lew Wallace on the extreme right, and Grant's weary troops occupying the space between. The movement began unopposed, except by small unsupported parties which were quickly forced to retreat.

The Confederates had been unable to reorganize their widely scattered forces during the night. Therefore, when the Union advance began on Monday the opposing line of battle was yet unformed. The Confederates were still back in the vicinity of the captured Union camps vainly trying to reorganize their broken commands. They did not succeed in forming a line until after the enemy had advanced beyond the Peach Orchard and the Hornets' Nest, regaining much of the territory they had lost the day before.

Young Confederate enlisted men from the Washington Artillery of New Orleans. From a photograph made prior to the Battle of Shiloh.

The Confederates, one brigade strong, were first encountered by Lew Wallace a short distance in front of his Sunday night bivouac. In a brief but spirited engagement, the Confederates were attacked in front and on the left flank by the Union division. To keep from being surrounded, they fell back almost a mile in the direction of Shiloh Church to take their place in the forming line of battle.

In the meantime, Buell moved his troops rapidly forward until they developed the Confederate line of battle west of the Peach Orchard. The Southerners boldly charged the advancing Union infantry which had moved forward so rapidly that its artillery was still far to the rear. Without artillery support, the Federals were unable to withstand the violent assault of the Confederates and were forced to make a hasty retreat. The timely arrival and effective use of two batteries of artillery permitted the Union line again to advance, only to be driven back once more by the stubborn Confederates.

The battle now raged the entire length of the field. Charge followed by countercharge moved the fitfully swaying line first toward the river and then toward the church. The advantage would seem to rest momentarily with the weary Southerners, but would soon be lost to their greatly strengthened opponent. Commands became so intermingled and confused that it was often impossible to distinguish between friend and foe. The Confederates, clad in a variety of colored uniforms, with no well-defined line and on an ever-changing front, suffered the heavier losses from the fire of their own troops.

Meanwhile, General Beauregard, at Shiloh Church, anxiously awaited the return of couriers he had dispatched to Corinth to hurry forward Gen. Earl Van Dorn's army of about 20,000 men, daily expected there from Van Buren, Ark. He had promised to make a junction with General Beauregard as soon as possible, but was delayed because he had no means of transporting his troops across the Mississippi. Unaware that Van Dorn was still in Arkansas, General Beauregard maintained his largest troop concentration in the vicinity of the church to defend the Corinth-Pittsburg Road so that reinforcements could be quickly moved onto the field. As soon as it became known that additional troops were not on the way, Beauregard realized that the road would have to be kept open as a possible line of retreat. The Union commanders were equally determined to drive the Confederates from the position. Consequently, furious fighting raged before the church long after the tempo of the battle had slackened on each flank.

Despite all efforts of the Confederates, the Union line continued slowly to advance. In desperation the Confederates made a gallant charge, first expending their ammunition and then relying on the bayonet. The charge carried the surging line through waist-deep Water Oaks Pond, beyond which the fire from the adversary became so strong that the line was brought to an abrupt halt. Taking cover at the edge of a woods, they repulsed every attempt by the Federals to advance.

Arrival of Federal reinforcements.

The first tent field hospital ever used for the treatment of the wounded on the battlefield was established at Shiloh, April 7, 1862.

By 2 p. m. General Beauregard decided it was useless to prolong the unequal struggle. Since early morning, his lines had been forced back, step by step, with heavy losses. From all parts of the field his subordinates were sending urgent requests for reinforcements, which he was unable to supply. Even his position at the church was in danger of being taken. A continuation of the battle could bring only additional disasters upon his already greatly depleted ranks. To forestall a complete rout, he ordered a rear guard with artillery support to be put in position on the ridge west of the church and instructed his corps commanders to begin withdrawing their troops. By 4 o'clock, the last of the Confederate Army, or what was left of it, had retired from the field and was leisurely making its way back to Corinth without a single Federal soldier in pursuit.

The Union armies did not attempt to harass the retreating Southern columns or attack them when they went into bivouac for the night. Instead, Grant's troops, from the privates to the highest commanders, appear to have been content to return to their recaptured camps, while the Confederates returned to their former positions in and around Corinth to recruit and reorganize.

In explanation of his inactivity Grant said: "My force was too much fatigued from two days' hard fighting and exposure in the open air to a drenching rain during the intervening night, to pursue immediately. Night closed in cloudy and with heavy rain, making roads impracticable for artillery by the next morning."

The next morning, April 8, however, Gen. Thomas J. Wood, with his division, and Sherman, with two brigades and the 4th Illinois Cavalry, went in pursuit. Toward evening they came upon the Confederate rear guard at Fallen Timbers, about 6 miles from the battlefield. The Southern cavalry, commanded by Col. Nathan Bedford Forrest, charged the Federals, putting the skirmishers to flight and throwing the Union cavalry into confusion. The Confederates, pursuing too vigorously, came suddenly upon the main body of Federal infantry and were repulsed, after Colonel Forrest had been seriously wounded in the side. Before returning to camp, the Northerners tarried long enough to bury their 15 dead, gather up their 25 wounded, and find out that they had lost 75 as prisoners. The spirited action of the Confederate rear guard at Fallen Timbers put an end to all ideas of further pursuit by the Federals.

Results of the Battle

The losses on each side at Shiloh were unusually heavy. Grant's army of 39,830 had been reinforced by 25,255 during the night between the 2 days' battle, swelling the total number of Union troops engaged to 65,085, excluding a guard detachment of 1,727 men left at Crump's Landing. Of that total number 1,754 were reported killed, 8,408 wounded, and 2,885 missing; presenting an aggregate of 13,047 casualties.

The army under Generals Johnston and Beauregard had gone into battle with 43,968 men of all arms and condition. They received no reinforcements, except 731 men of Col. Munson R. Hill's Tennessee Regiment who had reached the front unarmed and were furnished with arms and equipment picked up from the field. The Southerners lost 1,728 killed, 8,012 wounded, and 959 captured or missing, or a total of 10,699 casualties.

"Present" and "Casualties" at Shiloh

	Present for duty	Casualties			
		Killed	Wounded	Missing	Total
UNION					
Army of the Tennessee (April 6)............	39, 830	1, 433	6, 202	2, 818	10, 453
Reinforcements (April 7)					
Army of the Tennessee....................	7, 337	80	399	12	491
Army of the Ohio......................	17, 918	241	1, 807	55	2, 103
Total Federals engaged [1]............	65, 085	1, 754	8, 408	2, 885	13, 047
CONFEDERATE					
Army of the Mississippi (April 6)..........	43, 968	1, 728	8, 012	959	10, 699
Reinforcements (April 7)					
Hill's 47th Tennessee....................	731	......	......	......	......
Total Confederates engaged.........	44, 699	1, 728	8, 012	959	10, 699
GRAND TOTAL......................	109, 784	3, 482	16, 420	3, 844	23, 746

[1] Does not include 1, 727 troops left at Crump's Landing as rear guard.

During the first few weeks following the battle, both sides claimed a victory. The Confederates based their claim upon the facts that they had inflicted an almost complete rout on the Federals on Sunday, April 6, and that they had been able to hold a part of the field until they withdrew in good order on Monday. Furthermore, they said, the Union armies were so battered that they were unable to pursue.

The Federals claimed the victory upon the grounds that on Monday evening they had recovered their encampments and had possession of the field from which the Confederates had retired, leaving behind a large number of their dead and wounded.

After the Battle of Shiloh the Confederates were compelled to withdraw southward. Corinth was abandoned to the North on May 30th, severing the railroad from Memphis to Chattanooga. By the end of June 1862, only those forts on the Mississippi River near Vicksburg remained in Southern hands. After a long siege, Vicksburg fell to the North on July 4, 1863, cutting the Confederacy in two.

Bloody Pond.

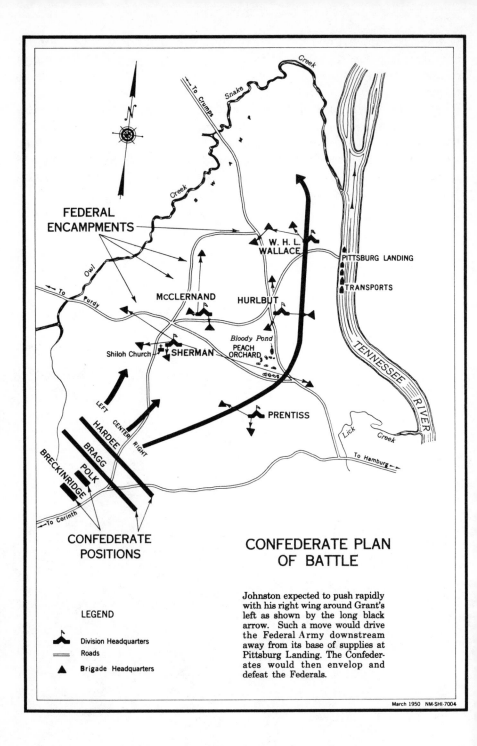

FEDERAL
ENCAMPMENTS

W. H. L.
WALLACE

PITTSBURG LANDING

TRANSPORTS

McCLERNAND

HURLBUT

TENNESSEE RIVER

Bloody Pond

PEACH
ORCHARD

Shiloh Church   SHERMAN

To Purdy

To

Owl   Creek

Snake   Creek

To Crumps

Creek

PRENTISS

Lick   Creek

To Hamburg

LEFT   CENTER   RIGHT

HARDEE

BRAGG

POLK

BRECKINRIDGE

To Corinth

CONFEDERATE
POSITIONS

CONFEDERATE PLAN
OF BATTLE

Johnston expected to push rapidly
with his right wing around Grant's
left as shown by the long black
arrow. Such a move would drive
the Federal Army downstream
away from its base of supplies at
Pittsburg Landing. The Confederates would then envelop and
defeat the Federals.

LEGEND

Division Headquarters
Roads
Brigade Headquarters

March 1950 NM-SHI-7004

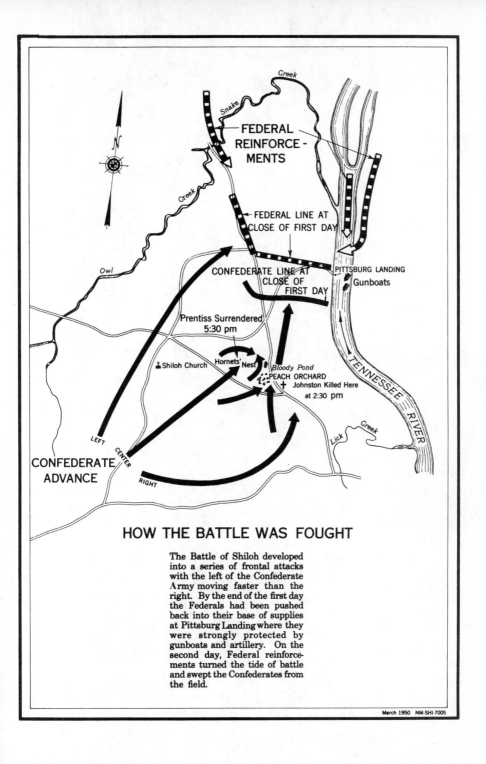

HOW THE BATTLE WAS FOUGHT

The Battle of Shiloh developed
into a series of frontal attacks
with the left of the Confederate
Army moving faster than the
right. By the end of the first day
the Federals had been pushed
back into their base of supplies
at Pittsburg Landing where they
were strongly protected by
gunboats and artillery. On the
second day, Federal reinforcements turned the tide of battle
and swept the Confederates from
the field.

March 1950 NM-SHI-7005

Richmond, 1858. From a contemporary sketch.

CHAPTER IV
Peninsula Campaign

Richmond

In session at Montgomery, Ala., in May 1861, the Confederate Congress voted to remove the Capital of the Confederate States to Richmond, Va. This decision, in effect, made Richmond a beleaguered city for 4 years. Essentially, the move was dictated by political and military considerations. The prestige of Virginia, richest and most populous State in the South, was considered necessary for the success of the Confederacy. For political reasons it was believed that the Capital should be near the border States and the heavy fighting expected there.

Second only to New Orleans, Richmond was the largest city in the Confederacy, having a population of about 38,000. It was also the center of iron manufacturing in the South. The Tredegar Iron Works, main source of cannon supply for the Southern armies, influenced the choice of Richmond as the Confederate Capital and demanded its defense. During the course of the war, Tredegar made over 1,100 cannon, in addition to mines, torpedoes, propeller shafts, and other war machinery. It expanded to include rolling mills, forges, sawmills, and machine shops. The Richmond Laboratory made over 72 million cartridges, along with grenades, gun carriages, field artillery, and canteens, while the Richmond Armory had a capacity for manufacturing 5,000 small arms a month.

Thus Richmond became the political, military, and manufacturing center of the South, and the symbol of secession to the North.

Situated near the head of the navigable waters of the James River, and within 110 miles of the National Capital at Washington, Richmond was the key to the military planning of both sides. For 4 years the city remained the primary military objective of the Union armies in the east. As one southern newspaper stated: "To lose Richmond is to lose Virginia, and to lose Virginia is to lose the key to the Southern Confederacy."

The Army of the Potomac

In July 1861 the untrained Union Army of the Potomac suffered disaster at Manassas (Bull Run) in the first attempt to drive into Virginia and capture Richmond. President Abraham Lincoln then appointed Gen. George B. McClellan the new commander of the demoralized army. McClellan reported: "I found no army to command * * * just a mere collection of regiments cowering on the banks of the Potomac."

To this chaotic situation he brought order and discipline. During the long winter months, the raw recruits were marshalled and drilled into an efficient fighting machine of over 100,000 men—the largest army ever commanded by one man in the history of the western hemisphere. By the spring of 1862 this army was ready for the supreme test—the goal was Richmond.

THE PENINSULA CAMPAIGN, SUMMER, 1862

On To Richmond

Instead of marching overland, McClellan decided to take advantage of Union control of the inland waters and transport his army, with its vast supplies and materiel, down the Potomac River and across Chesapeake Bay to the tip of the peninsula between the York and James Rivers. Then with his supply ships steaming up the York, he planned to march northwestward up the peninsula, join another force under Gen. Irvin McDowell marching overland from Washington, and together, converge on Richmond.

McClellan's plan of attack. Painting by Sidney King.

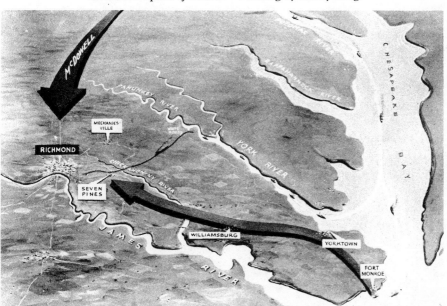

To accomplish this, McClellan undertook the largest amphibious operation ever attempted in the western world. Over 400 steam vessels, brigs, schooners, sloops, ferry boats, and barges assembled on the Potomac River. In March 1862 these vessels ferried the Army of the Potomac, with its 3,600 wagons, 700 ambulances, 300 pieces of artillery, 2,500 head of cattle, and over 25,000 horses and mules, to the southeast coast of Virginia. As Q. M. Gen. Rufus Ingalls reported: "Operations so extensive and important as the rapid and successful embarkation of such an army, with all its vast equipment, its transfer to the peninsula, and its supply while there, had scarcely any parallel in history."

Up The Peninsula

After landing at Fortress Monroe the Federal troops pushed aside the thinly held Confederate defenses at Yorktown and Williamsburg and proceeded up the peninsula according to plan. But progress was slow. Every day 500 tons of forage and subsistence were required to keep the army in the field. Early in May it rained and kept raining, day after dreary day. Federal soldiers had a saying: "Virginia used to be in the Union—now it's in the mud." Dirt roads turned into bottomless muck—creeks and gullies became swift flowing streams—fields were swamps. Roads and bridges had to be built and rebuilt, and still the thousands of wagons, horses, and mules continually stuck in the mud.

Sumner's troops crossing Grapevine Bridge to reinforce Couch at Seven Pines. From a contemporary sketch.

Realizing that an effective overland pursuit of the retreating Confederate forces under Gen. Joseph E. Johnston was out of the question because of the weather and the condition of the roads, McClellan on May 6 sent Gen. William B. Franklin's division up the York River by transport to West Point, terminus of the Richmond and York River Railroad, in an attempt to cut off the Confederate wagon train. Johnston anticipated the move, however, and on May 7 ordered Gen. W. H. C. Whiting's troops to attack Franklin in the battle of West Point, or Eltham's Landing.

The attack was repulsed, but, even so, the wagon train managed to continue safely to Richmond. McClellan, however, had cleared the way to his next objective—the landing at White House on the Pamunkey River, a tributary of the York. Here the railroad crossed the Pamunkey on its way to West Point. This would be the Union base of supply for the contemplated attack on Richmond. This battle also cleared the way for the right wing of the Union army, which would have to stay north and east of Richmond in order to hook up with McDowell's anticipated overland march from Washington.

General Johnston, falling back steadily in front of McClellan's slow advance, was the target of severe criticism from Richmond newspapers for not making a determined stand. But he wrote to Gen. Robert E. Lee: "We are engaged in a species of warfare at which we can never win. It is plain that Gen. McClellan will adhere to the system adopted by him last summer, and depend for success upon artillery and engineering. We can compete with him in neither."

Drewry's Bluff

After the fall of Norfolk on May 10 to the Union forces under Gen. John Wool, the crew of the *Virginia (Merrimack)* scuttled their ship. River pilots had advised that the iron-clad vessel could not navigate the treacherous channel up the James River to Richmond. Loss of the *Virginia* opened the river to Federal gunboats, and McClellan immediately telegraphed the War Department: "I would now most earnestly urge that our gunboats and the iron-clad boats be sent as far as possible up the James river without delay. Instructions have been given so that the Navy will receive prompt support wherever and whenever required."

Five Union gunboats, including the famous *Monitor*, started up the James under Comdr. John Rogers in the *Galena*. By May 15 they reached Drewry's Bluff, just 7 miles below Richmond. Here, at a sharp bend, the Confederates had effectively obstructed the river and erected powerful batteries on a 90-foot bluff.

Battle of Drewry's Bluff. Diorama, Richmond National Battlefield Park Visitor Center.

At 7 that morning the Federal gunboats opened fire on Fort Darling. The battle raged for 4 hours while the fate of Richmond hung in the balance, and near panic spread through the city. However, the accurate fire of the heavy guns on the bluff, combined with effective sharpshooting along the riverbanks, finally proved too much for the gunboats, and the Federal fleet retreated down the river. One Confederate officer observed: "* * * had Commander Rogers been supported by a few brigades, landed at City Point or above on the south side, Richmond would have been evacuated."

Although the Secretary of the Navy requested "a cooperating land force" to help the gunboats pass Fort Darling and take Richmond, McClellan, despite his earlier promise of cooperation, wired the War Department: "Am not yet ready to cooperate with them." He neglected to say when he would be ready. Richmond was never again seriously threatened by water.

Seven Pines (Fair Oaks)

Slowed by the heavy rains and the bad condition of the roads, where "teams cannot haul over half a load, and often empty wagons are stalled," McClellan finally established his base of supply at White House on May 15. Five days later his advance crossed the Chickahominy River at Bottoms Bridge. By the 24th the five Federal corps were established on a front partly encircling Richmond on the north and east, and less than 6 miles away. Three corps lined the

Gen. George B. McClellan. Courtesy, Library of Congress.

north bank of the Chickahominy, while the two corps under Generals E. D. Keyes and Samuel P. Heintzelman were south of the river, astride the York River Railroad and the roads down the peninsula.

With his army thus split by the Chickahominy, McClellan realized his position was precarious, but his orders were explicit: "General McDowell has been ordered to march upon Richmond by the shortest route. He is ordered * * * so to operate as to place his left wing in communication with your right wing, and you are instructed to cooperate, by extending your right wing to the north of Richmond * * *."

Then, because of Gen. Thomas J. ("Stonewall") Jackson's brilliant operations in the Shenandoah Valley threatening Washington, Lincoln telegraphed McClellan on May 24: "I have been compelled to suspend McDowell's movements to join you." McDowell wrote disgustedly: "If the enemy can succeed so readily in disconcerting all our plans by alarming us first at one point then at another, he will paralyze a large force with a very small one." That is exactly what Jackson succeeded in doing. This fear for the safety of Washington—the skeleton that haunted Lincoln's closet—was the dominating factor in the military planning in the east throughout the war.

Lincoln's order only suspended McDowell's instructions to join McClellan; it did not revoke them. McClellan was still obliged to keep his right wing across the swollen Chickahominy.

Learning of McDowell's withdrawal, Johnston decided to attack the two Federal corps south of the river, drive them back and destroy the Richmond and York River Railroad to White House. Early in the morning on May 31, after a violet rainstorm that threatened to wash all the Federal bridges into the river, Johnston fell upon Keyes and Heintzelman with 23 of his 27 brigades at Seven Pines.

The initial attack was sudden and vicious. Confederate Gen. James Longstreet threw Gen. D. H. Hill's troops against Gen. Silas Casey's division of Keyes' corps, stationed about three-quarters of a mile west of Seven Pines. Longstreet overwhelmed the Federal division, forcing Casey to retreat a mile east of Seven Pines. Keyes then put Gen. D. N. Couch's division on a line from Seven Pines to Fair Oaks, with Gen. Philip Kearney's division on his left flank. Not until 4 that afternoon, however, did Confederate Gen. G. W. Smith send Whiting's division against Couch's right flank at Fair Oaks. The delay was fatal. Although Couch was forced back slowly, he drew up a new line of battle facing south towards Fair Oaks, with his back to the Chickahominy River. Here he held until Gen. Edwin V. Sumner, by heroic effort, succeeded in getting Gen. John Sedgwick's division and part of Gen. I. B. Richardson's across the tottering Grapevine Bridge to support him. Led by Sumner himself, Sedgwick's troops repulsed Smith's attack and drove the Confederates back with heavy losses.

The battle plan had been sound, but the attack was badly bungled. Directed by vague, verbal orders instead of explicit, written ones, whole brigades got lost, took the wrong roads, and generally got in each other's way. Nine of the 23 attacking brigades never actually got into the fight at all. Towards nightfall Johnston was severely wounded in the chest and borne from the field. The command then fell to G. W. Smith. Fighting ceased with darkness.

Early next morning, June 1, Smith renewed the attack. His plan called for Whiting on the left flank to hold defensively, while Longstreet on the right swung counterclockwise in a pivot movement to hit Richardson's division, which was facing south with its right near Fair Oaks. The Federal troops repulsed the assault, however, and when Heintzelman sent Gen. Joseph Hooker's division on the Federal left on the offensive, the Confederates withdrew and the battle was over before noon.

That afternoon President Jefferson Davis appointed his chief military advisor, Gen. Robert E. Lee, as commander of the Southern forces. Lee promptly named his new command the Army of Northern Virginia—a name destined for fame in the annals of the Civil War.

McClellan's troops repairing Grapevine Bridge. Courtesy, Library of Congress.

Although the battle itself was indecisive, the casualties were heavy on both sides. The Confederates lost 6,184 in killed, wounded, and missing; the Federals, 5,031. Undoubtedly the most important result of the fight was the wounding of Johnston and the resultant appointment of Lee as field commander.

Lee Takes Command

Lee immediately began to reorganize the demoralized Southern forces, and put them to work digging the elaborate system of entrenchments that would eventually encircle Richmond completely. For this the troops derisively named him the "King of Spades." But Lee was planning more than a static defense. When the time came these fortifications could be held by a relatively small number of troops, while he massed the bulk of his forces for a counteroffensive. He was familiar with and believed in Napoleon's maxim: "* * * to manoeuver incessantly, without submitting to be driven back on the capital which it is meant to defend * * *."

On June 12 Lee sent his cavalry commander, Gen. J. E. B. ("Jeb") Stuart, with 1,200 men, to reconnoiter McClellan's right flank north

97

Gen. Robert E. Lee. Courtesy, National Archives.

of the Chickahominy, and to learn the strength of his line of communication and supply to White House. Stuart obtained the information, but instead of retiring from White House the way he had gone, he rode around the Union army and returned to Richmond on June 15 by way of the James River, losing only one man in the process.

Lee's fortifications east of Mechanicsville Turnpike. From a contemporary sketch.

Chickahominy swamps.   Courtesy, National Archives.

It was a bold feat, and Stuart assured his chief that there was nothing to prevent his turning the Federal right flank.   But the daring ride probably helped McClellan more than Lee.   Alerted to the exposed position of his right flank and base of supply, McClellan withdrew his whole army south of the Chickahominy, with the exception of Gen. Fitz-John Porter's corps, which stretched from Grapevine Bridge to the Meadow Bridge west of Mechanicsville.   On June 18 he started the transfer of his enormous accumulation of supplies with the shipment of 800,000 rations from White House to Harrison's Landing on the James River.   After Jackson's success in the Shenandoah Valley at Cross Keys and Port Republic, it was becoming apparent even to McClellan that McDowell probably never would join him, in which case he wanted his base of operations to be the James rather than the York River.

Meanwhile, pressure from Washington for an offensive movement against Richmond was mounting. But because of the wettest June in anyone's memory, McClellan was having trouble bringing up his heavy siege guns, corduroying roads, and throwing bridges across the flooded Chickahominy swamps. As one bedraggled soldier wrote: "It would have pleased us much to have seen those 'On-to-Richmond' people put over a 5 mile course in the Virginia mud, loaded with a 40-pound knapsack, 60 rounds of cartridges, and haversacks filled with 4 days rations."

Also, McClellan believed erroneously that the Confederates had twice as many available troops as he had. Consequently, his plan of action, as he wrote his wife, was to "make the first battle mainly an artillery combat. As soon as I gain possession of the 'Old Tavern' I will push them in upon Richmond and behind their works; then I will bring up my heavy guns, shell the city, and carry it by assault."

The Seven Days Begins

McClellan's plan probably would have succeeded had Lee been willing to stand still for it. But the Confederate commander did not intend to let McClellan fight that type of warfare. As he wrote to Jackson: "Unless McClellan can be driven out of his entrenchments he will move by positions under cover of his heavy guns within

Lee's plan of attack. Painting by Sidney King.

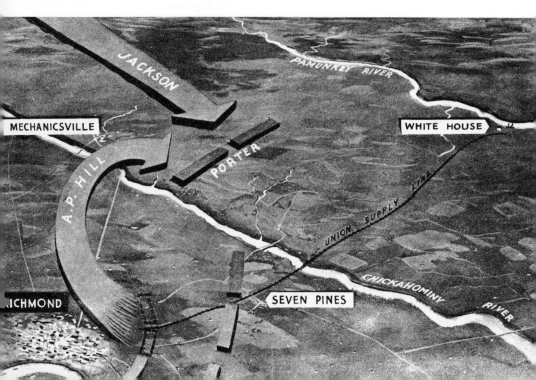

shelling distance of Richmond." It was almost as if Lee had read McClellan's letter to his wife.

Lee's plan to drive McClellan away from Richmond was bold and daring, and strategically brilliant. He would bring Jackson's forces down from the valley quickly and secretly to turn McClellan's right flank at Mechanicsville. At the same time Gen. A. P. Hill's division would cross the Chickahominy at Meadow Bridge, turn east and clear the Federal forces from Mechanicsville, thereby opening the Mechanicsville Turnpike bridge for D. H. Hill and Longstreet's troops to cross. Then, in echelon, the four divisions would sweep down the north side of the Chickahominy, annihilate Porter's corps, capture the supply base at White House, then turn and destroy the rest of the Union army. With Jackson's forces and other reinforcements from farther south, Lee would have about 90,000 men, the largest army he would ever command in the field.

To protect Richmond, he planned to leave about one-third of his army, under Generals John B. Magruder and Benjamin Huger, in the entrenchments around the city to hold back the main part of McClellan's force, about 70,000 men, from marching into the Confederate Capital. If this force started to withdraw, then Magruder and Huger would attack.

Lee apparently believed that McClellan would try to retreat to his base at White House, or failing that, would retire back down the peninsula. He assured Jefferson Davis that "any advance of the enemy toward Richmond will be prevented by vigorously following his rear and crippling and arresting his progress." The strategy was just about perfect, but, unfortunately for Lee, the tactics were not.

On the morning of June 25 the Seven Days began with the advance of Hooker's division along the Williamsburg road at Oak Grove, preparatory to a general advance McClellan planned for the next day. But Hooker ran into strong opposition from Huger's troops, and when McClellan received intelligence of Jackson's approach, Hooker was ordered back. McClellan wired Washington: "I incline to think that Jackson will attack my right and rear." He had delayed too long—the next day Lee wrested the initiative from him.

Beaver Dam Creek (Ellerson's Mill)

According to Lee's plan, Jackson was to march from Ashland on June 25 and encamp that night just west of the Central Railroad. At 3 a.m. on the 26th he was to advance and envelop Porter's right flank at Beaver Dam Creek. Then, wrote Lee, "A. P. Hill was to cross the Chickahominy at Meadow Bridge when Jackson's

Confederate attack at Beaver Dam Creek.   From a contemporary sketch.

advance beyond that point should be known and move directly upon Mechanicsville."

But from the beginning, unforeseen circumstances upset the operation and timing of this plan.   McClellan suspected Jackson's approach, so the element of surprise was lacking.   And when the action of the Union pickets in destroying bridges and felling trees in Jackson's path, as well as the fatigue of his weary troops, combined to delay him, the all-important time element was lost.

As the day wore on with no word from Jackson, A. P. Hill became impatient and fearful for the success of Lee's plan.   He decided to attack regardless.   At 3 that afternoon he crossed the Chickahominy and swept the Union outposts from Mechanicsville, thus clearing the way for D. H. Hill and Longstreet's troops to cross.   Porter withdrew to a prepared position behind Beaver Dam Creek, a mile east of Mechanicsville.   This naturally strong position was further fortified by felled trees and the banks of a millrace.   Here, atop the high banks of the stream, he placed Gen. George McCall's division, extending from near the Chickahominy on the south, across Old Church road (now U.S. 360) on the north.   Gen. Truman Seymour's brigade held the left and Gen. John Reynold's the right, with Gen. George G. Meade's brigade in reserve.   The only approaches to the position were across open fields, commanded by the Federal artillery, and down the steep banks of the stream, covered by the soldiers' muskets.

Hill recklessly hurled his brigades forward in a hopeless frontal assault. The gray-clad infantry charged bravely down the steep banks and up to the stream before the murderous fire of artillery and musketry from the surrounding slopes forced a bloody withdrawal. Casualties in killed and wounded were: Confederate 1,485; Union, 258.

Despite the successful defense, when Jackson's forces finally appeared on his right flank later that night, Porter's position became untenable and McClellan ordered him to withdraw to a previously prepared position behind Boatswain Swamp, near Gaines' Mill. At the same time he ordered his quartermaster general at White House to reship all the supplies he possibly could to Harrison's Landing on the James, and send all the beef cattle to the vicinity of Savage Station. Early next morning, June 27, the herd of 2,500 head of cattle started on its drive from White House.

Battle of Gaines' Mill. From *Battles and Leaders of the Civil War.*

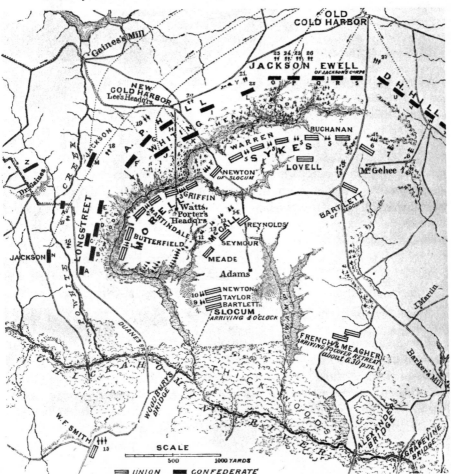

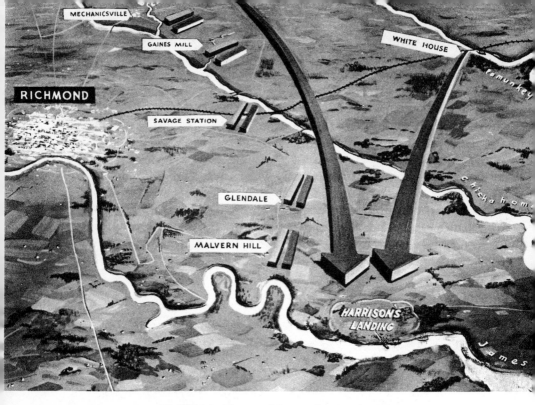

McClellan's change of base. Painting by Sidney King.

Gaines' Mill

The tactical situation was now extremely critical for both Lee and McClellan. Because of the repulse at Beaver Dam, Lee had not yet achieved his first objective, which, according to his battle order, was to "drive the enemy from his position above New Bridge," about 4 miles east of Mechanicsville. Lee's whole plan for the defense of Richmond, in the event McClellan should elect to march on the city with his main force south of the Chickahominy, hinged on his ability to cross the river quickly and attack the Federal rear. Lacking control of New Bridge this would be impossible. Although the Union position behind Boatswain Swamp was actually east of New Bridge, the approaches to the bridge could be covered by Porter's artillery.

The situation was equally serious for McClellan. With Jackson enveloping his right flank and rear, and believing he "had to deal with at least double" his numbers, White House would have to be abandoned. Having made the decision to change his base to the James, he desperately needed time to perfect the arrangements and to get the thousands of wagons and the herd of cattle safely started. His order to Porter was explicit, "hold our position at any cost until night * * *"

104

Porter's corps now occupied a semicircular line of battle along the crest of the partially wooded plateau behind Boatswain Swamp, with both extremes resting on the Chickahominy River. It was another naturally strong position further strengthened by felling trees and digging rifle pits. The approaches to the position were over an open plain and across a sharp ravine. Gen. George Morell's division held the left and Gen. George Sykes' right, with McCall's weary troops in reserve. Gen. Philip St. George Cooke's cavalry was on Porter's extreme left, in the lowlands bordering the Chickahominy. During the course of the impending battle of Gaines' Mill, Porter would be reinforced by Gen. Willard Slocum's division, giving him a total strength of about 35,000, as opposed to about 60,000 for Lee.

On the Confederate side, Longstreet was on Lee's right opposite Morell, A. P. Hill in the center, and Jackson and D. H. Hill on the left. Lee was convinced that the greater part of the Federal army was in his front, and he still thought McClellan would try to protect his base and retreat toward White House. On these erroneous assumptions he made his plans.

A. P. Hill would attack the center while Longstreet made a feint on the Union left. Then when Jackson appeared on the Union right, Lee believed Porter would shift part of his troops to meet Jackson's threat in order to keep him from getting between the Union army and its base at White House. As soon as Porter did this, Longstreet would turn the feint into a full assault, and together with Hill drive the Union forces into Jackson and D. H. Hill, waiting on Lee's left.

About 2:30 p.m. Hill attacked the center of the Federal line, but under a devastating fire of artillery and musketry, "where men fell like leaves in an autumn wind," his troops were hurled back with heavy losses. Longstreet, realizing a feint now would not help Hill, ordered a full-scale attack, but he too suffered a bloody repulse. Jackson, sensing that "Porter didn't drive worth two cents," as he quaintly put it, threw D. H. Hill against Sykes on Porter's right.

By now A. P. Hill's division was badly cut up, and on Lee's request Jackson sent Whiting's division, consisting of Gen. E. M. Law's and John B. Hood's brigades, over to support him. Porter then threw in Slocum's division of Franklin's corps, to protect threatened points along the line. The vicious battle waged furiously for 4 hours. "The noise of the musketry," said one veteran, "was not rattling, as ordinarily, but one intense metallic din."

Finally, just as darkness covered the bloody field, Hood's Texas brigade, along with Gen. George Pickett's brigade on Longstreet's left, penetrated the right of Morell's line in a courageous bayonet charge that broke the morale of the Federal troops. They went streaming back across the plateau to the safety of the Chickahominy

River. In a last desperate attempt to stem the tide, General Cooke ("Jeb" Stuart's father-in-law) sent his cavalry in a wild charge against the pressing Confederates. But the retreating Union infantry and artillery obstructed the cavalry and broke its attack. The only result was the loss of several more artillery pieces in the confusion.

With darkness closing in and the Confederate troops disorganized after the breakthrough, Lee did not attempt to pursue the Federals farther. Porter withdrew the remnants of his corps across the river and rejoined the main Union army. Total casualties in this crucial battle, the most costly and vicious of the Seven Days, were: Union, 6,837; Confederate, 8,751.

In a sense, both sides had achieved their immediate objectives. Porter had held until night, so McClellan could get his army safely started for Harrison's Landing. Lee had cleared the north side of the Chickahominy of all Federal forces, broken their supply line to White House, controlled strategic New Bridge, and had turned back McClellan's advance on Richmond.

Savage Station

McClellan was now engaged in the most difficult move an army can be called upon to make in the face of an aggressive enemy—a flanking movement to effect a change of base. There was no thought

Battle of Savage Station. From *Battles and Leaders of the Civil War.*

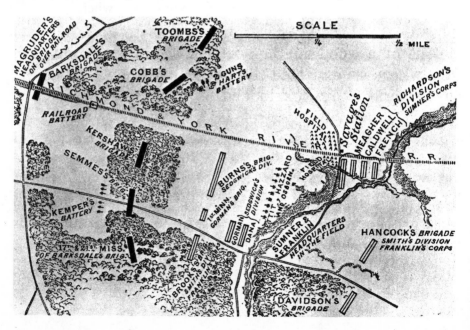

given to any offensive movement. President Lincoln telegraphed: "Save your army at all events." This was now McClellan's only objective.

That McClellan had not tried to fall back on White House surprised Lee, as he had believed he was facing the main part of the Federal army at Gaines' Mill. The next day, June 28, he spent burying the dead, reorganizing for another offensive movement, and attempting to divine McClellan's plans. Lee reported to Jefferson Davis that "the bridges over the Chickahominy in rear of the enemy were destroyed, and their reconstruction impracticable in the presence of his whole army and powerful batteries. We were therefore compelled to wait until his purpose should be developed." By nightfall, however, he realized that McClellan was headed for the James River, and made his plans accordingly.

Early next morning, June 29, Longstreet and A. P. Hill were to cross the Chickahominy at New Bridge and take the Darbytown road to where it met the Long Bridge road. Huger and Magruder, already on the south side of the river in front of Richmond, were ordered in pursuit of the Federal forces—Huger by Charles City road and Magruder by the Williamsburg road. In the meantime, Jackson would cross Grapevine Bridge and sweep down the south side of the river to get in McClellan's rear.

Again, Lee's strategy was brilliant. The Charles City road met the Long Bridge road at a place called Glendale or Frayser's Farm. Lee planned to have all his divisions converge there at about the time the middle of McClellan's long column should be passing. The impact of the expected blow would undoubtedly split the Union army. and with Jackson's corps in the rear of one half, the other half could be cut off and annihilated. Once again, however, the staff work and tactics were pitiful.

McClellan's rearguard was posted about Savage Station on the Richmond and York River Railroad, facing west. Richardson's division, of Sumner's corps, was in an open field north of the railroad tracks in back of the station. Sedgwick's division held the center in another open field south of the tracks, with its left resting on the Williamsburg road. Gen. William F. ("Baldy") Smith's division, of Franklin's corps, took position in the woods south of the Williamsburg road.

Magruder reached the vicinity of Savage Station about noon, June 29, but did not attack as he realized his four brigades were badly outnumbered. He halted and waited for Jackson, who was supposed to turn the Federal right flank along the Chickahominy and get in their rear. But Jackson "was delayed by the necessity of reconstructing Grapevine Bridge." Magruder then mistakenly reported McClellan advancing and sent for two brigades from Huger to support him. Lee cancelled the order when he realized that what Magruder had hit was only the rearguard covering the Federal army's passage across White Oak swamp. What Lee did not realize, however, was that Jackson was not in position and would not reach Savage Station until 3 the following morning. Finally, about 5 that afternoon, Magruder attacked with his four brigades and two regiments, but it was too late with too little. The Federals withdrew hastily but safely. In their haste they were forced to leave 2,500 sick and wounded men in the field hospital at Savage Station and to abandon or destroy a vast amount of supplies and equipment.

Battle of Savage Station.   From a contemporary sketch.

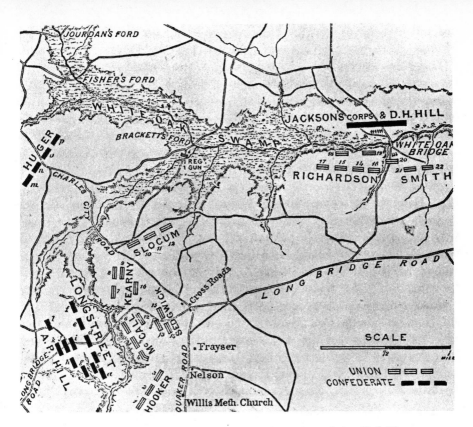

Battle of Glendale. From *Battles and Leaders of the Civil War.*

Glendale (Frayser's Farm)

Lee now ordered Magruder to follow Longstreet and A. P. Hill down the Darbytown road. The next day, June 30, Longstreet and Hill came upon the Union troops of McCall and Kearney across the Long Bridge road about a mile west of the Charles City road intersection at Glendale. Hooker held the left or south flank, with Slocum on the right guarding the Charles City road approach. Sedgwick was in the rear in reserve. Longstreet and Hill halted and waited for Huger, coming down the Charles City road, and Jackson, supposedly coming on the Federal rear from White Oak Swamp.

Meanwhile, Gen. T. H. Holmes, who had come from the south side of the James River with part of his division and Gen. Henry A. Wise's brigade, had been sent by Lee down the River, or New Market, road in an attempt to get between McClellan and the James River. McClellan anticipated the move, however, and Warren of Sykes' division stopped Holmes south of Malvern Hill. Lee then ordered Magruder on the Darbytown road to reinforce him, but Magruder's forces did not get there in time to help.

Huger was delayed by obstructions, mostly felled trees, with which the Federals had blocked his path. Instead of going around the obstructions, Huger continually halted to clear the road. Thus it resolved itself into a question of whether Huger could clear the trees as fast as the Union soldiers cut them down. In this so-called "battle of the axes" Huger lost, and did not get to Glendale in time to participate in the engagement.

About 4 that afternoon, however, Longstreet heard artillery firing from Huger's direction which "was supposed to indicate his approach," and expecting Jackson's appearance momentarily, he opened with one of his batteries and thus brought on the battle. Jackson never did show up, being held north of White Oak Swamp by the artillery of Richardson and Smith, and did not get to Glendale until the next day. The fight was particularly vicious with many pockets of hand-to-hand combat, but, without the expected support of Huger and Jackson, Longstreet could not break the Union lines in time to inflict any serious damage or to interrupt the withdrawal. Lee stated in his report: "Could the other commands have cooperated in the action the result would have proved most disastrous to the enemy." Gone was Lee's last chance to cut McClellan's army in two.

Malvern Hill

McClellan had already selected another naturally strong position, this time on Malvern Hill, for the last stand before reaching the James River. On the morning of July 1, Morell and Sykes' divisions of Porter's corps were drawn up on the crest of the hill west of the Quaker road. East of the road Couch's division of Keyes' corps held the front, with Kearney and Hooker of Heintzelman's corps flanked to the right and rear. Sumner's troops were in the rear in reserve. The position was flanked on either side by creeks in deep ravines less than a mile apart, and across this narrow front, Porter placed his batteries with the guns almost hub to hub. In front, the ground was open, sloping down to woods, marshes, and swamps, through which the Confederate forces had to form for attack within range of the Federal artillery.

Lee had Jackson on his left facing Kearney, Hooker, and Couch's right. D. H. Hill was in the center opposite Couch's left and Morell's right. Lee then ordered Magruder to the right of Hill, but Magruder was delayed by taking the wrong road; so instead two brigades of Huger's were placed on Hill's right. Longstreet and A. P. Hill, their ranks decimated from the actions at Gaines' Mill

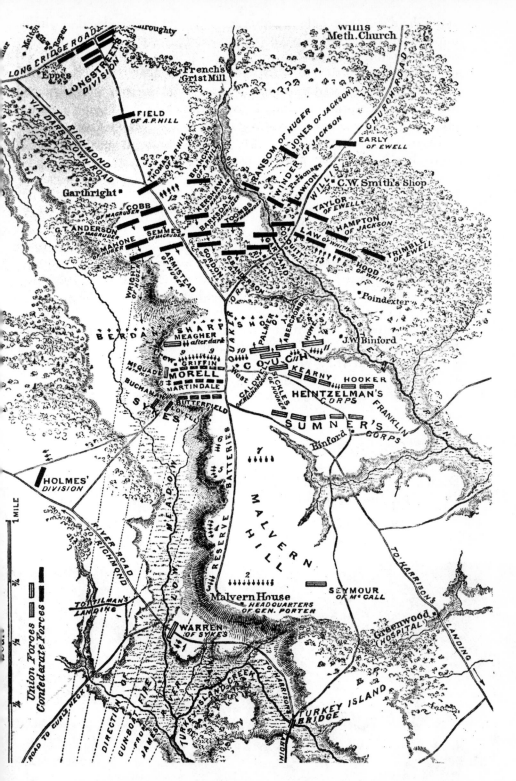

Battle of Malvern Hill. From *Battles and Leaders of the Civil War.*

and Glendale, were held in reserve. The terrain rendered it almost impossible for effective use of Confederate artillery, and the few batteries that did get into position were quickly cut to pieces by the massed Union guns.

"Owing to ignorance of the country, the dense forests impeding necessary communications, and the extreme difficulty of the ground," Lee reported, "the whole line was not formed until a late hour in the afternoon." The first real assault did not take place until after 5, and then it was uncoordinated and confused. The signal for the attack was to be a yell from one of Huger's brigades, after the Confederate artillery had blasted a hole in the Union lines. This put the responsibility of where and when to begin the attack on a mere brigade commander.

The artillery was unable to put concentrated fire in any one spot, but Huger attacked regardless and was beaten back with heavy losses. Then D. H. Hill attacked, only to suffer the same fate. Magruder finally sent his troops in a gallant charge across the open fields right up to the cannons' muzzles, only to be mowed down like wheat at harvest time. Late in the battle Jackson sent his own division to Magruder's and Hill's support, but in the heavily wooded and swampy ground they got lost and did not arrive in time to help. Darkness finally put an end to these hopeless attacks. As D. H. Hill declared bitterly, "It was not war—it was murder."

End of Campaign

During the night McClellan continued his withdrawal, and the next day found the Army of the Potomac safe at Harrison's Landing

McClellan's withdrawal. From a contemporary sketch.

Army of the Potomac at Harrison's Landing.   From a contemporary sketch.

under the protection of the Federal gunboats on the James. The Seven Days were over. Total casualties: Army of Northern Virginia, 20,614; Army of the Potomac, 15,849.

In his official report of the campaign Lee stated: "Under ordinary circumstances the Federal Army should have been destroyed. Its escape was due to * * * the want of correct and timely information. This fact, attributable chiefly to the character of the country, enabled Gen. McClellan skillfully to conceal his retreat and to add much to the obstructions with which nature had beset the way of our pursuing columns * * *." But his other objective had been achieved—Richmond was safe, at least for the time being.

While McClellan had successfully changed his base of operations from the York to the James River and saved his army in the process, he had failed in his first objective of capturing Richmond and possibly ending the war. The decision to remove the army from the peninsula, rather than reinforce it for another attempt on Richmond, was made in Washington over McClellan's strong objections. He wrote to Gen. Henry W. Halleck: "It is here on the banks of the James, that the fate of the Union should be decided."

McClellan's cartographers. Courtesy, Library of Congress.

Although McClellan wisely realized the advantages of another assault on Richmond on the line of the James, it was his own mistaken view of Lee's strength that was the major reason for the withdrawal. As Halleck explained to him:

> You and your officers at one interview estimated the enemy's forces in and around Richmond at 200,000 men. Since then you and others report that they have received and are receiving large re-enforcements from the South. General Pope's army covering Washington is only about 40,000. Your effective force is only about 90,000. You are 30 miles from Richmond, and General Pope 80 or 90, with the enemy directly between you, ready to fall with his superior numbers upon one or the other, as he may elect. Neither can re-enforce the other in case of such an attack. If General Pope's army be diminished to re-enforce you, Washington, Maryland, and Pennsylvania would be left uncovered and exposed. If your force be reduced to strengthen Pope, you would be too weak to even hold the position you now occupy should the enemy turn around and attack you in full force. In other words, the old Army of the Potomac is split into two parts * * * and I wish to unite them.

In August the Army of the Potomac was transported by water back to Washington to support Pope's campaign in Northern Virginia. McClellan's failure to capture the Confederate Capital, combined with Lee's failure to destroy the Union Army, assured the nation a long, bitter war that became one of the great turning points in American history.

Richmond, summer of 1862.   From a contemporary sketch.

The Years Between

In August 1862 Lee wrote to Jefferson Davis: "If we are able to change the theater of the war from the James River to the north of the Rappahannock we shall be able to consume provisions and forage now being used in supporting the enemy." So Lee moved into Northern Virginia to meet Pope's threatened overland campaign against Richmond. At Second Manassas (Bull Run) the Union army was defeated again and withdrew into the fortifications around Washington.

Lee took advantage of this opportunity and made his first invasion north into Maryland, only to be defeated by McClellan at Antietam (Sharpsburg) in September. Lee then withdrew into Virginia, and at Fredericksburg in December he severely repulsed Gen. Ambrose Burnside's move on Richmond. In the spring of 1863 the Union army, now under Hooker, attempted to flank Lee's left and rear to cut him off from Richmond, but it was decisively defeated at Chancellorsville and driven back across the Rapidan. Lee then made his second thrust north, penetrating into Pennsylvania, but was beaten back by Meade at Gettysburg in the summer of 1863 and, once again, retired into Virginia.

These gallant armies fought each other across the fields of Pennsylvania, Maryland, and Virginia before they clashed again in the outskirts of Richmond 2 years later.

***Jackson's troops pillaging Federal supplies at Manassas Junction just prior to
the Second Battle of Manassas.*** From "Battles and Leaders of the Civil War."

CHAPTER V

Second Battle of Bull Run

Second Battle of Manassas

FIRST PHASE—BRISTOE AND MANASSAS, AUGUST 27. Pope, now advised of the presence of Jackson in his rear, immediately ordered a concentration of his forces in order to crush him. McDowell's and Sigel's corps, together with the division of Reynolds, were to move to Gainesville, while Reno's corps, with Kearny's division of Heintzelman's corps, was to concentrate at Greenwich. By these dispositions Pope hoped to intercept any reinforcements coming to Jackson by way of Thoroughfare Gap. With Hooker's division of Heintzelman's corps Pope moved along the railroad to Manassas Junction.

On the afternoon of August 27, Hooker attacked Ewell and drove him back upon Bristoe. During the night, Ewell retired to Manassas where he joined the rest of Jackson's force. Pope now learned for the first time that the whole of Jackson's command was at Manassas. New orders were issued for a concentration at that point. Porter was ordered to march at 1 a. m. of the 28th from Warrenton Junction and be in position at Bristoe by daylight. McDowell, Sigel, and Reno were to move at dawn upon Manassas Junction, while Kearny was to advance at the same hour upon Bristoe.

About 3 a. m., August 28, Jackson began to move out of Manassas toward Groveton. In order to mystify and mislead Pope, he sent Taliaferro along the Manassas-Sudley Road, Ewell along the Centreville Road via Blackburn's Ford and the Stone Bridge to Groveton, and A. P. Hill to Centreville and thence along the Warrenton Pike to a position near Sudley Church.

Moving with Kearny's division, Pope arrived at Manassas Junction at noon, to find the town deserted. Later in the day, word was received that the Confederates had been seen in Centreville. Pope thereupon ordered a concentration at this place in the belief that Jackson's whole force was there. The corps of Heintzelman and Reno moved along the Centreville Road; Sigel and Reynolds along the Manassas-Sudley Road; King's division of McDowell's corps along the Warrenton Pike.

Longstreet's troops skirmishing at Thoroughfare Gap. From
"Manassas to Appomattox."

SECOND PHASE—GROVETON, AUGUST 28.   Jackson had but a short time
before concentrated north of the turnpike when word was received that
King's Federal column was approaching from Gainesville. There was now
need for a quick decision. To allow King to pass unmolested would
defeat the purpose of the campaign by permitting Pope to assume an
impregnable position on the heights at Centreville. To attack, without
assurance as to when Longstreet would arrive, was to invite the assault
of Pope's whole force with possible fatal consequences. Without hesitation he ordered the divisions of Taliaferro and Ewell to advance. A
fierce and stubborn fight ensued which resulted in heavy losses on both
sides. Finally, about 9 p. m., King withdrew towards Manassas.

In the meantime, Longstreet had reached Thoroughfare Gap at about
3 p. m. of the same day to find his way blocked by Federal troops under
Ricketts. Outmaneuvering his opponent by way of Hopewell Gap, he
forced him to fall back to Gainesville. That night, without informing
Pope of their intentions, King and Ricketts decided to move towards
Manassas. This enabled Longstreet to effect an easy junction with Jackson in the afternoon of the following day.

THIRD PHASE—MAIN BATTLE, AUGUST 29–30.   When Pope learned of
the engagement of Groveton he mistakenly decided that King had met
the head of Jackson's column in retreat. Confident of success, he ordered
a concentration of his leg weary troops to crush the Confederate force.
Sigel and Reynolds were to attack at dawn, reinforced by Heintzelman
and Reno. McDowell and Porter were ordered to reverse their course
and push toward Gainesville in an effort to cut off Jackson's retreat.

119

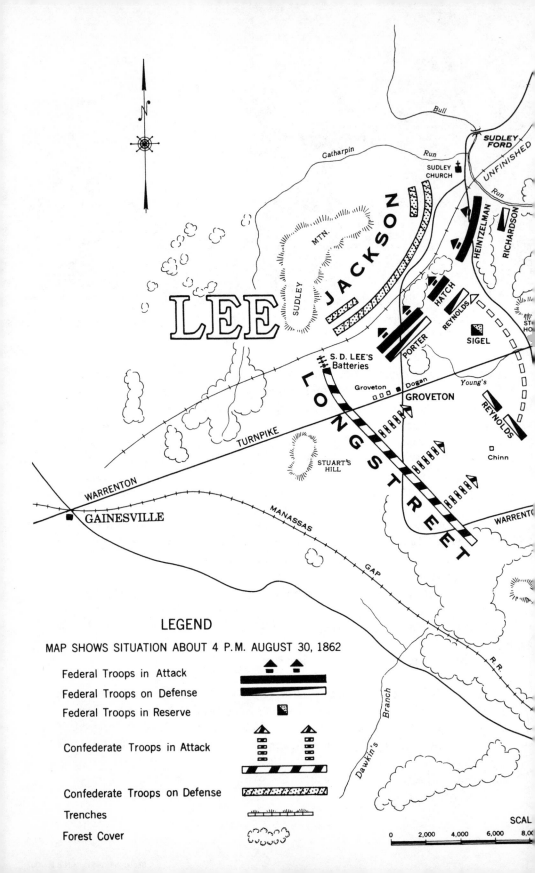

N

Bull

SUDLEY
FORD

Catharpin

Run

UNFINISHED

SUDLEY
CHURCH

Run

SUDLEY MTN.

JACKSON

HEINTZELMAN

RICHARDSON

LEE

HATCH

REYNOLDS

ST.
HO...

S. D. LEE'S
Batteries

LONGSTREET

PORTER

SIGEL

Groveton

Dogan

Young's

GROVETON

REYNOLDS

TURNPIKE

STUART'S
HILL

Chinn

WARRENTON

WARRENTO...

GAINESVILLE

MANASSAS

GAP

R R

LEGEND

MAP SHOWS SITUATION ABOUT 4 P.M. AUGUST 30, 1862

Federal Troops in Attack

Federal Troops on Defense

Federal Troops in Reserve

Confederate Troops in Attack

Confederate Troops on Defense

Trenches

Forest Cover

Branch

Dawkin's

SCAL...

0   2,000   4,000   6,000   8,0...

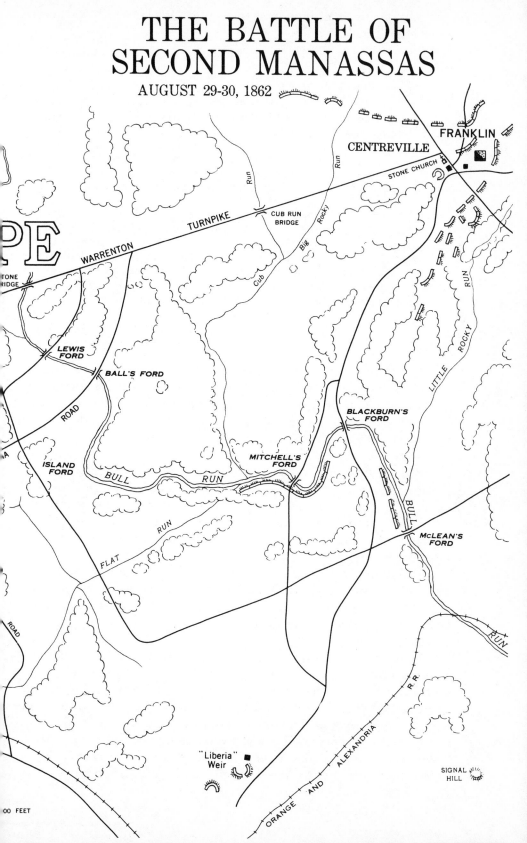

THE BATTLE OF
SECOND MANASSAS

AUGUST 29-30, 1862

FRANKLIN

CENTREVILLE

STONE CHURCH

Run

Run

PE

TURNPIKE

CUB RUN
BRIDGE

Big
(Rocky)

WARRENTON

Cub

TONE
RIDGE

LITTLE ROCKY RUN

LEWIS
FORD

BALL'S FORD

ROAD

BLACKBURN'S
FORD

ISLAND
FORD

MITCHELL'S
FORD

BULL

RUN

A

RUN

BULL

McLEAN'S
FORD

FLAT

ROAD

R.R.

"Liberia"
Weir

SIGNAL
HILL

00 FEET

ORANGE AND ALEXANDRIA

RUN

The text of this order known as the "Joint Order," which was received about noon, reads as follows:

HEADQUARTERS ARMY OF VIRGINIA
Centreville, August 29, 1862.

Generals McDowell and Porter:

You will please move forward with your joint commands toward Gainesville. I sent General Porter written orders to that effect an hour and a half ago. Heintzelman, Sigel, and Reno are moving on the Warrenton turnpike, and must now be not far from Gainesville. I desire that as soon as communication is established between this force and your own the whole command shall halt. It may be necessary to fall back behind Bull Run at Centreville to-night. I presume it will be so, on account of our supplies. . . .

If any considerable advantages are to be gained by departing from this order it will not be strictly carried out. One thing must be had in view, that the troops must occupy a position from which they can reach Bull Run to-night or by morning. The indications are that the whole force of the enemy is moving in this direction at a pace that will bring them here by to-morrow night or the next day. My own headquarters will be for the present with Heintzelman's corps or at this place.

Jno. Pope,
Major-General, Commanding.

Prior to the receipt of the "Joint Order," Porter had reversed his course to Centreville and had moved as far as Dawkin's Branch, located about 3 miles from Gainesville. Finding the Confederates strongly posted in his front, he deployed a brigade of his leading division and waited. McDowell, who arrived shortly thereafter, showed him a dispatch he had received a few minutes before from Buford, who commanded the Union cavalry on the right. The dispatch stated that 17 regiments, 1 battery, and 500 cavalry had passed through Gainesville about 8:45 a. m. This was the advance of Longstreet's command which had left Thoroughfare Gap early that morning and now, followed by heavy reinforcements, was moving into position on Jackson's right (Porter's front).

This information, the generals felt, had not reached Pope. After a conference, it was decided that in face of this new development they would take advantage of the latitude the order granted: McDowell would move towards Groveton, while Porter would remain in the vicinity of his present position.

The relative quiet in this sector was in sharp contrast to the heavy fighting now taking place along Jackson's front. With about 18,000 infantry and 40 guns, Jackson had taken up a position along an unfinished railroad bed which extended from near Sudley Springs 2 miles southwesterly to Groveton. The grades and cuts of this road provided ready-made entrenchments and formed a very strong position. There, shortly after sunrise, Sigel's and Reynolds' columns were seen at a distance deploying for the attack. About 7 a. m., the Federal batteries opened fire.

Maj. Gen. Fitz-John Porter, in command of the Fifth Army Corps at the Second Battle of Manassas. Courtesy Library of Congress.

By 10:30 a. m., a number of sharp skirmishes had taken place, but no general assault had been made. About this time Federal reinforcements of Reno and Kearny reached the field. It was not until 2 p. m., however, that the battle reached its height. All afternoon in violent but uncoordinated attacks, blue columns gallantly assaulted Jackson's line. At one point the Confederate left was pushed back dangerously near the breaking point, but the gray line steadied and held. Towards dusk, King's division, of McDowell's corps, arrived in time to take part in the action, engaging a part of Longstreet's command which was then advancing on a reconnaissance.

Pope, still unaware of the arrival of Longstreet on the field, late in the day sent Porter the following order to attack Jackson's right at once:

HEADQUARTERS IN THE FIELD,
August 29—4:30 p. m.

Major-General Porter:

Your line of march brings you in on the enemy's right flank. I desire you to push forward into action at once on the enemy's flank, and, if possible, on his rear, keeping your right in communication with General Reynolds. The enemy is massed in the woods in front of us, but can be shelled out as soon as you engage their flank. Keep heavy reserves and use your batteries, keeping well closed to your right all the time. In case you are obliged to fall back, do so to your right and rear, so as to keep you in close communication with the right wing.

John Pope,
Major-General, Commanding.

This order, dated 4:30 p. m., was received by Porter at Bethlehem Church about 6:30 p. m. Upon receipt of the order Porter immediately sent his chief of staff, Locke, to order Morell's division to attack. Shortly thereafter Porter rode to the front to find Morell's preparations for the attack complete. By this time, however, it was so late that Porter decided to rescind the order.[1]

During the night the Confederates retired from the advanced positions gained during the day to their original battleline. This fact was reported from the field early on the morning of the 30th and later confirmed by a reconnaissance by McDowell and Heintzelman. This led Pope falsely to assume that Lee was in retreat to Thoroughfare Gap. Immediately, plans were initiated to press a vigorous pursuit. At midday the following order was issued:

Special Orders,   HEADQUARTERS NEAR GROVETON,
No. —   *August* 30, 1862—12 M.

The following forces will be immediately thrown forward and in pursuit of the enemy, and press him vigorously during the whole day. Major-General McDowell is assigned to the command of the pursuit.

Major-General Porter's corps will push forward on the Warrenton turnpike, followed by the divisions of Brigadier-Generals King and Reynolds. The division of Brigadier-General Ricketts will pursue the Hay Market road, followed by the corps of Major-General Heintzelman. . . .

At 3 a. m. of the 30th, Porter received Pope's dispatch ordering him to march his command immediately to the field of battle of the previous day. In compliance with this order he promptly withdrew from his position facing Longstreet and marched rapidly along the Sudley Road to the center of the battlefield where he reported to Pope for orders. Though this movement strengthened the center, it dangerously weakened the Federal left.

From its contracted left near Groveton, the Federal line now extended approximately 3 miles to Bull Run near Sudley Church. The opposing Confederate line was about 4 miles long. Jackson held the left along the unfinished railroad, while Longstreet held the right, with the main body of his troops "bent to the front" south of the Warrenton Pike. A heavy concentration of artillery was placed on high ground between the two wings. These guns commanded the open fields and the stretch of woods near Jackson's right and center.

[1] For his failure to carry out Pope's order of the 29th to attack Jackson, Porter was court-martialed and dismissed from the army on January 21, 1863. In 1879, a board of general officers who reviewed the case held that Porter could not have attacked Jackson successfully, as ordered, because Longstreet's corps had moved up into position on the right of Jackson and opposite Porter, and that this was known to the latter. Thus, Pope's order, which was written without knowledge of this development, could not be carried out. President Arthur, in 1882, remitted that part of the sentence which disqualified Porter from holding any office of trust or profit under the Government of the United States. On August 5, 1886, Porter was reappointed colonel of infantry, and 2 days later placed on the retirement list. To this day, despite his final vindication, the controversy over Porter's action on August 29, 1862, at Second Manassas has not died down among military students.

Preparations completed about midafternoon, the Federal columns of Porter and Heintzelman advanced three lines deep, preceded by a swarm of skirmishers and supported by great masses of men and guns in the rear. A strange quiet pervaded the fields as the unsuspecting troops pushed forward. Behind their protective cover, the Confederates watched the lines draw closer; then suddenly opened upon them a rapid artillery fire. Instantly, the infantry bugles sounded the alarm alerting Jackson's men to action. The Federal advance line halted and staggered back. Other brigades quickly pushed forward only to be broken by the raking force of the fire.

Soon it was apparent that the main Federal assault was being directed by Porter and Hatch against Jackson's right and center held by the divisions of Starke and Lawton. In gallant style, a third line moved up and impetuously pressed the attack. The force of this forward movement pushed back the famous Stonewall brigade, but later it reestablished its lines in a desperate countercharge. Heavy fighting at close quarters now ensued. At one point in their line near a section of the railroad bed known as the "Deep Cut," Jackson's veterans, with ammunition exhausted, partially repelled an attack with stones from the embankment.

Some of Jackson's Confederates, their ammunition exhausted, hurling rocks at the advancing Federals, during the Second Battle of Manassas. From "Battles and Leaders of the Civil War."

Finally, the pressure became so great that Jackson sent an urgent request for reinforcements. Lee then ordered forward a brigade from Longstreet's command. Anticipating the request, Longstreet had already moved up the batteries of Stephen D. Lee, which now opened a withering fire on the Federal columns on Jackson's right and center. The effect was devastating. Within 15 minutes the whole aspect of the battle had changed.

Shortly after the Federal brigades had engaged Jackson along the unfinished railroad, Pope had ordered Reynolds' division from his left at Bald Hill to move up and support the attack on the right. The weight of his numbers, however, proved insufficient to stem the tide of retreat that had now set in. Quickly, Jackson ordered up two brigades to press a counterattack, moving forward his artillery as the infantry advanced.

The transfer of Reynolds' division had again greatly weakened the Federal left. Lee saw this and realized that here at last was the opportunity for which he had been waiting. The order was sent immediately to Longstreet to deliver the counterstroke. Every regiment, battery, and squadron of both wings of the army were to be employed. By sheer weight of numbers the attack was to be driven home in successive waves of assault, piling one upon the other.

"The battle of Groveton or Second Bull Run between the Union Army commanded by Genl. Pope and Con. Army under Genl. Robert E. Lee. Sketched from Bald face hill (Henry Hill) on Saturday afternoon half past three o'clock . . . Looking toward the village of Groveton." From original wartime sketch, with title by E. Forbes. Courtesy Library of Congress.

Again, Longstreet had anticipated the order for which he had been preparing since dawn. The long gray lines of infantry, restive for the fray, now swept forward in a furious assault. In advance came Hood's Texans, their colors gleaming red in the evening sun. Above the thunderous roar of artillery and the noise of battle could be heard the shrill cries of the rebel yell echoing through the Groveton valley. So intense was the excitement that only with the greatest difficulty could the officers restrain their men. Rapidly moving up in support came the divisions of Anderson, Kemper, and D. R. Jones. Across the rolling fields the attack pushed to gain the promontory of Chinn Ridge despite a stubborn defense by the Union brigades of McLean, Tower, and Milroy, while Jackson's veterans successfully assailed Buck Hill.

On Henry Hill, poignant with memories of the previous year, were now assembled Reynolds' divisions, Sykes' regulars, and other available troops. With courage and gallantry that matched the crisis of battle, they hurled back repeated Confederate assaults that continued until dark. The successful defense of Henry Hill made possible Pope's retreat over

Note. *The artist identified the following points:*

1. *Thoroughfare Gap through which Genl. Lee's Army passed.*
2. *Rebs line of battle.*
3. *The old R.R. embankment behind which the Con. were posted.*
4. *The old Stone House on the Turnpike used as a hospital.*
5. *Warrenton Turnpike.*
6. *Bald face hill {Henry Hill}.*
7. *Henry Hill {Buck Hill}.*
8. *Union line of battle.*
9. *McDowell's corps moving to the left flank to repel Longstreet's attack which had just commenced.*
10. *Sudley Springs road."*

The "Deep Cut" where Porter's troops made a gallant bid for victory. Here a Federal flag held its position for half an hour within 10 yards of a Confederate regimental flag. Six times it fell, only to be raised again. From "Battles and Leaders of the Civil War."

Bull Run, by the Stone Bridge and other fords, to the strong defenses of the Centreville plateau.

FOURTH PHASE—CHANTILLY, SEPTEMBER 1.   Considering the Centreville position as unfavorable for attack, Lee sent Jackson by Sudley Ford to the Little River Turnpike in an effort to turn the Federal right and threaten communications with Washington. The movement, however, was anticipated by Pope, and the divisions of Stevens and Kearny were sent to check it. In a sharp contest, fought in a rainstorm at Chantilly on September 1, Stevens and Kearny were killed; but Jackson was repulsed. During the next 2 days Pope retired to the defenses of Washington.

The Federal retreat over the Stone Bridge on Saturday evening, August 30, 1862. From "Battles and Leaders of the Civil War."

Ruins of the Henry House after the Second Battle of Manassas.
Wartime photograph. Courtesy National Archives.

RESULTS OF SECOND BATTLE OF MANASSAS.   Second Manassas offers an interesting contrast to the opening battle which had found two armies of raw, undisciplined volunteers courageously but falteringly battling for supremacy. The raw volunteers had now been replaced by seasoned veterans, hardened by months of strenuous campaigning. The campaign just ended had been one to test to the utmost the endurance and discipline of the men in the ranks of both armies—a test they had met with valor and high honor. In contrast to the rout of First Manassas, the Federal army which now retired upon Washington was a weary but defiant fighting machine. Its defeat had been accomplished by exceptional daring, combined with a skillful coordination of Confederate commands. Gambling with long chances, Lee had succeeded in removing some 150,000 invading troops from deep in Virginia and reversing the threat of impending attack upon the opposing capital.

Commenting upon the battle, Henderson, the English soldier and historian, writes:

> . . . If, as Moltke avers, the junction of two armies on the field of battle is the highest achievement of military genius, the campaign against Pope has seldom been surpassed; and the great counter-stroke at Manassas is sufficient in itself to make Lee's reputation as a tactician. . . . It was not due to the skill of Lee that Pope weakened his left at the crisis of battle. But in the rapidity with which the opportunity was seized, in the combination of the three arms, and in the vigour of the blow, Manassas is in no way inferior to Austerlitz or Salamanca.

This brilliant success did much to offset Confederate reverses in the West—the loss of Missouri, the defeats of Forts Henry and Donelson,

Shiloh, and the fall of Nashville, New Orleans, and Memphis. Contrary to the inactivity that followed First Manassas, Lee pressed his victory by the first invasion of the North. On September 4, he began moving his troops across the Potomac with the hope of winning the support of Maryland and possibly the recognition of the Confederacy by foreign powers. In the desperately fought battle of Antietam, September 17, at Sharpsburg, Md., however, these hopes were dashed by McClellan, now returned to Federal command.

	FEDERAL	CONFEDERATE
Strength	73, 000 (*approx.*)	55, 000
CASUALTIES		
Killed	1, 747	1, 553
Wounded.	8, 452	7, 812
Captured or missing	4, 263	109
Total	14, 462	9, 474

The War After Second Manassas

From Antietam, Lee retired to Virginia. With the coming of winter snows he bloodily repelled Maj. Gen. Ambrose E. Burnside in the Battle of Fredericksburg, December 13, 1862. In the spring, Confederate arms achieved brilliant success in the defeat of Maj. Gen. Joseph E. Hooker in the Battle of Chancellorsville, May 1–6, 1863. Capitalizing on his victory, Lee again invaded the North. At Gettysburg, July 1–3, he was defeated by Maj. Gen. George Gordon Meade. The next day saw the end of one of the most brilliant and decisive operations of the war with the surrender of Vicksburg to Maj. Gen. Ulysses S. Grant. Its fall cut the Confederacy in two and opened the Mississippi to Federal commerce and control. From the telling force of these simultaneous blows the Confederacy never recovered.

On March 9, 1864, Grant was placed in supreme command of all Federal armies. Now as never before, the full strength and resources of the republic were marshalled for a great offensive to be delivered simultaneously on all fronts. Attaching himself to Meade's army, Grant crossed the Rapidan on May 4 to launch his overland campaign against Richmond, while Sherman began the famous march that was to carry him to Atlanta and the sea.

In the fiercely contested battles of the Wilderness and Spotsylvania Court House, May 5–6 and 8–21, respectively, Grant largely succeeded in destroying Lee's offensive power, forcing his retirement upon Richmond. Repulsed with heavy losses at Cold Harbor, June 3, Grant moved upon Petersburg again to encounter Lee's army.

Ten months of siege followed as Grant methodically cut the Confed-

*View northwest across Henry Hill. The present Henry House is
seen in center background.*

erate lifeline. On April 2, Lee evacuated Petersburg with the hope of
reaching the Danville railroad and possibly effecting a junction with
Johnston's forces in North Carolina. Grant's pursuit, however, was rapid
and relentless. The cutting of the escape route by the Danville line and
the disastrous defeat of a large segment of his army in the Battle of
Sayler's Creek forced Lee to move farther westward to Appomattox
Court House. There at dusk, April the 8th, the widening circle of Federal
campfires brought realization that the end had been reached. The next
day Lee surrendered to the magnanimous terms of Grant. On April 26,
Johnston yielded to Sherman and by June all isolated units of the Confederate forces had laid down their arms.

CHAPTER VI

Battle of Antietam

Focal point of the early morning attacks, the Dunkard Church and some who de-fended it.   From photograph attributed to James Gardner.   Courtesy, Library of Congress.

I N WESTERN MARYLAND *is a stream called Antietam Creek.*
*Nearby is the quiet town of Sharpsburg. The scene is pastoral, with
rolling hills and farmlands and patches of woods. Stone monuments and
bronze tablets dot the landscape. They seem strangely out of place. Only some
extraordinary event can explain their presence.*

*Almost by chance, two great armies collided here. Gen. Robert E. Lee's
Army of Northern Virginia was invading the North. Maj. Gen. George
B. McClellan's Army of the Potomac was out to stop him. On September
17, 1862—the bloodiest day of the Civil War—the two armies fought the
Battle of Antietam to decide the issue.*

*Their violent conflict shattered the quiet of Maryland's countryside. When
the hot September sun finally set upon the devastated battlefield, 23,000
Americans had fallen—nearly eight times more than fell on Tarawa's beaches
in World War II. This single fact, with the heroism and suffering it im-
plies, gives the monuments and markers their meaning. No longer do they
presume upon the land. Rather, their mute inadequacy can only hint of the
great event that happened here—and of its even greater consequences.*

Across the Potomac

On September 5-6, 1862, a ragged host of nearly 55,000 men in butternut and gray splashed across the Potomac River at White's Ford
near Leesburg, Va. This was Gen. Robert E. Lee's Army of North-

ern Virginia embarked on the Confederacy's first invasion of the North. Though thousands of Lee's men were shoeless, though they lacked ammunition and supplies, though they were fatigued from the marching and fighting just before the historic crossing into Maryland, they felt invincible.

Only a week before, August 28-30, they had routed the Federals at the Battle of Second Manassas, driving them headlong into the defenses of Washington. With this event, the strategic initiative so long held by Union forces in the East had shifted to the Confederacy. But Lee recognized that Union power was almost limitless. It must be kept off balance—prevented from reorganizing for another drive on Richmond, the Confederate capital. Only a sharp offensive thrust by Southern arms would do this.

Because his army lacked the strength to assault Washington, General Lee had decided on September 3 to invade Maryland. North of the Potomac his army would be a constant threat to Washington. This would keep Federal forces out of Virginia, allowing that ravaged land to recuperate from the campaigning that had stripped it. It would give Maryland's people, many of whom sympathized with the South, a chance to throw off the Northern yoke.

From Maryland, Lee could march into Pennsylvania, disrupting the east-west rail communications of the North, carrying the brunt of war into that rich land, drawing on its wealth to refit his army.

Lee's army crossing the Potomac; Union scouts in foreground. From wartime sketch by A. R. Waud. Courtesy, Library of Congress.

Larger political possibilities loomed, too. The North was war weary. If, in the heartland of the Union, Lee could inflict a serious defeat on Northern arms, the Confederacy might hope for more than military dividends—the result might be a negotiated peace on the basis of Southern independence. Too, a successful campaign might induce England and France to recognize the Confederacy and to intervene for the purpose of mediating the conflict.

So it was that the hopes of the South rode with this Army of Northern Virginia as it marched into Frederick, Md., on September 7.

McClellan in Command

On that same September 7, another army assembled at Rockville, Md., just northwest of Washington. Soon to be nearly 90,000 strong, this was Maj. Gen. George B. McClellan's Army of the Potomac. Its goal: To stay between Lee's army and Washington, to seek out the Confederate force, and, as President Abraham Lincoln hoped, to destroy it.

Hastily thrown together to meet the challenge of Lee's invasion, this Union army was a conglomerate of all the forces in the Washington vicinity. Some of its men were fresh from the recruiting depots—they lacked training and were deficient in arms. Others had just returned from the Peninsular Campaign where Lee's army had driven them from the gates of Richmond in the Seven Days' Battles, June 26–July 2. Still others were the remnants of the force so decisively beaten at Second Manassas.

Gen. Robert E. Lee. From photograph by Julian Vannerson. Courtesy, Library of Congress.

Maj. Gen. George B. McClellan.
From photograph by Matthew B. Brady
or assistant. Courtesy, National Archives.

In McClellan the Union army had a commander who was skilled at organization. This was the reason President Lincoln and Commander in Chief of the Army Henry Halleck had chosen him for command on September 3. In 4 days he had pulled together this new army and had gotten it on the march. It was a remarkable achievement.

But in other respects, McClellan was the object of doubt. He was cautious. He seemed to lack that capacity for full and violent commitment essential to victory. Against Lee, whose blood roused at the sound of the guns, McClellan's methodical nature had once before proved wanting—during the Seven Days' Battles. At least so thought President Lincoln.

But this time McClellan had started well. Could he now catch Lee's army and destroy it, bringing the end of the war in sight? Or, failing that, could he at least gain a favorable decision? A victory in the field would give the President a chance to issue the Emancipation Proclamation, which he had been holding since midsummer. The proclamation would declare free the slaves in the Confederate States. By this means, Lincoln hoped to infuse the Northern cause with regenerative moral power. Spirits were lagging in the North. Unless a moral purpose could be added to the North's primary war aim of restoring the Union, Lincoln questioned whether

137

the will to fight could be maintained in the face of growing casualty lists.

And so, followed by mingled doubt and hope, McClellan started in pursuit of the Confederate army. McClellan himself was aware of these mingled feelings. He knew that Lincoln and Halleck had come to him as a last resort in a time of emergency. He knew they doubted his energy and ability as a combat commander. Even his orders were unclear, for they did not explicitly give him authority to pursue the enemy beyond the defenses of Washington.

Burdened with knowledge of this lack of faith, wary of taking risks because of his ambiguous orders, McClellan marched toward his encounter with the victorious and confident Lee.

Lee Divides His Forces

Maryland was a disappointment to Lee. On September 8, he had issued a dignified proclamation inviting the men of that State to join his command and help restore Maryland to her rightful place among the Southern States. His words concluded with assurance that the Marylanders could make their choice with no fear of intimidation from the victorious Confederate army in their midst.

Maryland took him at his word. Her people did not flock to the Confederate standard, nor were they much help in provisioning his army. No doubt Lee's barefooted soldiers were a portent to

First Virginia Cavalry at a halt during invasion of Maryland. From wartime sketch by Waud. Courtesy, Library of Congress.

these people, who had previously seen only well-fed, well-equipped Federal troops.

Deprived of expected aid, Lee had to move onward to Pennsylvania quickly. For one thing, unless he could get shoes for his men, his army might melt away. Straggling was already a serious problem, for Maryland's hard roads tortured bare feet toughened only to the dirt lanes of Virginia.

By now, Lee's scouts were bringing reports of the great Federal army slowly pushing out from Rockville toward Frederick.

Lee's proposed route into Pennsylvania was dictated by geography. West of Frederick—beyond South Mountain—is the Cumberland Valley. This is the northern half of the Great Valley that sweeps northeastward through Virginia, Maryland, and Pennsylvania. That part of the Great Valley immediately south of the Potomac is called the Shenandoah Valley.

Lee planned to concentrate his army west of the mountains near Hagerstown, Md. There he would be in direct line with his supply base at Winchester in the Shenandoah Valley. After replenishing his supplies and ammunition, he could strike northeast through the Cumberland Valley toward Harrisburg, Pa., where he could destroy the Pennsylvania Railroad bridge across the Susquehanna River. Once loose in the middle of Pennsylvania he could live off the country and threaten Philadelphia, Baltimore, and Washington.

Before launching this daring maneuver, Lee must first clear his line of communications through the Shenandoah Valley to Winchester and to Richmond. Blocking it were strong Federal garrisons at Harpers Ferry and Martinsburg. Unaccountably, they had remained at their posts after the Confederate army crossed the Potomac. Now they must be cleared out.

Lee decided to accomplish this mission by boldly dividing his army into four parts. On September 9, he issued Special Order 191. Briefly, it directed Maj. Gen. James Longstreet and Maj. Gen. D. H. Hill to proceed across South Mountain toward Boonsboro and Hagerstown. Three columns cooperating under Maj. Gen. Thomas J. "Stonewall" Jackson were ordered to converge on Harpers Ferry from the northwest, northeast, and east. En route, the column under Jackson's immediate command was to swing westward and catch any Federals remaining at Martinsburg. Maj. Gen. Lafayette McLaws, approaching from the northeast, was to occupy Maryland Heights, which overlooks Harpers Ferry from the north side of the Potomac. Brig. Gen. John Walker, approaching from the east, was to occupy Loudoun Heights, across the Shenandoah River from Harpers Ferry. Maj. Gen. J. E. B. Stuart's cavalry was to screen these movements from McClellan by remaining east of South Mountain.

(At this point a fateful event occurred—one which was destined to change the subsequent course of the campaign. D. H. Hill, Jackson's

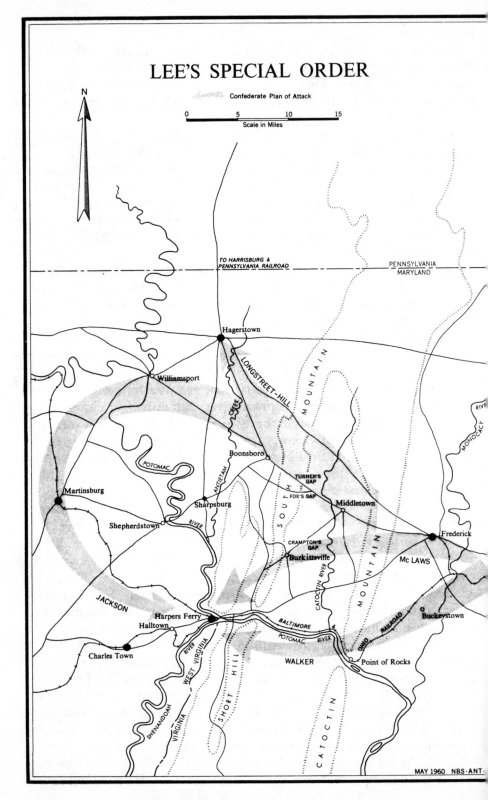

LEE'S SPECIAL ORDER

Confederate Plan of Attack

0 ___ 5 ___ 10 ___ 15
Scale in Miles

N

TO HARRISBURG &
PENNSYLVANIA RAILROAD

PENNSYLVANIA
MARYLAND

Hagerstown

LONGSTREET-HILL

Williamsport

CREEK

MOUNTAIN

Boonsboro

POTOMAC

ANTIETAM

TURNER'S
GAP

MONOCACY

RIVER

Martinsburg

Sharpsburg

FOX'S GAP

Middletown

SOUTH

Shepherdstown

RIVER

Frederick

CRAMPTON'S
GAP

Burkittsville

CATOCTIN RIVER

MOUNTAIN

Mc LAWS

JACKSON

Harpers Ferry

Halltown

BALTIMORE

POTOMAC   RIVER

OHIO   RAILROAD

Buckeystown

Charles Town

SHENANDOAH

VIRGINIA

WEST VIRGINIA

RIVER

SHORT   HILL

WALKER

Point of Rocks

CATOCTIN

MAY 1960 NBS·ANT

brother-in-law, had until this time been under Jackson's command. Unaware that a copy of Lee's order had already been sent to Hill, Jackson now prepared an extra copy for that officer. Hill kept the copy from Jackson; the other was to provide the script for much of the drama that followed.)

Lee was courting danger by thus dividing his force in the face of McClellan's advancing army. Against a driving opponent, Lee probably would not have done it. But he felt certain that McClellan's caution would give Jackson the margin of time needed to capture Harpers Ferry and reunite with Longstreet before the Federal army could come within striking distance. That margin was calculated at 3 or 4 days. By September 12, Jackson's force should be marching north toward Hagerstown. As soon as the army reconcentrated there, Lee could begin his dash up the Cumberland Valley into Pennsylvania.

So confident was Lee of the marching capacities of the Harpers Ferry columns, and so certain was he that McClellan would approach slowly, that he made no provision for guarding the gaps through South Mountain.

The Lost Order

Lee's army departed Frederick on September 10. Two days later leading elements of McClellan's army entered that city. On September 13, came McClellan himself with his usual cavalcade of staff officers.

Maj. Gen. James Longstreet.
Courtesy, Library of Congress.

Maj. Gen. Thomas J. "Stonewall" Jackson. From photograph by George W. Minnes. Courtesy, Library of Congress.

That same afternoon a copy of Lee's Special Order 191 was discovered in the encampment grounds previously used by the Confederate army. Quickly it was passed to McClellan. The handwriting was recognized as that of Col. R. H. Chilton, Lee's assistant adjutant general; the document's authenticity could not be doubted.

The fate of Lee's army literally lay in McClellan's hands. If he slashed swiftly through the South Mountain gaps and planted his army squarely between Longstreet's force near Hagerstown and Jackson's columns at Harpers Ferry, he could overwhelm the Confederate detachments in turn.

But again McClellan was methodical. Not until the next morning, September 14, did his heavy columns get underway. This crucial delay was to give Lee the chance to pull his army together at the small town of Sharpsburg.

Fighting for Time at South Mountain

By September 12, Lee had begun to worry. Stuart's scouts had reported the Federal approach to Frederick. McClellan was moving too fast. Next evening things looked worse. Jackson had not yet captured Harpers Ferry, and already McClellan's forward troops were pushing Stuart back toward the South Mountain gaps. Delay at Harpers Ferry made these passes through South Mountain the key to the situation. They must be defended.

South Mountain is the watershed between the Middletown and

The Battle of South Mountain. From lithograph by Endicott. Courtesy, Library of Congress.

Cumberland Valleys. The Frederick-Hagerstown road leads through Middletown, then goes over South Mountain at Turner's Gap. At the eastern base of the mountain, the old road to Sharpsburg turned south from the main road and passed through Fox's Gap, a mile south of Turner's Gap. Four miles farther south is Crampton's Gap, reached by another road from Middletown.

On the night of September 13, Lee ordered all available forces to defend these three passes. D. H. Hill, with Longstreet coming to his aid, covered Turner's and Fox's Gaps. McLaws sent part of his force back from Maryland Heights to hold Crampton's Gap.

Next morning the thin-stretched Confederate defenders saw McClellan's powerful columns marching across Middletown Valley. Up the roads to the gaps they came—ponderous and inexorable. The right wing of McClellan's army under Maj. Gen. Ambrose Burnside assaulted Turner's and Fox's Gaps. The left wing under Maj. Gen. William Franklin struck through Crampton's Gap. By nightfall, September 14, the superior Federal forces had broken through at Crampton's Gap; and Burnside's men were close to victory at the northern passes. The way to the valley was open.

By his stubborn defense at South Mountain, Lee had gained a day. But was it enough? McClellan's speed and shrewd pursuit, together with Jackson's inability to meet the demanding schedule set forth in Special Order 191, had fallen upon Lee with all the weight of a strategic surprise. No longer could he command events, pick his own objectives, and make the Federal army conform to his moves. Rather, the decision at South Mountain had snatched the initiative away from Lee. His plan for an offensive foray into Pennsylvania was wrecked. Now it was a question of saving his army.

The first step was to call off the attack on Harpers Ferry. At 8 p.m., September 14, Lee sent a dispatch to McLaws stating,

Harpers Ferry looking east toward confluence of Potomac and Shenandoah Rivers. Ruins of armory in right foreground. Maryland Heights, left; Loudoun Heights, right. From 1862 photograph by Brady. Courtesy, Library of Congress.

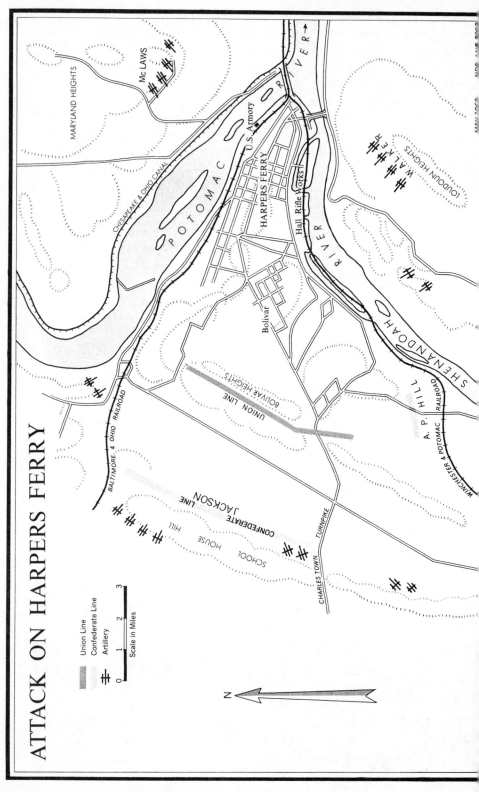

ATTACK ON HARPERS FERRY

Union Line
Confederate Line
Artillery

Scale in Miles
0 1 2 3

N

MARYLAND HEIGHTS

Mc LAWS

POTOMAC

CHESAPEAKE & OHIO CANAL

U.S. Armory

HARPERS FERRY

Hall Rifle Works

LOUDOUN HEIGHTS

WALKER

R I V E R

Bolivar

SHENANDOAH

HILL

A. P.

BALTIMORE & OHIO RAILROAD

BOLIVAR HEIGHTS

UNION LINE

JACKSON

CONFEDERATE LINE

SCHOOL HOUSE HILL

HILL

CHARLES TOWN TURNPIKE

WINCHESTER & POTOMAC RAILROAD

The day has gone against us and this army will go by Sharpsburg and cross the river. It is necessary for you to abandon your position tonight. . . . Send forward officers to explore the way, ascertain the best crossing of the Potomac, and if you can find any between you and Shepherdstown leave Shepherdstown Ford for this command." Jackson was ordered ". . . to take position at Shepherdstown to cover Lee's crossing into Virginia."

But then came a message from Jackson: Harpers Ferry was about to fall. Perhaps there was still hope. If Jackson could capture Harpers Ferry early the next day, the army could reunite at Sharpsburg. Good defensive ground was there; a victory over McClellan might enable Lee to continue his campaign of maneuver; and should disaster threaten, the fords of the Potomac were nearby.

At 11:15 p.m., Lee countermanded his earlier order; the attack on Harpers Ferry was to proceed. Shortly after, Longstreet's divisions began to march through the night toward Sharpsburg.

Harpers Ferry Surrenders

The village of Harpers Ferry lies at the gateway cut through the mountains by the Potomac and Shenandoah Rivers, whose waters join there. Situated at the apex of the triangle of land between the rivers, the town is completely dominated by Loudoun and Maryland Heights. By nightfall of September 14, McLaws and Walker had artillery on these heights ready for plunging fire into the town; Jackson had stretched his lines across the base of the triangle between the rivers.

Caught in this trap were nearly 12,000 Federal troops commanded by Col. D. S. Miles. Their position was indefensible.

At daybreak on September 15, the surrounding Confederate artillery opened fire. At 8 a.m., the hopelessness of his position confirmed, Miles ordered the surrender; he was killed in the last moments of the battle.

Jackson immediately sent word of his victory to Lee. Then, after assigning Maj. Gen. A. P. Hill's division to dispose of prisoners and booty, he prepared the rest of his troops for the hard march ahead.

The same dawn that signaled Jackson's guns to open fire on Harpers Ferry revealed Longstreet's tired soldiers taking position on the rolling hills around Sharpsburg. As he watched them, Lee still did not know whether to fight or to withdraw across the Potomac. Decision waited upon word from Jackson. The word came; it was good; the crisis was past. Even now Lee's messenger hurried to direct Jackson's veterans toward Sharpsburg. Confident that the entire army would soon be at hand, certain that he could whip McClellan, Lee decided to fight.

Sharpsburg shortly after the Battle of Antietam. Taken from crest of Sharpsburg Ridge, looking west down Boonsboro Pike toward Potomac River. Hagerstown Pike heads north (right) just beyond large tree in left-center. Lee's headquarters were in Oak Grove in distance, just to right of Boonsboro Pike.

Lee Takes a Stand on Sharpsburg Ridge

Lee's decision to make his stand on the low ridge extending north and south of Sharpsburg might well have led to disaster for the Confederate army. A large part of his force was still scattered and several miles away. Backed against the coils of the Potomac River, with only the ford near Shepherdstown offering an avenue of withdrawal, a reversal in battle could result in rout and consequent loss of thousands of men and scores of guns. Longstreet voiced disapproval of battle at Sharpsburg. Jackson, hurriedly examining the ground on his arrival from Harpers Ferry, strongly favored Lee's choice.

The village of Sharpsburg lies in a small valley at the western base of Sharpsburg Ridge. From the village, the Boonsboro Pike leads east across the ridge, then across Antietam Creek. The Hagerstown Pike extends northward on the crest of the ridge.

From the Hagerstown Pike, gently rolling farmland spreads a mile eastward to Antietam Creek and the same distance westward to the winding Potomac River. A mile north of Sharpsburg was a heavy patch of trees known as West Woods; it was about 300 yards wide at its southern limits, tapering to 200 yards or less as it stretched away northwest from the pike. Half a mile east of Hagerstown Pike was another patch of trees called East Woods; it was 200 yards wide and extended a quarter mile south across the Smoketown Road. North Woods, a triangular plot of trees, stretched east from the Hagerstown Pike over the Poffenberger farm. Half a mile to the west looms Nicodemus Hill, a prominent landmark near the Potomac. Artillery on its heights would command the open ground lying between the patches of woodland. In this open area east of the Hagerstown Pike lay a 40-acre cornfield. West of the pike were outcroppings of rock running nearly parallel to the road—ready-made fortifications. Adjacent to the Hagerstown Pike, on a slight rise near the lower end of West Woods, stood a Dunkard Church, a small white building framed by massive oaks. Southeast of Sharpsburg, rolling land broken by deep ravines extends a mile beyond to a sharp bend in Antietam Creek.

Crossings of swiftly flowing Antietam Creek were readily available. The road extending northwest from Keedysville went over the stream at the Upper Bridge, the road to Sharpsburg from Boonsboro over the Middle Bridge, and the road to Sharpsburg from Pleasant Valley over the Lower Bridge. The stream could be crossed, also, at Pry's Mill Ford, a half mile south of the Upper Bridge, at Snavely's Ford, nearly a mile south of the Lower Bridge, and at other unnamed fording places.

With its advantages of woodland and outcroppings of rock ledges, Lee believed that the ridge north of Sharpsburg offered a strong battle position. Though he had ample time to construct earthworks, the Confederate commander chose to rely wholly on natural defenses.

As Lee's men approached from Boonsboro during the morning hours of September 15, they turned left and right off the pike to form their lines on Sharpsburg Ridge. Brig. Gen. John Hood, with only two brigades, held the ground at the fringe of the West Woods—from the Dunkard Church northwest to Nicodemus Hill near the Potomac. Here, Stuart's cavalry protected the left end or flank of the line. From Hood's position southward to Sharpsburg, D. H. Hill placed his five brigades east of and paralleling the Hagerstown Pike. Brig. Gen. Nathan Evan's brigade occupied the center of the line in front of Sharpsburg; his men straddled the Boonsboro Pike. The six brigades of Maj. Gen. D. R. Jones extended the Confederate front southeast nearly a mile to the Lower Bridge over Antietam Creek. The fords over the Antietam at the extreme right of the line were guarded by Col. Thomas Munford's cavalry brigade. Artillery was placed at vantage points on the ridges.

Throughout the 15th, Lee presented a show of strength with 14 brigades of infantry and 3 of cavalry—about 18,000 men.

Army supply train crosses Middle Bridge over Antietam Creek. After ascent of ridge in background, Boonsboro Pike dips into a ravine, then ascends Sharpsburg Ridge and enters the village. Courtesy, National Archives.

McClellan Concentrates at the Antietam

Against this pretense of power, General McClellan marched cautiously on the forenoon of the 15th, over good roads and in fine weather. By noon, he arrived at the Confederate front with a force of nearly 75,000 men. McClellan hesitated, and the day wore away.

As the early morning fog of the 16th cleared, Lee's artillerists caught sight of Federal guns on the high bank beyond Antietam Creek. The thunder of a prolonged duel between Lee's guns and Brig. Gen. Henry Hunt's powerful Federal batteries soon rolled through the hills. There was no question in McClellan's mind now that Lee intended to hold Sharpsburg Ridge.

In midafternoon of the 16th, McClellan prepared for battle. Maj. Gen. Joseph Hooker's I Corps was instructed to take position opposite the Confederate left on the Hagerstown Pike. Maj. Gen. Joseph Mansfield's XII Corps and Maj. Gen. Edwin Sumner's II Corps were to extend the battleline from Hooker's left to the Smoketown Road and on to Antietam Creek near Pry's Mill Ford. The V Corps, Maj. Gen. Fitz-John Porter commanding, was directed to occupy the center of the Federal line on the Boonsboro Pike.

Burnside was to place his IX Corps just east of the Lower Bridge over Antietam Creek. Maj. Gen. William Franklin's VI Corps was to support the entire front. In the center, on the high east bank of Antietam Creek, and south of the Boonsboro Pike, General Hunt placed four batteries of 20-pounder Parrott rifles, the most powerful cannon on the field.

McClellan's plan called for an initial attack on the Confederate left flank on the Hagerstown Pike with the two corps of Hooker and Mansfield. McClellan intended to support this mass charge with Sumner's entire force and, if necessary, with Franklin's corps. If the powerful thrust against the Confederate left should succeed, McClellan would send Burnside's corps across Antietam Creek at the Lower Bridge and strike the Confederate right flank on the ridge southeast of Sharpsburg. Should Burnside succeed in turning the southern end of Lee's line, he would be expected to carry the attack northwest toward Sharpsburg. Finally, if either of these flanking movements appeared successful, McClellan would drive up the Boonsboro Pike with all available forces to smash the Confederate center.

It was a good plan. If the Federal attacks could be delivered in concert, McClellan's preponderance of power must stretch Lee's smaller force to the breaking point. But the story of Antietam is one of piecemeal Federal attacks—a corps here, a division there. This failure in execution allowed Lee to shift troops from momentarily quiet sectors to plug the gaps torn by the succession of Federal attacks. As each threat developed, Lee rushed his troops there and beat it back. Taking advantage of his interior lines, he re-

Meadow just beyond trees bordering Antietam Creek marks top of bluffs where many of Hunt's Union batteries were placed. This view from one-half mile in front of Confederate gun emplacements on Sharpsburg Ridge.

Brig. Gen. W. N. Pendleton, Lee's
chief of artillery. From Miller's Photographic History of the Civil War.

Brig. Gen. Henry Hunt, McClellan's
chief of artillery.

peatedly achieved a local advantage of numbers, though larger Federal
contingents were always nearby.

The Lines Are Poised for Action

At 2 p.m. on the 16th, Hooker marched from his camp near
Keedysville, crossed the Upper Bridge, and late in the afternoon
reached the Hagerstown Pike. Under cover of the North Woods,
his divisions formed for the attack on both sides of the pike. A
massed force of more than 12,000 men was ready to advance on
the Confederates.

Lee's thin line, 3 miles long, had been reinforced early on the
16th by the arrival of Jackson's troops from Harpers Ferry. They
were placed where they could support the northern part of the

Union artillery in battery line. From 1863 photograph. Courtesy, Library of Congress.

Confederate line. John Walker's division, arriving from Harpers Ferry in the afternoon, took position south of Sharpsburg.

Jackson now commanded the Confederate front north of Sharpsburg; Longstreet, with a part of his force north of the village, extended the line nearly a mile south.

When Lee's outposts near Antietam Creek informed him in mid-afternoon that Hooker's Federals were massing north of Sharpsburg, Lee moved some of his men to advance positions. Hood established a line east of the Hagerstown Pike, with part of his troops in a cornfield and others extending the front to the East Woods. Skirmishers spread out far in front. Additional troops were rushed from reserve near Lee's headquarters at the Oak Grove west of Sharpsburg; they extended the line west across the Hagerstown Pike.

It was dusk by the time Hooker's force was ready to charge. With Maj. Gen. George Meade's men leading the way, they struck Hood's Confederates at the edge of the East Woods and in the adjacent fields. A brisk artillery fire from opposing batteries forced the men to seek cover. The gathering darkness made it difficult for the forces on either side to locate their marks. Gradually the opening skirmish at Antietam ended. The thrust of the Federal skirmishers, however, made it clear to Lee just where the next Federal blow would fall.

Even as Hooker's Federals withdrew to the cover of the North

Brig. Gen. John B. Hood.

Maj. Gen. Joseph Hooker. From photograph by Brady or assistant. Courtesy, Library of Congress.

Woods, strong forces were moving to their aid—the two powerful corps under Mansfield and Sumner. Mansfield would lead the XII Corps across Antietam Creek about midnight and encamp 1½ miles northeast of Hooker. Sumner's II Corps would cross the Antietam at Pry's Mill Ford at 7:30 the next morning to lend additional support.

Lee, too, was counting on reinforcements. McLaws' division was expected to arrive on the field by midmorning. A. P. Hill, who had been left at Harpers Ferry to handle details of the surrender, would arrive late in the day.

On the evening of September 16, picket lines were so close that the men on both sides, though unable to see each other, could hear footsteps. They knew that a tremendous struggle would begin at dawn. Some tried to sleep, but scattered firing throughout the night made this difficult. Others cleaned and cleaned again their rifled muskets, whose huge bullets made holes as big as silver dollars. Artillerists brought up ammunition for their smooth-bore Napoleons—so deadly at close range—and for the long-range rifled Parrott guns. And so these men got through the night, each one facing the impending crisis in his own way.

Union signal station on Elk Ridge. From here, McClellan's observers spotted Confederate troop movements during the battle. Courtesy, National Archives.

Hooker Strikes at Daybreak

A drizzling rain fell during the night. The morning of the 17th broke gray and misty, but the skies cleared early. As rays of light outlined the fringe of trees about the Dunkard Church, restless Federal skirmishers opened fire. A line of rifle fire flashed from the Southern muskets far out in front of the church. Soon, powerful Federal guns on the bluffs beyond Antietam Creek poured a raking fire of shot and shell into the Confederate lines. The first stage of McClellan's plan of crushing Lee—folding up the Confederate left flank—was about to begin.

Hooker struck with tremendous force. With skirmishers still hotly engaged, 10 brigades moved out from the cover of the North Woods. Brig. Gen. Abner Doubleday's men advanced along the Hagerstown Pike. Brig. Gen. James Ricketts' force charged down the Smoketown road toward the Dunkard Church. Part of Meade's division in the center was held in reserve. Hooker's artillery, massed on the ridge near the Poffenberger house, raked the Confederate lines. Heads down and bent to the side, like people breasting a hailstorm, the wave of Federals charged southward, spreading over the front from East Woods to the fringe of West Woods.

From left and from right, Confederate brigades poured into the fray to buttress Jackson's line of battle. D. H. Hill sent three brigades from the Sunken Road, dangerously weakening his own line—but then, first things first, and this is the story of the Confederate defense throughout the day. Hood's two brigades stood in reserve in the woods adjoining the Dunkard Church. Eight thousand Confederates awaited Hooker's assault.

While most of Jackson's men formed a line from east to west in front of the Dunkard Church, Brig. Gen. A. R. Lawton had sent a strong force into the Miller cornfield, 300 yards in advance, concealed, he believed, from the enemy.

East Woods on left; Miller cornfield, where Lawton's men were hidden, on right. This view looking south, as Hooker's men saw it at dawn.

View from the south, as Jackson's men saw it. Cornfield ahead; East Woods at right.

Doubleday's Federals came upon the cornfield. "As we appeared at the edge of the corn," related Maj. Rufus Dawes, "a long line of men in butternut and gray rose up from the ground. Simultaneously, the hostile battle lines opened a tremendous fire upon each other. Men, I cannot say fell; they were knocked out of the ranks by dozens." Hooker, nearby, saw farther in the field the reflection of sunlight from the enemy's bayonets projecting above the corn. Ordering all of his spare batteries to the left of this field, the Federal guns at close range raked the cornfield with canister and shell. "In the time I am writing," Hooker later wrote, "every stalk of corn in the northern and greater part of the field was cut as closely as could have been done with a knife, and the slain lay in rows precisely as they had stood in their ranks a few moments before. It was never my fortune to witness a more bloody, dismal battlefield."

Those Confederates who survived the slaughter in the cornfield now fled before the Federal onslaught. Heading for West Woods, they had to clamber over the picket-and-rail fence bordering the Hagerstown Pike; many were shot in the attempt and lay spread-eagled across the fence or piled on either side.

One soldier recalled the hysterical excitement that now gripped the Union troops: The only thought was victory. Without regard for safety, they charged forward, loading, firing, and shouting as they advanced. In contrast were the fallen—as waves of blue-clad troops swept by, wounded men looked up and cried for aid, but there was no time to stop.

Cornfield Avenue, marking southern limit of "bloody cornfield." Federals charged from right; Confederates counterattacked from left. From photograph taken on anniversary of battle, showing corn as it stood when the fighting began.

While Doubleday's division charged through the cornfield, Rickett's men, on the left of the attacking columns, pushed through the East Woods to its southern fringe. Capt. Dunbar Ransom's battery broke from the cover of the East Woods and fired shot and shell into the staggering Confederate lines.

For more than an hour, the battlefront flamed along an extended semicircular line from the open fields of the Mumma farm northwest through the cornfield to the rocky ledges in West Woods. The fury of the Federal attack had carried Doubleday's and Ricketts' men deep into the Confederate line, and now Meade's reserve brigades rushed forward.

In this critical stage, Jackson launched a driving counterattack. Hood's men, supported by D. H. Hill's brigades, battered the Federals back to the cornfield but were halted by the pointblank fire of Union guns in East Woods.

Mansfield Renews the Attack

As the remnants of Hooker's command sought shelter under the cover of powerful Federal batteries in front of East Woods, a new threat faced the Confederates. Mansfield's XII Corps, which had encamped more than a mile to the rear of Hooker during the night, had marched at the sound of Hooker's opening guns. At 7:30 a.m., almost an hour and a half later, Mansfield's force was

155

approaching from the north in heavy columns.

Seeing Hooker's plight, Mansfield now rushed to the forefront of his men, urging them to the attack. But his work was cut short by a Confederate ball; mortally wounded, he was carried from the field.

Without pause, Brig. Gen. Alpheus Williams moved up to command and the attack swept on over ground just vacated by Hooker. On the right, Brig. Gen. Samuel Crawford's division bore down the Hagerstown Pike toward the Confederates in West Woods. Attacking in separate units, however, their lines were shattered by Brig. Gen. J. R. Jones' men, fighting from the cover of projecting rocks. J. E. B. Stuart's artillery, from the hill a half mile to the west, rapidly dispersed the remnants.

On the left, the Federals fared better. They pounded Hood's men back across the fields toward the Dunkard Church and opened a great gap in the Confederate line. Into the hole plunged Brig. Gen. George S. Greene's Union division. Only a desperate Confederate stand stopped Greene's men at the Dunkard Church. There they remained, an isolated salient beyond support—the Federal assault had shot its bolt.

Attacking separately, the two corps of Hooker and Mansfield had each come within a hair of breaking Jackson's line. What if they had attacked together? Again and again through this long day, the same question—changing only the names—would apply.

Taken back of the picket-and-rail fence on the Hagerstown Pike, where Jackson's men attempted to rally in the face of Hooker's charge. From photograph by Alexander Gardner. Courtesy, National Archives.

Maj. Gen. Joseph Mansfield.
Courtesy, Library of Congress.

It may have been while observing this critical fight near the Dunkard Church, that General Lee saw a straggler heading back toward camp lugging a pig that he had killed. With disaster so close, and straggling one of its chief causes, Lee momentarily lost control and ordered Jackson to shoot the man as an example to the army. Instead, Jackson gave the culprit a musket and placed him where action was hottest for the rest of the day. He came through unscathed and was afterward known as the man who had lost his pig but saved his bacon.

Jackson Prepares an Ambush

By 9 a.m., 3 hours of killing had passed. The Miller cornfield had become a no-mans' land, its tall stalks trampled to the ground

Going into Action. From etching by W. H. Shelton. Courtesy, Library of Congress.

and strewn with blood-soaked corpses. Firing had been so intense, had so fouled the men's muskets, that some of them were using rocks to pound their ramrods home.

For a moment, the fighting ceased. Then powerful reserves were rushed forward by commanders of both armies to renew the battle.

Jackson was in extreme danger. Green's Federals still lurked near the Dunkard Church, waiting only for support to renew their attack on the frayed Confederate line. And at this very moment a mass of blue-clad infantry could be seen emerging from the East Woods half a mile away—it was part of Sumner's II Corps moving up for the morning's third major Federal attack.

Swiftly Jackson gathered together reinforcements from other sectors of the battlefield. Some had just arrived from Harpers Ferry; these were McLaws' men. With hardly a pause they moved north and disappeared into the West Woods. Lee ordered Walker's two brigades north from the Lower Bridge; they too disappeared into the West Woods. Thus they came, racing from far and near.

As soon as they came in, Jackson craftily placed these men behind the rocks and ridges at the western fringe of the woods. Soon they formed a great semicircle whose outer points perfectly encompassed the 5,000 men in Sumner's approaching column. Ten-thousand Confederates were there. Now they disappeared into the landscape and waited.

Sumner's II Corps, under orders to support the attack on the Confederate left, had prepared at dawn to cross Antietam Creek at Pry's Mill Ford. Impatiently, Sumner had awaited the signal to march while the battle raged with increasing violence on the ridge beyond the stream. Finally, at 7:30 a.m., he led Maj. Gen. John

Knap's Independent Pennsylvania Battery "E" supported Mansfield's corps. Courtesy, National Archives.

Closeup of Dunkard Church where Greene's men were halted. From Gardner's
Photographic Sketch Book. Courtesy, Library of Congress.

*Federal artillery at Antietam. Note the observer in foreground, and the smoke of
battle.* From photograph by Alexander Gardner. Courtesy, Library of Congress.

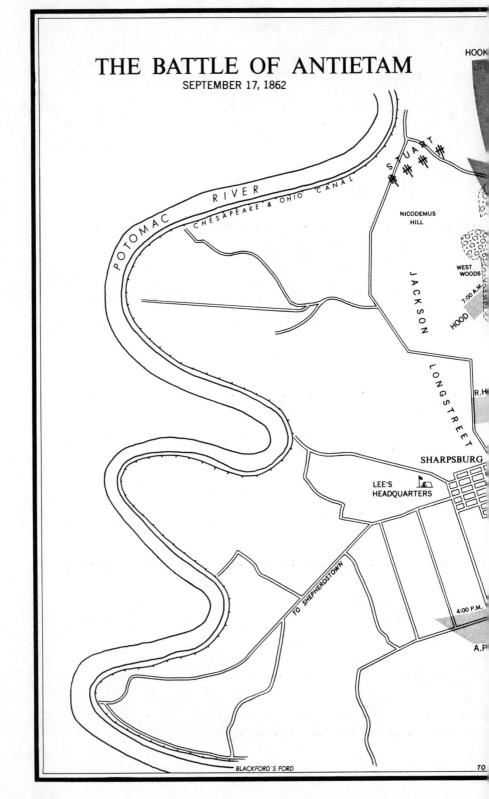

THE BATTLE OF ANTIETAM
SEPTEMBER 17, 1862

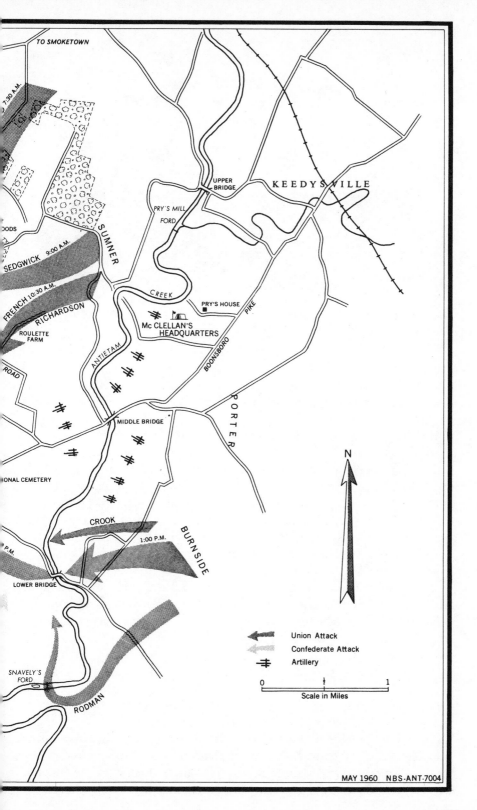

TO SMOKETOWN

7:30 A.M.

UPPER
BRIDGE

K E E D Y S V I L L E

PRY'S MILL
FORD

WOODS

SUMNER

SEDGWICK 9:00 A.M.

CREEK

PRY'S HOUSE

FRENCH 10:30 A.M.

RICHARDSON

McCLELLAN'S
HEADQUARTERS

ROULETTE
FARM

BOONSBORO PIKE

ROAD

ANTIETAM

PORTER

MIDDLE BRIDGE

IONAL CEMETERY

N

CROOK

BURNSIDE

1:00 P.M.

P.M.

LOWER BRIDGE

Union Attack

Confederate Attack

Artillery

SNAVELY'S
FORD

0   ½   1

Scale in Miles

RODMAN

MAY 1960   NBS-ANT-7004

161

Maj. Gen. Edwin V. Sumner. From photograph by Brady or assistant. Courtesy, Library of Congress.

Maj. Gen. John Sedgwick.

Sedgwick's division across the ford. Brig. Gen. William French's division followed, but soon drifted to the south and lost contact with Sedgwick.

Believing that he still led two divisions, Sumner continued his march past the East Woods. By now he knew that the earlier Federal attackers could give him no support, but he believed that the Confederates who had repulsed them must be equally exhausted and disorganized. Striking now—immediately—he might turn the tide before the enemy had time to recover. In his hurry, Sumner neglected to make sure that French's division followed closely in his rear. Neither had he taken time to reconnoiter the Confederate front in the West Woods.

Soon after 9 a.m., Sedgwick's heavy column, with Sumner at the head, started toward the Hagerstown Pike. Battleflags waving, bayonets glistening, the division marched forward in brigade front—long swaying lines of two ranks each.

Unmolested, they crossed the pike and passed into the West Woods. Almost surrounding them were Jackson's quietly waiting 10,000. Suddenly the trap was sprung. Caught within a pocket of almost encircling fire, in such compact formation that return fire was impossible, Sedgwick's men were reduced to utter helplessness. Completely at the mercy of the Confederates on the front, flank, and rear, the Federal lines were shattered by converging volleys. So appalling was the slaughter, nearly half of Sedgwick's 5,000 men, were struck down in less than 20 minutes.

The Halt of the Line of Battle. From the wartime sketch by Edwin Forbes. Courtesy, Library of Congress.

Scene of the ambush. Sedgwick's men marched in from left; note rock outcroppings where Jackson's men were hidden.

Part of the ground over which Sedgwick's men fought, possibly near Hagerstown Pike.
Courtesy, National Archives.

But the trap had not been completely closed. In the confusion of the surprise assault, many regiments on the Federal right found an opening. Hastily withdrawing to the northeast, they soon found cover under the protecting fire of Sedgwick's artillery in the cornfield. Other batteries in the East Woods and to the north joined in the cannonade.

Eagerly grasping the opportunity for a counterattack, Jackson's line now swept across the open fields and charged the Federal batteries in front of East Woods. But the fire was more than sheer valor could overcome. Blasted with grape and canister from the crossfire of 50 guns, the Confederates staggered, then gave way and drew back to the cover of West Woods. There, protruding rock strata protected them. Meanwhile, from his menacing position near the Dunkard Church, Greene was driven back by Confederate reserves.

Three-quarters of Lee's army was now north of Sharpsburg. The successive Federal attacks had punched the northeast salient of the Confederate left and center inward toward the Dunkard Church. Now these two sectors were merged into one long line that ran roughly southeast from Nicodemus Hill, past the Dunkard Church, to end along the Sunken Road. What had been the right (southern)

Sunken Road in 1877.
The same view today.

Maj. Gen. Lafayette McLaws, who led Jackson's counterattack after the ambush. Courtesy, Frederick Hill Meserve Collection.

Maj. Gen. D. H. Hill. Courtesy, Library of Congress.

end of the long Confederate line was now the rear. Properly speaking, Lee had no center. He had two separate lines—the main one, facing northeast toward East Woods; and a detached guard force, facing southeast toward the Lower Bridge. Between them was only a thin line of riflemen. If McClellan now delivered simultaneous hammer blows from northeast, east, and southeast, he would surely destroy Lee's weak defensive setup. But if he continued his piecemeal attacks, Lee could keep on shuttling his brigades back and forth to meet them. And this is what they both did.

The Fight for the Sunken Road

Sedgwick may have wondered, in the moments before the Confederate onslaught in the West Woods, why General French was not closely following him. Nor is it clear, in view of French's instructions, why he did not do so.

French's troops had crossed Pry's Mill Ford in Sedgwick's wake. After marching about a mile west, they had veered south toward the Roulette farmhouse, possibly drawn that way by the fire of enemy skirmishers. Continuing to advance, they became engaged with Confederate infantry at the farmhouse and in a ravine which inclines southward to a ridge. On the crest of this ridge, a strong enemy force waited in a deeply cut lane—the Sunken Road.

Mumma farm, left; Roulette farmhouse, far right. This view looking east from Hagerstown Pike. French's division advanced from left toward the Sunken Road, which is off picture to the right. Both farmhouses seen in this modern view were here at time of the battle.

Worn down by farm use and the wash of heavy rains, this natural trench joins the Hagerstown Pike 500 yards south of the Dunkard Church. From this point the road runs east about 1,000 yards, then turns south toward the Boonsboro Pike. That first 1,000 yards was soon to be known as Bloody Lane.

Posted in the road embankment were the five brigades of D. H. Hill. At dawn these men had faced east, their line crossing the Sunken Road. But under the pressure of the Federal attacks on the Confederate left, they had swung northward. Three of Hill's brigades had been drawn into the fight around the Dunkard Church. Then Greene's Federals had driven them back toward the Sunken Road. There Hill rallied his troops. About 10:30 a.m., as the men were piling fence rails on the embankment to strengthen the position, a strong enemy force appeared on their front, steadily advancing with parade-like precision. It was French's division, heading up the ravine toward Sunken Road Ridge.

Crouched at the road embankment, Hill's men delivered a galling fire into French's ranks. The Federals fell back, then charged again. One Union officer later wrote: "For three hours and thirty minutes the battle raged incessantly, without either party giving way."

But French's division alone could not maintain its hold on the ridge. Hurt by fire from Confederates in the road and on either side, the Union men gave way. Still it was not over. French's reserve brigade now rushed up, restoring order in the disorganized ranks; once again the division moved forward.

Now, opportunely, Maj. Gen. Israel Richardson's Federal division—also of Sumner's corps—arrived on the left of French and was about to strike Hill's right flank in the road embankment.

It was a critical moment for the Confederates. Aware that loss of the Sunken Road might bring disaster, Lee ordered forward his last reserve—the five brigades of Maj. Gen. R. H. Anderson's division. At the same time Brig. Gen. Robert Rodes of Hill's division launched a furious attack to hold the Federals back until Anderson's men could arrive. This thrust kept French's men from aiding Richardson, who even now prepared to assault the Confederates in the road.

As French's attack halted, Richardson swept forward in magnificent array. Richardson was a tough old fighter—bluff and courageous, a leader of men. One of his officers recalled his leading the advance, sword in hand: "Where's General ————?" he cried. Some soldiers answered, "Behind the haystack!" "G-- d--- the field officers!" the old man roared, pushing on with his men toward the Sunken Road. In three units they passed to the east of the Roulette farmhouse and charged the Confederates at the crest of the ridge.

As the struggle increased in fury, R. H. Anderson's brigades arrived in the rear of Hill's troops in the road. But Anderson fell wounded soon after his arrival, and suddenly the charging Confederate counteroffensive lost its punch. By a mistaken order, Rodes' men in the Sunken Road near the Roulette lane withdrew to the rear. A dangerous gap opened on the Confederate front. The artillerist Lt. Col. E. P. Alexander wrote later, "When Rodes' brigade left the sunken road . . . Lee's army was ruined, and the end of the Confederacy was in sight."

Union Col. Francis Barlow saw the gap in the Confederate front opened by Rodes' withdrawal. Quickly swinging two regiments astride the road, he raked its length with perfectly timed volleys. Routed by this devastating enfilade, the Confederate defenders fled the road and retreated south toward Sharpsburg. Only a heroic rally by D. H. Hill's men prevented a breakthrough into the town.

The Sunken Road was now Bloody Lane. Dead Confederates lay so thick there, wrote one Federal soldier, that as far down the road as he could see, a man could have walked upon them without once touching ground.

The Federals had suffered heavily, too. Their bodies covered the

On the Firing Line. By Gilbert Gaul. Courtesy, Library of Congress.

169

Bloody Lane.   Courtesy, Library of Congress.

170

approaches to the ridge. In the final moments, while leading his men in pursuit, Colonel Barlow had been seriously wounded; and shortly after, his commander, General Richardson, had fallen with a mortal wound.

The fight for the Sunken Road had exhausted both sides. At 1 p.m. they halted, and panting men grabbed their canteens to swish the dust and powder from their rasping throats.

The Confederate retreat from Bloody Lane had uncovered a great gap in the center of Lee's line. A final plunge through this hole would sever the Confederate army into two parts that could be destroyed in detail. "Only a few scattered handfuls of Harvey Hill's division were left," wrote Gen. William Allen, "and R. H. Anderson's was hopelessly confused and broken. . . . There was no body of Confederate infantry in this part of the field that could have resisted a serious advance." So desperate was the situation that General Longstreet himself held horses for his staff while they served two cannon supporting Hill's thin line.

But McClellan's caution stopped the breakthrough before it was born. Though Franklin's VI Corps was massed for attack, McClellan restrained it. "It would not be prudent to make the attack," he told Franklin after a brief examination of the situation, "our position on the right being . . . considerably in advance of what it had been in the morning."

So McClellan turned to defensive measures. Franklin's reserve corps would not be committed, but would remain in support of the Federal right. And in the center, McClellan held back Fitz-John Porter's V Corps. After all, reasoned the Federal commander, was not this the only force that stood between the enemy and the Federal supply train on the Boonsboro Pike?

But Porter was not quite alone. The entire Federal artillery reserve stood with him. Further, Brig. Gen. Alfred Pleasonton had placed his cavalry and artillery on a commanding ridge west of the Middle Bridge during the morning. From here he had already supported the attack by Sumner's corps on the Sunken Road, and he had aided Burnside's efforts on the left. Now he stood poised for further action. Pleasonton was to wait in vain. His dual purpose of obtaining ". . . an enfilading fire upon the enemy in front of Burnside, and of enabling Sumner to advance to Sharpsburg" was nullified by McClellan's decision to halt and take the defensive.

In striking contrast to McClellan's caution, General Lee was at that very moment considering a complete envelopment of the Federal flank at the North and East Woods. By this means he might relieve the pressure on D. H. Hill; for despite the lull, Lee could not believe that McClellan had halted the attack there. If the attack in the North Woods succeeded, Lee hoped to drive the Federal remnants to the banks of Antietam Creek and administer a crushing defeat.

Jackson and J. E. B. Stuart, early in the afternoon, shifted northward and prepared to charge the Federal lines. When they arrived close to the powerful Federal artillery on Poffenberger Ridge, they saw that a Confederate attack there would be shattered by these massed guns. A wholesome respect for Federal artillerists now forced Lee to withdraw his order. As he did so, heavy firing to the south heralded a new threat developing there.

Burnside Takes the Lower Bridge

During the morning of the 17th, Confederate observers on the ridge north of Sharpsburg had spotted masses of Federals moving southward beyond Antietam Creek. These were the four divisions of Burnside's IX Corps concentrating for the attack on the Lower Bridge.

Topography at the Lower Bridge heavily favored the few hundred Georgia men who defended it under the leadership of Brig. Gen. Robert Toombs. The road approaching the east end of the bridge swings on a course paralleling that of Antietam Creek; in the last few hundred yards before reaching the bridge, the road plunges into a funnel-like depression between the opposing bluffs of the creek. Toombs' men were in rifle pits on the west bluff overlooking the bridge and the approach road.

Because of faulty reconnaissance, Burnside did not know that fords were nearby where his men could have waded across the stream. Instead, the Federal plan of attack forced the advancing columns to pile into this funnel and storm across the bridge.

Soon after 9 a.m., the Federal divisions began to assault the bridge. One after another, their gallant charges were broken by deadly short-range fire from Toombs' Georgians. By noon, when the agony at the Sunken Road was reaching its highest pitch, and despite repeated orders from McClellan to get across Antietam Creek at all costs, the bottleneck at the bridge was still unbroken.

Meanwhile, Brig. Gen. Isaac Rodman's Union division had moved slowly downstream from the bridge in search of a crossing. Rounding a sharp bend in the creek, nearly a mile south, scouts came upon shallow water at Snavely's Ford. Late in the morning Rodman crossed the stream and began to drive against the right flank of the Georgians guarding the bridge. About the same time, Col. George Crook's scouts located a ford a few hundred yards above the bridge; there he sent his brigade across. Capt. Seth J. Simonds' battery was placed in position to command the bridge.

Maj. Gen. Ambrose E. Burnside. From photograph by Brady or assistant. Courtesy, Library of Congress.

Burnside or Lower Bridge shortly after the battle. Toombs' men were on the bluff in background. Courtesy, Library of Congress.

Burnside's men storm the bridge.   From wartime sketch by Forbes.

The same view today.   Note how tree at near end of bridge has grown.

Zouaves of Burnside's IX Corps charge toward Sharpsburg. From wartime sketch by Forbes. Courtesy, Library of Congress.

At 1 p.m., the defending Confederates saw a sudden stir across Antietam Creek. Two regiments, the 51st New York and the 51st Pennsylvania, marched swiftly out from the cover of the wooded hill and charged for the bridge. Supported now by converging artillery fire, they quickly formed into columns and were over the bridge before Confederate artillery could halt them. Soon a wide gap split the Confederate defense. Masses of Federal troops poured across the bridge while Rodman and Crook hammered the Confederate flanks. Burnside's men had gained the west bank of the creek.

But again there was fateful delay as Burnside paused to reorganize. By the time he was ready to drive the Southern defenders from the ridge in his front, 2 critical hours had passed.

Close to 3 p.m., the mighty Federal line moved slowly up the hill toward Sharpsburg, then gained momentum. "The movement of the dark column," related an observer, "with arms and banners glittering in the sun, following the double line of skirmishers, dashing forward at a trot, loading and firing alternately as they moved, was one of the most brilliant and exciting exhibitions of the day."

First brushing aside the depleted ranks in the rifle pits above the bridge, the Federals struck D. R. Jones' four lonely brigades on the hills southeast of Sharpsburg—whence every other Confederate infantry unit had been withdrawn to reinforce the line to the north. Unable to stem the massive Federal attack, Jones' men were driven back toward the town.

To halt the Federal tide, Lee shifted all available artillery south-

A Confederate battery on this site on the Harpers Ferry Road fired on Burnside's men as they charged toward the left across the low ground in the middle distance. A. P. Hill's division marched behind these guns, going left, then turned off the road and passed through the cornfield to hit Burnside's corps in flank.

ward. By 4 p.m., however, the Federals were approaching the village itself; only a half mile lay between them and Lee's line of retreat to the Potomac. Disaster seemed at hand for Lee's decimated force.

A. P. Hill Turns the Tide

But now came a great moment in Confederate military annals. A. P. Hill's notable Light Division, having hurriedly crossed the Potomac, 3 miles away, was driving hard toward the jubilant Federals charging on Sharpsburg. Some of Hill's artillery had already arrived from Harpers Ferry with the cheering news that Hill's brigades of infantry were close by.

At Lee's urgent order, Hill had left Harpers Ferry early. Sensing the critical role they would play, urged on at sword point by their grim commander, Hill's veterans had covered the 17 miles from Harpers Ferry to the Potomac in 7 hours. Hundreds of men had fallen out, unable to keep the pace. Now, across the river, the stalwart survivors pounded on toward the sound of the guns.

Suddenly the head of Hill's column appeared on the road to the south. Hill rode up to Lee's headquarters at the Oak Grove, then quickly to D. R. Jones, whose exhausted troops formed the last de-

Maj. Gen. A. P. Hill. From an engraving by A. H. Ritchie.

fense line in front of Sharpsburg. Hill's five brigades now rushed toward the Federal flank. Confusion gripped Burnside's men as this unexpected onslaught plowed into their lines. Men broke and started to run. In moments the tide had turned. The Federal lines, sagging from the overwhelming charge of the Southerners, and with gaping holes cut by artillery, fell back across the hills to the sheltering banks of Antietam Creek.

Powerful Federal artillery continued to thunder across the hills; heavy blue columns could still be seen in overmastering strength across Antietam Creek and far to the north. But the Federal commander had called a halt.

An hour and a half after the timely arrival of A. P. Hill's division from Harpers Ferry, the battle ended. With sunset, the firing died away. That night, the tired men lay on their arms in line of battle. Neither side would admit defeat; neither could claim the victory.

Retreat from Sharpsburg

Seldom had Lee's army fought a battle so strenuous and so long. "The sun," a soldier wrote, "seemed almost to go backwards, and it appeared as if night would never come." From dawn to sunset, the Confederate commander had thrown into battle every organized unit north of the Potomac. Straggling in the days preceding Antietam had reduced Lee's army from 55,000 to 41,000 men. This small force had sustained five major attacks by McClellan's 87,000-

Blackford's Ford from the Maryland side of the Potomac.

man army—three in the West Woods and the Miller cornfield, and those at the Sunken Road and the Lower Bridge—each time the outcome hanging in the balance.

In the stillness of the night, Lee called his commanders to his headquarters west of Sharpsburg. Of each in turn he asked the condition of the men, and each, even Jackson, spoke against renewal of battle on the morrow. "Still too weak to assume the offensive," Lee wrote later, "we waited without apprehension the renewal of the attack."

Early on the following morning, it became apparent that McClellan was not going to attack, though during the night he had received strong reinforcements, and more were on the way. Still undaunted, Lee returned to his plan of striking the Federal right at Poffenberger Ridge. But after surveying the ground, his officers informed him that Federal batteries completely dominated the narrow strip of land over which the attack must be launched. An attempt against the Federal guns would be suicidal.

Balked in his last hope of a counteroffensive, Lee realized that he could not recall the decision won by McClellan at South Mountain: The campaign was lost. During the afternoon, he announced to his lieutenants his intention of withdrawing that night across the Potomac. At midnight Longstreet led the way across Blackford's Ford and formed a protective line on the south bank. Steadily through the night and early morning, the Confederate columns crossed over into Virginia.

McClellan did not actively pursue. As the days passed and Lee's army withdrew into the Shenandoah Valley, President Lincoln became impatient. The time was at hand, he thought, for the decisive blow. Calling upon McClellan on the field of Antietam, October 1, Lincoln urged a vigorous pursuit of the Confederate army. McClellan insisted that his army required reorganization and new equipment. The President, having lost all confidence in McClellan, removed him from command on November 7.

The Battle and the Campaign

Tactically, Antietam was a draw. Strategically, however, it was a Northern victory because it halted Lee's invasion.

Though McClellan failed to destroy Lee's army, his contribution was in many ways notable. In the 3 weeks after he was chosen for command on September 3, he provided for Washington's defense, created a new field army, fought two major actions, compelled Lee's evacuation of Maryland, and established Federal control of the Potomac River from Washington to Williamsport. That he was not a daring commander of Lee's stripe cannot detract from these solid achievements.

Lee, on the other hand, may have been too daring. Because of this he made two major miscalculations. First, his invasion of Maryland imposed a strain that his poorly equipped and exhausted army could not support; heavy straggling was the surest evidence of this. Second, he misjudged the capacity of the enemy to recuperate from the effects of Second Manassas and quickly put a reliable field army on his trail. He did achieve one of his objectives: The delay of the Federal armies in resuming major offensive operations in Virginia until the next winter. But the price was high and the South could not afford the kind of attrition suffered in the campaign.

Casualties were so heavy in the Battle of Antietam that September 17, 1862, is termed the bloodiest day of the Civil War. Of McClellan's 26,023 killed, wounded, and captured during the Maryland Campaign (including Harpers Ferry), he counted 12,410 at Antietam. Of Lee's 13,385 casualties during the campaign, 10,700 fell at Antietam.

The War for the Union Takes on a New Purpose

After Antietam there was no serious threat of foreign recognition or intervention on behalf of the Confederacy. And the repulse inflicted on Lee's Army of Northern Virginia gave Abraham Lincoln

Lincoln visits McClellan and his staff after the battle.   McClellan is the fourth man to the left from the President.   Courtesy, National Archives.

Lincoln and McClellan confer on the field of Antietam.

the opportunity he had sought: On September 22—just 5 days after the battle—the President issued the preliminary Emancipation Proclamation. It declared that upon the first day of January next all slaves within any State or district then in rebellion against the United States ". . . shall be then, thenceforward, and forever free."

With the formal Emancipation Proclamation of January 1, 1863, the war took on new purpose. In the North, and in many foreign lands, the cause of American Union had become one with that of human liberty.

Clara Barton at Antietam

At Antietam, also, was Clara Barton, founder of the American Red Cross. On this field of desolation, long after the guns had ceased, Miss Barton was still busily rendering care to the wounded and dying. Having arrived early in the day in the northern area of battle, she witnessed the wounded men of Sedgwick's depleted ranks streaming to the cover of North and East Woods. By midmorning her wagonload of supplies, donated by the citizens of Washington, had arrived. She worked tirelessly with army surgeons at the field hospital on the Joseph Poffenberger farm. Her supply of bandages, linens, anesthetics, and oil lanterns replenished the surgeons' urgent need of dressings and provided light to carry on through the night. So outstanding were her services on the field of battle that she later received official recognition by the United States Army Medical Corps. Her work here and later would become basic to the establishment of the American Red Cross.

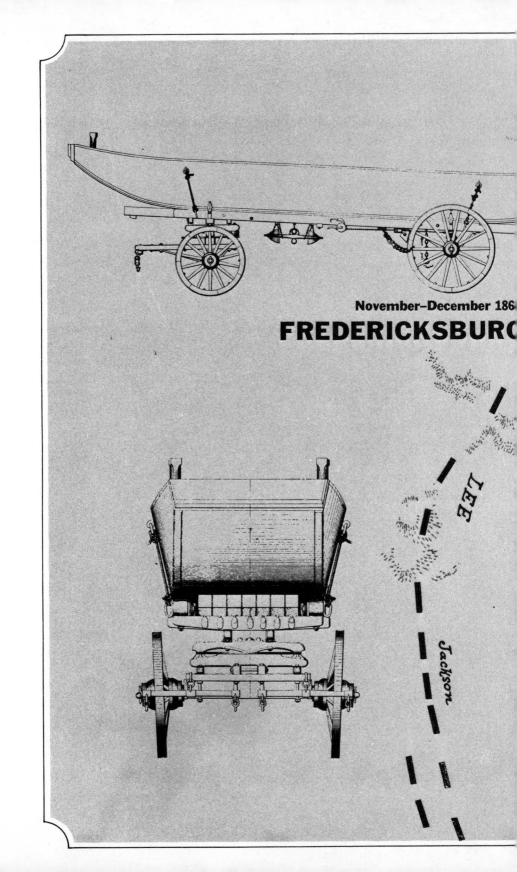

LEE

Jackson

CHAPTER VII

Battle of Fredericksburg

At the head of the navigable waters of the Rappahannock River, Fredericksburg lay midway between the Confederate Capital at Richmond, Va., and the National Capital at Washington, a scant 100 miles apart. Founded in 1727, Fredericksburg by the 1850's was a thriving commercial city of almost 5,000 people, carrying on a direct trade with Europe and the West Indies. Large three-masted schooners, moored at the wharves, gave an air of bustling prosperity to the area. In 1861, however, its importance laÿ in the obstacle it presented, along with the Rappahannock River, to any overland march from Washington on Richmond. As the political, manufacturing, and military center of the South, Richmond became the symbol of secession to the North and the key to military planning on both sides. For 4 years it remained the primary objective of the Union armies in the east. "On to Richmond" was the cry.

There were two main avenues of approach to the Confederate capital: The direct overland route southward through Fredericksburg; and the approach by water down the Potomac, across Chesapeake Bay to the tip of the peninsula between the York and the James Rivers, and then northwestward up the peninsula. In the summer of 1861 the Federal Government, in its first attempt to drive into Virginia and capture Richmond, decided on the overland approach.

Astride this road to Richmond lay Manassas, a small railroad settlement a few miles east of the Bull Run mountains and north of Fredericksburg. Here, Confederate Gen. P. G. T. Beauregard blocked the road with a force of about 22,000 men, while Gen. Joseph E. Johnston commanded a smaller force of some 11,000

troops at Winchester in the Shenandoah Valley. And here, on July 21, Gen. Irvin McDowell brought his 35,000 Union troops on their way to Richmond.

In this first major engagement of the Civil War the Federal army suffered disaster in a nightmare battle of mistakes. Routed from the field, it fled back to Washington in disorder and panic.

President Abraham Lincoln then appointed Gen. George B. McClellan the new commander of the demoralized army. McClellan restored order and discipline and in the spring of 1862 decided to try the water approach to Richmond. This Peninsular Campaign, as it was called, culminated in the famous Seven Days' Battle, when the Army of the Potomac's drive on Richmond was repulsed by Gen. Robert E. Lee's Army of Northern Virginia on the outskirts of the city.

Lee now chose to try to stop the next "On-to-Richmond" move before it could penetrate very deeply into Virginia. On August 23 he wrote Confederate President Jefferson Davis: "If we are able to change the theater of the war from the James River to the north of the Rappahannock we shall be able to consume provisions and forage now being used in supporting the enemy."

So Lee moved into northern Virginia to meet Gen. John Pope's threatened overland campaign against Richmond. At Second Manassas (Bull Run) the Union Army was defeated again and withdrew into the fortifications around Washington.

Lee took advantage of this opportunity and made his first invasion north into Maryland, only to be stopped by McClellan at Antietam (Sharpsburg) in September. He then retired into Virginia and prepared to spend the winter recruiting and reprovisioning his army.

Robert E. Lee

A
FAST
MARCH

President Lincoln used the victory at Antietam to issue the Emancipation Proclamation, but both the Government and the Northern people generally were disappointed at McClellan's failure to pursue vigorously the retreating Confederates. When he gave the poor condition of his horses as one excuse for not moving, Lincoln telegraphed: "I have read your dispatch about sore-tongued and fatigued horses. Will you pardon me for asking what the horses of your army have done since the battle of Antietam that fatigues anything?"

Finally, late in October, the Army of the Potomac advanced cautiously into Virginia, concentrating in the Warrenton-Manassas area. McClellan's immediate objective was Gordonsville, but the movement was so slow, averaging only 5 to 6 miles a day, that Lincoln relieved him of command on November 5 and appointed Gen. Ambrose E. Burnside. General-in-Chief Henry W. Halleck telegraphed from Washington: "Immediately on assuming command of the Army of the Potomac, you will report the position of your troops, and what you propose doing with them."

Burnside, a quiet, unassuming man, had a creditable record as a corps commander and was not generally regarded as being overly ambitious. He did not particularly want the job of army commander. "Had I been asked to take it, I should have declined," he informed Halleck, "but being ordered, I cheerfully obey." From his headquarters at Warrenton he promptly proposed a new plan:

> To concentrate all the forces near this place, and impress upon the enemy a belief that we are to attack Culpeper or Gordonsville, and at the same time accumulate a four or five days' supply for the men and animals; then make a rapid move of the whole force to Fredericksburg, with a view to a movement upon Richmond from that point.

There were many advantages to this plan, Burnside was careful to explain. It would enable him to take advantage of Union control of the waterways to establish supply bases at Aquia Creek and Belle Plain on the Potomac; it would allow him to use the Richmond, Fredericksburg, and Potomac Railroad from Aquia Creek to Richmond; the Army of the Potomac would always be between the enemy and Washington; and it was the shortest overland route to the Confederate capital. At the same time he requested permission to reorganize the Army of the Potomac into three "grand divisions" of about two corps each.

The key to the whole plan, as Lincoln shrewdly realized, was contained in the words "a rapid move of the whole force on Fredericksburg." On November 14 Halleck told Burnside: "The President has just assented to your plan. He thinks it will succeed, if you move rapidly; otherwise not."

Burnside moved rapidly. Early the next morning Gen. E. V.

A Federal column moves along the river on the night of December 11, as flames rise from the city after the day-long bombardment.

Waud's sketch of a captured Confederate.

Sumner's Right Grand Division, consisting of Gen. D. N. Cou[
II Corps and Gen. O. B. Wilcox's IX Corps, moved out, follo[
the next day by Gen. W. B. Franklin's Left Grand Division of G
J. F. Reynolds' I Corps and Gen. W. F. Smith's VI Corps, [
Gen. Joseph Hooker's Center Grand Division of Gen. Geo
Stoneman's III Corps and Gen. Daniel Butterfield's V Corp[

Sumner's advance reached Falmouth, opposite Fredericksb[
on the 17th after a march of about 40 miles, and he immedia
requested permission for part of his command to cross the r[
fords, the bridges having been destroyed. Burnside, howe[
deemed the plan "impracticable." He did not want "to
sending a portion of the command on the opposite side of
river until I had the means for crossing the main body." In
event the fords became impassable, he feared the troops wo
be cut off. Consequently, he decided to await the arrival of
pontoon boats, expected momentarily, to enable him to br[
the river. By November 19 Burnside and the rest of the A[
of the Potomac were encamped on Stafford Heights oppo
Fredericksburg.

The suddenness of the move surprised Lee. He had rece[
reorganized the Army of Northern Virginia into two corps un
Gens. James Longstreet and Thomas J. "Stonewall" Jack
and his plan of defense against McClellan's slow advance [
been "to attempt to baffle his designs by maneuvering, ra[
than to resist his advance by main force." As a result, Jacks[

corps was now in the vicinity of Winchester in the Shenandoah Valley, while Longstreet's was encamped at Culpeper, about 35 miles northwest of Fredericksburg. Only a token force held the city itself.

Despite the sudden Federal move, Lee showed no inclination to unite the separated wings of his army. He was not yet convinced that Fredericksburg was Burnside's only immediate objective. On November 18 he wrote Davis: "It is possible that he may attempt to seize Winchester, Culpeper, and Fredericksburg . . . ." But even if Fredericksburg was the only objective, Lee at this time did not desire to make a stand there, as he saw no particular military advantage in the position. He told Jackson November 19: "I do not now anticipate making a determined stand north of the North Anna River," which was approximately midway between Fredericksburg and Richmond. As a precautionary measure, he ordered Longstreet's corps to Fredericksburg, although admitting as late as November 23 that he was "as yet unable to discover what may be the plan of the enemy."

Finally, on November 26 he ordered Jackson to join him. Lee had now decided to resist the Federal advance along the Rappahannock. "My purpose was changed," he stated, "not from any advantage in this position, but from an unwillingness to open more of our country to depredation than possible, and also with a view of collecting such forage and provisions as could be obtained in the Rappahannock Valley."

These Confederate pickets, sketched by Arthur Lumley, fell while opposing the Federal crossing of the Rappahannock.

THE
FATAL DELAY

Fortunately for Lee, Burnside was not hurrying either. Th
the pontoons needed to bridge the river were late arriving w
not his fault, to be sure. But even after they finally arrived
November 25, Burnside made no attempt to cross for almost
weeks. His feeble explanation for this inexcusable delay w
contained in his official report:

> By this time [November 25] the enemy had concen-
> trated a large force on the opposite side of the river,
> so that it became necessary to make arrangements to
> cross in the face of a vigilant and formidable foe. These
> arrangements were not completed until about Decem-
> ber 10.

The "large force" referred to was Longstreet's corps of abc
35,000 men (Jackson's corps had not yet arrived). Burnsi
commanded an army of approximately 130,000 men.

Lee took advantage of the delay to make his position behi
Fredericksburg almost impregnable. He would not attempt
dispute the Federal crossing of the river because of the top
raphy of the area. The Rappahannock here takes a wide sw
to the south to cut between two elevated ridges. The Feder
occupied Stafford Heights on the east, commanding the ri
and the city. Had the Confederates opposed the crossing, F
eral artillery literally would have been looking down their throa
Instead, Lee chose to fortify the heights west of the city, vary
from 1 to 2 miles distant from the river. Here, along a 7-m
front that stretched from the Rappahannock to Massappo
Creek, he placed Longstreet on the left and Jackson on the rig
with over 300 pieces of artillery in support. His force in t
line consisted of approximately 75,000 men.

Longstreet's position, along a ridge behind the city known
Marye's Heights, was further fortified by a sunken road an
stone wall at the base of the heights, providing excellent
protection for infantry. An open plain about 2 miles
wide lay between Jackson's position and the river.
To facilitate troop movements during the battle,
Lee constructed a military road between
the two corps.

Burnside's delay was confusing, even to the Confederates. As days passed with no attempt made to force a crossing, Lee continued to strengthen his position, although he became somewhat apprehensive that Burnside's hesitation suggested "the probability that he is waiting for expected operations elsewhere."

Actually, Lee had no cause for alarm. Burnside was merely trying to decide what to do. It is a military axiom that strategy is the art of bringing the enemy to battle on terms disadvantageous to him and advantageous to yourself. In the positions of the two armies at Fredericksburg after Burnside's delay, it was obvious even to the men in the ranks that Lee had all the advantages. Despite this strategic handicap, Burnside finally decided to attack.

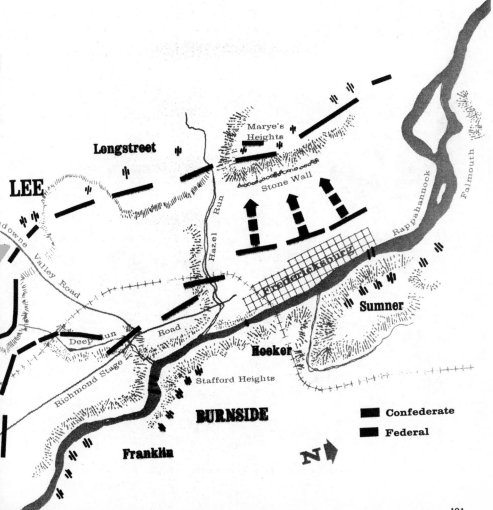

The Battle of Fredericksburg, December 13, 1862.

191

Building Pontoon Bridge at Fredericksburg Dec

Working under a brisk and accurate rifle fire, Federal engineers begin laying a pontoon bridge across the Rappaha

ACROSS
THE
RAPPAHANNOCK

Wednesday, December 10, dawned gray and blustery. Snow blew across the tents and guns and covered the fields. The cold wind cut through the men, as couriers galloped from Burnside's headquarters with the orders that finally set the Army of the Potomac in motion.

Franklin's Left Grand Division would cross the river below Fredericksburg and advance on Jackson's position; Sumner's Right Grand Division was to cross opposite the city and attack Longstreet on Marye's Heights; Hooker's Center Grand Division was held in reserve, ready to support either wing if the occasion warranted.

Early the next morning under cover of a heavy fog, Federal soldiers began laying the pontoon bridges, six in all, varying in length from 400 to 440 feet. Below the city the work proceeded as scheduled, but opposite Fredericksburg it was a different story. As the first rays of sun pierced the mist, Confederate sharp-shooters, concealed in the houses and streets, opened a deadly fire. The bridge building stopped.

Burnside ordered a bombardment. The massed Federal artillery on Stafford Heights opened with a frightful roar. A storm of shot and shell tore through the streets, alleys, and houses, spreading death and destruction. Thick clouds of smoke swirled high in the air as buildings caught fire. Walls and chimneys crashed to the ground. Yet when the bombardment lifted and the smoke drifted away, the sharpshooters were still there.

In desperation the Federal officers called for volunteers who were ferried across the river in a daring bridgehead operation. After bitter house-to-house fighting, the outnumbered Confederates withdrew to the heavily fortified heights behind the town, enabling the engineers to complete the bridges.

The next day Federal troops poured over the river. Franklin put Reynolds' I Corps on his left opposite Jackson's right at Hamilton's Crossing where the Mine Road crossed the Richmond, Fredericksburg, and Potomac Railroad. Smith's VI Corps formed on Reynolds' right, opposite Jackson's left at Lansdowne Valley. Sumner had Couch's II Corps in Fredericksburg, and Willcox's IX Corps just south of the city connecting with Smith's right near Deep Run. By nightfall everything seemed set. Corps and division commanders waited anxiously for their attack orders. Behind them was the river; in front were the heights, bristling with Confederate cannon and bayonets.

orning of December 11.

ck on the rebel works
Fredericksburg
Dec. 15th

BURNSIDE'S
FAILURE

Even with most of his army safely across the river, Burnsi
still had no definite plan of attack. Not until early the ne
morning did he issue his orders, and then they were vague a
confused, couched in generalities. Corps and division co
manders had no clear conception of what was expected of the
Franklin with one division was ordered "to seize, if possible" t
heights at Hamilton's Crossing. Sumner was ordered to push
division through the city "with a view to seizing the heights in t
rear," whatever that was supposed to mean. Incredible as
seems, with an army of 130,000 men under his command Bur
side's so-called battle orders basically did nothing but commit tv
divisions to action, one to "seize if possible," the other "with
view to seizing."

Reynolds picked Gen. George Meade's division of Penns
vanians to make the attack near Hamilton's Crossing, support
by Gen. John Gibbon's division on his right, with Gen. Abr
Doubleday's division in reserve on the left. Meade formed l
men along the Richmond Stage Road hidden by a heavy fc
Shortly after 9 a.m. the fog lifted. The Union soldiers march
bravely out across the open plain to attack Gen. A. P. Hi
division of Jackson's corps, concealed in the woods at the base
the heights and behind the shelter of the railroad embankme

As the attack on the Federal left below the town foundered, Burnside ordered his right wing to assault the heavily defended heights behind Fredericksburg. In this sketch by Waud, waves of infantry push across the broken plain on December 13 in the face of fierce Confederate musket and artillery fire. The Marye mansion is at right.

At Lee's command post, on top of a hill that has borne his name ever since, Confederate officers were treated to an awe-inspiring spectacle. They had a panoramic view of thousands of blue-clad soldiers in battle formation, marching with parade-ground precision out across the open fields to the attack. Bugles blared, and drums rolled. Horse-drawn artillery wheeled into line in skilled maneuvers. Steel bayonets flashed in the pale winter sun. The rich colors of the regimental flags unfurled in the breeze. Officers, on horseback shouting orders, charged up and down the line. It was a breathtaking sight—a picture-book study of war that prompted Lee to remark: "It is well that war is so terrible— we should grow too fond of it."

Then the Confederate artillery opened, ripping holes in the blue lines. The charging Federals were obscured in smoke as regiment after regiment behind the railroad embankment erupted into action. Still they came on, up to the embankment, over it, clubbing and stabbing with musket and bayonet.

Without knowing it, Meade had hit a weak spot between Archer's and Lane's brigades of Hill's division and pierced the Confederate line. But in the process he lost contact with Gibbon on his right and, unsupported on his left, was forced to retreat when Jackson quickly threw in his reserves. The gallant charge was wasted, since the Federals were driven back to the vicinity of the Richmond Stage Road.

"THAT TERRIBLE STONE WALL"

Sumner, on the Federal right, fared even worse. On Marye's Heights and in the sunken road behind the stone wall at the base of the Heights, Longstreet had placed Ransom's division and Cobb's Georgia brigade of Gen. Lafayette McLaws' division.

As Gen. William French's division of Couch's II Corps formed for the attack on the edge of the city, it came under a devastating artillery fire from the Confederate guns on the surrounding hills. Then as the brigades swung out in battle formation across the open fields, their alinement was broken by a canal drainage ditch that Burnside obstinately refused to admit existed. The blue line staggered and slowed as men fell like leaves in an autumn wind. Regrouped under fire, the men sprang forward again, passing under the range of the artillery on the hills, only to be met by a sheet of flame as the Confederates behind the stone wall, reinforced by Gen. Joseph Kershaw's brigade, exploded into action. When the smoke eddied away, remnants of the Federal regiments could be seen retreating across the fields to the shelter of a slight rise in the ground.

Burnside stubbornly refused to admit his mistakes. He continued to hurl brigade after brigade against the stone wall, first committing to action Gen. Winfield Hancock's division, then Gen. Oliver O. Howard's and later two divisions from the IX Corps. As one soldier described it: "They reach a point within a stone's throw of the stone wall . . . that terrible stone wall. No farther. They try to go beyond but are slaughtered. Nothing could advance farther and live."

It was hopeless and useless, a waste of life, a horrible mistake. Nothing was accomplished by the attack. Darkness mercifully put an end to it. And that night, as the snow lay hard on the hills, many of the wounded slowly froze to death. "It is fearful to wake at night," one veteran wrote, "and to hear the sounds made by the men about you. All night long the sounds go up of men coughing, heavy and hoarse with halfchoked throats, moaning and groaning with acute pain, a great deal of sickness and suffering on all sides . . . ."

Even then, Burnside hesitated. Not until 2 days later did he finally make up his mind to withdraw. During the night of December 15, under cover of a violent rainstorm, the Army of the Potomac retreated across the Rappahannock and went into its old camp on the heights beyond the city. The Federals had suffered 12,653 casualties in killed, wounded, and missing; the Confederates 5,309.

Frederic Cavada, a Union lieutenant, recorded Sumner's vast and futile charge against the strong Confederate line along Marye's Heights on the afternoon of December 13.

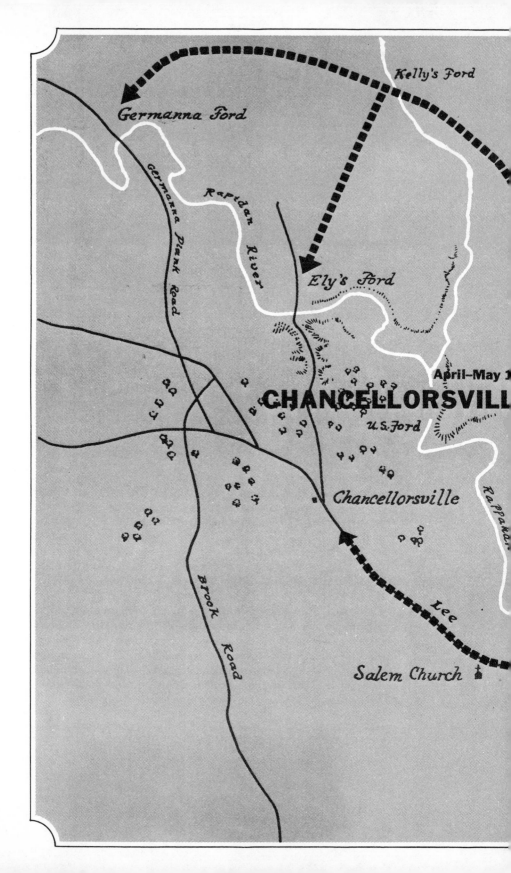

Kelly's Ford

Germanna Ford

Rapidan River

Germanna Plank Road

Ely's Ford

April–May 1

CHANCELLORSVILL

U.S. Ford

Chancellorsville

Rappaha

Brook Road

Lee

Salem Church ✝

Hooker

almouth

CHAPTER VIII

Battle of Chancellorsville

A NEW COMMANDER

AFTER the Fredericksburg disaster President Lincoln appointed Gen. Joseph ("Fighting Joe") Hooker to succeed Burnside. Hooker realized his first job was to restore morale and discipline to the demoralized Union army, and in this he showed rare administrative ability that few suspected he possessed. Abandoning Burnside's unwieldy Grand Divisions, he reorganized the army on the corps level, forming the cavalry into a separate corps. The quality and quantity of the rations was increased, camp sanitation and living conditions improved. By spring of 1863 the Army of the Potomac, numbering about 135,000 men, was probably the best equipped and supplied army in the world. It was now becoming evident that the South could win victories and emerge permanently weakened, and that the North could suffer defeats and emerge still stronger.

Yet when Lincoln reviewed the army early in April, he seemed to have a premonition of disaster. What bothered him was Hooker, who prefaced almost every sentence with the words "When I get to Richmond . . . ." This led Lincoln to remark that "the hen is the wisest of all of the animal creation because she never cackles until the egg is laid." And he gave Hooker and Couch, next in command, some sage advice. "In your next fight gentlemen," he told them, "put in all of your men." Unfortunately for the North, the suggestion went unheeded.

HOOKER'S
PLAN

Hooker did develop a good plan, however. He would take three corps up the Rappahannock to a point northwest of Fredericksburg, then cross both the Rappahannock and the Rapidan to get on Lee's left flank and rear. Two corps would stay in front of Frederickburg to hold the Confederates in their defensive positions, while the remaining two corps would be held ready to go wherever the best opportunity presented itself. The men would carry 60 rounds of ammunition, and 8-days' rations of hardtack, salt pork, coffee, sugar, and salt. Each ration weighed 3 pounds. For the first time in the east, 2,000 pack mules would be used instead of the usual supply wagons to speed up the movement. The cavalry corps would take off on a raid to disrupt Lee's communications with Richmond.

Hooker reasoned that with three Federal corps on his rear, Lee would have to retreat toward Richmond, and in retreating would, in effect, be executing a flank movement across Hooker's front, a movement generally regarded as suicidal if performed in front of an aggressive commander. Hooker was supposed to be aggressive. His orders to his cavalry commander certainly sounded that way when he reminded him that "celerity, audacity and resolution are everything in battle. Let your watchword be fight, fight, fight."

The campaign got underway April 27 when Meade's V, Howard's XI, and Gen. Henry Slocum's XII Corps started up the Rappahannock, crossing it the next day at Kelly's Ford. "For miles nothing could be heard but the steady tramp of the men," wrote one campaigner, "the rattling and jingling of canteens and accouterments, and the occasional 'close-up-men-close-up' of the officers." On April 29 they crossed the Rapidan at Ely's and Germanna Fords and by April 30 reached Chancellorsville, a strategic crossroads on the edge of an area known as the Wilderness.

While this flanking march of some 40 miles was taking place, Couch's II Corps and Gen. Daniel Sickles' III Corps bluffed a crossing at U.S. Ford on the Rappahannock in an attempt to deceive Lee as to Hooker's intentions. When he completed the flank march, Hooker order the two corps to cross the river and join him at Chancellorsville. This left Reynolds' I Corps and Gen. John Sedgwick's VI Corps opposite Lee at Fredericksburg.

So far everything had worked perfectly. "I have Lee in one hand and Richmond in the other," Hooker boasted.

LEE'S
RESPONSE

Surprisingly, there was some truth in Hooker's statement. Le
had been outflanked. He had not believed that Hooker wou.
move his army that far up the Rappahannock, knowing he wou.
have to cross two rivers instead of one. By April 29, howeve
his cavalry commander, Gen. J. E. B. ("Jeb") Stuart, had ca
tured enough Federal stragglers to inform Lee that Hooker ha
undoubtedly split his army into two wings, either of which cou
be as large as the total Confederate force. Longstreet, wi
Pickett's and Hood's divisions, was on a foraging expedition dow
on the Peninsula. This left Lee with only Jackson's corps ar
the divisions of Gens. R. H. Anderson and McLaws, for a total
about 60,000 men. At least three Federal corps were on his le
and rear. Heavily outnumbered, the logical move seemed to
to retreat and join Longstreet somewhere between Fredericksbu
and Richmond, probably at the North Anna River.

But Lee undoubtedly realized that that was exactly what Hook
expected him to do, so he refused even to consider retreat. T
only question in his mind was which of the Federal wings
attack. Finally convinced that the troops in front of Frederic
burg were merely a diversion, he decided to attack the force
Chancellorsville. Consequently, on May 1 Jackson was order
to Chancellorsville to join Anderson and McLaws. Gen. Jub
Early's division was left to hold the heights at Fredericksburg.

That morning the Federal corps commanders at Chancellorsvi
were impatiently awaiting the order to advance. They realiz
Hooker had outflanked Lee, but a delay now could lose all t
advantages gained by the maneuver. Most of their men we
still in the Wilderness, a dense forest of second-growth pine ar
scrub oak, with numerous creeks, gullies, swamps, heavy tanglefo
underbrush, and few farms or open spaces. Two or three mi
east on the Orange Turnpike toward Fredericksburg, howeve

May 1, 1863, was a day of maneuvering for both armies. Here the Federals concentrate at Chancellorsville, the home of the Chancellor family at the important road junction of the Orange Turnpike and Ely's Ford Road. The house standing at right was Hooker's headquarters and a hospital during the battle. It later burned.

would bring them to open areas where they could maneuver effectively.

Finally, late in the morning, Hooker ordered Meade and Slocum forward. Meade sent two divisions down the River Road and one down the turnpike. Slocum took the Orange Plank Road farther south. The only force in front was Anderson's and McLaws' divisions near Zoan Church, about 3 miles east of Chancellorsville. But when they made contact with the Confederate force, Hooker suddenly abandoned the whole idea and ordered them back, despite the strong protests of his corps commanders. "The position thus abandoned was high ground," Couch reported, "more or less open in front, over which an army might move and artillery be used advantageously." Meade grumbled disgustedly, "If he can't hold the top of the hill, how does he expect to hold the bottom of it."

A well known fact of military history is that by the faulty disposition of troops a battle can be lost before it starts. Hooker not only committed this error, but by dropping the offense and assuming a defensive attitude, he voluntarily surrendered the initiative to his opponent. This despite the fact that the one clear lesson from all the campaigns of the great military commanders was that a defensive posture should never be assumed except as a means of passing to the offensive under more favorable conditions. The strength of the offensive lies in maneuvering at will, screening forces for surprise, and, the primary duty of a good strategist, massing superior power at the opponent's weak point.

Lee quickly decided to take full advantage of the opportunity Hooker had given him. The Federal right flank extended just west of Wilderness Church on the Turnpike. When Stuart reported that it was not resting on a natural obstacle and seemed ill-prepared to resist, Lee decided this would be the main point of his attack. The risk was high, for the attacking force would have to make a flanking march of some 12 miles across the front of the Union Army, the most dangerous military maneuver in the book.

JACKSON DISAPPEARS INTO THE FOREST

At a conference that night between Lee and Jackson it was decided that Jackson's corps would make the attack. A local guide was found who knew a seldom-used trail through the woods that would keep them out of sight of the Federals for most of the march. Lee would keep pressure on Hooker as best he could with his limited force until Jackson was in position. Stuart's cavalry was to screen the movement.

The Union Army's right flank was held by Howard's XI Corps, stretching west about a mile from Wilderness Church and generally facing south. East of Howard was Sickles' III Corps with Slocum's XII and Couch's II curved around the Chancellorsville crossroads. Meade's V Corps held the left flank, with its own flank resting on the Rappahannock.

Saturday, May 2, broke clear and hot. As the sun burned down, Jackson's column, 6 miles long, wound its way across the Union front. Shortly after the march began, Federal observers posted atop tall trees, reported a heavy movement in front of Sickles. Hooker declared jubilantly, "Lee is in full retreat towards Gordonsville."

Sickles requested permission to attack. But it took Hooker until noon to make up his mind, and then his orders were hesitant and timid. "Move out cautiously and harass the movement." The word "attack" was not even mentioned, and only Sickles was ordered to move. Strange orders, indeed, for a commanding general who earlier had informed his cavalry commander that the secret of success in battle is to "fight, fight, fight."

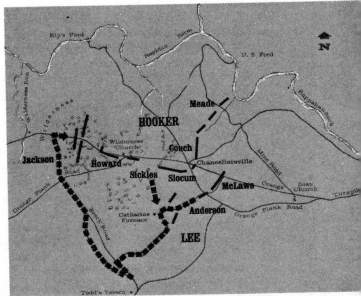

Jackson's flank march, May 2, 1863.

Sickles moved out with two divisions. About 2:30 p.m. he hit the Confederate rear guard near Catharine Furnace and killed or captured most of the 23d Georgia Regiment. But by 2:30 Jackson's leading regiment, the 5th Alabama, was already forming for the attack across the turnpike west of Hooker's right flank.

As the other Confederate regiments gradually came up and formed in the woods, the Union pickets were aware that something was afoot. Junior officers of the line tried to alert corps headquarters, but Howard, imbued with Hooker's belief that Lee was fleeing and convinced that the woods were too thick on his flank for a major assault, refused to take any action. At Army headquarters back at Chancellorsville, the warnings also went unheeded. In desperation, one officer in command of some pickets sent a final message to Howard that the enemy was forming in strength in the woods on his flank, and ended with, "For God's sake make disposition to receive him." About that time Hooker was informing Sedgwick: "We know the enemy is fleeing, trying to save his trains."

Thomas J. Jackson

Shortly after 5 o'clock Jackson was ready. Many of the Union soldiers, their muskets stacked, were preparing supper, some were playing cards, others were sleeping. At the shouted orders the gray-clad regiments exploded out of the woods to the sound of the rebel yell and rolled up Hooker's right flank. Most of Howard's corps was quickly shattered into a frightened, disorganized mob and streamed back toward Chancellorsville. A soldier in the 13th Mass. Volunteers remembered that "along the road it was pandemonium; on the side of the road it was chaos."

In the shadows of dusk the initial charge lost its momentum as scattered Federal units were brought into line to stem the tide. Their alinement broken by the charge through the woods and the excitement of the attack, the Confederate regiments halted to reorganize. In the hope that he could continue the assault, Jackson himself went forward on the turnpike in the growing darkness to study the situation at firsthand. But in returning to his lines he was mistakenly shot and mortally wounded by his own men, ending any chance of another major attack before morning.

205

Under a darkening late afternoon sky, units of Couch's I Corps move up to Jackson's fierce onslaught, while Howard's corps (foreground) flees from the

During the night the XI Corps was reorganized and hel
Chancellorsville. Reynolds' I Corps, which had previously
ordered up from Fredericksburg and arrived on the field du
the attack, now held the Federal right flank, with its own f
resting on the Rapidan River and facing west rather than sc

Lee's strategy was successful. The whole movement had
a model of maneuvering, screening, and massing. Yet Lee
gained little. His situation was almost as critical as when
flanking movement was being made. The Army of Northern
ginia was split into three parts, with Sickles' corps and mo
Slocum's between Lee and Jackson's corps, now commande
Stuart. Until he could reunite these two wings Lee was in da
of being destroyed piecemeal.

THE
COMMANDER
WHO WOULD
NOT DARE

The Army of the Potomac had not been seriously hurt by Jackson's surprise attack. Howard's corps, though temporarily routed in panic, suffered only 2,412 casualties during the whole campaign, while Sickles' corps, for example, lost 4,119 and Slocum's 2,824. During the night Howard reorganized his men, and by morning they were ready and willing to fight, if given a chance. Moreover, with the arrival of Reynolds' corps from Fredericksburg, Hooker now had approximately 90,000 men around Chancellorsville to throw against Lee's divided 48,000. Unfortunately for

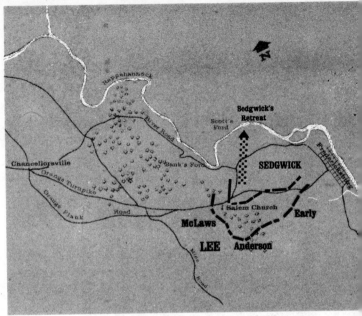

Lee turns back Sedgwick at Salem Church, May 4, 1863.

the Army of the Potomac, Hooker was thinking only of defer
Strategically, most of the advantages were still his, but the Un
commander had lost his nerve.

Early the next morning Lee and Stuart resumed the assa
fighting desperately to connect with each other. Then Hoo
suddenly made it easy for them. He voluntarily withdrew Sick
to strengthen his new, shorter defensive line to the north. T
not only enabled Lee to unite the two wings of his army, it a
gave him strategic high ground at Hazel Grove, just south
Chancellorsville, from where his artillery could inflict sev
damage on the Federals. This forced Hooker to withdraw fr
Chancellorsville entirely into a new defensive position closer
the rivers. The Union army now arched between the Rapic
and the Rappahannock. Behind the strong defensive wo
that he had built, Hooker should have felt safe even though
90,000 men were "surrounded" by Lee's 48,000.

In the meantime, Sedgwick's VI Corps had been ordered
seize Marye's Heights behind Fredericksburg from Early's divisi
then march to Hooker's assistance. In a daring bayonet cha
Sedgwick drove Early off the heights and back toward Ri
mond. Pausing only long enough to regroup, he then procee
west on the turnpike toward Chancellorsville.

When Lee learned that Early had lost the heights and a Fed
force was marching on his rear, he again boldly split his ar
Showing his complete contempt for Hooker, he marched McLa
and Anderson's divisions back toward Fredericksburg, leav
Stuart with about 25,000 men to hold the Union army of 90,0

Late that afternoon Lee met Sedgwick's advance division r
Salem Church on the Orange Turnpike and halted it, w
Sedgwick waited for his other divisions to come up. The r
day, May 4, Early advanced on the Federals from Fredericksb

Attacked furiously on three sides, Sedgwick wisely abandoned any idea of joining Hooker. Instead, he gradually swung his corps around toward the Rappahannock to protect his flanks and that night crossed the river to safety at Scott's Ford, just below Banks' Ford. Hooker made no move to help Sedgwick at any time.

Lee promptly marched his weary men back to Chancellorsville to join Stuart, intending to attack Hooker again in his strongly fortified position. Fortunately for the exhausted Confederate troops, the Army of the Potomac retreated across the Rappahannock before Lee could mount another assault. The battle of Chancellorsville was over. The Union loss in killed, wounded, and missing totaled 17,287; the Confederate, 12,821.

LEE
MOVES
NORTH

While Richmond rejoiced at the brilliant victory, the deep despair in Washington was summed up by Lincoln's anguished statement: "My God! What will the country say?"

The situation for the North was not as bad as it first seemed. In a sense, the Army of the Potomac had not been defeated, only its general. At no time during the battle had it been committed to action as an army. Over 40,000 troops had seen no action at all, despite Lincoln's admonition to Hooker to use all his men. The losses suffered in the campaign were soon made good by new recruits, and when Lincoln appointed George Meade to succeed Hooker, the Army of the Potomac was stronger than ever. Although few people realized it, while the North was losing battles it was at the same time inexorably winning the war by consistently whittling away at Southern resources.

And while Richmond celebrated, the truth was that the South had gained little if anything from the victory. To be sure, another "On-to-Richmond" drive had been stopped, but that was the extent of it. The loss of "Stonewall" Jackson was a serious blow to the Confederacy. Without him, the Army of Northern Virginia never again executed the bold and vigorous strategy that had characterized it. "I have lost my right arm," Lee declared sadly.

Nevertheless, the decision was made to attempt a second invasion of the North. The Confederate government believed that the victory at Chancellorsville had seriously affected Northern morale and hoped that an invasion now would put so much pressure on Lincoln that he would be forced to call a halt to the war. So Lee moved into Pennsylvania, only to be defeated by Meade at Gettysburg in July 1863. He then retreated back into Virginia and prepared to spend the winter in the Mine Run area behind the Rapidan.

Merchant steamers unloading supplies at Vicksburg after the surrender. Courtesy Library of Congress.

CHAPTER IX
Battle of Vicksburg

ACROSS THE IMPERISHABLE CANVAS *of the American Civil War are vividly recorded feats of arms and armies, and acts of courage and steadfast devotion which have since become a treasured heritage for all Americans. Among the military campaigns, few, if any, present action over so vast an area, of such singular diversity, and so consequential to the outcome of the war, as the great struggle for control of the Mississippi River. Seagoing men-of-war and ironclad gunboats engaged shore defenses and escorted troops along river and bayou; cavalry raids struck far behind enemy lines as the armies of the West marched and countermarched in a gigantic operation which culminated in the campaign and siege of Vicksburg. Protected by heavy artillery batteries on the riverfront and with land approaches to the north and south guarded by densely wooded swamplands, Vicksburg defied large-scale land and river expeditions for over a year. Finally the tenacious Grant, in a campaign since accepted as a model of bold strategy and skillful execution, forced the surrender of Vicksburg on July 4, 1863, splitting the Confederacy in two and securing for the North its great objective in the Western Theater.*

VICKSBURG AND THE MISSISSIPPI. Control of the Mississippi River, whose course meandered over 1,000 miles from Cairo, Ill., to the Gulf of Mexico and divided the Confederacy into almost equal parts, was of inestimable importance to the Union from the outbreak of hostilities. The agricultural and industrial products of the Northwest, denied their natural outlet to markets down the great commercial artery to New Orleans, would be afforded uninterrupted passage. It would provide a safe avenue for the transportation of troops and their supplies through a tremendous area ill-provided with roads and railroads; the numerous navigable streams tributary to the Mississippi would offer ready routes of invasion into the heart of the South. Union control would cut off and isolate the section of the Confederacy lying west of

"Johnny Reb." A volunteer soldier of the Confederacy. Courtesy Confederate Museum, Richmond.

the river—Texas, Arkansas, and most of Louisiana—comprising almost half of the land area of the Confederacy and an important source of food, military supplies, and recruits for the Southern armies. Forcefully emphasizing the strategic value of the Mississippi was the dispatch of the General in Chief of the Union armies to Maj. Gen. U. S. Grant on March 20, 1863, as Grant prepared to launch his Vicksburg campaign:

> The great objective on your line now is the opening of the Mississippi River, and everything else must tend to that purpose. The eyes and hopes of the whole country are now directed to your army. In my opinion, the opening of the Mississippi River will be to us of more advantage than the capture of forty Richmonds.

To protect this vital lifeline, the Confederacy had erected a series of fortifications at readily defensible locations along the river from which the Union advance could be checked. Pushing southward from Illinois by land and water, and northward from the Gulf of Mexico by river, Union army and naval units attacked the Confederate strongpoints from both ends of the line. They captured post by post and city by city until, after the first year of the war, Vicksburg alone barred complete Union possession of the Mississippi River. From the city ran the only railroad west of the river between Memphis and New Orleans. Through the city most of the supplies from the trans-Mississippi were shipped to Confederate armies in the East. The city's batteries on the bluffs, commanding a 5-mile stretch of the river, effectively prevented Union control of the Mississippi. Vicksburg was indeed the key, declared Lincoln, and the war could not be brought to a successful conclusion "until that key is in our pocket."

THE FIRST MOVES AGAINST VICKSBURG. David Farragut, first admiral of the United States Navy, early in May 1862, headed his Western Gulf Squadron of oceangoing vessels up the Mississippi. In a spectacular

"Billy Yank." A volunteer soldier of the Union. Courtesy Library of Congress.

engagement he passed the forts protecting New Orleans and captured the South's largest port city. Proceeding 400 miles up river, Farragut received the surrenders of Baton Rouge, capital of Louisiana, and Natchez, Miss., arriving before Vicksburg on May 18, just 1 year before Grant's army invested the city from the rear. At the same time, Flag Officer C. H. Davis was moving down the Mississippi River from the north, commanding a flotilla whose striking power was largely provided by a ram fleet under Col. Charles Ellet, Jr., and the seven "Pook Turtles"—ironclad gunboats, built on the Northern rivers, which mounted 13 guns in an armored casemate resting on a flat-bottomed hull.

After capturing Memphis in June 1862 and completely destroying the Confederate fleet of converted river steamboats, Davis pushed southward and on July 1 dropped anchor beside Farragut's fleet just north of Vicksburg. All of the Mississippi River was now in Union possession, except for a section at and below Vicksburg.

The batteries of Vicksburg had been passed for the first time on June 28. On that day Farragut blasted the city and its defenses with broadsides from his ships and a devastating fire from Comdr. David Dixon Porter's mortar boats in an unsuccessful attempt to reduce the city by naval attack. It was clearly evident from this experience that a powerful land force would be required to capture fortress Vicksburg. Only 3,000 troops under Brig. Gen. Thomas Williams had accompanied the expedition, and they were put to work with pick and shovel to dig a cut off which might permit river traffic to bypass the Vicksburg batteries. As the fleets idled above Vicksburg, the sweltering monotony was spectacularly interrupted by the short but battle-filled career of the Confederate ironclad ram *Arkansas,* which performed at Vicksburg one of the great feats of arms on the Western waters.

The energy and skill of Lt. Isaac N. Brown, who commanded the *Arkansas,* had enabled the ram to be readied for action despite almost impossible handicaps in securing materials. Routing the Union vessels sent to apprehend her, the venturesome man-of-war stood for the two Federal fleets lying at anchor just above Vicksburg and, with guns blazing, passed entirely through the massed flotillas to safety under the Vicksburg batteries. Here the *Arkansas* withstood all attempts to destroy her and presented a formidable threat to Farragut's wooden ships.

By the end of July, conditions indicated to Farragut that a withdrawal from Vicksburg was necessary. In the hot, fetid atmosphere of the river the disease rate had so increased that only 800 of Williams' 3,000 men were fit for duty. At the same time, the steadily falling waters threatened to maroon his deep-draught vessels. Farragut, with Williams' troops aboard, moved down river to New Orleans, while

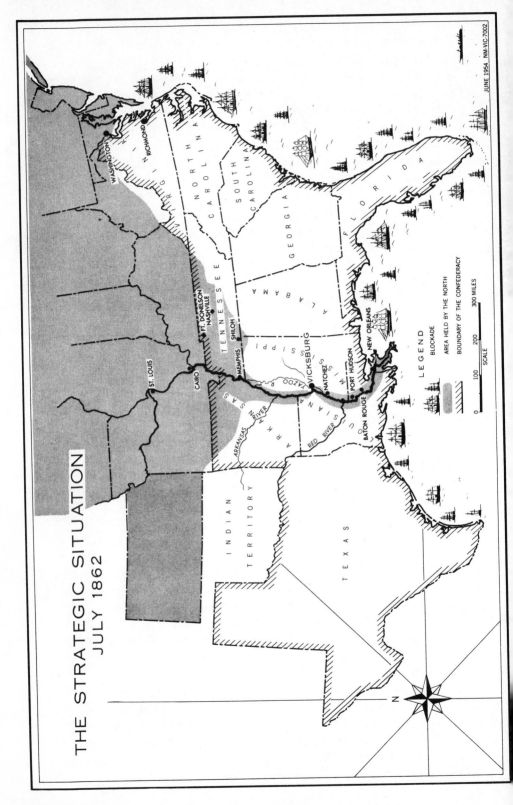

THE STRATEGIC SITUATION
JULY 1862

LEGEND

▦ BLOCKADE

░ AREA HELD BY THE NORTH

— · — BOUNDARY OF THE CONFEDERACY

SCALE

0   100   200   300 MILES

JUNE 1954   NM-VIC-7002

WASHINGTON
RICHMOND
VIRGINIA
NORTH CAROLINA
SOUTH CAROLINA
GEORGIA
FLORIDA
ALABAMA
MISSISSIPPI
TENNESSEE
FT. DONELSON
NASHVILLE
SHILOH
MEMPHIS
ST. LOUIS
CAIRO
ARKANSAS
ARKANSAS RIVER
RED RIVER
YAZOO
VICKSBURG
NATCHEZ
PORT HUDSON
BATON ROUGE
NEW ORLEANS
LOUISIANA
INDIAN TERRITORY
TEXAS

N

Scene of Sherman's assault against the Bluffs at Chickasaw Bayou. From *Battles and Leaders of the Civil War.*

Davis steamed up river, leaving Vicksburg unopposed. The initial expedition against Vicksburg had failed.

With the Union withdrawal, communications between the sections of the Confederacy east and west of the Mississippi, which had been temporarily curtailed, were resumed. From Vicksburg to Port Hudson, a distance of 250 miles by river, the Mississippi was now in Confederate hands. Into the Mississippi, just above Port Hudson, emptied the Red River which drained much of the trans-Mississippi South, and down which great stores of food were being floated to supply the armies of the Confederacy. It was imperative for the North to close off this important supply route.

GRANT'S FIRST FAILURE AT VICKSBURG. In October 1862, Grant, who had won the sobriquet of "Unconditional Surrender" at Fort Donelson and had rallied his army from near defeat at bloody Shiloh, was placed in command of the Department of the Tennessee with headquarters at Memphis; his objective—to clear the Mississippi River. The same month, Lt. Gen. John C. Pemberton, a West Pointer, born and raised in Pennsylvania, who had served with Grant in the Mexican War, was placed in command of the Confederate troops defending the Mississippi; his objective—to keep the Southern supply line open and prevent loss of the river. Vicksburg would be the focus of military operations for both commanders.

217

The first full-scale expedition against Vicksburg was initiated in December 1862, with Grant pushing southward through the State of Mississippi to strike Vicksburg from the rear as Maj. Gen. William Tecumseh Sherman, with an army of 32,000 men aboard 60 transports, proceeded down river from Memphis. Grant anticipated that his advance would pull Pemberton's army away from Vicksburg, permitting Sherman to make a lodgment on the bluffs immediately north of the city against a greatly reduced garrison. On December 20, Maj. Gen. Earl Van Dorn, with a striking force of 3,500 Confederate cavalry, swung in behind the Union line of march, capturing and burning $1,500,000 of military goods at Grant's supply base in Holly Springs. Unwilling to wage a campaign without a base of supply, Grant abandoned his campaign and returned to Memphis.

Sherman made his assault on December 29 at Chickasaw Bayou, 5 miles north of Vicksburg. The land here was a low, swampy shelf lying between the Yazoo River and the bluffs. The few dry causeways over which the Federal infantry could advance were completely covered by Confederate rifle and artillery fire from the bluffs 200 feet above. The Union Army lost nearly 2,000 men against Confederate casualties of less than 200. Tersely, Sherman reported his defeat: "I reached Vicksburg at the time appointed, landed, assaulted and failed."

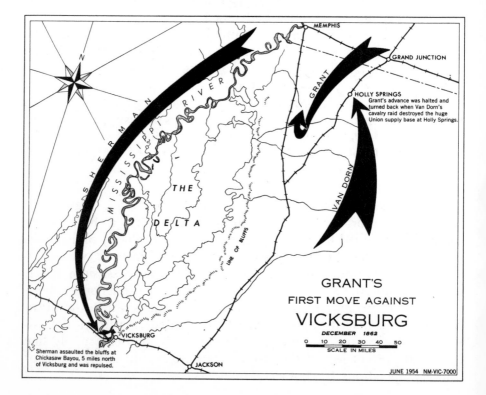

GRANT'S
FIRST MOVE AGAINST
VICKSBURG
DECEMBER 1862
0 10 20 30 40 50
SCALE IN MILES

Grant's advance was halted and turned back when Van Dorn's cavalry raid destroyed the huge Union supply base at Holly Springs.

Sherman assaulted the bluffs at Chickasaw Bayou, 5 miles north of Vicksburg and was repulsed.

JUNE 1954 NM-VIC-7000

The Confederate ironclad ram Arkansas *engaging the combined Union fleets at* *Vicksburg.* From *Battles and Leaders of the Civil War.*

The Bayou Expeditions: Grant Moves Against Vicksburg— and Fails

By the end of January, Grant had arrived at the Union encampment at Milliken's Bend, 30 miles north of Vicksburg, and assumed leadership of the operations against Vicksburg. His army, numbering about 45,000, was divided into three corps under General Sherman, Maj. Gen. John McClernand, and Maj. Gen. James Birdseye McPherson. Cooperating with the army, and providing aid without which the bayou expeditions would not have been possible, was the Western Flotilla under Porter. This fleet consisted of 11 ironclads, 38 wooden gunboats, rams, and sundry auxiliary craft mounting over 300 guns and carrying a complement of 5,500. The war in the West now hinged upon the effectiveness of this combined land and naval force. Under Grant's direction it maneuvered over hundreds of miles of river and bayou seeking to outflank Vicksburg. The capture of the city would result not from great battles but from a war of movement.

THE GEOGRAPHICAL PROBLEM OF VICKSBURG. The capture of Vicksburg proved difficult partly because of the topography of the area, which so favored defense of the city as to render the fortress almost impregnable

219

to attack. To move against the city it was necessary to reach the bluffs which extended north and south and on which Vicksburg had been built. Behind the bluffs, to the east, lay dry ground on which an army might maneuver; below the bluffs, on both sides of the river, flooded swamplands prevented ground movements. With his army behind the bluffs, either above or below, Grant might come to grips with Pemberton's Army of Vicksburg. Unless he reached the bluffs, capture of the city would be impossible; it could not be assaulted from the river.

The line of bluffs which marks the eastern boundary of the Mississippi Valley leaves the river at Memphis, curves in a great 250-mile arc away from the river, and then swings back to reach the river again at Vicksburg. Enclosed between the bluffs and the river is the "Delta"—a strip of land averaging some 60 miles in width, which is now a fertile, well-drained, cotton-growing region. In 1863, it was a swampy bottom land containing numerous rivers and bayous, subject to incessant floods. It was covered with thick forests and dense undergrowth, a condition, which, according to Grant's engineer officer, "renders the country almost impassable in summer, and entirely so, except by boats, in winter." This impenetrable swampland, lying before the bluffs, effectively guarded Vicksburg's right flank. Unless the waterways of the Delta might provide a passage to the bluffs, operations against Vicksburg to the north were hopeless.

Maj. Gen. U. S. Grant, commanding the Union Army of the Tennessee. Courtesy National Archives.

Lt. Gen. John C. Pemberton, commanding the Confederate Army of Vicksburg. Courtesy Flohr Studio, Vicksburg.

South of Vicksburg the prospect for the Union Army was equally dismal. After meeting the river at Vicksburg, the bluffs follow the river course closely to the south and were accessible, therefore, to troops from the Mississippi River. But the river batteries of the city prevented passage of transports to the river below; for troops to get below the city it was necessary to move through the Louisiana lowlands west of the river. This region was like the Delta north of Vicksburg—flooded bottom lands interspersed with bayous, rivers, and lakes. It would prove equally obstinate to land movements.

To increase Grant's difficulties, his campaign against Vicksburg was begun during the wet season when streams were overflowing and lowlands impassable. The winter of 1862–63 was a period of unusually high water, the Mississippi cresting higher than its natural banks from December until April. Had Grant reached Vicksburg during the dry season, his problem would have been less formidable.

Until the bottoms were dry enough to permit land movements, the Union commander felt himself compelled to keep the army active. Even if success along the water routes seemed unlikely, he reasoned that prolonged idleness would be injurious to the health and morale of his troops. Grant had come to believe that military success was won by the aggressive. To Grant's critics, who demanded that he open the Mississippi without delay or be replaced by someone who could, Lincoln replied, "I can't spare this man; he fights."

As Pemberton prepared to defend Vicksburg he was beset by difficulties rivaling those of his opponent, despite the topography which was friendly to his defensive purpose. Vicksburg would be secure only so long as the Confederate Army could prevent Grant from achieving a foothold on the high ground above or below the city. Yet, to prevent such a lodgment, it was necessary for Pemberton to defend a wide front extending 200 miles above and below Vicksburg, at any point along which Grant might strike. To cover this large area the Confederate commander would have to disperse his limited garrison dangerously and at the same time retain sufficient troops to protect the city—his primary responsibility. Under such conditions it was essential for Pemberton to receive information of Federal movements in order to concentrate his troops rapidly to meet the advance. Yet Pemberton was almost wholly lacking in cavalry and had no navy to interfere with and report Union progress through the rivers and bayous. Both Pemberton and Grant faced exacting problems in command during the Vicksburg operations.

GRANT'S CANAL. Vicksburg's location on the horseshoe bend of the river had suggested a solution to the Vicksburg problem the previous summer. By digging a canal across the peninsula below Vicksburg and diverting the river through it, unarmored transports could bypass the

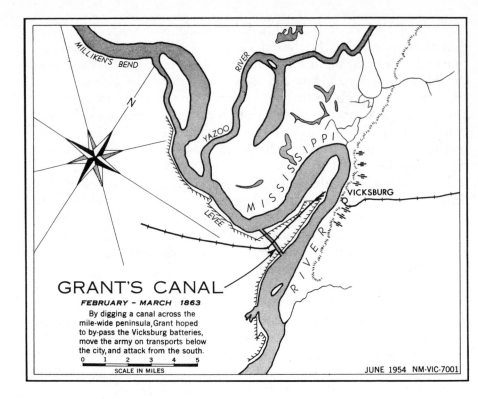

GRANT'S CANAL

FEBRUARY – MARCH 1863

By digging a canal across the mile-wide peninsula, Grant hoped to by-pass the Vicksburg batteries, move the army on transports below the city, and attack from the south.

0   1   2   3   4   5
SCALE IN MILES

JUNE 1954 NM-VIC-7001

city batteries and deliver troops safely to the bluffs below. In January, Sherman's Corps, assisted by dredging machines, began excavation of the mile-long canal. This project continued until March when a sudden rise in the river flooded the peninsula, driving the troops to the levees, and destroying much of their work.

DUCKPORT CANAL. A similar effort to turn Vicksburg's left flank was essayed by cutting a canal at Duckport, between Milliken's Bend and Vicksburg. By this avenue it was hoped vessels might leave the Mississippi above Vicksburg, pass through a series of circuitous bayous and emerge again on the Mississippi 20 miles below the city. The route was laboriously opened for navigation and one small steamer safely passed to the river below. Then the level of the river fell and blocked the Duckport attempt.

LAKE PROVIDENCE EXPEDITION. While the canal work was in progress, McPherson's Corps was assigned the opening of the Lake Providence route. The objective of this activity was the turning of Vicksburg's left flank by passing southward through the Louisiana waterways to reach the bluffs below the city. A canal was cut to provide entrance from the Mississippi into Lake Providence, 75 miles above Vicksburg. From Lake Providence a route was surveyed through the labyrinth of

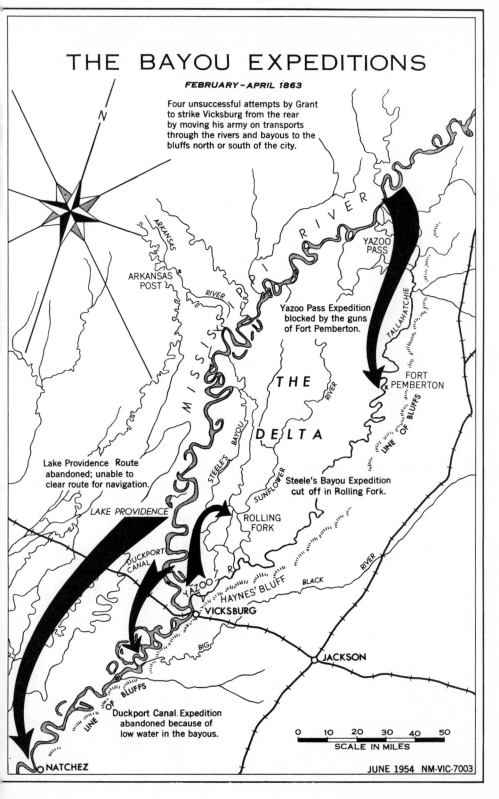

THE BAYOU EXPEDITIONS

FEBRUARY – APRIL 1863

Four unsuccessful attempts by Grant
to strike Vicksburg from the rear
by moving his army on transports
through the rivers and bayous to the
bluffs north or south of the city.

N

ARKANSAS

ARKANSAS
POST

RIVER

MISSISSIPPI

RIVER

YAZOO
PASS

Yazoo Pass Expedition
blocked by the guns
of Fort Pemberton.

TALLAHATCHIE

THE

RIVER

FORT
PEMBERTON

LINE OF BLUFFS

DELTA

Lake Providence Route
abandoned; unable to
clear route for navigation.

STEELE'S BAYOU

SUNFLOWER

Steele's Bayou Expedition
cut off in Rolling Fork.

LAKE PROVIDENCE

ROLLING
FORK

DUCKPORT
CANAL

YAZOO

R.

HAYNES' BLUFF

BLACK

RIVER

VICKSBURG

BIG

JACKSON

LINE

OF

BLUFFS

Duckport Canal. Expedition
abandoned because of
low water in the bayous.

0   10   20   30   40   50
SCALE IN MILES

NATCHEZ

JUNE 1954 NM-VIC-7003

bayous, lakes, and rivers by which a fleet might emerge again on the Mississippi 200 miles below the city and move on Vicksburg from the south. While presenting great difficulties to navigation, the entire 400 miles would be safe from enemy action. By the end of March 1863, McPherson's men had almost cleared the route for navigation. The dredging of shoals and the sawing off of trees far enough below the water to permit passage of the transports proved the most severe obstacles. Before this long and extremely difficult route could be completed, however, other, more likely, plans were formulated, and the Lake Providence expedition was recalled.

THE YAZOO PASS EXPEDITION. The Yazoo Pass project, which sought to turn the right flank of Vicksburg by sending an expedition through the Delta waterways to the bluffs north of the city, was for a time the most promising of the bayou attempts. By exploding a mine in the Yazoo Pass, 325 river miles north of Vicksburg, access from the Mississippi into the rivers of the Delta was secured. With paddle wheels reversed against the roaring current which surged through the crevasse, and suffering extensive damage in collisions with trees and floating debris, the gunboats and transports carrying a division of infantry began the hazardous journey. Almost a month was required to reach the calmer waters of the Coldwater River.

Notified of the threat, Pemberton dispatched Maj. Gen. W. W. Loring's Division to halt the Union advance. Fort Pemberton, overlooking the Yalabusha River 90 miles north of Vicksburg, was quickly constructed of earth and cotton bales. The land surrounding the fort was completely flooded, permitting approach by water only. On March 11, the Union gunboats began an artillery bombardment and were promptly greeted by a heavy return fire as "Old Blizzards" Loring gained his nickname by pacing the parapet and urging his gunners to, "Give them blizzards, boys! Give them blizzards!" Grant had planned to send 30,000 men through the Yazoo Pass; but Loring's gunners blasted back every attempt to pass the fort, forcing the fleet to withdraw. The Yazoo Pass expedition was one of the great flanking attempts of the war—the route from Milliken's Bend to the rear of Vicksburg through the pass was over 700 miles, yet it was only 30 miles direct from Milliken's Bend to Vicksburg.

THE STEELE'S BAYOU EXPEDITION. The last and most extraordinary of Grant's unsuccessful attempts to reach Vicksburg was the Steele's Bayou expedition through 200 miles of narrow, twisting bayous north of Vicksburg. Like the Yazoo Pass operation, it was an effort to turn the city's right flank. This shorter route had been originally scouted in order to send aid to the Yazoo Pass expedition when that column seemed in great danger of being cut off and captured. Further exploration suggested the route to the bluffs by way of Steele's Bayou might prove the best of all possible approaches to Vicksburg, and Porter himself commanded the squadron of 11 vessels which entered Steele's Bayou from the Yazoo River on March 16.

The route was heavily obstructed by natural hazards, but Porter, warned by apprehensive officers who feared that superstructures would be carried away in crashing through the closely overhung waterways, answered with the declaration, "All I need is an engine, guns, and a hull to float them." Progress was slow through winding streams barely wide enough to admit passage of the gunboats. This time alert Confederates, aided by treacherous obstructions in the mouth of the Rolling Fork, nearly succeeded in shutting up and capturing the entire fleet by felling huge trees across the bayou to block Porter's retreat.

Sherman, following behind the fleet with infantry, received word of Porter's danger, and an eerie night march ensued. By the flaring light of candles held in the muzzles of their rifles, the Federal soldiers splashed through the canebrake hip deep in water and arrived in time to drive off the Confederates who had moved in behind the Union fleet. Three days were required to back the fleet to safety on the Mississippi, which was reached late in March. Grant had now tested

Skirmishing in the heavily wooded and flooded bottom lands during the bayou expeditions. From a wartime sketch.

all possible approaches to Vicksburg as he attempted to swing wide around its flanks to the north and south. Every effort had failed. In April, the Union Army was no closer to Vicksburg than it had been in December. The Southern bastion on the Mississippi had successfully withstood Union land and naval attacks for almost a year.

The Vicksburg Campaign: Grant Moves Against Vicksburg— and Succeeds

In the eyes of many in the North, Grant's Army had floundered in the swamps for months with nothing to show for it except a steadily mounting death list from disease. Criticism of the Union commander mounted. "I don't know what to make of Grant, he's such a quiet little fellow," said Lincoln, thinking of the more flamboyant leaders who had led his Eastern armies, "The only way I know he's around is by the way he makes things *git*." Lincoln had grown increasingly fond of Grant, whose army, while ineffective, had never been inactive. Now he declared to Grant's critics, "I think we'll try him a little longer."

Although Grant had made every effort to navigate the bayous and reach Vicksburg, he was later to record that little hope had been entertained that success would greet these ventures. While waiting for the dry season which would permit land operations, however, he had determined to exhaust every possibility and to retain the fighting edge of his army by keeping it constantly on the move. As April arrived and the roads began to emerge from the slowly receding waters, Grant prepared to execute the movement which he had believed from the first to be the logical approach against Vicksburg—marching down the west bank of the Mississippi through Louisiana, crossing the river south of the city, and laying siege to it from the rear.

PORTER RUNS THE VICKSBURG BATTERIES. Grant's Vicksburg campaign officially began on March 29, 1863, when he ordered McClernand's Corps to open a road for the army from Milliken's Bend to the river below the city. Considerable work had been done previously when it was contemplated that a canal from Duckport to the river below Vicksburg might offer passage to the fleet. Falling waters had finally defeated this plan and, during April, McClernand's engineers labored to bridge streams, corduroy roads, and build flatboats to cross areas still covered by flood waters. During that month also, elements of the Army of the Tennessee accomplished the 70-mile march and assembled at a small hamlet appropriately named, Hard Times, in view of Grant's unpleasant bayou experiences. Here they were across the river from the Confederate stronghold of Grand Gulf, 25 miles below Vicksburg.

Adm. David Dixon Porter, commanding the Union naval operations on the inland waters. Courtesy National Archives.

Porter's gunboats running the Vicksburg batteries on the night of April 16, 1863. From a wartime sketch.

This remarkable wartime photograph, taken by a Confederate Secret Service agent, shows Grierson's cavalrymen near the end of their 600-mile raid behind the Confederate lines. From *Photographic History of the Civil War.*

To ferry the Union Army across the Mississippi, it was necessary for Porter's fleet, in anchorage north of Vicksburg, to run the batteries and rendezvous with Grant below. While naval craft singly and in groups had, on occasion, passed these batteries successfully before, it was still a formidable undertaking for which careful preparation was required. As protection against shellfire, each vessel had its port side, which would face the Vicksburg guns in passage, piled high with bales of cotton, hay, and grain. Coal barges were lashed alongside as an additional defense.

Shortly before midnight, April 16, Confederate pickets in skiffs at the bend of the river above Vicksburg saw the muffled fleet bearing down upon them and quickly gave the alarm. Tar barrels along the bank were ignited and buildings in the small village of De Soto across the river were set afire. The blinding light of a great flare helped illuminate the river and outline the fleet for the Confederate gunners. Tier upon tier of the river batteries thundered down on the Union vessels. In return, these boats delivered their broadsides into the city as they passed so close that the clatter of bricks from falling buildings could be heard on board.

Through this "magnificent, but terrible" spectacle—one of the most fearful pageants of the war—steamed the fleet in single file. "Their heavy shot walked right through us," related Porter. Every one of the 12 boats was hit repeatedly. Many went out of control and revolved slowly with the current. Despite the furious bombardment, only one craft was sunk; within a few days damages were repaired and the fleet joined the army at the village of Hard Times. Because of the difficulty of supplying the army by wagon train over the wretched road from Milliken's Bend, 6 transports and 12 barges loaded with supplies ran the batteries a few nights later with the loss of 1 transport and 6 barges.

THE RIVER CROSSING. Grant's plan was to make an assault landing at Grand Gulf, a fortified road junction on the bluffs at the mouth of the Big Black River. On April 29, the Union gunboats pounded the Grand Gulf fortifications for 6 hours, seeking to neutralize the defenses and clear the landing for 10,000 Federal infantry aboard transports just beyond range of the Confederate cannon. The naval attack failed to reduce the Confederate works, and that night Grant marched southward along the Louisiana shore to a landing opposite Bruinsburg. There he was met by the fleet which then slipped downstream under cover of darkness. By noon of the following day, April 30, Grant was across the Mississippi, experiencing

> a degree of relief scarcely ever equaled since. . . . I was now in the enemy's country, with a vast river and the stronghold of Vicksburg between me and my base of supplies. But I was on dry ground on the same side of the river with the enemy. All the campaigns, labors, hardships, and exposures, from the month of December previous to this time, that had been made and endured, were for the accomplishment of this one object.

Grant's landing was unopposed, partly because of two diversionary movements and partly because of Pemberton's decision to hold his army close to Vicksburg and fight a defensive campaign. Both diversions were completely successful. On April 17, the day after Porter's running of the batteries had indicated Grant's strategy of striking from the south, Col. B. H. Grierson with 1,000 cavalrymen moved out from southwestern Tennessee on one of the celebrated cavalry raids of the war. They rode entirely through the State of Mississippi behind Pemberton's army to a junction with Union forces at Baton Rouge, La. In 16 days Grierson covered 600 miles, interfering with Confederate telegraph and railroad communications and forcing Pemberton to detach a division of infantry to protect his supply and communication lines. Sherman, whose corps had not yet made the march from Milliken's Bend, made an elaborate feint above Vicksburg. Loading his men aboard every available gunboat, transport, and tug, he landed at

Haynes' Bluff, north of Vicksburg, leading Pemberton to expect the real attack from that direction. Both moves helped screen Grant's true objective.

The events immediately following Grant's landing revealed a basic difference in tactical concepts between Pemberton, commanding the Army of Vicksburg, and Gen. Joseph E. Johnston, his superior, who was in charge of Confederate operations in the West. Johnston believed that to defeat Grant it would be necessary for Pemberton to unite his whole force in order to smash the Union Army, preferably before Grant could consolidate his position on the east bank. Accordingly, he wired Pemberton on May 2 "If Grant's army crosses, unite all your troops to beat him; success will give you back what was abandoned to win it."

It was Pemberton's concept that holding Vicksburg was vital to the Confederacy and that he must primarily protect the city and its approaches. To have marched his army to meet Grant "would have stripped Vicksburg and its essential flank defenses of their garrisons, and the city itself might have fallen an easy prey into the eager hands of the enemy." This inability of Pemberton and Johnston to reach agreement upon the tactics that might thwart Grant's invasion seriously affected subsequent Confederate operations and prevented effective cooperation between the two commanders in the Vicksburg campaign.

Maj. Gen. William Tecumseh Sherman, commanding the Union XV Corps. Courtesy National Archives.

Gen. Joseph E. Johnston, commanding Confederate military operations in the West. Courtesy National Archives.

THE BATTLE OF PORT GIBSON. McClernand's Corps, immediately upon debarking on April 30, headed for the bluffs 3 miles inland. By nightfall the Federal soldiers had reached the high ground and pushed on toward Port Gibson, 30 miles south of Vicksburg. From this point, roads led to Grand Gulf, Vicksburg, and Jackson. Maj. Gen. John S. Bowen moved his Grand Gulf command toward Port Gibson to intercept the threat, and, at daylight on May 1, leading elements of the Union advance clashed with Bowen's troops, barring the two roads which led to Port Gibson.

The battle of Port Gibson was a series of furious day-long engagements over thickly wooded ridges cut by deep, precipitous gullies and covered with dense undergrowth. While greatly outnumbering Bowen, McClernand was prevented by the rugged terrain from bringing his whole force into action. Slowly forced backward, Bowen conducted an orderly retreat through the town, which he evacuated. The holding action had cost Bowen 800 casualties from his command of 8,000; Union losses were about the same from a force at hand of about 23,000. Pemberton determined not to contest Grand Gulf lest he risk being cut off from Vicksburg and withdrew across the Big Black River. Thus he permitted Grant to occupy Grand Gulf and gave him a strong foothold on the east bank of the Mississippi.

THE STRATEGY OF THE VICKSBURG CAMPAIGN. Grant's overall strategy, up to the capture of Grand Gulf, had been first to secure a base on the river below Vicksburg and then to cooperate with Maj. Gen. Nathaniel P. Banks in capturing Port Hudson. After this he planned to move the combined force against Vicksburg. Port Hudson, a strong point on the Mississippi near Baton Rouge, was garrisoned by Confederate troops after Farragut's withdrawal the previous summer. At Grand Gulf, Grant learned that Bank's investment of Port Hudson would be delayed for some time. To follow his original plan would force postponement of the Vicksburg campaign for at least a month, giving Pemberton invaluable time to organize his defense and receive reinforcements. From this delay the Union Army could expect the addition of no more than 12,000 men. Grant now came to one of the most remarkable decisions of his military career.

Information had been received that a new Confederate force was being raised at Jackson, 45 miles east of Vicksburg. Against the advice of his senior officers, and contrary to orders from Washington, Grant resolved to cut himself off from his base of supply on the river, march quickly in between the two Confederate forces, and defeat each separately before they could join against him. Meanwhile, he would subsist his army from the land through which he marched. The plan was well conceived, for in marching to the northeast toward Edwards Station, on the railroad midway between Jackson and Vicksburg,

Grant's vulnerable left flank would be protected by the Big Black River. Moreover, his real objective—Vicksburg or Jackson—would not be revealed immediately and could be changed to meet events. Upon reaching the railroad, he could also sever Pemberton's communications with Jackson and the East. It was Grant's belief that, although the Confederate forces would be greater than his own, this advantage would be offset by their wide dispersal and by the speed and design of his march.

But this calculated risk was accompanied by grave dangers, of which Grant's lieutenants were acutely aware. It meant placing the Union Army deep in alien country behind the Confederate Army where the line of retreat could be broken and where the alternative to victory would not only be defeat but complete destruction. The situation was summed up in Sherman's protest, recorded by Grant, "that I was putting myself in a position voluntarily which an enemy would be glad to maneuver a year—or a long time—to get me."

The action into which Pemberton was drawn by the Union threat indicated the keenness of Grant's planning. The Confederate general believed that the farther Grant campaigned from the river the weaker his position would become and the more exposed his rear and flanks. Accordingly, Pemberton elected to remain on the defensive, keeping his army as a protective shield between Vicksburg and the Union Army and awaiting an opportunity to strike a decisive blow—a policy which permitted Grant to march inland unopposed.

With the arrival of Sherman's Corps from Milliken's Bend, Grant's preparations were complete and, on May 7, the Union Army marched out from Grand Gulf to the northeast. His widely separated columns moved out on a broad front concealing their objective. When assembled, Grant's Army numbered about 45,000 during the campaign. To oppose him, Pemberton had available about 50,000 troops, but these were scattered widely to protect important points. On the day of Grant's departure from Grand Gulf, Pemberton's defensive position was further complicated by orders from President Jefferson Davis that both Vicksburg and Port Hudson must be held at all cost. The Union Army, however, was already between Vicksburg and Port Hudson and would soon be between Vicksburg and Jackson.

In comparison with campaigns in the more thickly populated Eastern Theater, where a more extensive system of roads and railroads was utilized to provide the tremendous quantities of food and supplies necessary to sustain an army, the campaign of Grant's Western veterans ("reg'lar great big hellsnorters, same breed as ourselves," said a charitable "Johnny Reb") was a new type of warfare. The Union supply train largely consisted of a curious collection of stylish carriages, buggies, and lumbering farm wagons stacked high with ammunition boxes and drawn by whatever mules or horses could be found. (Grant

Troops on the march, going into bivouac at night. From a wartime sketch.

began his Wilderness campaign in Virginia the following year requiring over 56,000 horses and mules for his 5,000 wagons and ambulances, artillery caissons, and cavalry.) Lacking transportation, food supplies were carried in the soldier's knapsack. Beef, poultry, and pork "requisitioned" from barn and smokehouse enabled the army which had cut loose from its base to live for 3 weeks on 5 days' rations.

A noted historian described this campaign: "The campaign was based on speed—speed, and light rations foraged off the country, and no baggage, nothing at the front but men and guns and ammunition, and no rear; no slackening of effort, no respite for the enemy until Vicksburg itself was invested and fell."

THE BATTLES OF RAYMOND AND JACKSON. When it became likely that Grant might strike the railroad in the vicinity of Edwards Station, Pemberton moved from Vicksburg toward that point with his main force, leaving a strong reserve in this city. At the same time he ordered the units collecting at Jackson to hit Grant's flank and rear if the opportunity presented itself. Maj. Gen. John A. Logan's Division, in

233

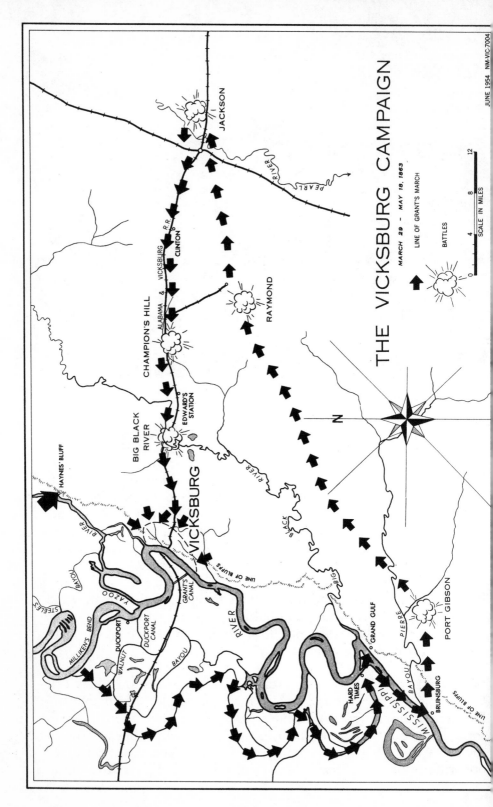

THE VICKSBURG CAMPAIGN

MARCH 29 - MAY 18, 1863

—— LINE OF GRANT'S MARCH

BATTLES

0   4   8   12
SCALE IN MILES

JUNE 1954 NM-VIC-7004

234

advance of McPherson's Union Corps, reached the vicinity of Raymond, a crossroads village 15 miles from Jackson on May 12, and was there engaged by a Confederate brigade under Brig. Gen. John Gregg. A sharp clash lasting several hours followed, Gregg's outmanned infantry being driven back toward Jackson. Each side lost about 500 men during the engagement. Confederate resistance at Raymond indicated to Grant that Jackson might be held more strongly than had been anticipated, and rumors reached the Union Commander that strong reinforcements under Johnston were expected there. Grant then determined to make sure of Jackson and, on May 13, wheeled his entire army toward the east.

Johnston arrived by rail in Jackson, on the night of the Raymond engagement, in order to take field command of all troops defending Vicksburg, and was notified that Grant's Army was between Pemberton's forces and those in Jackson. About 12,000 troops were at Jackson, against which the entire Union Army was reported to be moving. Johnston telegraphed Richmond, "I am too late."

In a pouring rain, Sherman and McPherson approached Jackson on the morning of May 14. Johnston posted the brigades of General Gregg and Brig. Gen. W. H. T. Walker on the approaches to the city with instructions to hold just long enough for valuable stores to be removed from Jackson northward to Canton where he hoped to combine forces with Pemberton. Delaying their attack until the rain

Photograph of Vicksburg taken from across the Mississippi River by a Union surgeon during a bombardment. From *Photographic History of the Civil War.*

A Union assault during the battle of Champion's Hill. From a wartime sketch.

(which would spoil their powder) slackened, the Union infantry charged the Confederate entrenchments, driving the defenders before them and capturing the city along with 35 guns and much equipment. Having intercepted a dispatch from Johnston to Pemberton ordering a junction of all Confederate troops, Grant put his men on the road toward Edwards Station at daylight the following morning. His plan was to drive a wedge between the Confederate forces before Johnston, circling to the north, could effect a junction with Pemberton. Sherman remained in Jackson to destroy the railroad yards and stores.

THE BATTLE OF CHAMPION'S HILL. Events preceding the battle of Champion's Hill emphasized the opposing tactical views held by the two Confederate commanders. Pemberton believed the retention of Vicksburg so imperative that no move which might endanger the city should be considered. It was Johnston's view that Admiral Porter's successful passage of the batteries and Grant's approach from the rear had already doomed the city, and that it was consequently valuable only for the military supplies and troops which it contained. Johnston believed that the South's only chance to prevent loss of the Mississippi was for Pemberton and himself to join forces and fight the great battle which might smash and destroy Grant's Army.

On the morning of May 14, Pemberton, at Edwards Station, received the dispatch from Johnston (a copy of which Grant had already intercepted) informing him of the position of Union troops at Clinton, between the two Confederate forces, and ordering him "if practicable, come up on his [Grant's] rear at once." Pemberton considered the order "suicidal." Convinced that Johnston's recent arrival on the field and separation from the main body did not give him sufficient information to survey the situation accurately, Pemberton called a council of war and placed the order before his commanders. Although a majority of his council favored obedience to Johnston's order, Pemberton was unwilling to endorse a movement which might endanger Vicksburg. It was decided to move instead against Grant's supposed communications which were believed essential to the Union Army's existence away from the river.

On May 15, Pemberton marched to the southeast with 17,000 men, his route further separating him from Johnston to the north. Grant, meanwhile, prepared to head westward, his line of march threatening to pierce the gap between Johnston and Pemberton and beat both of them in the race for Vicksburg. On the morning of the 16th, a second order was received from Johnston ordering Pemberton to move to the north and join Johnston. This order was obeyed, but as Pemberton's troops were countermarching they were struck by Union troops.

The battle of Champion's Hill centered around a crescent-shaped ridge of about 75 feet elevation near the Champion plantation home and involved three parallel roads leading from Edwards Station to Raymond. Each of Pemberton's three divisions—led by General Bowen, General Loring, and Maj. Gen. Carter L. Stevenson—covered one of these roads. The battle opened shortly before noon on the 16th when Brig. Gen. A. P. Hovey's Union Division, supported by Logan's Division, attacked along the north road which passed over the slope of Champion's Hill. From the crest of the hill, Stevenson's Confederate Division opened a heavy fire on the advancing Union lines which steadily mounted the ridge, driving the Confederates back and capturing 11 guns. To meet this threat to the Confederate left flank, Bowen's Division was shifted to the north to prevent a breakthrough. Re-forming his lines, Bowen counterattacked the ridge position. He dislodged the Federal infantry, driving them from the slope, and recaptured all but two of the lost guns.

Grant, in turn, was now compelled to reinforce his hard-pressed right, and at 3:30 p. m. massed Union batteries concentrated fire on the ridge. The Federal infantry followed with heavy and repeated attacks along the entire line, and for the third time the hill changed hands. Pemberton was unable to rally his troops against these attacks, and the divisions of Bowen and Stevenson began to retreat toward Baker's Creek. Loring was detailed to hold the road open for the withdrawal of the

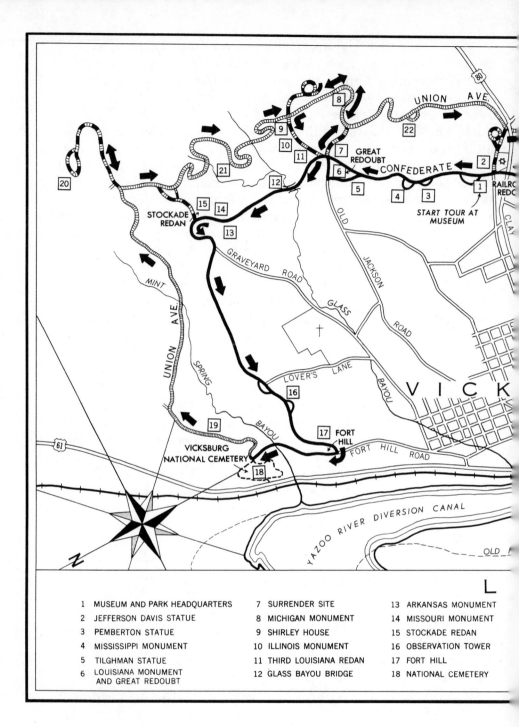

1 MUSEUM AND PARK HEADQUARTERS	7 SURRENDER SITE	13 ARKANSAS MONUMENT
2 JEFFERSON DAVIS STATUE	8 MICHIGAN MONUMENT	14 MISSOURI MONUMENT
3 PEMBERTON STATUE	9 SHIRLEY HOUSE	15 STOCKADE REDAN
4 MISSISSIPPI MONUMENT	10 ILLINOIS MONUMENT	16 OBSERVATION TOWER
5 TILGHMAN STATUE	11 THIRD LOUISIANA REDAN	17 FORT HILL
6 LOUISIANA MONUMENT AND GREAT REDOUBT	12 GLASS BAYOU BRIDGE	18 NATIONAL CEMETERY

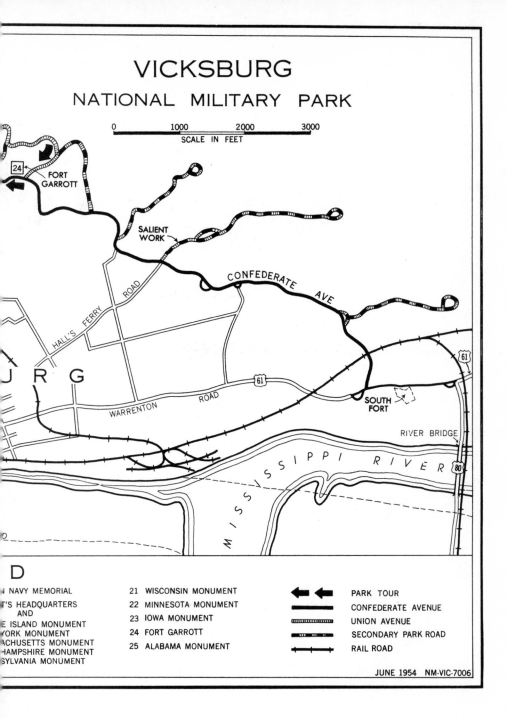

VICKSBURG
NATIONAL MILITARY PARK

0   1000   2000   3000
SCALE IN FEET

FORT
GARROTT

24

SALIENT
WORK

CONFEDERATE AVE

HALL'S FERRY ROAD

U R G

61

WARRENTON ROAD

61

SOUTH
FORT

RIVER BRIDGE

80

M I S S I S S I P P I   R I V E R

D

NAVY MEMORIAL
T'S HEADQUARTERS
AND
E ISLAND MONUMENT
ORK MONUMENT
ACHUSETTS MONUMENT
HAMPSHIRE MONUMENT
SYLVANIA MONUMENT

21 WISCONSIN MONUMENT
22 MINNESOTA MONUMENT
23 IOWA MONUMENT
24 FORT GARROTT
25 ALABAMA MONUMENT

PARK TOUR
CONFEDERATE AVENUE
UNION AVENUE
SECONDARY PARK ROAD
RAIL ROAD

JUNE 1954 NM-VIC-7006

Wartime photograph of a Union supply station on the Big Black River in rear of Vicksburg. Courtesy Library of Congress.

Confederate Army. Before Loring could rejoin the main body, after its crossing of the stream, the Union Army secured the crossings. Loring was thus cut off, and he was only able to join Johnston after a long 3-day march around the Union Army. Pemberton retreated toward Vicksburg and that night took position at Big Black River, 12 miles east of the city.

The battle of Champion's Hill (or Baker's Creek) was the bloodiest action of the Vicksburg campaign. The numbers actually engaged were relatively equal, although a large Union reserve was close at hand. Pemberton lost nearly 4,000 men, not counting the entire division of Loring which was lost to his army. Grant listed casualties of 2,500, with Hovey losing one-third of his entire division killed and wounded.

THE BATTLE OF BIG BLACK RIVER. Not knowing that Loring's Division had been cut off, Pemberton made a stand at the Big Black River in order to hold the bridges open for Loring to joint the main force. The Confederate entrenchments spanned the river at a readily defensible location where the stream made a horseshoe bend. Across the mile-wide neck of the river the Confederates constructed a line of works, and behind the earthworks, with their backs to the river, were placed 4,000 infantry of Bowen's Division supported by artillery.

Before dawn on the 17th the Union Army pushed on toward Vicksburg. Grant, still hoping to win the race for Vicksburg, had dispatched Sherman's Corps to the north to pass the retreating Confederate Army as Grant engaged it from the front. At an early hour the Federal troops came in sight of the Confederate line, whereupon they opened an artillery barrage and deployed to assault. Before the deployment was complete, Brig. Gen. Eugene A. Carr's Division charged "with a shout" from the woods fronting the Confederate position. Realizing the danger of their position, where they might be cut off from the crossing to their rear, the Confederate troops broke and headed for the bridges in disorder. After the withdrawal, the bridges were burned, effectively halting Union pursuit. In the confusion, Grant captured over 1,000 prisoners along with 18 artillery pieces.

While Pemberton's Army retreated into the defenses of Vicksburg, Grant's engineers immediately began construction of bridges across the Big Black River, using trees, cotton bales, and lumber from nearby buildings as bridging materials. Sherman's Corps, which had struck the river 11 miles to the north attempting to outflank Pemberton and prevent his retreat to Vicksburg, threw a pontoon bridge across the river at that point. By light of pitch torches, the bridges were completed during the night. On the following morning, May 18, troops crossed en route to Vicksburg.

THE CAMPAIGN ENDED. The Union Army, now within a few miles of its long-sought objective, had, in the 18 days since it crossed the Mississippi, completed one of the most noteworthy campaigns of the war.

A regiment drawn up in line of battle. From a wartime sketch.

"Whistling Dick." This Confederate cannon which guarded Vicksburg gained widespread fame among Union soldiers and sailors because of the peculiar whistle of its projectiles. From *Photographic History of the Civil War.*

The terrain of the siege of Vicksburg—looking from the Confederate line to the Union position on the far ridge.

Marching deep into enemy territory, the Army of the Tennessee had successfully lived off the country while fighting and winning five engagements and inflicting critical losses in men and equipment, had prevented Johnston and Pemberton from joining forces, and had driven the Army of Vicksburg into the defenses of the city.

By noon of May 18, with Grant's advance expected momentarily, Pemberton believed the defenses of Vicksburg strong enough to stand off the Union Army until Johnston received sufficient reinforcements to raise the expected siege and prevent loss of the Mississippi River. There, while inspecting his defenses, Pemberton received a dispatch from Johnston advising the evacuation of Vicksburg which, Johnston felt, was already doomed. Military necessity demanded that "instead of losing both troops and place, we must, if possible, save the troops. If it is not too late, evacuate Vicksburg and its dependencies and march to the northeast."

Unwilling to yield the city without a fight, Pemberton placed the order before his senior officers. They were of unanimous opinion that it would be "impossible to withdraw the army from this position with such *morale* as to be of further service to the Confederacy." As the council of war reached its decision to remain and fight, Union guns opened on the works. The siege of Vicksburg had begun.

The Siege of Vicksburg

THE CONFEDERATE DEFENSE LINE.   From his assumption of command 7 months before, Pemberton had put his engineers to work constructing a fortified line which would protect Vicksburg against an attack from the rear. A strong line of works had been thrown up along the crest of a ridge which was fronted by a deep ravine. The defense line began on the river 2 miles above Vicksburg and curved for 9 miles along the ridge to the river below, thus enclosing the city within its arc. So long as this line could be held, the river batteries denied to the North control of the Mississippi River.

At salient and commanding points along the line, artillery positions and forts (lunettes, redans, and redoubts) had been constructed. The earth walls of the forts were up to 20 feet thick. In front of these was dug a deep, wide ditch so that assaulting troops which climbed the steep ridge slope and reached the ditch would still have a high vertical wall to climb in order to gain entrance into the fort. Between the strong points, which were located every few hundred yards, was constructed a line of rifle pits and entrenchments, for the most part protected by parapets and ditches. Where spurs jutted out from the main ridge, advanced batteries were constructed which provided a deadly crossfire against attacking lines. The Confederates had mounted 128 artillery pieces in these works, of which 36 were heavy siege guns; the remainder, field pieces.

Greatly strengthening the Confederate position was the irregular topography which resulted from the peculiar characteristics of the region's loess soil. Possessing an unusual tenacity, except when eroded by the action of running water, the loess had over the centuries been cut into deep gullies and ravines with abrupt faces separated by narrow, twisting ridges. This resulted in a broken and complicated terrain which would seriously obstruct the Union movement. To permit a clear field of fire and to hinder advancing troops, all the trees fronting the Confederate line were cut down. Several hundred yards away from the Confederate position and roughly parallel to it was a ridge system not so continuous and more broken than that occupied by Pemberton's Army. Along this line, the Union Army took position and began its siege operations.

On the scattered natural bridges of high ground, which spanned the ravines and provided approaches to Vicksburg, were located the six roads and one railroad leading into that city. Nine forts had been constructed overlooking each of these routes into Vicksburg, their guns completely commanding the approaches—Fort Hill on the river north of the city, Stockade Redan, Third Louisiana Redan, Great Redoubt, Second Texas Lunette, Railroad Redoubt, Fort Garrott (also known as Square Fort), Salient Works, and South Fort on the river below Vicksburg. (All but two of these works are well preserved today.) The Confederate divisions, left to right, were commanded by Maj. Gen. M. L. Smith, General Bowen, Maj. Gen. John H. Forney, and General Stevenson. The Army of Vicksburg, at the beginning of the siege, numbered about 31,000 men, of which Pemberton listed 18,500 effectives as available to man his defense line. Grant gave his strength, shortly after the siege began, as 50,000 effectives; his army was steadily enlarged during the siege by reinforcements from Memphis.

THE ASSAULT OF MAY 19. By midday of May 19, Grant had completed his investment of the city. In the north, Sherman's Corps was in position opposite the Confederate left from the river (at the present location of the national cemetery) to the Graveyard Road, at an average distance of about 500 yards. McPherson's Corps took position on Sherman's left from the Graveyard Road to near the Baldwin's Ferry Road; the front of McClernand's Corps extended from the Baldwin's Ferry Road southward.

Considerable skirmishing had preceded the Union approach, as the Confederate pickets fell slowly back inside the defenses, thus preventing a close inspection of the Confederate fortifications. Grant determined, however, to attack immediately, before Pemberton had time to post his defenses strongly. The Union general ordered an assault

Confederate Railroad Redoubt. Plaques mark angle where fort wall was breached and entered by Union troops during the assault of May 22, 1863.

at 2 p. m. on the 19th. Sherman's troops, whose early arrival had enabled them better to prepare for attack, moved under heavy fire against the Confederate left. Although they succeeded in making a close lodgment against the walls of the Stockade Redan, they failed to breach the works and were repulsed. McPherson and McClernand, not yet in good position for attack, were unable to do more than advance several hundred yards closer to the siege line. Grant lost 1,000 men testing the Vicksburg defenses and discovered an unyielding army manning the works. Confederate losses were slight.

THE ASSAULT OF MAY 22. While the probing operation of the 19th had failed, Grant further considered the important results which a successful assault would achieve. Such a move, however costly, would save a long siege. In the end, fewer men might be lost, and a growing threat to the Union rear—General Johnston raising troops near Jackson for the relief of Vicksburg—could be eliminated by quickly capturing Vicksburg and throwing the entire Union strength against Johnston. In addition, the Federal troops, spirited by recent victories and impatient to seize the prize for which they had campaigned so long, would not work so zealously in the trenches with pick and shovel unless

The heavy guns of this Union siege battery were borrowed from the Federal gunboats and used against the Confederate siege defenses. From *Photographic History of the Civil War.*

assault had failed. On the 21st, Grant issued orders for a general assault against Vicksburg the following day.

The Union assault of May 22 was delivered against the center of the Confederate siege line along a 3-mile front from Stockade Redan to Fort Garrott. The felled trees and thick undergrowth, as well as the precipitous faces of the ravines, restricted the scope of Union maneuver. Only a portion of Grant's full strength could be brought into action, reserves being posted to exploit a breakthrough. Careful preparations preceded the attack: field batteries were run forward and emplaced to provide a covering fire for the infantry, and troops were advanced into concealed positions—in places, within 200 yards of their objective. Watches of all Union commanders were synchronized, the attack to begin simultaneously at 10 a. m. in order to prevent Pemberton from shifting his forces from one threatened point to another.

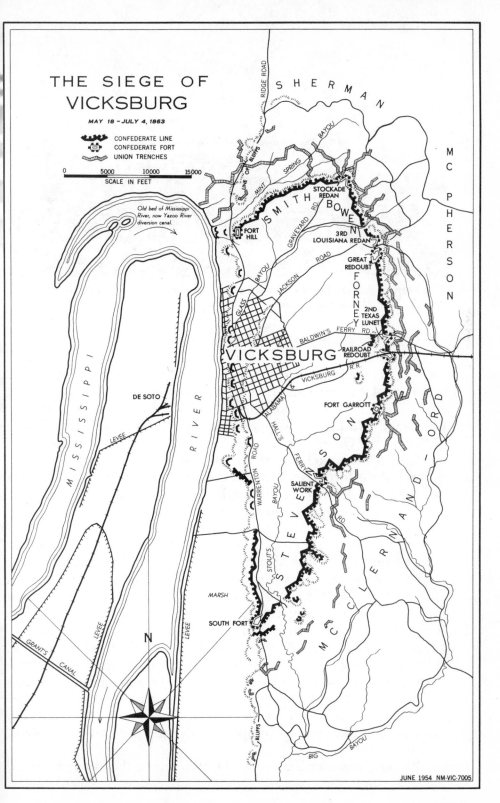

THE SIEGE OF VICKSBURG

MAY 18 – JULY 4, 1863

CONFEDERATE LINE
CONFEDERATE FORT
UNION TRENCHES

0   5000   10000   15000
SCALE IN FEET

Old bed of Mississippi
River, now Yazoo River
diversion canal.

SHERMAN

MC PHERSON

SMITH

BOWEN

STOCKADE REDAN

FORT HILL

3RD LOUISIANA REDAN

GREAT REDOUBT

FORNEY

2ND TEXAS LUNET

BALDWIN'S FERRY RD.

VICKSBURG

RAILROAD REDOUBT

R.R.

& VICKSBURG R.R.

FORT GARROTT

DE SOTO

ORD

STEVENSON

SALIENT WORK

MISSISSIPPI RIVER

ALABAMA

HALL'S FERRY ROAD

WARRENTON ROAD

MARSH

SOUTH FORT

STOUT'S BAYOU

MCCLERNAND

LEVEE

GRANT'S CANAL

LEVEE

LEVEE

N

BLUFFS

BIG BAYOU

JUNE 1954 NM-VIC-7005

247

This hospital ship provided medical care for the sick and wounded of Grant's Army during the Vicksburg operations. From *Photographic History of the Civil War.*

Of the six forts in the area of the grand assault, the Stockade Redan, under attack by Maj. Gen. Frank Blair's Division of Sherman's Corps, exemplified the day's action in method and result. Blair's men were faced with two formidable obstacles: the fort could be reached only by way of the Graveyard Road because of the deep ravines bordering the road, and the road was completely covered by the guns of the fort. In front of the fort was a deep ditch which protected it from attempts to climb the wall and enter the works. The night before, Sherman had decided that a bridge would be needed by his men to span the ditch. Only one source of lumber could be found—a frame house in which General Grant was sleeping. Informed of the need, Grant dressed and watched the house quickly torn down for bridging materials.

At the stroke of 10, the artillery bombardment of the fort ceased and the "Forlorn Hope"—a volunteer company of 150 men—raced from their position over the Graveyard Road toward the Stockade Redan, carrying the planks to bridge the ditch for the regiments to follow. Until the Federal troops almost reached the Confederate line, there was no sign of its defenders. Then the Southern soldiers "rose from their reclining position behind the works, and gave them such a terrible volley of musketry" that the road soon was nearly obstructed by the bodies of the killed and wounded, "the very sticks and chips, scattered over the ground jumping under the hot shower of Rebel bullets."

Although two color-bearers climbed the wall of the fort and planted their flags near the crest, the remnants of regiments which reached the ditch were unable to storm the walls and enter the redan. Attempting to prevent the fort garrison from firing down into the ditch, the Federal infantry swept the top of the wall with rifle fire. The toll was costly among the Confederate defenders, who fought back, using artillery shells as hand grenades and rolling them down among the Union troops in the ditch. After 4 hours of fighting, the attack was stalemated at Stockade Redan.

Union flags were placed also on the walls of the Great Redoubt and Second Texas Lunette, but it was at the Railroad Redoubt that a momentary breach was made in the Confederate defenses. Here, McClernand's men reached the fort in force, and Sgt. Joseph E. Griffith and several comrades of the 22nd Iowa crawled through a gap in the wall, which had been blasted by Union artillery, and entered the outer works. All were shot down but Griffith. He was able to back out through the opening, bringing a dozen prisoners with him. When the Union assault threatened to engulf the fort, there was a call for Confederate volunteers to regain the lost ground. A volunteer company from the Texas Legion counterattacked and drove the Union troops from the outer defenses.

Encouraged by his partial success, McClernand asked Grant for reinforcements and a renewal of the attack which, he felt, would enable his men to break the Confederate line. Grant ordered Sherman and McPherson to commit their reserves and create a diversion in McClernand's favor. The renewed assault was shattered by the resolute Confederate defense. It served only to increase Union losses and to

Union Battery Hickenlooper during the siege, within 100 yards of the Confederate line. From a wartime sketch.

intensify an already bitter controversy over McClernand's military ability, which eventually resulted in his removal from command and the appointment of Maj. Gen. Edward Ord to head the XIII Corps. More than 3,000 Union soldiers lay dead or wounded in the ditches and on the slopes of the ridge. It was the last assault against Vicksburg.

UNION SIEGE OPERATIONS. To bring the Union Army close against the Confederate defense line, construction of protected approaches was begun. As the siege progressed, "saps" or "approach trenches," deep enough to conceal troops, zigzagged their way toward the works protecting Vicksburg. Ten major approaches were carried forward by pick and shovel details, each with a network of parallels, bomb proofs, and artillery emplacements. Over 60,000 feet of trenches and 89 artillery positions, mounting 220 guns, were completed. In the siege of Vicksburg "Spades were trumps."

A Federal infantryman was later to recall that

> Every man in the investing line became an army engineer day and night. The soldiers worked at digging narrow, zigzag approaches to the rebel works. Entrenchments, rifle pits, and dirt caves were made in every conceivable direction. When entrenchments were safe and finished, still others, yet farther in advance were made, as if by magic, in a single night. Other zigzag underground saps and mines were made for explosion under forts. Every day the regiments foot by foot, yard by yard, approached nearer the strongly armed rebel works. The soldiers got so they bored like gophers and beavers, with a spade in one hand and a gun in the other.

With an almost limitless ammunition supply, Federal sharpshooters and artillerymen kept up a relentless fire, giving the Confederates little opportunity to pick off the work parties which continued digging operations during the day. Pemberton's ammunition supply dwindled each day. Considering the possible duration of the siege until an effective relief army might be assembled, the Confederate commander considered it "a matter of vital importance that every charge of ammunition on hand should be hoarded with the most jealous care." He therefore issued strict orders that both rifle and cannon should be fired only when absolutely necessary. This prevented the Confederates from keeping up the steady, harrassing fire needed to hold in check the Union siege activities.

Trench life for Grant's soldiers was not so rigorous or dangerous as for the Vicksburg defenders. Food supplies were ample, although lack of pure water was a problem for both armies and resulted in considerable disease. The burning sun and frequent rains made life miserable for both "Yank" and "Reb." Particularly as a result of the low ammunition stores of the Vicksburg army, Union losses during the siege, after the assaults of May 19 and 22, were comparatively light.

After the unsuccessful assault of May 22, only two attempts were made to break through the Confederate defenses, neither of which succeeded. Sherman, holding the Union right opposite the strong Fort Hill position, determined to reduce the fort with naval aid, and on May 27 the gunboat *Cincinnati,* protected by logs and bales of hay, moved into position and engaged the several batteries of that sector. Subjected to a deadly plunging fire which "went entirely through our protection—hay, wood, and iron," the *Cincinnati* went down with her colors nailed to the stump of a mast.

The other attempt to pierce the defense line was by exploding a mine under the Third Louisiana Redan. Logan's approach trench had reached the fort walls and from here a shaft was sunk under the fort and a powder charge prepared for its demolition. The Confederate garrison, hearing the miners' picks at work beneath the fort, began countermines in a grim race for survival. On June 25, as the entire Union line opened fire to prevent shifting of reinforcements, a charge of 2,200 pounds of powder was exploded beneath the Third Louisiana Redan, creating a large crater into which elements of the 23rd Indiana and 45th Illinois raced from the approach trench. Anticipating this result, General Forney had prepared a second line of works in the rear of the fort where survivors of the blast and supporting regiments met the Union attack and drove it back. Still other mines -were also being prepared by Union engineers at the time of the surrender.

CONFEDERATE TRENCH LIFE. Siege life for the Confederate soldier was a hazardous ordeal; nearly 3,500 were killed or wounded. Because of the limited number of effective troops available to Pemberton, almost the entire Vicksburg Army had to be placed in the trenches; sufficient numbers were not available to rotate frontline duty as was done by the Federal Army. Never knowing when an attempt might be made to assault the defense line, it was necessary for them to be on guard at all times, enduring sun, rain, mud, poor and inadequate food, as well as the bullets and shells of the Union Army for 47 days and nights. The unending barrage of small arms and artillery fire, one Confederate exclaimed, "can be compared to men clearing land—the report of musketry is like the chopping of axes and that of the cannon like the felling of trees."

Rations were generally prepared by details of soldiers behind the lines and carried to the troops at the breastworks. Coffee, the soldier's staple, was soon unobtainable and an ersatz beverage introduced, the somewhat questionable ingredients of which included sweet potatoes, blackberry leaves, and sassafras. To replace the exhausted flour supply, a substitute was devised from ground peas and cornmeal. When this was baked over a fire, one soldier complained, "it made a

Bombproofs of the 45th Illinois in Union siege line. Shirley House in background is only surviving wartime building in the park. From *Photographic History of the Civil War.*

nauseous composition, as the corn-meal cooked in half the time the peas-meal did, so this stuff was half raw. . . . It had the properties of india-rubber and was worse than leather to digest." Its effect on the digestive systems of the Confederate soldiers was possibly the equivalent of a secret Yankee weapon. A more famous, although not necessarily a more palatable, item of the besieged soldiers' diet was the mule meat introduced late in the siege. General Pemberton heartily approved of its appearance, observing that mule proved "not only nutritious, but very palatable, in every way preferable to poor beef."

For protection against artillery fire, the Confederate troops dug bombproofs in the reverse slope of their fortified ridge. From these dugouts, bulwarked by heavy timbers, trenches connected with the fortifications, affording the besieged some degree of relaxation in reading or playing cards a few yards from the front line. To defend against surprise night attacks, they were forced to sleep on their arms in the trenches.

At night the unending bombardment from Porter's fleet provided the troops of both armies with an awesome pyrotechnic display. Especially popular with the pickets were the giant 13-inch mortar

Fort Hill, on the Confederate left flank above Vicksburg, commanding the bend of the Mississippi.

South Fort, on the Confederate right flank below Vicksburg, overlooking the Mississippi.

Each of Porter's mortar boats carried one of these giant 17,000-pound mortar
which hurled 200-pound shells into Vicksburg throughout the campaign and siege
Courtesy National Archives.

The General Price. *This merchant steamer was converted into a ram by the*
Confederate Navy, captured by the Union Fleet at Memphis and used as a Federal
gunboat against Vicksburg. From *Photographic History of the Civil War.*

shells whose sputtering fuses described a tremendously high arc in the blackness before disappearing into the city. It was a "wonderful spectacle," one soldier remembered, "to see the fuse from the shells—and you could see them plainly—the comet or star-like streams of fire and then hear them coming down into the doomed city. We used to watch them while on picket at night."

Only when the Union trenches approached close to the defensive works were determined efforts made to halt the Union threat. Then the Union sap rollers (woven cane cylinders filled with earth or cotton rolled in front of the open end of the trench to protect the work party) became targets for destruction. Fuses were set on artillery shells which were then rolled down against the sap rollers, or they were ignited by Minié balls dipped in turpentine. Occasional night sallies succeeded temporarily in driving off Union work parties and filling up trenches, but no daylight forays were attempted by the Confederates.

CIVILIAN LIFE IN VICKSBURG DURING THE SIEGE. For the civilian population of Vicksburg, the siege was a grim and harrowing experience. Ordered to evacuate the city or prepare to face siege, many of the townspeople preferred to remain and share the fate of the army. They were joined by refugees accompanying the Confederate retreat into the city. Vicksburg had been subjected to periodic naval bombardment during the year of preliminary action and continuously during the siege. For relief and protection against shellfire, many of the townspeople occupied caves dug into the city's plentiful hillsides.

To the civilians, as to the Confederate soldiers, there seemed only three intervals during the day when the shelling ceased—8 a. m., noon, and 8 p. m.—when the Union artillerymen ate their meals. However, much of the accustomed social life of the town continued. Men and women passed along the streets despite frequent shell explosions, and the town's newspaper continued to appear—finally printed on wallpaper. Despite the artillery fire, few civilians were killed, although many dwellings were destroyed or badly damaged. Over more and more buildings, as the siege progressed, the yellow hospital flags floated. Thousands of Confederate sick and wounded were brought into the city, many being cared for by the women of Vicksburg. In the latter stages of the siege the food stores of the city were badly depleted, placing the people of Vicksburg on extremely short rations.

FRATERNIZATION. A unique feature of the American Civil War was the inclination of the private soldier—Union and Confederate—to fight with unrelenting ferocity during the engagements of the war and yet to engage in friendly intercourse with each other once the battle had ended, or even during lulls in the fighting. Swapping of Northern coffee for Southern tobacco was a commonplace picket activity in all

A Civil War drummer boy. From a wartime sketch.

theaters of the war. In the long, weary siege of Vicksburg, the monotony was often lightened by jeers and pleasantries exchanged between lines. Many examples of soldier humor were recorded. The Confederates, taking grim delight in their ability to withstand the onslaughts of a steadily increasing Federal Army, would shout "When are you coming in Vicksburg for a visit?" To which a grimy, sweating Federal private would yell, "Not till you show better manners to strangers."

To prevent surprise attacks, both armies posted pickets in advance of their lines at night. With the lines so close in the latter stages of the siege, pickets would often stand within a few feet of one another, or even side by side. Discussions of good shots and bad officers, or vice versa, helped to pass the long night watches. By common agreement, out of respect for the exposed and unprotected position of the sentinels, there was no firing at men on picket duty.

One Union veteran best remembered the siege of Vicksburg for

Maj. Gen. John S. Bowen, commanding the Confederate troops at the battle of Port Gibson. Courtesy Confederate Museum, Richmond.

Maj. Gen. John A. McClernand, commanding the Union XIII Corps. Courtesy National Archives.

the nightly verbal exchanges with the "Rebs" when "we used to talk to each other after fighting all day."

> In the evening when everything had stopped for the day, some of our men or some of the Johnnies would yell, "hello Johnnie" or "hello Yank" "how did you enjoy the day?" The other would say "Fine;" then some one would say, "Johnnie, how do you like mule meat?" and they answer "Fine;" then "How do you like beef dried on the bone?" to which they would reply "Not so well; it is too close to the bone to be good." Then some one would say, "Come over and we will give you some 'sow belly' to fry it in." They would reply, "We can't eat meat alone;" then the reply was, "We will give you some hardtack." Then they would reply, "The tack you sent over today was so hard we could not chew it." So you see how soon those on both sides forgot their troubles when night came, but in the morning about daylight, when the business of the day was about to open, we would say, "Watch out Johnnie, and hunt your hole," and things were on in earnest for the day.

JOHNSTON'S DILEMMA. Pemberton's foremost objective in prolonging the siege had been to afford Johnston and the Confederate government time to collect sufficient troops to raise the siege. But shortly after Grant had invested the city, Gen. Robert E. Lee's Army of Northern

The Surrender Site. The monument was erected and inscribed by Union soldiers on spot where Grant and Pemberton met.

Virginia began its invasion of the North, which ended on the field of Gettysburg. No troops could be spared from that point. To have removed troops from Lt. Gen. Braxton Bragg's army in Tennessee would have dangerously weakened that place in a desperate attempt to save the Mississippi. Johnston wired Secretary of War James A. Seddon "We cannot hold both."

During June, General Johnston had succeeded in increasing his force to about 30,000, many of whom were green troops, but efforts to secure adequate weapons, ammunition and wagons to equip the regiments had been only partly successful. Preparing to encounter an expected move by Johnston against his rear, Grant used reinforcements arriving from Memphis to construct and man a strong outer defense line facing Johnston's line of advance. Grant then had two lines of works, one to hold Pemberton in, the other to hold Johnston out. While Seddon notified Johnston "Rely upon it, the eyes and hopes of the whole Confederacy are upon you, with the full confidence that you will act, and with the sentiment that it is better to fail nobly daring, than, through prudence even, to be inactive," Johnston notified his government on June 15 "I consider saving Vicksburg hopeless."

On July 1, Johnston moved his army of 4 infantry and 1 cavalry divisions to the east bank of the Big Black River, seeking a vulnerable place to attack Grant's outer defenses. His reconnaissance during the next 3 days convinced him that no move against the Federal position was practicable. Receiving word of the surrender on July 4, he withdrew to Jackson.

THE SURRENDER OF VICKSBURG.   By July, the Army of Vicksburg had held the line for 6 weeks, but its unyielding defense had been a costly one. Pemberton reported 10,000 of his men so debilitated by wounds and sickness as to be no longer able to man the works, and the list of ineffectives swelled daily from the twin afflictions of insufficient rations and the searching fire of Union sharpshooters. Each day the constricting Union line pushed closer against the Vicksburg defenses, and there were indications that Grant might soon launch another great assault which, even if repulsed, must certainly result in a severe toll of the garrison. (Grant had actually ordered a general assault for July 6, 2 days after the surrender.)

General Pemberton, faced with dwindling stores and no help from the outside, saw only two eventualities, "either to evacuate the city and cut my way out or to capitulate upon the best attainable terms." Contemplating the former possibility, he asked his division commanders on July 1 to report whether the physical condition of the troops would favor such a hazardous stroke. His lieutenants were unanimous in their replies that siege conditions had physically distressed so large a number of the defending army that an attempt to cut through the Union line would be disastrous. Pemberton's only alternative, then, was surrender.

Although not requested, Pemberton also received the verdict of his army in a message from an unknown private, signed "Many Soldiers."

The Union ironclad gunboat Cairo, *sunk by a Confederate "torpedo" (mine) near* Vicksburg. From *Photographic History of the Civil War.*

David and Goliath of the Union fleet, photographed at Vicksburg after the surrender.
Above: A patrol boat, the "tinclad" Silver Lake.
Below: The powerful ironclad ram **Choctaw.** From *Photographic History of the Civil War.*

Maj. Gen. M. L. Smith, commanding the Confederate left at Vicksburg.
Courtesy Library of Congress.

Maj. Gen. James B. McPherson, commanding the Union XVII Corps.
Courtesy Library of Congress.

Taking pride in the gallant conduct of his fellow soldiers "in repulsing the enemy at every assault, and bearing with patient endurance all the privations and hardships," the writer requested his commanding general if he would "Just think of one small biscuit and one or two mouthfuls of bacon per day," concluding with the irrefutable logic of an enlisted man, "If you can't feed us, you had better surrender us, horrible as the idea is."

On July 3, white truce flags appeared along the center of the Confederate works. A few hours later, Grant and Pemberton met beneath an oak tree, on a slope between the lines, to arrange for the capitulation of Vicksburg and its army of 29,500. It had been 14 months since Farragut's warships had first engaged the Vicksburg batteries, 7 months since Grant's first expedition against the city, and 47 days since the beginning of the siege. On the morning of July 4, 1863, while Northern cities celebrated Independence Day, Vicksburg was formally surrendered. The Confederate troops marched out from their defenses and stacked their rifles, cartridge boxes, and flags before a hushed Union Army which witnessed the historic event without cheering—a testimonial of their respect for the courageous defenders of Vicksburg, whose line was never broken.

Into the city which had defied him for so long, and which nearly proved the graveyard rather than the springboard of his military career, rode General Grant. At the courthouse, where the Stars and Bars had floated in sight of the Union Army and Navy throughout the siege, he watched the national colors raised on the flagstaff, and then proceeded to the waterfront. With every vessel of the Navy sounding its whistle in celebration, he went aboard Porter's flagship to express gratitude for the work of the fleet.

THE SIGNIFICANCE OF THE FALL OF VICKSBURG. Vicksburg, and the simultaneous repulse of Lee's invasion at the battle of Gettysburg, marked the beginning of the end for the Confederacy. Previously, there had been confidence that victory, although demanding desperate measures, could yet be achieved. Afterward, there was only the hope that the North might sicken of the frightful cost of continuing the war and terminate hostilities. The great objective of the war in the West—the opening of the Mississippi River and the severing of the Confederacy— had been realized with the fall of Vicksburg. While in the East the Union armies battled on in bloody stalemate before Richmond, the armies of the West would now launch their columns deep into the vitals of the Confederacy.

Grant emerged from the Vicksburg campaign with a hard-won reputation as a master strategist, which prompted President Lincoln to place him in supreme command of all the armies of the United States. From this position he was destined to direct the final campaigns of the Civil War and to receive Lee's surrender at Appomattox. As for Pemberton, the fall of Vicksburg subjected him to painful criticism from those who held that a more resourceful defense might have saved the city, or his army, or both. Essentially, both commanders had disobeyed orders in like manner—Grant in striking behind Vicksburg alone rather than waiting to combine forces with Banks; Pemberton in deciding to protect Vicksburg at all cost rather than joining Johnston and risking loss of the city. But Grant's gamble had succeeded and Pemberton's had failed; and in war, as a leading Confederate commander had soberly remarked, the people measure a general's merit by his success. "I thought and still think that you did right to risk an army for the purpose of keeping command of even a section of the Mississippi River," President Davis wrote to General Pemberton after the fall of Vicksburg. "Had you succeeded none would have blamed, had you not made the attempt few if any would have defended your course."

In the Confederate capital, Gen. Josiah Gorgas, one of the most able of Southern leaders, confided to his diary the implications of the calamitous change in fortune to the South attending the twin disasters of Gettysburg and Vicksburg:

Events have succeeded one another with disastrous rapidity. One brief month ago we were apparently at the point of success. Lee was in Pennsylvania threatening Harrisburgh, and even Philadelphia. Vicksburgh seemed to laugh all Grant's efforts to scorn. . . . All looked bright. Now the picture is just as somber as it was bright then. Lee failed at Gettysburgh. . . . Vicksburgh and Port Hudson capitulated, surrendering thirty-five thousand men and forty-five thousand arms. It seems incredible that human power could effect such a change in so brief a space. Yesterday we rode on the pinnacle of success—today absolute ruin seems to be our portion. The Confederacy totters to its destruction.

In Washington, a grateful President sat at his desk seeking words to express appreciation to Grant "for the almost inestimable service you have done the country." Explaining the fear he had entertained that the Union Army might be destroyed during its daring thrust in the rear of Vicksburg, which he believed at the time to be "a mistake," Lincoln wrote to Grant, "I wish now to make the personal acknowledgement that you were right and I was wrong."

On July 9, the Confederate commander at Port Hudson, upon learning of the fall of Vicksburg, surrendered his garrison of 6,000 men. One week later the merchant steamboat *Imperial* tied up at the wharf at New Orleans, completing the 1,000-mile passage from St. Louis undisturbed by hostile guns. After 2 years of land and naval warfare, the Mississippi River was open, the grip of the South had been broken, and merchant and military traffic had now a safe avenue to the gulf. In the words of Lincoln, "The Father of Waters again goes unvexed to the sea."

The Union Army passing the courthouse as it took possession of Vicksburg on July 4, 1863. From a wartime sketch.

"The Battle of Gettysburg" (Pickett's Charge), by Peter F. Rothermel. Courtesy Pennsylvania Historical and Museum Commission.

CHAPTER X

Battle of Gettysburg

O N THE GENTLY ROLLING FARM LANDS surrounding the little town of Gettysburg, Pa., was fought one of the great decisive battles of American history. For 3 days, from July 1 to 3, 1863, a gigantic struggle between 75,000 Confederates and 97,000 Union troops raged about the town and left 51,000 casualties in its wake. Heroic deeds were numerous on both sides, climaxed by the famed Confederate assault on July 3 which has become known throughout the world as Pickett's Charge. The Union victory gained on these fields ended the last Confederate invasion of the North and marked the beginning of a gradual decline in Southern military power.

Here also, a few months after the battle, Abraham Lincoln delivered his classic Gettysburg Address at the dedication of the national cemetery set apart as a burial ground for the soldiers who died in the conflict.

The Situation, Spring 1863

The situation in which the Confederacy found itself in the late spring of 1863 called for decisive action. The Union and Confederate armies had faced each other on the Rappahannock River, near Fredericksburg, Va., for 6 months. The Confederate Army of Northern Virginia, commanded by Gen. R. E. Lee, had defeated the Union forces at Fredericksburg in December 1862 and again at Chancellorsville in May 1863, but the nature of the ground gave Lee little opportunity to follow up his advantage. When he began moving his army westward, on June 3, he hoped, at least, to draw his opponent away from the river to a more advantageous battleground. At most, he might carry the war into northern territory, where supplies could be taken from the enemy and a victory could be fully exploited. Even a fairly narrow margin of victory might enable Lee to capture one or more key cities and perhaps increase northern demands for a negotiated peace.

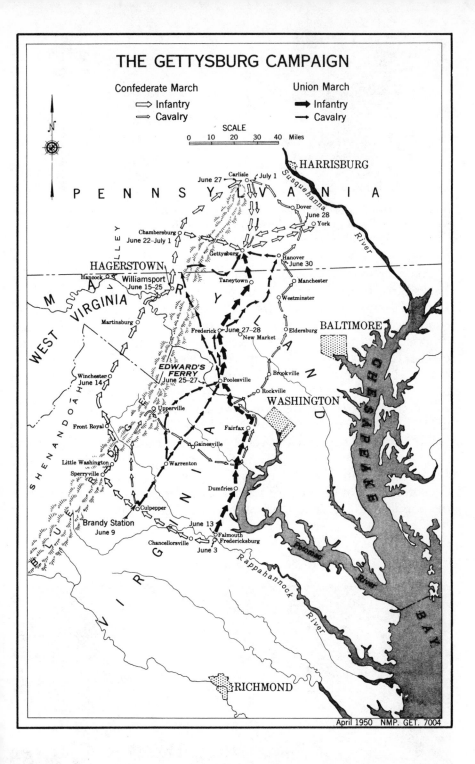

THE GETTYSBURG CAMPAIGN

Confederate March
⟹ Infantry
⟹ Cavalry

Union March
➡ Infantry
→ Cavalry

SCALE
0 10 20 30 40 Miles

HARRISBURG

P E N N S Y L V A N I A

June 27 Carlisle | July 1

Dover
June 28
York

Chambersburg
June 22–July 1

Gettysburg

HAGERSTOWN
Hancock

Williamsport
June 15–25

Hanover
June 30

Taneytown

Manchester

Westminster

Martinsburg

M A

W E S T
V I R G I N I A

S H E N A N D O A H

Winchester
June 14

Front Royal

Little Washington

Sperryville

Upperville

Gainesville

Warrenton

Brandy Station
June 9

Culpepper

June 13

Chancellorsville
June 3

Frederick June 27–28
New Market

EDWARD'S FERRY
June 25–27

Poolesville

Rockville

Brookville

Eldersburg

BALTIMORE

WASHINGTON

Fairfax

Dumfries

Falmouth
Fredericksburg

Rappahannock River

Potomac River

C H E S A P E A K E

B A Y

Susquehanna River

V I R G I N I A

RICHMOND

April 1950   NMP. GET. 7004

Maj. Gen. George Gordon Meade, Commander of the Union Forces at Gettysburg. Courtesy National Archives.

Gen. Robert E. Lee, Commander of the Confederate Army at Gettysburg. Courtesy National Archives.

Confederate strategists had considered sending aid from Lee's army to Vicksburg, which Grant was then besieging, or dispatching help to General Bragg for his campaign against Rosecrans in Tennessee. They concluded, however, that Vicksburg could hold out until climatic conditions would force Grant to withdraw, and they reasoned that the eastern campaign was more important than that of Tennessee.

Both Union and Confederate governments had bitter opponents at home. Southern generals, reading in Northern newspapers the clamors for peace, had reason to believe that their foe's morale was fast weakening. They felt that the Army of Northern Virginia would continue to demonstrate its superiority over the Union Army of the Potomac and that the relief from constant campaigning on their own soil would have a happy effect on Southern spirit. Events were to prove, however, that the chief result of the intense alarm created by the invasion was to rally the populace to better support of the Union government.

General Meade and staff, July 2. Artist unknown. From the W. H. Tipton Collection, Gettysburg National Military Park.

Gettysburg, as it appeared from Seminary Ridge a short time after the battle. Brady photograph.

The Plan of Campaign

Lee's plan of campaign was undoubtedly similar to that of his invasion which ended in the battle of Antietam in September 1862. He then called attention to the need of destroying the bridge over the Susquehanna River at Harrisburg and of disabling the Pennsylvania Railroad in order to sever communication with the west. "After that," he added, "I can turn my attention to Philadelphia, Baltimore, or Washington as may seem best for our interest."

Lee had suffered an irreparable loss at Chancellorsville when "Stonewall" Jackson was mortally wounded. Now reorganized into three infantry corps under Longstreet, A. P. Hill, and R. S. Ewell, and a cavalry division under J. E. B. Stuart, a changed Army of Northern Virginia faced the great test that lay ahead. "Stonewall" Jackson, the right hand of Lee, and in the words of the latter "the finest executive officer the sun ever shone on," was no longer present to lead his corps in battle.

The long lines of gray started moving on June 3 from Fredericksburg, Va., first northwestward across the Blue Ridge, then northward in the Shenandoah Valley. On June 9, one of the greatest cavalry engagements of the war occurred at Brandy Station. Union horsemen, for the first time, held Stuart's men on even terms. The Confederates then continued their march northward, with the right flank constantly protected by Stuart's cavalry, which occupied the passes of the Blue Ridge. Stuart was ordered to hold these mountain gaps until the advance into Pennsylvania had drawn the Union Army north of the Potomac. On June 28, Hill and Longstreet reached Chambersburg, 16 miles north of the Pennsylvania boundary. Rodes' division of Ewell's corps reached Carlisle on June 27. Early's command of 8,000 men had passed through Gettysburg on June 26 and on the 28th had reached York. Early planned to take possession of the bridge over the Susquehanna at

Columbia, and to move on Harrisburg from the east. Lee's converging movement on Harrisburg seemed to be on the eve of success.

An unforeseen shift of events between June 25 and 28, however, threatened to deprive Lee of every advantage he had thus far gained in his daring march up the Shenandoah and Cumberland Valleys. The cavalry engagement between Stuart and Pleasonton at Brandy Station convinced Gen. Joseph Hooker, then in command of the Union Army, that the Confederate Army was moving northward. President Lincoln and General in Chief Halleck, informed of this movement, ordered Hooker to proceed northward and to keep his command between the Confederate Army and Washington. When he was refused permission to abandon Harpers Ferry, and to add the garrison of 10,000 men to his army, Hooker asked to be relieved of command. Gen. George G. Meade received orders to assume command of the army at Frederick, Md., on June 28, and he at once continued the march northward.

General Stuart, in command of the Confederate cavalry, had obtained conditional approval from Lee to operate against the rear of the Union Army as it marched northward and then to join Lee north of the Potomac. As he passed between Hooker's army and Washington, the unexpected speed of the Union Army forced Stuart into detours and delays, so that on June 28 he was in eastern Maryland, wholly out of touch with the Confederate force. The eyes and ears of Lee were thus closed at a time when their efficient functioning was badly needed.

"Old Dorm" of Pennsylvania (now Gettysburg) *College. It was used as a shelter for wounded.*

In this state of affairs, a Confederate agent reported to Lee at Chambersburg, Pa., on the night of June 28, that the Union forces had crossed the Potomac and were in the vicinity of Frederick. With the entire Union Army close at hand and with many miles between him and his base, Lee decided to abandon his original plan and to concentrate for battle. He moved his army at once across the mountains to Cashtown, 8 miles from Gettysburg. Here, near Cashtown, he planned to establish his battle position. Rodes, then at Carlisle, and Early, at York, were at once ordered to this point.

The First Day

THE TWO ARMIES CONVERGE ON GETTYSBURG.   The men of Heth's division, leading the Confederate advance across the mountain, reached Cashtown on June 29. Pettigrew's brigade was sent on to Gettysburg the following day to obtain supplies, but upon reaching the ridge a mile west of the town, they observed a column of Union cavalry approaching. Not having orders to bring on an engagement, Pettigrew withdrew to Cashtown.

In the intervening 2 days since he had assumed command of the Union forces, General Meade had moved his troops northward and instructed his engineers to survey a defensive battle position at Pipe Creek, near Taneytown, in northern Maryland. Buford's cavalry, which had effectively shadowed Lee's advance from the mountaintops of the Blue Ridge, was ordered to make a reconnaissance in the Gettysburg area. It was

Cavalry outpost,
by
Charles A. Morgenthaler.

Maj. Gen. John F. Reynolds. Courtesy National Archives.

Lt. Gen. Ambrose P. Hill. Courtesy National Archives.

these troops that Pettigrew's men saw posted on the roads leading into the town. Neither Lee nor Meade yet foresaw Gettysburg as a field of battle. Each expected to take a strong defensive position and force his adversary to attack.

A. P. Hill, in the absence of Lee, who was still beyond the mountains, now took the initiative. At daybreak of July 1, he ordered the brigades of Archer and Davis, of Heth's division, to advance along the Chambersburg Road to Gettysburg for the purpose of testing the strength of the Union forces. As these troops reached Marsh Creek, 4 miles from Gettysburg, they were fired upon by Union cavalry pickets who hurriedly retired to inform their commander of the enemy's approach. In the meantime, Buford's division of cavalry had moved from their camp just southwest of Gettysburg to McPherson Ridge, a mile west of the town. Buford prepared to hold out against heavy odds until aid arrived. Thus, subordinate field commanders had chosen the ground for battle.

It was 8 a. m., July 1, when the two brigades of Archer and Davis, the former to the right and the latter to the left of the Chambersburg Road, deployed on Herr Ridge. Supported by Pegram's artillery, they charged down the long slope and across Willoughby Run against Buford's men. The cavalry had an advantage in their rapid-fire, breech-loading carbines. Dismounted, and fighting as infantrymen, they held their ground against the spirited attacks of Heth's superior numbers. At 10 o'clock timely aid arrived as troops from Gen. John F. Reynolds' First Infantry corps began streaming over Seminary Ridge from the south and relieved Buford's exhausted fighters. Calef's battery, one of whose guns had fired the first Union cannon shot at Gettysburg, was replaced by Hall's Maine artillery. But, in a few moments, Union joy at receiving aid was offset by tragedy. Reynolds, close to the front lines, was killed instantly by a sharpshooter's bullet.

The struggle increased in scope as more forces reached the field. When Archer's Confederates renewed the attack across Willoughby Run, Union troops of Meredith's Iron Brigade, arriving opportunely, struck the flank of the Confederates, routing them and capturing close to 100 men, including General Archer. Relieved from the threat south of the Chambersburg Pike, the 14th Brooklyn and 95th New York regiments shifted to the north of the Pike where the Confederates were overwhelming the Union defenders. With renewed effort, these troops, joined by Dawes' 6th Wisconsin, drove the Confederates steadily back, capturing 200 Mississippians in a railroad cut. The Confederates then withdrew beyond striking distance. There was a lull in the fighting during the noon hour. The first encounter had given Union men confidence. They had held their ground against superior numbers and had captured Archer, a brigadier general, the first Confederate general officer taken since Lee assumed command.

THE BATTLE OF OAK RIDGE.   While the initial test of strength was being determined west of Gettysburg by advance units, the main bulk of the two armies was pounding over the roads from the north and south, converging upon the ground chosen by Buford. Rodes' Confederates, hurrying southward from Carlisle to meet Lee at Cashtown, received orders at Biglerville to march to Gettysburg. Early, returning from York with

McPherson Ridge and Woods, the Federal position on July 1. In the woods at the right, General Reynolds was killed. The cupola of the Theological Seminary appears in the background. Brady photograph.

Chambersburg Pike, looking westward from the Federal position toward Herr Ridge, where the Confederate attack began.

Cashtown as his objective, learned at Heidlersburg of the action at Gettysburg and was ordered to approach by way of the Harrisburg Road.

Employing the wooded ridge as a screen from Union cavalry north of Gettysburg, Rodes brought his guns into position on Oak Ridge about 1 o'clock and opened fire on the flank of Gen. Abner Doubleday, Reynolds' successor, on McPherson Ridge. The Union commander shifted his lines northeastward to Oak Ridge and the Mummasburg Road to meet the new attack. Rodes' Confederates struck the Union positions at the stone wall on the ridge, but the attack was not well coordinated and resulted in failure. Iverson's brigade was nearly annihilated as it made a left wheel to strike from the west. In the meantime, more Union troops had arrived on the field by way of the Taneytown Road. Two divisions of Howard's Eleventh corps were now taking position in the plain north of the town, intending to make contact with Doubleday's troops on Oak Ridge.

Doles' Confederate brigade charged across the plain and was able to force Howard's troops back temporarily, but it was the opportune approach of Early's division from the northeast on the Harrisburg Road which rendered the Union position north of Gettysburg indefensible. Arriving in the early afternoon as the Union men were establishing their position, Early struck with tremendous force, first with his artillery and then with his infantry, against General Barlow. Soon he had shattered the entire Union force. The remnants broke and turned southward through Gettysburg in the direction of Cemetery Hill. In this headlong

Lt. Gen. Richard S. Ewell. Courtesy National Archives.

Maj. Gen. Winfield S. Hancock. Courtesy National Archives.

and disorganized flight General Schimmelfenning was lost from his command, and, finding refuge in a shed, he lay 2 days concealed within the Confederate lines. In the path of Early's onslaught lay the youthful Brigadier Barlow severely wounded, and the gallant Lieut. Bayard Wilkeson, whose battery had long stood against overwhelming odds, mortally wounded.

The Union men on Oak Ridge, faced with the danger that Doles would cut off their line of retreat, gave way and retired through Gettysburg to Cemetery Hill. The withdrawal of the Union troops from the north and northwest left the Union position on McPherson Ridge untenable. Early in the afternoon, when Rodes opened fire from Oak Hill, Heth had renewed his thrust along the Chambersburg Pike. His troops were soon relieved and Pender's division, striking north and south of the road, broke the Union line. The Union troops first withdrew to Seminary Ridge, then across the fields to Cemetery Hill. Here was advantageous ground which had been selected as a rallying point if the men were forced to relinquish the ground west and north of the town. Thus, by 5 o'clock, the remnants of the Union forces (some 6,000 out of the 18,000 engaged in the first day's struggle) were on the hills south of Gettysburg.

Ewell was now in possession of the town, and he extended his line from the streets eastward to Rock Creek. Studiously observing the hills in his front, he came within range of a Union sharpshooter, for suddenly he heard the thud of a minie ball. Calmly riding on, he remarked to General Gordon at his side, "You see how much better fixed for a fight I am than you are. It don't hurt at all to be shot in a wooden leg."

A momentous decision now had to be made. Lee had reached the field at 3 p. m., and had witnessed the retreat of the disorganized Union troops through the streets of Gettysburg. Through his glasses he had watched their attempt to reestablish their lines on Cemetery Hill. Sensing his advantage and a great opportunity, he sent orders to Ewell by a staff officer to "press those people" and secure the hill (Cemetery Hill) if possible. However, two of Ewell's divisions, those of Rodes and Early, had been heavily engaged throughout the afternoon and were not well in hand. Johnson's division could not reach the field until late in the evening, and the reconnaissance service of Stuart's cavalry was not yet available. General Ewell, uninformed of the Union strength in the rear of the hills south of Gettysburg, decided to await the arrival of Johnson's division. Cemetery Hill was not attacked, and Johnson, coming up late in the evening, stopped at the base of Culp's Hill. Thus passed Lee's opportunity of July 1.

When the Union troops retreated from the battleground north and west of the town on the evening of July 1, they hastily occupied defense positions on Cemetery Hill, Culp's Hill, and a part of Cemetery Ridge. Upon the arrival of Slocum by the Baltimore Pike and Sickles by way of the Emmitsburg Road, the Union right flank at Culp's Hill and Spangler's Spring and the important position at Little Round Top on the left were consolidated. Thus was developed a strong defensive battle line in the shape of a fish hook, about 3 miles long, with the advantage of high ground and of interior lines. Opposite, in a semicircle about 6 miles long, extending down Seminary Ridge and into

Scene north of Gettysburg from Oak Ridge. The Federal position may be seen near the edge of the open fields in the middle distance.

the streets of Gettysburg, stood the Confederates who, during the night, had closed in from the north and west.

The greater part of the citizenry of Gettysburg, despite the prospect of battle in their own yards, chose to remain in their homes. Both army commanders respected noncombatant rights to a marked degree. Thus, in contrast with the fields of carnage all about the village, life and property of the civilian population remained unharmed, while the doors of churches, schools, and homes were opened for the care of the wounded.

General Meade, at Taneytown, had learned early in the afternoon of July 1 that a battle was developing and that Reynolds had been killed. A large part of his army was within 5 miles of Gettysburg. Meade then sent General Hancock to study and report on the situation. Hancock reached the field just as the Union troops were falling back to Cemetery Hill. He helped to rally the troops and left at 6 o'clock to report to Meade that in his opinion the battle should be fought at Gettysburg. Meade acted on this recommendation and immediately ordered the concentration of the Union forces at that place. Meade himself arrived near midnight on July 1.

The Second Day

PRELIMINARY MOVEMENTS AND PLANS. The small college town of Gettysburg, with 2,400 residents at the time of the battle, lay in the heart of a fertile country, surrounded by broad acres of crops and pastures. Substantial houses of industrious Pennsylvania farmers dotted the countryside. South of the town and hardly more than a musket shot from the houses on its outer edge, Cemetery Hill rose somewhat abruptly from the lower ground. Extending southward from the hill for nearly 2 miles was a long roll of land called Cemetery Ridge. At its southern ex-

Spangler's Spring, the right of the Federal battle line, July 2 and 3. This Tipton photograph shows the wartime appearance of the spring.

Lunettes, or artillery defense works, on the crest of East Cemetery Hill. The entrance gateway to the public cemetery, which is still in use, appears in the background on the Baltimore Pike. Brady photograph.

Jennie Wade House, located on Baltimore street between the battle lines. Jennie Wade, the only civilian killed during the battle, was accidentally struck by a bullet which passed through a door of the house.

tremity a sharp incline terminated in the wooded crest of Little Round Top and a half mile beyond was the sugar-loaf peak of Big Round Top, the highest point in the vicinity of Gettysburg. Paralleling Cemetery Ridge, at an average distance of two-thirds of a mile to the west, lay Seminary Ridge, which derived its name from the Lutheran Seminary that stood upon its crest a half mile west of Gettysburg. In 1863, 10 roads radiated from Gettysburg, the one leading to Emmitsburg extending diagonally across the valley between Seminary and Cemetery Ridges.

By noon of July 2, the powerful forces of Meade and Lee were at hand, and battle on a tremendous scale was imminent. That part of the Union line extending from Cemetery Hill to Little Round Top was strongly

East Cemetery Hill, the objective of the Confederate charge on the evening of July 2.

held. Late in the forenoon, Sickles, commanding the Third Corps which lay north of Little Round Top, sent Berdan's sharpshooters and some of the men of the 3rd Maine Regiment forward from the Emmitsburg Road to Pitzer's Woods, a half mile to the west. As they reached the woods, a strong Confederate force fired upon them, and they hurriedly retired to inform their commander. To Sickles, the extension of the Confederate line southward meant that his left flank was endangered. He at once began moving forward to the advantageous high ground at the Peach Orchard, and by 3:30 p. m. his battle front extended from Devil's Den northwestward to the Orchard and northward on the Emmitsburg Road. In this forward movement, the strong position on the crest of Little Round Top was left unoccupied. This was the situation when Meade finally turned his attention from his right flank at Culp's Hill and Spangler's Spring—the cause of his great concern throughout the forenoon—to review Sickles' line.

Lee planned to attack, despite the advice of Longstreet who continually urged defensive battle. On July 2, Longstreet recommended that Lee swing around the Union left at Little Round Top, select a good position, and await attack. Lee observed that while the Union position was strong if held in sufficient numbers to utilize the advantage of interior lines, it presented grave difficulties to a weak defending force. A secure lodgment on the shank of the hook might render it possible to sever the Union Army and to deal with each unit separately. Not all of Meade's force had reached the field, and Lee thought he had the opportunity of destroying his adversary in the process of concentration. He resolved to send Longstreet against the Federal left flank which he believed was then on

Maj. Gen. Gouverneur K. Warren.
Courtesy National Archives.

Maj. Gen. Daniel E. Sickles.
Courtesy National Archives.

Trostle farmhouse. Here the 9th Massachusetts battery, taking position in the yard, lost 80 out of 88 horses during the battle of July 2. Brady photograph.

lower Cemetery Ridge, while Ewell was to storm Cemetery Hill and Culp's Hill.

LONGSTREET ATTACKS ON THE RIGHT.   In the execution of this plan, Longstreet was ordered to take position across the Emmitsburg Road and to attack what was thought to be the left flank of the Union line on Cemetery Ridge. From his encampment on the Chambersburg Road, 3 miles west of Gettysburg, he started toward his objective, using Herr Ridge to conceal the movement from Union signalmen on Little Round Top. After marching to Black Horse Tavern on the Fairfield Road, he realized that his troops were in sight of the signal unit and at once began retracing his course. Employing the trees on Seminary Ridge as a screen, he marched southward again in Willoughby Run Valley, arriving in position on the Emmitsburg Road about 3:30 p.m. Immediately in front, and only 700 yards away, Longstreet saw Sickles' batteries lined up in the Peach Orchard and on the Emmitsburg Road. Col. E. P. Alexander, commanding Longstreet's artillery battalions, opened with full force against the Union guns. A moment later, Law's Alabama brigade stepped off, with Robertson's Texans on the left. They advanced east, then swung toward the north, with Devil's Den and the Round Tops in their path.

WARREN SAVES LITTLE ROUND TOP.   Gen. G. K. Warren, Meade's Chief of Engineers, after reviewing Sickles' line with Meade, rode to the crest of Little Round Top and found the hill, "the key to the Union position," unoccupied except by a signal station. Warren was informed by

Little Round Top from the northwest. Brady photograph.

the signalmen that they believed Confederate troops lay concealed on the wooded ridge a mile to the west. Smith's New York battery, emplaced at Devil's Den, immediately was ordered to fire a shot into these woods. The missile, crashing through the trees, caused a sudden stir of the Confederates "which by the gleam of the reflected sunlight on their bayonets, revealed their long lines outflanking the position." Warren realized Longstreet would strike first at Little Round Top and he observed, too, the difficulty of shifting Sickles' position from Devil's Den to the hill.

At this very moment, Sykes' Fifth Corps, marching from its reserve position, began streaming across Cemetery Ridge toward the front. Warren sought aid from this corps. In answer to his plea for troops, the brigades of Vincent and Weed sprinted to Little Round Top. Law's Alabama troops were starting to scale the south slope of the hill when Vincent's men rushed to the attack. Weed's brigade, following closely, drove over the crest and engaged Robertson's Texans on the west slope. The arrival of Hazlett's battery on the summit of the hill is thus described by an eyewitness: "The passage of the six guns through the roadless woods and amongst the rocks was marvelous. Under ordinary circumstances it would have been considered an impossible feat, but the eagerness of the men . . . brought them without delay to the very summit, where they went immediately into battle." A desperate hand-to-hand struggle ensued. Weed and Hazlett were killed, and Vincent was mortally wounded—all young soldiers of great promise.

While Law and Robertson fought on Little Round Top, their comrades struggled in the fields below. The Confederate drive was taken up in turn by the brigades of Benning, Anderson, Kershaw, Semmes, Barksdale, Wofford, Wilcox, Perry, and Wright against the divisions of three Federal corps in the Wheatfield, the Peach Orchard, and along the Emmitsburg Road. Four hours of desperate fighting broke the Peach Orchard salient, an angle in the Union line which was struck from the south and the west. It left the Wheatfield strewn with dead and wounded, and the base of Little Round Top a shambles. Sickles' men had been driven back, and Longstreet was now in possession of the west slope of Big Round Top, of Devil's Den, and the Peach Orchard. Little Round Top, that commanding landmark which, in Confederate hands would have unhinged the Union line on Cemetery Ridge, still remained in Union possession.

CULP'S HILL.   In the Confederate plan, Ewell on the left was directed to attack Cemetery Hill and Culp's Hill in conjunction with Longstreet's drive. At the appointed time, the guns of Latimer's battalion on Benner's Hill, east of Gettysburg, opened a well-directed fire against the Union positions on East Cemetery Hill and Culp's Hill, but the return fire soon shattered many of Latimer's batteries and forced the remnants to retire out of range. In the final moments of this action the youthful Major Latimer was mortally wounded.

Dead Confederate sharpshooter at Devil's Den. Gardner photograph.

Field hospital. From the Cyclorama.

About dusk, long after the artillery fire had ceased, Johnson's division charged the Union works on Culp's Hill. Although his right failed to make headway because of the steep incline and the strength of the Union positions, Steuart's brigade on the left had better luck. Here, on the southern slope of the hill, the Union works were thinly manned. An hour earlier, the divisions of Geary and Ruger had been called from these works to reinforce the Union center. Johnson, finding the works weakly defended, took possession of them but did not press the attack further. Only a few hundred yards away on the Baltimore Pike lay the Union supply trains. Failure of Confederate reconnaissance here again was critically important. Thus passed another opportunity to strike a hard blow at the Union Army.

Closely timed with Johnson's assault, Early's infantry started a charge toward East Cemetery Hill. Seldom if ever surpassed in its dash and desperation, Early's assault reached the crest of the hill where the defenders, as a last resort in the hand-to-hand encounter, used clubbed muskets, stones, and rammers. Long after dark, Early's Louisiana and North Carolina troops fought to hold the crest of the hill and their captured guns. But the failure of Rodes to move out of the streets of Gettysburg and attack the hill from the west enabled Hancock to shift some of his men to aid in repelling Early's attack. Faced by these Union reserves, Early's men finally gave way about 10 o'clock and sullenly retired to their lines. The Union troops stood firm.

The Third Day

CANNONADE AT DAWN: CULP'S HILL AND SPANGLER'S SPRING. Night brought an end to the bloody combat at East Cemetery Hill, but this was not the time for rest. What would Meade do? Would the Union Army remain in its established position and hold its lines at all costs? At midnight Meade sought the advice of his Council of War in the east room of his headquarters. The corps commanders—Gibbon, Williams, Sykes, Newton, Howard, Hancock, Sedgwick, and Slocum—without exception advised holding the positions established. Meade, approving, turned to the officer whose division held the Union center, and said, "Gibbon, if Lee attacks me tomorrow it will be in your front."

Despite this prediction, Meade took no unusual measures next day to fortify the center of his line. In fact, by morning he seemed convinced that the Confederate attack would continue against his left. Thus the strong forces there, three corps, were left in place. Hancock's Second Corps, holding the center, did strengthen the stone wall running along its front. And General Hunt, Chief of Artillery, brought up reserve batteries to hold in readiness for replacement of front line guns.

Meanwhile, important movements were occurring elsewhere on the field. Ruger's division and Lockwood's brigade, which had been called from their lines on the south slope of Culp's Hill the previous evening to buttress the weakened Federal forces on Cemetery Ridge, had countermarched, under cover of darkness, to reoccupy their ground. Geary, who had misunderstood orders and had marched down the Baltimore

*Interior of breastworks on **Little Round Top**. Brady photograph.*

Lt. Gen. James Longstreet.
Courtesy National Archives.

Col. Edward Porter Alexander.
Courtesy National Archives.

Pike, had also returned to his works. Ruger's men, upon reaching the Pike, learned from scouts that their entrenchments south of Culp's Hill and at Spangler's Spring had been occupied by the Confederates. Ruger, resolving upon an attack at daybreak, organized his forces along the Pike. Powerful artillery units under Muhlenberg were brought into place along the road; Rigby's Maryland battery was stationed on Power's Hill, a prominent knoll a half mile to the south; and another battery was emplaced on McAllister Hill.

As dawn broke on July 3, Union guns on the Baltimore Pike opened with a heavy cannonade on Johnson's Confederates at Spangler's Spring. The heavily wooded area about the Confederate lines prevented them from bringing guns into position to return the fire. Union skirmishers began streaming across the field toward the Confederate entrenchments. The full force of Ruger's and Geary's divisions was soon committed. Throughout the forenoon the opposing lines exchanged extremely heavy fire.

It was about 10 o'clock that Ruger, believing that a flank attack might break the resistance of Johnson's men, ordered Col. Silas Colgrove to strike the Confederate left flank near the spring. The troops of the 2d Massachusetts and the 27th Indiana regiments started across the swale from the cover of the woods on the little hill south of the spring. A withering fire slowed their pace, but they charged on, only to have their ranks decimated by the Confederates in strong positions back of a stone wall. Colonel Mudge, inspiring leader of the Massachusetts regiment, fell mortally wounded. Forced to fall back, the men soon learned their efforts had not been in vain. On Ruger's and Geary's front the Confederates were now giving way and soon had retired across Rock Creek, out of striking range. By 11 o'clock, the Union troops were again in possession of their earthworks; again they could quench their thirst in the cooling waters of the spring.

*Repulse of General Johnson's Confederates near Spangler's
Spring on July 3, by Peter F. Rothermel.* Courtesy Pennsylvania
Historical and Museum Commission.

LEE PLANS A FINAL THRUST.   General Lee must have learned by mid-
forenoon, after the long hours of struggle at Culp's Hill and Spangler's
Spring, that his troops could not hold the Union works which they had
occupied with so little effort the previous evening. He had seen, also,
that in the tremendous battling during the preceding afternoon no important gains had been made at Little Round Top and its vicinity.
Longstreet had gained the advantageous ridge at the Peach Orchard and
had brought his batteries forward from Pitzer's Woods to this high
ground in preparation for a follow-up attack. Wright's brigade, the last
unit to move forward on July 2 in the echelon attack begun by General
Law, had charged across the open fields at dusk and pierced the Union
center just south of the copse of trees on Cemetery Ridge. Wright's
success could not be pressed to decisive advantage as the brigades on his
left had not moved forward to his support, and he was forced to retire.
Again, lack of coordination in attack was to count heavily against the
Confederates.

The failure to make any pronounced headway on July 2 at Culp's Hill
and Little Round Top, and the momentary success of Wright on
Cemetery Ridge, doubtless led Lee to believe that Meade's flanks were
strong and his center weak. A powerful drive at the center might pierce
the enemy's lines and fold them back. The shattered units might then
be destroyed or captured at will. Such a charge across open fields and in
the face of frontal and flank fire would, Lee well understood, be a gamble
seldom undertaken. Longstreet strongly voiced his objection to such a
move, insisting that "no 15,000 men ever arrayed for battle can take that
position."

Devil's Den, a formation of large granite boulders used as defense positions by Confederate sharpshooters.

Time now was the important element. Whatever could be done must be done quickly. Hood's and McLaws' divisions, who had fought bravely and lost heavily at Round Top and the Wheatfield, were not in condition for another severe test. Early and Johnson on the left had likewise endured long, unrelenting battle with powerful Union forces in positions of advantage. The men of Heth's and Pender's divisions had not been heavily engaged since the first day's encounter west of Gettysburg. These were the men, along with Pickett's division, whom Lee would have to count on to bear the brunt of his final great effort at Gettysburg.

LEE AND MEADE SET THE STAGE.   Late in the forenoon of July 3, General Meade had completed his plan of defense. Another Confederate attack could be expected: "Where?" was still the question. General Hunt, sensing the danger, placed a formidable line of batteries in position on the crest of Cemetery Ridge and alerted others in the rear for emergency use. As a final act of preparation, Meade inspected his front at the stone wall, then rode southward to Little Round Top. There, with General Warren, he could see the long lines of massed Confederate batteries, a sure indication of attack. Meade rode back to his headquarters.

Lee, on his part, had spent the forenoon organizing his attack formations on Seminary Ridge. Having reached his decision to strike the Union center, he had ordered the movement of batteries from the rear to points of advantage. By noon, about 140 guns were in line from the Peach Orchard northward to the Seminary buildings, many of them only 800 yards from the Union center. To Colonel Alexander fell the lot of directing the artillery fire and informing the infantry of the best opportunity to advance.

Massed to the west of Emmitsburg Road, on low ground which screened their position from the Union lines, lay Gen. George Pickett's three brigades commanded by Kemper, Armistead, and Garnett. Pickett's men had arrived the previous evening from Chambersburg, where they had guarded Lee's wagons on July 1 and 2. As a division these units had seen little fighting. Soon they would gain immortality. On Pickett's left, the attacking front was fast being organized. Joseph Pettigrew, a brigadier, was preparing to lead the division of the wounded Major General Heth, and Maj. Gen. Isaac Trimble took the command of Pender. Nearly 10,000 troops of these two divisions—including such units as the 26th North Carolina whose losses on the first day were so heavy that the dead marked their advance "with the accuracy of a line at a dress parade"—now awaited the order to attack. Many hours earlier, the Bliss farm buildings, which lay in their front, had been burned. Their objective on the ridge was in clear view. The brigades of Wilcox and Lang were to move forward on the right of Pickett in order to protect his flank as he neared the enemy position.

General Stuart, in the meantime, had been out of touch with Lee. Moving northward on the right flank of the Union Army, he became involved in a sharp engagement at Hanover, Pa., on June 30. Seeking to regain contact with Lee, he arrived at Carlisle on the evening of July 1. As he began shelling the barracks, orders arrived from Lee and he at once marched for Gettysburg, arriving north of the town the next day.

The Round Tops as they appear from Longstreet's battle line one mile away.

Meade's headquarters today.

Early on July 3 he was ordered to take position on the Confederate left. This movement usually has been interpreted as an integral part of Lee's assault plan. But battle reports leave Stuart's role vague, except for covering the Confederate left. Doubtless he would have exploited any significant success achieved by the infantry assault.

Except for the intermittent sniping of sharpshooters, an ominous silence prevailed over the fields. The orders had now been given; the objective had been pointed out. Men talked of casual things. Some munched on hard bread, others looked fearfully to the eastward, where, with the same mixed feelings, lay their adversary.

Far to the south, on another crucial front, General Pemberton was penning a letter to General Grant asking terms for the surrender of Vicksburg. In Richmond, the sick and anxious Jefferson Davis looked hopefully for heartening word from his great field commander at Gettysburg. The outcome of this bold venture would count heavily in the balance for the cause of the Confederacy.

ARTILLERY DUEL AT ONE O'CLOCK. At 1 p.m. two guns of Miller's Battery, posted near the Peach Orchard, opened fire in rapid succession. It was the signal for the entire line to let loose their terrific blast. Gunners rushed to their cannon, and in a few moments the massed bat-

Panorama of the battlefield from Cemetery Ridge. The Angle, left; Emmitsburg Road, center; Seminary Ridge, right. The

teries shook the countryside. Firing in volleys and in succession, the air was soon filled with smoke and heavy dust, which darkened the sky. Union gunners on Cemetery Ridge waited a few minutes until the positions of the Confederate batteries were located; then 80 guns, placed in close order, opened fire. For nearly 2 hours the duel continued, then the Union fire slackened. Hunt had ordered a partial cessation in order to cool the guns and conserve ammunition.

Colonel Alexander, in position on the Emmitsburg Road near the Peach Orchard, could observe the effectiveness of his fire on the Union lines and also keep the Confederate troops in view. To him, it appeared that Union artillery fire was weakening. His own supply of ammunition was running low. Believing this was the time to attack, Alexander sent a message to Pickett who in turn rode over to Longstreet. General Longstreet, who had persistently opposed Lee's plan of sending 15,000 men across the open ground, was now faced with a final decision. Longstreet merely nodded approval and Pickett saluted, saying, "I am going to move forward, sir." He rode back to his men and ordered the advance. With Kemper on the right, Garnett on the left, and Armistead a few yards to the rear, the division marched out in brigade front, first northeastward into the open fields, then eastward toward the Union lines. As Pickett's men came into view near the woods, Pettigrew and Trimble gave the order to advance. Sons of Virginia, Alabama, North Carolina, Tennessee, and Mississippi, comprising the brigades of Mayo, Davis, Marshall, and Fry in front, followed closely by Lane and Lowrance, now

Confederate charge of July 3 crossed the open fields from right to left.

moved out to attack. A gap between Pickett's left and Pettigrew's right would be closed as the advance progressed. The units were to converge as they approached the Union lines so that the final stage of the charge would present a solid front.

CLIMAX AT GETTYSBURG.   Billows of smoke lay ahead of the Union men at the stone wall, momentarily obscuring the enemy. But trained observers on Little Round Top, far to the south, could see in the rear of this curtain of smoke the waves of Confederates starting forward. Pickett, finding his brigades drifting southeastward, ordered them to bear to the left, and the men turned toward the copse of trees. Kemper was now approaching on the south of the Codori buildings; Garnett and Armistead were on the north. Halted momentarily at the Emmitsburg Road to remove fence rails, Pickett's troops, with Pettigrew on the left, renewed the advance. Pickett had anticipated frontal fire of artillery and infantry from the strong Union positions at the stone walls on the ridge, but now an unforeseen attack developed. Union guns as far south as Little Round Top, along with batteries on Cemetery Hill, relieved from Confederate fire at the Seminary buildings, opened on the right and left flanks. As Pickett's men drove toward the Union works at The Angle, Stannard's Vermont troops, executing a right turn movement from their position south of the copse, fired into the flank of the charging Confederates. The advancing lines crumbled, re-formed, and again pressed ahead under terrific fire from the Union batteries.

Maj. Gen. J. E. B. Stuart.
Courtesy National Archives.

Maj. Gen. George E. Pickett.
Courtesy National Archives.

But valor was not enough. As the attackers neared the stone wall they lost cohesion in the fury that engulfed them. All along the wall the Union infantry opened with volley after volley into the depleted ranks of Garnett and Fry. Armistead closed in, and with Lane and Lowrance joining him, made a last concerted drive. At this close range, double canister and concentrated infantry fire cut wide gaps in the attacking front. Garnett was mortally wounded; Kemper was down, his lines falling away on the right and left. Armistead reached the low stone fence. In a final surge, he crossed the wall with 150 men and, with his cap on his sword, shouted "Follow me!" At the peak of the charge, he fell mortally wounded. From the ridge, Union troops rushed forward and Hall's Michigan regiments let loose a blast of musketry. The gray column was surrounded. The tide of the Confederacy had "swept to its crest, paused, and receded."

Two of the divisions in the charge were reduced to mere fragments. In front of the Union line, 20 fallen battle flags lay in a space of 100 yards square. Singly and in little clumps, the remnants of the gray columns that had made the magnificent charge of a few minutes earlier now sullenly retreated across the fields toward the Confederate lines. Lee, who had watched anxiously from Spangler's Woods, now rode out to meet his men. "All this has been my fault," he said to General Wilcox who had brought off his command after heavy losses. "It is I that have lost this fight, and you must help me out of it in the best way you can." And again that night, in a moment of contemplation, he remarked to a comrade, "Too bad! too bad! Oh! too bad!"

CAVALRY ACTION.   As the strength of Lee's mighty effort at The Angle was ebbing and the scattered remnants of the charge were seeking shelter, action of a different kind was taking place on another field not far distant. Early in the afternoon, Stuart's cavalry was making its way down the valley of Cress Run, 3 miles east of Gettysburg. The brigades of Hampton and Fitzhugh Lee, at the rear of the line of march, momentarily lost the trail and came out into open ground at the north end of Rummel's Woods. Stuart, soon learning of the mistake, attempted to

The High Water Mark Monument,
where Pickett's Charge was stopped.

Section of the Cyclorama painting of Pickett's Charge by Paul Philippoteaux. Courtesy Times and News Publishing Company.

The harvest of the guns. From Brady Collection.

bring them into line and to proceed southward. But at this point, Gen. D. M. Gregg's Union cavalry, in position along the Hanover Road a mile southeast, saw the Confederates. Gregg prepared at once to attack, and Stuart had no choice but to fight on this ground. As the two forces moved closer, dismounted men opened a brisk fire, supported by the accurate shelling of artillerists.

Then came the initial cavalry charge and countercharge. The Confederate Jenkins was forced to withdraw when his small supply of ammunition became exhausted. Hampton, Fitzhugh Lee, and Chambliss charged again and again, only to be met with the equally spirited counterattack of McIntosh. Custer's Michigan regiments assailed the front of the charging Confederate troopers, and Miller's squadron of the 3d Pennsylvania, disobeying orders to hold its position, struck opportunely on the Confederate left. The thrusts of the Union horsemen, so well coordinated, stopped the onslaught of Stuart's troopers. After 3 hours of turbulent action, the Confederates left the field and retired to the north of Gettysburg. The Union horsemen, holding their ground, had successfully cut off any prospect of Confederate cavalry aid in the rear of the Union lines on Cemetery Ridge.

End of Invasion

Lee, as he looked over the desolate field of dead and wounded and the broken remnants of his once-powerful army still ready for renewed battle, must have realized that not only was Gettysburg lost, but that eventually it might all end this way. Meade did not counterattack, as expected. The following day, July 4, the two armies lay facing each other, exhausted and torn.

Late on the afternoon of July 4, Lee began an orderly retreat. The wagon train of wounded, 17 miles in length, guarded by Imboden's cavalry, started homeward through Greenwood and Greencastle. At night, the able-bodied men marched over the Hagerstown Road by way of Monterey Pass to the Potomac. Roads had become nearly impassable from the heavy rains that day, hindering the movements of both armies. Meade, realizing that the Confederate Army was actually retreating and not retiring to the mountain passes, sent detachments of cavalry and infantry in pursuit and ordered the mountain passes west of Frederick covered. Lee, having the advantage of the more direct route to the Potomac, reached the river several days ahead of his pursuers, but heavy rains had swollen the current and he could not cross. Meade arrived on the night of July 12 and prepared for a general attack. On the following night, however, the river receded and Lee crossed safely into Virginia. The Confederate Army, Meade's critics said, had been permitted to slip from the Union grasp.

The Eternal Light Peace Memorial, dedicated on the 75th anniversary of the battle, commemorates "Peace Eternal in a Nation United." Union Pacific Railroad photograph.

The Alexander Gardner portrait of Lincoln, taken 4 days before the Gettysburg Address. Meserve Collection.

Lincoln and Gettysburg

ESTABLISHMENT OF A BURIAL GROUND.   For the residents of Gettysburg the aftermath of battle was almost as trying as the 3 days of struggle that had swirled about them. The town's 2,400 inhabitants, and the nearby country folk, bore a heavy share of the burden of caring for the 21,000 wounded and dying of both sides, who were left behind when the armies moved on. Spacious rooms in churches and schools and hundreds of homes were turned over to the care of the wounded; and kindly folk from neighboring towns came to help those of Gettysburg in ministering to the needs of the maimed and shattered men.

Adequate attention to the wounded was an immediate necessity, but fully as urgent was the need of caring for the dead. Nearly 6,000 had been killed in action, and hundreds died each day from mortal wounds. In the earlier stages of the battle, soldiers of both armies performed the tasks of burying their fallen comrades, but the struggle had reached such large proportions and the scene of battle had so shifted that fallen men had come within enemy lines. Because of the emergencies of battle, therefore, hundreds of bodies had been left unburied or only partially covered. It was evident that the limited aid which could be offered by local authorities must be supported by a well-organized plan for dis-interment of the dead from the temporary burial grounds on the field and reburial in a permanent place at Gettysburg or in home cemeteries.

A few days after the battle, the Governor of the Commonwealth, Hon. Andrew Curtin, visited the battlefield to offer assistance in caring for the wounded. When official duties required his return to Harrisburg, he appointed Attorney David Wills, of Gettysburg, to act as his special agent. At the time of his visit, the Governor was especially distressed by the condition of the dead. In response to the Governor's desire that the remains be brought together in a place set aside for the purpose, Mr. Wills selected land on the northern slope of Cemetery Hill and suggested that the State of Pennsylvania purchase the ground at once in order that interments could begin without delay. He proposed that contributions for the purpose of laying out and landscaping the grounds be asked from legislatures of the States whose soldiers had taken part in the battle.

Within 6 weeks, Mr. Wills had purchased 17 acres of ground on Cemetery Hill and engaged William Saunders, an eminent landscape gardener, to lay out the grounds in State lots, apportioned in size to the number of graves for the fallen of each State. Each of the Union States represented in the battle made contributions for planning and landscaping.

The reinterment of close to 3,500 Union dead was accomplished only after many months. Great care had been taken to identify the bodies on the field, and, at the time of reinterment, remains were readily identified by marked boards which had been placed at the field grave or by items found on the bodies. Even so, the names of 1,664 remained unknown, 979 of whom were without identification either by name or by State. Within a year, appropriations from the States made possible the enclosure of the cemetery with a massive stone wall and an iron fence on the Baltimore Street front, imposing gateways of iron, headstones for the graves, and a keeper's lodge. Since the original burials, the total of Civil War interments has reached 3,706. Including those of later wars, the total number now is close to 5,000.

The removal of Confederate dead from the field burial plots was not undertaken until 7 years after the battle. During the years 1870–73, upon the initiative of the Ladies Memorial Associations of Richmond, Raleigh, Savannah, and Charleston, 3,320 bodies were disinterred and sent to cemeteries in those cities for reburial, 2,935 being interred in Hollywood Cemetery, Richmond. Seventy-three bodies were reburied in home cemeteries.

The Commonwealth of Pennsylvania incorporated the cemetery in March 1864. The cemetery "having been completed, and the care of it by Commissioners from so many states being burdensome and expensive," the Board of Commissioners, authorized by act of the General Assembly of Pennsylvania in 1868, recommended the transfer of the cemetery to the Federal Government. The Secretary of War accepted title to the cemetery for the United States Government on May 1, 1872.

DEDICATION OF THE CEMETERY.   Having agreed upon a plan for the cemetery, the Commissioners believed it advisable to consecrate the grounds with appropriate ceremonies. Mr. Wills, representing the Governor of Pennsylvania, was selected to make proper arrangements for the event. With the approval of the Governors of the several States, he wrote to Hon. Edward Everett, of Massachusetts, inviting him to deliver the oration on the occasion and suggested October 23, 1863, as the date for the ceremony. Mr. Everett stated in reply that the invitation was a great compliment, but that because of the time necessary for the preparation of the oration he could not accept a date earlier than November 19. This was the date agreed upon.

Edward Everett was the outstanding orator of his day. He had been a prominent Boston minister and later a university professor. A cultured scholar, he had delivered orations on many notable occasions. In a distinguished career he became successively President of Harvard, Governor of Massachusetts, United States Senator, Minister to England, and Secretary of State.

The Gettysburg cemetery, at the time of the dedication, was not under the authority of the Federal Government. It had not occurred to those in charge, therefore, that the President of the United States might desire to attend the ceremony. When formally printed invitations were sent to a rather extended list of national figures, including the President, the acceptance from Mr. Lincoln came as a surprise. Mr. Wills was there-

The Soldiers' National Monument honors the Federal dead who fell at Gettysburg. Dedicated July 1, 1869, it stands where Lincoln stood when he delivered the Gettysburg Address.

The procession on Baltimore Street en route to the cemetery for the dedicatory exercises, November 19.

upon instructed to request the President to take part in the program, and, on November 2, a personal invitation was addressed to him.

Throngs filled the town on the evening of November 18. The special train from Washington bearing the President arrived in Gettysburg at dusk. Mr. Lincoln was escorted to the spacious home of Mr. Wills on Center Square. Sometime later in the evening the President was serenaded, and at a late hour he retired. At 10 o'clock on the following morning, the appointed time for the procession to begin, Mr. Lincoln was ready. The various units of the long procession, marshaled by Ward Lamon, began moving on Baltimore Street, the President riding horseback. The elaborate order of march also included Cabinet officials, judges of the Supreme Court, high military officers, Governors, commissioners, the Vice President, the Speaker of the House of Representatives, Members of Congress, and many local groups.

Difficulty in getting the procession under way and the tardy return of Mr. Everett from his drive over the battleground accounted for a delay of an hour in the proceedings. At high noon, with thousands scurrying about for points of vantage, the ceremonies were begun with the playing of a dirge by one of the bands. As the audience stood uncovered, a prayer was offered by Rev. Thomas H. Stockton, Chaplain of the House of Representatives. "Old Hundred" was played by the Marine Band. Then Mr. Everett arose, and "stood a moment in silence, regarding the battlefield and the distant beauty of the South Mountain range." For nearly 2 hours he reviewed the funeral customs of Athens, spoke of the purposes of war, presented a detailed account of the 3-days' battle, offered tribute to those who died on the battlefield, and reminded his audience of the bonds which are common to all Americans. Upon the conclusion of his address, a hymn was sung.

Four score and seven years ago our fathers brought forth, upon this continent, a new nation, conceived in Liberty, and dedicated to the proposition that all men are created equal.

Now we are engaged in a great civil war, testing whether that nation, or any nation, so conceived, and so dedicated, can long endure. We are met here on a great battlefield of that war. We have come to dedicate a portion of it, as a final resting place for those who here gave their lives, that that nation might live. It is altogether fitting and proper that we should do this.

But in a larger sense we can not dedicate— we can not consecrate— we can not hallow this ground. The brave men, living and dead, who struggled here, have consecrated it, far above our poor power to add or detract. The world will little note, nor long remember, what we say here, but can never forget what they did here. It is for us, the living, rather to be dedicated here to the unfinished work which they have thus far, so nobly carried on. It is rather

First page of the second draft of the Gettysburg Address. This copy, made by Lincoln on the morning of November 19, was held in his hand while delivering his address. Reproduced from the original in the Library of Congress.

This is the only known close-up photographic view of the rostrum (upper left) at the dedication of the National Cemetery. The view shows a part of the audience which was estimated at 15,000. Bachrach photograph.

Then the President arose and spoke his immortal words:

Four score and seven years ago our fathers brought forth on this continent, a new nation, conceived in Liberty, and dedicated to the proposition that all men are created equal.

Now we are engaged in a great civil war, testing whether that nation, or any nation so conceived and so dedicated, can long endure. We are met on a great battle field of that war. We have come to dedicate a portion of that field, as a final resting place for those who here gave their lives that that nation might live. It is altogether fitting and proper that we should do this.

But, in a larger sense, we cannot dedicate—we cannot consecrate—we cannot hallow—this ground. The brave men, living and dead, who struggled here, have consecrated it, far above our poor power to add or detract. The world will little note, nor long remember what we say here, but it can never forget what they did here. It is for us the living, rather, to be dedicated here to the unfinished work which they who fought here have thus far so nobly advanced. It is rather for us to be here dedicated to the great task remaining before us—that from these honored dead we take increased devotion to that cause for which they gave the last full measure of devotion—that we here highly resolve that these dead shall not have died in vain—that this nation, under God, shall have a new birth of freedom—and that government of the people, by the people, for the people, shall not perish from the earth.

A hymn was then sung and Rev. H. L. Baugher pronounced the benediction.

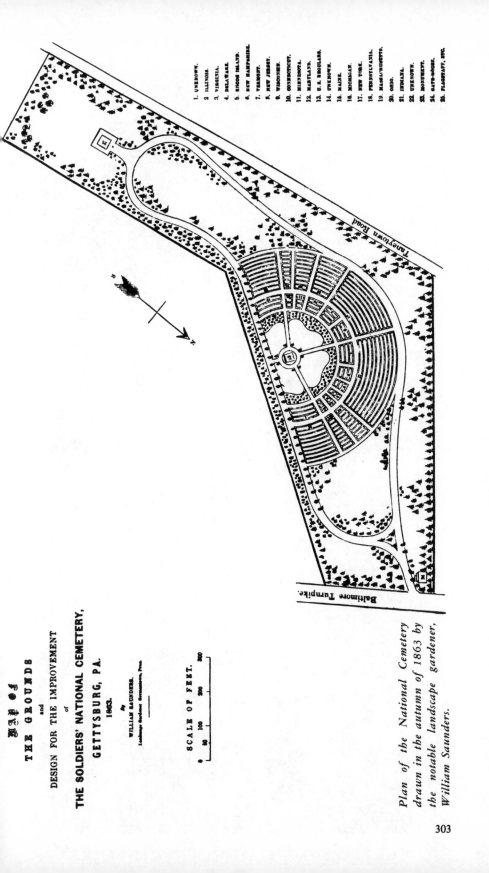

MAP OF
THE GROUNDS
and
DESIGN FOR THE IMPROVEMENT
of
THE SOLDIERS' NATIONAL CEMETERY,
GETTYSBURG, PA.
1863.
By
WILLIAM SAUNDERS.
Landscape Gardener Commission's, Penn.

SCALE OF FEET.

1. UNKNOWN.
2. ILLINOIS.
3. VIRGINIA.
4. DELAWARE.
5. RHODE ISLAND.
6. NEW HAMPSHIRE.
7. VERMONT.
8. NEW JERSEY.
9. CONNECTICUT.
10. MINNESOTA.
11. WISCONSIN.
12. MARYLAND.
13. U. S. REGULARS.
14. UNKNOWN.
15. MAINE.
16. MICHIGAN.
17. NEW YORK.
18. PENNSYLVANIA.
19. MASSACHUSETTS.
20. OHIO.
21. INDIANA.
22. UNKNOWN.
23. MONUMENT.
24. GATE-KEEP.
25. FLAGSTAFF, ETC.

Tineytown Road

Baltimore Turnpike.

Plan of the National Cemetery drawn in the autumn of 1863 by the notable landscape gardener, William Saunders.

Wartime view of Chattanooga from north bank of the Tennessee River. From Harper's Pictorial History of the Great Rebellion.

CHAPTER XI

Battles of Chickamauga and Chattanooga

IN AND AROUND STRATEGICALLY IMPORTANT Chattanooga, Tenn., in the autumn of 1863, there occurred some of the most complex maneuvers and hard fighting of the Civil War. The Confederate victory at Chickamauga (September 19–20) gave new hope to the South after the defeats at Gettysburg and Vicksburg in July of that year. At Chattanooga (November 23–25) Union forces under Maj. Gen. Ulysses S. Grant blasted this hope and prepared the way for the capture of Atlanta and Sherman's "March to the Sea." Chickamauga and Chattanooga National Military Park, oldest and largest of the national military parks, commemorates the heroic soldiers of both North and South in the battles for the control of Chattanooga.

The year 1863 proved to be one of victory for the Union forces. Three great campaigns took place which shaped the destiny of the war. The first, a decisive blow at Gettysburg, forced a Confederate army under Gen. Robert E. Lee to abandon its attempt to invade Northern soil. Lee began an orderly retreat to Virginia on July 4.

On the same day, but far removed from the fields of Gettysburg, Lt. Gen. John C. Pemberton surrendered his army and the City of Vicksburg, Miss., to General Grant. The fall of Vicksburg, simultaneous with the victory at Gettysburg, gave heart and strength to the North, while Confederate morale dropped.

The third campaign, Murfreesboro to Chattanooga, slow and uncertain in its first phases, and including later the great Confederate victory at Chickamauga, culminated nearly 5 months after the other two in ultimate victory for the North in the Battle of Chattanooga.

Wartime Importance of Chattanooga and East Tennessee

Chattanooga had only 2,545 inhabitants in 1860, but its importance was out of all proportion to its size. Situated where the Tennessee River passes through the Cumberland Mountains, forming gaps, it was called the "Key to East Tennessee" and "Gateway to the deep South." The possession of Chattanooga was vital to the Confederacy, and a coveted goal of the Northern armies.

Chattanooga's principal importance during the Civil War was its position as a railroad center. Four lines radiated in the four principal directions—to the North and Middle West via Nashville, to the western States via Memphis, to the South and southern seaboard via Atlanta, and to Richmond and the North Atlantic States via Knoxville.

By 1863 both sides were aware of the great advantages of strategic railroad lines. Lt. Gen. Braxton Bragg had made skillful use of the railroads in 1862, when he suddenly shifted his army from Mississippi to Chattanooga to begin his drive across Tennessee and into Kentucky. President Lincoln had long recognized the importance of railroads in this area. In the same year Lincoln said, "To take and hold the railroad at or east of Cleveland, in East Tennessee, I think fully as important as the taking and holding of Richmond." And in 1863 Lincoln wrote Maj. Gen. William S. Rosecrans, "If we can hold Chattanooga and East Tennessee, I think the rebellion must dwindle and die. I think you and [General]Burnside can do this, and hence doing so is your main object."

The armies that traversed this region found it a fertile farming area. East Tennessee's rich grain fields supplied not only wheat, corn, and hay, but beef, pork, bacon, horses, and mules. It was a vital region for the armies of the Confederacy. It not only supported the troops that occupied that region, but large quantities of provisions were shipped to other armies.

In addition to the military and economic reasons, a political factor had to be considered in the struggle for control of East Tennessee. The people there, living in a mountainous area unlike the rest of the State, wished to adhere to the Union. The people maintained their allegiance to the Old Whig party, and there was an attitude of suspicion and distrust toward the Democrats. They were mostly small farmers with little cash income, who had a dislike for the wealthy plantation- and slave-owning class.

After fighting broke out at Fort Sumter, neighbors began to take sides. An uneasy truce prevailed until November 1861 when small groups of Union men struck blows at widely dispersed railroad bridges. The cancellation of a projected northern campaign into East Tennessee left the Unionists there without support, and the Confederates took retaliatory measures. Many of the Unionists in East Tennessee fled to Kentucky to enlist in the Union Army; others hid in the mountains. While relief

Gen. Braxton Bragg, Commander Army of Tennessee. Courtesy National Archives.

Maj. Gen. William S. Rosecrans, Commander Army of the Cumberland. Courtesy National Archives.

to this section of Tennessee by the Union Army was not to come until 1863, it was not forgotten by President Lincoln.

Winter 1863

After the battle of Stones River, or Murfreesboro, Tenn., December 31, 1862, to January 2, 1863, the Union Army of the Cumberland, under Maj. Gen. William Rosecrans, and the Confederate Army of Tennessee, commanded by Gen. Braxton Bragg, remained relatively inactive for several months. During this time the Union forces entrenched themselves at Murfreesboro. General Bragg withdrew his forces southward and established his headquarters at Tullahoma. He placed his army in a defensive position to cover the routes, both rail and road, to Chattanooga.

Impatient at the inaction, the War Department in Washington urged Rosecrans to move against Bragg's army. Grant, conducting his Vicksburg campaign, wanted pressure applied against Bragg's army to prevent all or part of it from reinforcing the Confederates in Mississippi. At the same time Andrew Johnson, Military Governor of Tennessee, reminded the authorities in Washington of the plight of the East Tennesseans. During this period, Maj. Gen. Ambrose E. Burnside gathered a Union force and made plans to invade East Tennessee.

Rosecrans hesitated to move. His lack of cavalry was a disadvantage in gathering intelligence and prevented him from countering the Confederate cavalry which harassed him constantly. In June, Maj. Gen.

Henry W. Halleck, general in chief, U. S. Army, wired Rosecrans asking him, "Is it your intention to make an immediate movement forward? A definite answer, yes or no, is required." Rosecrans telegraphed: "In reply to your inquiry, if immediate means tonight or tomorrow, no. If it means as soon as all things are ready, say five days, yes." On June 24, General Rosecrans put his army of some 60,000 men in motion.

The Tullahoma Campaign

The Army of the Cumberland—the Union force—had undergone a reorganization since the Battle of Stones River. It now comprised three corps: The Fourteenth, Maj. Gen. George H. Thomas in command; the Twentieth, Maj. Gen. Alexander McD. McCook in command; and the Twenty-first, Maj. Gen. Thomas L. Crittenden in command. Maj. Gen. David S. Stanley commanded the Cavalry Corps. Maj. Gen. Gordon Granger commanded the Reserve Corps.

The left wing of General Bragg's defense line was at Shelbyville under Lt. Gen. Leonidas Polk and its right wing at Wartrace and Fairfield under Lt. Gen. William Hardee—a line nearly 13 miles long. Two Confederate cavalry corps occupied positions on either flank—that on the right at McMinnville under Maj. Gen. Joseph Wheeler, the other on the left at Columbia under Brig. Gen. Nathan B. Forrest. The total strength of the Army of Tennessee was approximately 43,000 men at this time.

The Confederate position was good. The terrain favored a defensive fight. To traverse the Cumberland Plateau the Union Army would have to move along roads that pierced the mountains by way of Hoover's, Liberty, and Guy's Gaps. The railroad to Chattanooga and another road passed through Bellbuckle Gap. This latter route and the road by way of Shelbyville were well fortified. Rosecrans resolved to make a feint toward Shelbyville with Granger's Reserve Corps and most of the cavalry while the rest of his army moved toward the Confederate right. After stubborn fights at Hoover's and Liberty Gaps the Confederates withdrew toward Tullahoma. So successful was Rosecrans' flanking movement that Col. John T. Wilder's mounted infantry brigade reached Decherd, on the main line of the Nashville and Chattanooga Railroad, and destroyed the depot and a few hundred yards of track. Although Wilder withdrew when superior Confederate forces appeared, his raid against the railroad was of great importance in forcing Bragg to evacuate Tullahoma.

Rough terrain and bad weather were the worst enemies of the Union Army. Brig. Gen. John Beatty records in his diary that "The road was exceedingly rough, and the rebels had made it impassable, for artillery, by rolling great rocks into it and felling trees across it." He frequently

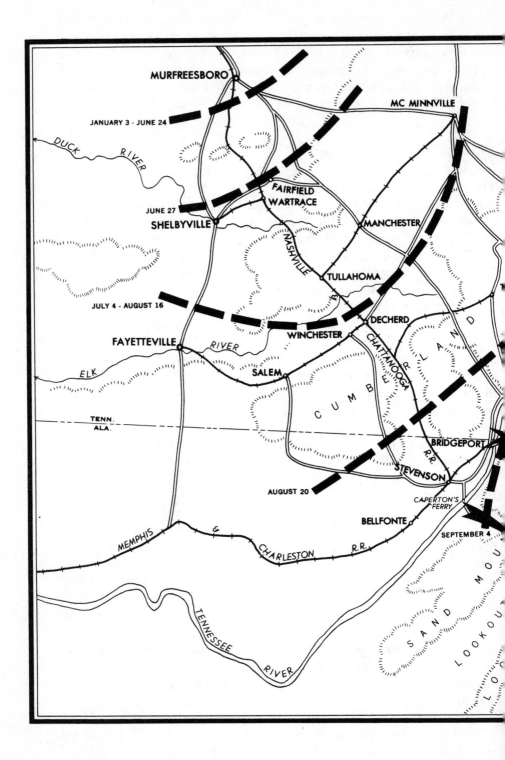

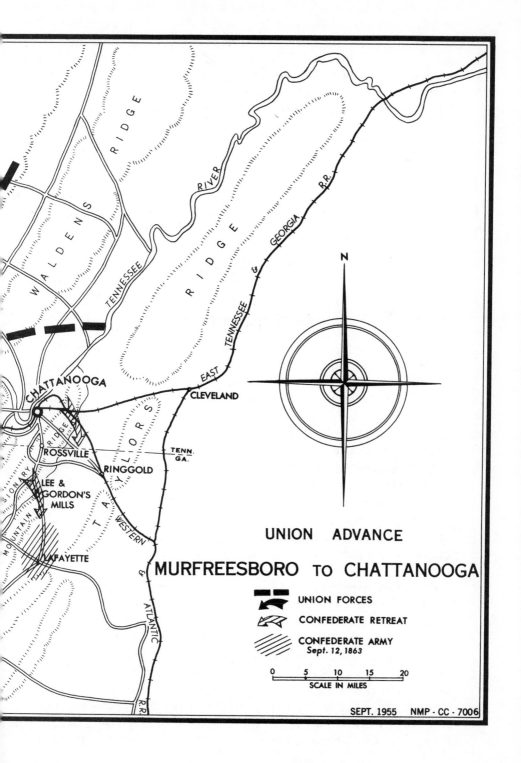

N

UNION ADVANCE
MURFREESBORO TO CHATTANOOGA

UNION FORCES

CONFEDERATE RETREAT

CONFEDERATE ARMY
Sept. 12, 1863

0   5   10   15   20
SCALE IN MILES

SEPT. 1955   NMP - CC - 7006

WALDENS RIDGE

RIDGE

TENNESSEE RIVER

RIDGE

TENNESSEE & GEORGIA R.R.

EAST TENNESSEE

CLEVELAND

CHATTANOOGA

ROSSVILLE

TENN.
GA.

RINGGOLD

LEE &
GORDON'S
MILLS

WESTERN

MISSIONARY RIDGE

TAYLORS

ATLANTIC

LAFAYETTE

R.R.

mentions the rain which fell incessantly during the campaign. His entry of July 5 states that "Since we left Murfreesboro (June 24) rain has been falling almost constantly; today it has been coming down in torrents, and the low grounds around us are overflowed." Yet, in spite of mountains and rain and the Confederate Army, Rosecrans, by this series of brilliant flanking maneuvers, forced Bragg to evacuate Tullahoma on July 1 and withdraw toward Chattanooga.

From Tullahoma to Chickamauga

After the Tullahoma campaign, the two armies adopted their previous policy of remaining stationary. Each began to gather forces and equipment for a future struggle. The Union Army occupied a line from Winchester to McMinnville—the same territory the Confederates had occupied previously—while the Confederate General Bragg established his headquarters at Chattanooga. There the Army of Tennessee strengthened its defensive position and prepared to close the "gate" to further advances of the Army of the Cumberland.

During July and August, Halleck again urged Rosecrans to move against Bragg's forces, but Rosecrans failed to budge. In the latter's judgment, three things were needed to insure a successful campaign. The first was ripe corn which would not be ready until August; the second was the repair of the railroad to the Tennessee River; and the third was support for his flanks. In spite of the constant flow of dispatches from Halleck to Rosecrans, it was not until August 16 that he began his movement southward to cross the river.

As Rosecrans moved toward the Tennessee River and Chattanooga, another Union army under command of General Burnside entered east Tennessee to threaten Knoxville. General Bragg, supposing that the two armies would join forces to attack him, made urgent appeals for help. Though the shortage of manpower at this time was a major problem of the Confederacy, troops were sent hurrying to Bragg from several directions.

Rosecrans' strategy, after viewing several possibilities, was to cross the river below Chattanooga, turn the Confederate left and interrupt his opponent's communications and supply line from Atlanta. This movement if successful would effectively cut all railroad lines to Chattanooga, and Bragg would find himself shut in between Burnside on the north and east and Rosecrans on the west and south. To deceive Bragg as to the point of crossing the Tennessee River, Rosecrans sent Hazen's and Wagner's infantry brigades, Wilder's mounted infantry, and Minty's cavalry, all under the command of Brig. Gen. William B. Hazen, to make a feint at the river north of the town and to annoy the enemy as much as possible.

Union troops constructing a pontoon bridge across the Tennessee River at Bridgeport, Ala. Ruins of Nashville and Chattanooga Railroad bridge shown. Courtesy Library of Congress.

The ruse was successful, and so thoroughly was Bragg deceived into thinking the attack would come from upstream on the north side of the Tennessee, he left the crossings below Chattanooga practically unguarded. Rosecrans with the bulk of his army then crossed the river in the vicinity of Bridgeport and Caperton's Ferry, Ala., and Shellmound, Tenn. By September 4, the Army of the Cumberland, thus meeting little opposition, was safely across a great barrier and was threatening Bragg from new positions.

When Bragg learned that the Union Army had crossed the Tennessee below Chattanooga and was threatening his supply lines, he decided after much deliberation to abandon his position and retreat southward.

Once the Union Army had crossed the river, Thomas' corps marched toward Trenton, Ga.; McCook's took the road to Alpine, Ga.; and Crittenden moved toward Chattanooga. On the 9th of September, Rosecrans, believing the Confederates to be in full retreat, ordered McCook to press forward toward Alpine, covered by the cavalry, and make attempts to cut Bragg off; Crittenden to garrison Chattanooga with one brigade and pursue Bragg by way of the Ringgold Road with the rest of his force; and Thomas to continue toward Trenton.

In order to understand the importance of the movements of both commanding generals, the geography of the country must be considered. When the Union commanders climbed to the top of the Lookout Mountain range and viewed the country, they began to have misgivings about their divided army. Thomas and McCook, 20 and 40 miles southwest of Chattanooga, respectively, found themselves on a mountain ribbed by ridges and hills, more than 1,000 feet above the valley floor. The few roads which ran over the mountain were narrow, rough, stony, and unusually steep.

Thomas, looking to the east, saw Pigeon Mountain, a spur that juts off Lookout Mountain and veers in a northeastwardly direction. The acute angle of these diverging mountains forms McLemore's Cove. Running into this cove from the northeast and ending there is the southern extremity of Missionary Ridge which begins immediately east of Chattanooga. Here, also, originates Chickamauga Creek which gave the ensuing battle its name.

As the two Union corps moved eastward they found the country sparsely populated. There were a few farms, but most of the land was covered with cedar thickets and tangled undergrowth. The roads connecting farm and village were dry and dusty.

The Union Army was now split into three distinct columns with its flanks more than 40 miles apart. In mountainous terrain, this made it impossible for them to support one another. In the period September 10–12, corps commanders began to receive reports that a large Confederate force was at LaFayette, Ga. It was Bragg's army. He had not retreated as far south as Rosecrans had thought—he had stopped at LaFayette behind Pigeon Mountain. There he concentrated his army and awaited reinforcements.

Reinforcements for General Bragg

General Bragg had purposely given the impression that his army was disorganized and in full flight before Rosecrans. Actually, however, he was not running away but was quietly preparing for battle and gathering strength as reinforcements began to reach him. Realizing that Maj. Gen. Simon Bolivar Buckner's Corps could not defend Knoxville from Burnside, and having no troops to spare for reinforcements, Bragg

Wooden railroad trestle at Cumberland Ravine, Ga., erected by Union Army to replace bridge destroyed by Confederates. Courtesy National Archives.

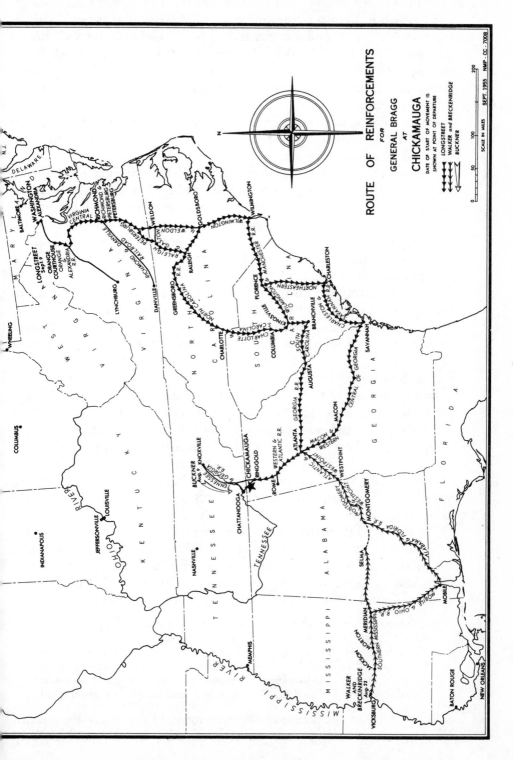

ROUTE OF REINFORCEMENTS
FOR
GENERAL BRAGG
AT
CHICKAMAUGA

DATE OF START OF MOVEMENT IS
SHOWN AT POINT OF DEPARTURE

LONGSTREET
WALKER and BRECKENRIDGE
BUCKNER

SCALE IN MILES   SEPT. 1955   NMP-CC-7008
0   50   100   200

ordered Buckner to rejoin the Army of Tennessee. Buckner's Corps of 8,000 men joined Bragg about the time the latter evacuated Chattanooga. Gen. Joseph E. Johnston from his army in Mississippi sent two divisions (about 9,000 men), under command of Major Generals John C. Breckinridge and W. H. T. Walker. A little later at Bragg's insistence Johnston sent two brigades, under command of Brigadier Generals John Gregg and Evander McNair. These brigades added 2,500 more troops to Bragg's Army.

About this same time preparations were under way to reinforce General Bragg further with Lt. Gen. James Longstreet's corps from the Army of Northern Virginia.

The movement of Longstreet's troops from Virginia to reinforce General Bragg in Georgia was an outstanding logistical achievement for the Confederacy. Even though by this time railroads had become an important factor in the strategy of war, no major troop movement involving so many lines over such a long distance had yet been attempted. It also shows the great concern the Southern War Department felt for the approaching battle.

From the Army of Northern Virginia to General Bragg's forces in Georgia was a distance of some 900 miles by railroad lines through Virginia, North Carolina, South Carolina, and Georgia. It was necessary for the troops to take this longer and roundabout route of reaching General Bragg because General Burnside had cut the railroad line by way of Knoxville.

By the summer of 1863 the railroads in the Confederacy were in very poor condition, for it had been extremely difficult to replace rails and rolling stock as the war continued. For the most part, the lines were comparatively short; were not connected at many points; lacked bridges across some of the major rivers; and like railroads everywhere, had different gauges. Sixteen different railroad lines were involved in the transfer as all parallel routes and all types of rolling stock were pressed into service.

In spite of all these difficulties, however, the movement was attended with dispatch and secrecy. Leaving the vicinity of Orange Courthouse, Va., on or about September 9, the advance brigades of Longstreet's Corps were joining General Bragg 9 days later. Mrs. Mary B. Chestnut recorded in her diary what she saw of this troop movement:

> At Kingsville (S. C.) on my way to Camden, I caught a glimpse of Longstreet's Corps going past. . . . It was a strange sight. What seemed miles of platform cars, and soldiers rolled in their blankets lying in rows with their heads all covered, fast asleep. In their grey blankets packed in regular order, they looked like swathed mummies. One man nearby was writing on his knee. He used his cap for a desk, and he was seated on a rail.

Information on the details of the movement, of the delays, the hazards encountered, as well as the number of men, animals, and artillery

Longstreet's soldiers detraining below Ringgold, Ga., September 18, 1863. From there they marched into battle at Chickamauga. A. R. Waud wartime sketch. *From Battlefields in Dixie Land and Chickamauga National Military Park.*

transported is difficult to find. A fair estimate of the number of troops is 15,000.

Only part of the infantry troops, and none of the artillery, arrived in time to participate in the Battle of Chickamauga; Longstreet himself was not present for the first day's fighting but three of his brigades were. The five brigades (about 9,000 men) which took part in the second day of battle became heroes along with their commander when they broke through the Union line.

Maneuver for Position

Bragg was aware of the isolated positions of the Union Army, and he saw an opportunity to strike his opponent in detail, one corps at a time, while they were not in supporting distance of each other. He issued orders to Maj. Gen. T. C. Hindman and Lt. Gen. D. H. Hill to strike Maj. Gen. James S. Negley's division of Thomas' corps, which was in an advanced position at McLemore's Cove, but Hill failed to carry out his order. Bragg ordered Buckner to join Hindman which he did on September 10. Instead of attacking Negley, the two Confederate commanders decided that a different plan was needed for the situation and sent their recommendation to Bragg. While this correspondence passed back and forth, Negley withdrew and rejoined the rest of Thomas' corps. The Confederates had now lost their opportunity to strike and possibly destroy this division.

Two days later a similar situation arose with the same result—loss of the opportunity to strike another corps in detail. This time Bragg ordered Polk to move his and Walker's corps to Lee and Gordon's Mills to strike Union General Crittenden's divided force. Two of Crittenden's divisions had marched toward Ringgold; one had moved to Lee and Gordon's Mills. Polk, instead of attacking, went on the defensive and asked for reinforcements. For the second time in 3 days, subordinate Confederate commanders allowed a Union corps to regroup.

Rosecrans now realized Bragg had concentrated and reinforced his army, and that his own force was in danger of annihilation in its divided condition. Accordingly he ordered General Granger, commanding the Reserve Corps in the vicinity of Bridgeport, Ala., to Chattanooga; General Crittenden to position at Lee and Gordon's Mills on Chickamauga Creek, some 12 miles south of Chattanooga; and General Thomas to move northward toward Crittenden as soon as he was joined by General McCook's Corps, which had been commanded to make haste in joining the other corps.

In the hurried concentration of the Army of the Cumberland, McCook withdrew from Alpine and chose to retrace his way by crossing over Lookout Mountain, thence up Lookout Valley where he had to recross the mountain to join General Thomas. It took McCook approximately 5 days (September 13 to 17) to complete this movement, greatly to the consternation of Rosecrans who had expected McCook to follow the shorter route on top of Lookout Mountain or roads through McLemore's Cove. Some of the troops, however, such as the Second Division, did forced marches in some instances of 25 miles in a day.

Bragg made no effort to prevent this concentration of the Union forces, and during the night of September 17 the three corps were within supporting distance of each other. The Union left was at Lee and Gordon's Mills, and from there the line extended west and south through McLemore's Cove to Stevens Gap through Lookout Mountain.

The Battle of Chickamauga

Chafing over the failure of his subordinate commanders to strike the divided units of Rosecrans' army and wishing to seize the initiative, General Bragg had his troops do an "about face." Turning northward, he planned an all-out attack on General Crittenden who had been following in his rear since the evacuation of Chattanooga and was now at Lee and Gordon's Mills. General Bragg moved his troops northward on the east side of the Chickamauga Creek. His plan was to cross the Chickamauga north of Lee and Gordon's Mills, seize the roads leading to Chattanooga, bear down on Crittenden, and crush this corps or drive it back into the Union center in McLemore's Cove. By turning the Union left in this manner, he hoped to force Rosecrans back into the mountains and to reoccupy Chattanooga.

Maj. Gen. John B. Hood (Longstreet's Corps) and Brig. Gen. Bushrod Johnson's troops were to cross at Reeds Bridge and turn left; Walker's Corps to cross at Alexander's Bridge; Buckner to cross at Tedford's Ford; Lt. Gen. Leonidas Polk's Corps to cross at Lee and Gordon's Mills; and Hill's Corps to cover the Confederate left.

Bragg did not seem to suspect that Rosecrans had guessed his intentions, and was hurriedly moving to support Crittenden and deploying his troops so as to protect the roads to Chattanooga.

SEPTEMBER 18—PRELIMINARIES.   On the morning of the 18th the three advanced brigades of Longstreet's Corps from Virginia arrived at Ringgold. One brigade immediately joined Bushrod Johnson's division as it prepared to cross Chickamauga Creek at Reed's Bridge. Union cavalry under Col. Robert H. G. Minty and mounted infantry under command of Col. John T. Wilder, guarding the bridges, offered stout resistance and delayed the crossing of the southern troops for several hours. During the skirmishing, Minty's men dismantled Alexander's Bridge and forced Walker to proceed to Lambert's Ford, a half-mile downstream. The Confederates used other fords and crossings throughout the late afternoon and night as all of Bragg's forces, except three divisions, crossed to the west side of Chickamauga Creek.

The Union forces were not idle, and during the night Rosecrans moved Thomas' corps northeastward above and back of Crittenden, so that Bragg would not outflank the Federal line. Negley's Division remained near Crawfish Springs (now Chickamauga), Maj. Gen. Joseph J. Reynolds' Division near Widow Glenn's, and Brigadier Generals Absalom Baird's and John M. Brannan's Divisions covered the roads leading to Reed's and Alexander's Bridges. General McCook's Corps moved to position in McLemore's Cove.

The situation at dawn on the 19th found the two armies facing each other over a stretch of several miles along the banks of the Chickamauga. Rosecrans had been able in a short time to maneuver the Army of the Cumberland into position so that it interposed between Bragg and Chattanooga. His Reserve Corps under General Granger was at McAfee's Church, near Rossville. Thomas' Fourteenth Army Corps composed the Union's left a few miles south of Granger, and formed a southwesterly line to Crawfish Spring where it joined McCook, forming the right in McLemore's Cove. Crittenden's Twenty-First Army Corps remained concentrated at Lee and Gordon's Mills, somewhat in front of the other two corps, to protect the Union center.

TABLE 1.—*Union Army at Chickamauga*

Army of the Cumberland—MAJ. GEN. WILLIAM S. ROSECRANS

Fourteenth Army Corps—MAJ. GEN. GEORGE H. THOMAS
    1st Division—Brig. Gen. Absalom Baird
    2d Division—Maj. Gen. James S. Negley
    3d Division—Brig. Gen. John M. Brannan
    4th Division—Maj. Gen. Joseph J. Reynolds

Twentieth Army Corps—MAJ. GEN. ALEXANDER McD. McCOOK
    1st Division—Brig. Gen. Jefferson C. Davis
    2d Division—Brig. Gen. Richard W. Johnson
    3d Division—Maj. Gen. Philip H. Sheridan

Twenty-first Army Corps—MAJ. GEN. THOMAS L. CRITTENDEN
    1st Division—Brig. Gen. Thomas J. Wood
    2d Division—Maj. Gen. John M. Palmer
    3d Division—Brig. Gen. H. P. Van Cleve

Reserve Corps—MAJ. GEN. GORDON GRANGER
    1st Division—Brig. Gen. James B. Steedman
    2d Division—Col. Daniel McCook

Cavalry Corps—BRIG. GEN. ROBERT B. MITCHELL
    1st Division—Col. Edward M. McCook
    2d Division—Brig. Gen. George Crook

"The First Gun at Chickamauga." Confederates open fire on Union cavalry at Reed's Bridge. A. R. Waud wartime sketch. From Brown, *The Mountain Campaign in Georgia.*

TABLE 2.—*Confederate Army at Chickamauga*

Army of Tennessee—GEN. BRAXTON BRAGG [1]

Right Wing—LT. GEN. LEONIDAS POLK

    Cheatham's Division—MAJ. GEN. B. F. CHEATHAM

    Hill's Corps—LT. GEN. DANIEL H. HILL
        Cleburne's Division—Maj. Gen. P. R. Cleburne
        Breckinridge's Division—Maj. Gen. J. C. Breckinridge

    Reserve Corps—MAJ. GEN. W. H. T. WALKER
        Walker's Division—Brig. Gen. S. R. Gist
        Liddell's Division—Brig. Gen. St. John R. Liddell

Left Wing—LT. GEN. JAMES LONGSTREET

    Hindman's Division—MAJ. GEN. T. C. HINDMAN

    Buckner's Corps—MAJ. GEN. SIMON B. BUCKNER
        Stewart's Division—Maj. Gen. Alexander P. Stewart
        Preston's Division—Brig. Gen. William Preston
        Johnson's Division—Brig. Gen. Bushrod R. Johnson

    Longstreet's Corps—MAJ. GEN. JOHN B. HOOD
        McLaw's Division—Brig. Gen. Joseph B. Kershaw
        Hood's Division—Maj. Gen. John B. Hood,
            Brig. Gen. E. McIver Law

    Corps Artillery [2]—COL. E. PORTER ALEXANDER

    Reserve Artillery, Army of Tennessee—Maj. FELIX H. ROBERTSON

    Cavalry—MAJ. GEN. JOSEPH WHEELER
        Wharton's Division—Brig. Gen. John A. Wharton
        Martin's Division—Brig. Gen. William T. Martin
        Forrest's Corps—Brig. Gen. N. B. Forrest
            Armstrong's Division—Brig. Gen. Frank C. Armstrong
            Pegram's Division—Brig. Gen. John Pegram

[1] General Bragg's army was composed of Polk's, Hill's, Buckner's, Longstreet's (Hood's), and Walker's (Reserve) Corps of infantry, and Wheeler's and Forrest's Corps of cavalry. For the second day's fight the army was divided into two wings, General Polk commanding the right and General Longstreet the left.
[2] In transit, did not take part in the battle.

Bragg's Army of Tennessee, except three divisions, was concentrated on the west side of the Chickamauga from Reeds Bridge almost to Dalton's Ford, near Lee and Gordon's Mills. The divisions had been shuffled around during the night, and remained so for the first day's battle. Brig. Gen. Nathan Bedford Forrest's cavalry held the right flank at Reeds Bridge; then, in succession toward the left (south), were Walker's Corps; Maj. Gen. Benjamin F. Cheatham's Division (Polk's Corps); Longstreet's Corps (under Maj. Gen. John B. Hood); and Buckner's Corps. On the east side of the stream and forming the

Maj. Gen. George H. Thomas, "The Rock of Chickamauga." Courtesy National Archives.

right were Maj. Gen. Patrick R. Cleburne's Division (Hill's Corps), preparing to cross at Tedford's Ford; Maj. Gen. T. C. Hindman's Division (Polk's Corps) opposite Lee and Gordon's Mills; and Maj. Gen. John C. Breckinridge's Division (Hill's Corps) forming the extreme left opposite Glass' Mill. Maj. Gen. Joseph Wheeler's cavalry, stationed at the upper fords of the Chickamauga, held the left flank.

Neither army knew the exact position of the other as they maneuvered for position during the night. The densely wooded area, covered with tangled undergrowth, brambles and cedar thickets, prevented easy movement or good observation, and many of the officers had difficulty keeping in touch with their own commands.

The armies were so close to each other, in some instances only a few hundred yards apart, that it was inevitable a clash would soon take place, but at what point no one could say.

SEPTEMBER 19—FIRST DAY. Early in the morning of September 19, Thomas ordered Brannan forward to reconnoiter the Confederate forces which had crossed the Chickamauga. In this manner, Col. John T. Croxton's brigade of infantry accidentally ran into some of Forrest's cavalry, which were dismounted and serving as infantry, at Jay's Mill near Reed's Bridge. And so the battle began.

Croxton drove Forrest back, but reinforcements hurried to the latter forced Croxton to give ground. Suddenly the commanding generals realized that a major conflict was upon them, and they hurriedly sent troops into the fight as first one side and then the other gained the upper hand. Rosecrans, by rapid and forced marches, brought up his troops from Crawfish Springs. Bragg ordered his left wing divisions to cross to the west side of the Chickamauga. By mid-afternoon major fighting had spread along a jagged line some 3 miles in length. All the Union divisions, with the exception of Granger's reserve force, became involved. The Confederate troops were also largely engaged, except Hindman and Breckinridge who crossed over during the late afternoon and night.

When the battle ended for the day, little progress could be shown by either side. The fighting had been furious and without much plan. Bragg's troops had reached the LaFayette-Chattanooga Road but were not able to hold the position. Neither side could claim a victory. Bragg had failed to crush the Union left, and Rosecrans remained in possession of the roads to Chattanooga. The losses on both sides were heavy.

As night fell and darkness settled over the battlefield the fighting stopped, but there was little rest for the weary soldiers. Rosecrans brought the Army of the Cumberland into a more compact defensive line; Thomas' Corps, heavily reinforced, formed the left in a bulge east of the LaFayette Road at Kelly's Field.

Throughout the night the Confederates heard the ring of axes as the Union troops cut trees and logs to form breastworks. McCook's Corps in the center faced LaFayette Road; Crittenden's Corps on the right was a little withdrawn west of the road.

During the night, Longstreet arrived with two more brigades ready for action. Bragg then decided to form the Army of Tennessee into two wings for offensive action the next day. He placed General Polk in command of the right wing and General Longstreet the left. The Confederate Army, facing west between Chickamauga Creek and the LaFayette Road formed a line more or less parallel with the road.

SEPTEMBER 20—SECOND DAY.   General Bragg issued orders to his subordinates to resume the battle at daybreak. On the Confederate right Breckinridge's Division was to begin the attack which would be taken up by successive divisions to the left. Sunday morning came. Daylight began to creep over the battlefield. The sun rose, but no attack came. Bragg waited impatiently. Finally, the orders reached Hill at 7:30 a. m. Further delay followed as the troops moved into position. About 9:30

Confederate line of battle in woods at Chickamauga.   From *Battles and Leaders of the Civil War.*

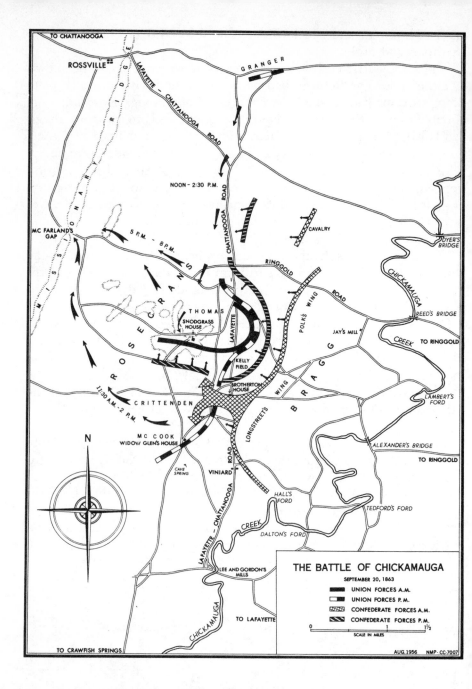

THE BATTLE OF CHICKAMAUGA
SEPTEMBER 20, 1863

UNION FORCES A.M.
UNION FORCES P.M.
CONFEDERATE FORCES A.M.
CONFEDERATE FORCES P.M.

0   1   1½
SCALE IN MILES

AUG. 1956   NMP·CC-7007

a. m. Breckinridge advanced to attack, followed by Cleburne. The extreme left of the Union line fell back, but the fire from the Union breastworks halted further Confederate advance. Reinforcements hurried to Thomas. In further fighting at this part of the line neither side made any considerable gain, as Rosecrans sought to hold his left against Polk's furious attacks. Almost equally matched, neither

Lt. Gen. James Longstreet. Courtesy National Archives.

Lt. Gen. Leonidas Polk. Courtesy National Archives.

Thomas nor Polk could show any appreciable gains throughout the morning. About 11 o'clock a lull occurred as Longstreet's wing prepared to move against the center in Bragg's plan of attack.

The Union center at which Longstreet pointed his attack was held by Brig. Gen. Thomas J. Wood's Division which had replaced Negley's Division in the line when the latter had reinforced Thomas early in the morning. To the immediate left of Wood were the troops of Brannan's Division, and on Brannan's left, Maj. Gen. Joseph J. Reynolds' Division.

An hour before noon as the Confederate right wing poised to strike, an irreparable blunder occurred on the Union side. A staff officer riding from Thomas' headquarters near Kelly Field reported to Rosecrans that he had noticed Brannan's Division was out of line and believed "General Reynolds' right was exposed." Rosecrans, without further investigation, immediately ordered Wood to "close up on Reynolds as fast as possible and support him." In order to do this, Wood had to pull his division out of line and march behind Brannan's Division toward Reynolds. Wood's division had left its place in the line, creating a true gap where none had actually existed before, and had started to march northward behind Brannan when Longstreet's column of five divisions accidentally struck into the gap.

Longstreet's attack hit Wood's and Brannan's Divisions on their exposed flank and drove them from the immediate field of battle. On the other side of the gap the Confederates struck Brig. Gen. Jefferson C. Davis' Division, which was marching up to take Wood's place in the line, and Maj. Gen. Philip H. Sheridan's Division in flank. In a very short time the entire Union right flank was in disorder and driven from the field. Wilder's brigade on the extreme right made a valiant stand for a while, employing to good effect the heavy fire power of the Spencer repeating carbine with which it was armed. Nothing, however, seemed to daunt the onrush of the Confederates, and Wilder withdrew for fear of being cut off from escape.

The routed divisions from the Union right withdrew northwestward through McFarland's Gap to Rossville. Generals Rosecrans, Crittenden, and McCook were caught in the breakthrough and fled the field. General Thomas was now in command of the Union forces left there.

The altered conditions of the battlefield now dictated a change in Confederate strategy. The original plan of enveloping the Union left changed to a sweep from the Union right to the left. A pause in the fighting enabled Thomas to form a new line quickly to his rear on Snodgrass Hill, almost at a right angle with the Union left. From this vantage point he met the onslaught of Longstreet's troops with such stubborn and determined resistance on that Sunday afternoon that he earned the name "Rock of Chickamauga."

The Union line on Snodgrass Hill was composed of Brannan's Division with fragments of Wood's, Negley's, and Van Cleve's Divisions. Longstreet vigorously assaulted the line again and again and nearly succeeded in enveloping Brannan's right. Confederate success seemed assured as Thomas' troops were hard hit and were short of ammunition, but at this moment unexpected reinforcements reached General Thomas.

General Granger, without orders and following the sound of battle, had hastened to the aid of Thomas. He arrived at Snodgrass Hill at a very opportune moment and just in time to stop the Confederates

The Battle of Chickamauga.   Scene from diorama in the Museum, Park Headquarters Building.

from enveloping Brannan's right. A fierce engagement took place as Brig. Gen. James B. Steedman's Division of Granger's Corps forced the southern troops from the crest of the hill.

Midafternoon found Longstreet once again attempting to wrest the hill from Thomas' troops, using McLaw's, Hindman's, and Bushrod Johnson's Divisions, and again he was repulsed. Later in the afternoon, Longstreet asked Bragg for reinforcements but was told none were available and that the right wing "had been beaten back so badly that they could be of no service" to him. Longstreet determined to make one more effort. He formed a column of such troops as were available and again assaulted the hill. The fight was desperate and lasted until nightfall. The Union troops repulsed some of the Confederate charges with the bayonet as their ammunition was nearly exhausted. Finally, Longstreet pushed Steedman back to the next ridge and occupied the ground to the right of Brannan.

The left of the Union line around Kelly Field spent a relatively quiet afternoon compared to their comrades on Snodgrass Hill. However, about 4 p. m., the divisions of Hill's corps and part of Walker's again assaulted the Union positions there. By 6 p. m., Cheatham's Division had joined the attack. This attack succeeded in enveloping the Union left, and the road to Rossville, through Rossville Gap, was cut off for the moment.

In the meantime, Thomas received orders from Rosecrans to "Assume command of all the forces, and with Crittenden and McCook take a strong position and assume a threatening attitude at Rossville." Although Thomas received these orders with little delay, it was late

Headquarters, Maj. Gen. Gordon Granger, Reserve Corps, Army of the Cumberland, at Rossville Gap. The house was built by John Ross, Cherokee Indian Chief, who lived in it until 1832. Ross gave his name to the village in the gap. From Elson, *The Civil War Through the Camera.*

afternoon before he sent instructions to Reynolds to begin the withdrawal and move into position to cover the retirement of the other troops on the left. In executing this movement, Reynolds was forced to drive off the Confederate troops who had begun to envelop the Union left. The Union army withdrew in relatively good order. The troops holding Kelly Field moved out first, followed by those who had stubbornly resisted Longstreet's attacks upon Snodgrass Hill.

While the retreat from the battlelines may have been in "good order," General Beatty's description of the march to Rossville amply describes the scene: "The march to Rossville was a melancholy one. All along the road, for miles, wounded men were lying. They had crawled or hobbled slowly away from the fury of the battle, become exhausted, and lain down by the roadside to die." Beatty reached Rossville between "ten and eleven" and reported, "At this hour of the night (eleven to twelve o'clock) the army is simply a mob. There appears to be neither organization nor discipline. The various commands are mixed up in what seems to be inextricable confusion."

Nevertheless, Thomas placed his forces at Rossville Gap and along Missionary Ridge in preparation against further attacks. The morning of the 21st found the Union Army of the Cumberland more or less reorganized. With the exception of some skirmishing, the Union forces were not molested.

The losses on both sides were appalling and the percentages surprisingly equal. The following tabulation of casualties at the Battle of Chickamauga is based on Thomas L. Livermore's *Numbers and Losses in the Civil War in America, 1861–65:*

Army	Total Strength	Total Casualties	Killed	Wounded	Missing	Percent Casualties
Union	58,222	16,170	1,657	9,756	4,757	.28
Confederate	66,326	18,454	2,312	14,674	1,468	.28

The Siege of Chattanooga

Thomas remained in position at Rossville throughout the 21st, but it was evident that the Confederates could turn his right flank and cut him off from Chattanooga. He suggested to Rosecrans that the Union Army concentrate at Chattanooga. In anticipation of receiving an order to withdraw to the town, Thomas instructed his officers to prepare their commands for the movement. Rosecrans adopted the suggestion and that evening Thomas withdrew the Union forces to Chattanooga. All wagons, ambulances, and surplus artillery had already departed for Chattanooga during the day. By morning of September 22, all Union troops were in position in the town.

Wartime view, Lee and Gordon's Mills, Chickamauga Battlefield. Courtesy National Archives.

The situation in which the men in blue found themselves in Chattanooga was not pleasant. The Tennessee River walled them in on the north, although a pontoon bridge and two ferries offered escape possibilities. Lookout Mountain blocked the way on the west, and Missionary Ridge to the east and south, now held by the Confederates, completed the circle.

Bragg issued orders for the pursuit of the Army of the Cumberland, then countermanded them. Instead, the Confederate troops began to take up siege positions around Chattanooga. In these positions the Confederates dominated the Union lines. Bragg's men controlled all the railroads leading into the town; Confederate batteries and sharpshooters commanded the Tennessee River, and river traffic ceased; they

Wartime view of Chattanooga in 1863 — Lookout Mountain in distance. Courtesy National Archives.

Maj. Gen. Ulysses S. Grant.
Courtesy National Archives.

Maj. Gen. William T. Sherman
Courtesy National Archives.

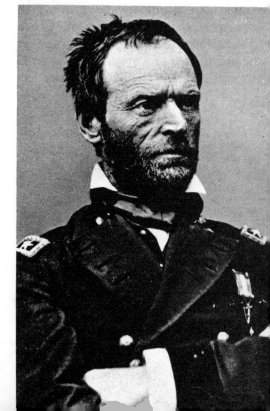

330

controlled the roads on the south side of the river and kept under fire the one road north of the river leading to Bridgeport, the nearest Union supply base. Only the road over Walden's Ridge and down through the Sequatchie Valley to Bridgeport was open to General Rosecrans.

Reinforcements for the Besieged Army

As early as September 13, General in Chief Halleck ordered reinforcements sent to Rosecrans. His dispatches on September 13, 14, and 15 to Major Generals Hurlbut at Memphis and Grant and Sherman at Vicksburg directed the troop movements. These dispatches, however, were delayed for several days en route from Cairo to Memphis and, in the meantime, the Battle of Chickamauga was fought. Grant received the orders on the 22nd and immediately instructed four divisions under Sherman to march to Chattanooga.

One division of the Seventeenth Corps, already in transit from Vicksburg to Helena, Ark., was ordered to proceed on to Memphis. General Sherman quickly brought three divisions of his Fifteenth Army Corps from the vicinity of the Big Black River into Vicksburg, where they embarked as fast as water transportation could be provided. By October 3, all of the movement of 17,000 men was under way.

The route of travel was by boat to Memphis, then by railroad and overland marches to Chattanooga. From Memphis the troops followed closely the Memphis and Charleston Railroad, which Sherman was ordered to repair as he advanced. By November 15, the troops were at Bridgeport, Ala., having traveled a distance of 675 miles.

When the War Department in Washington received word that the Army of the Cumberland was besieged in Chattanooga, it considered the situation so critical that President Lincoln was called out of bed late at night to attend a council meeting. This meeting occurred on the night of September 23, and is described by Nicolay and Hay:

> Immediately on receipt of Rosecrans' dispatch, Mr. Stanton sent one of the President's secretaries who was standing by to the Soldier's Home, where the President was sleeping. A little startled by the unwonted summons,—for this was "the first time" he said, Stanton had ever sent for him,—the President mounted his horse and rode in through the moonlight to the War Department to preside over an improvised council to consider the subject of reinforcing Rosecrans.
>
> There were present General Halleck, Stanton, Seward and Chase of the Cabinet; P. H. Watson and James A. Hardie of the War Department, and General D. C. McCallum, Superintendent of Military Transportation. After a brief debate, it was resolved to detach the Eleventh and Twelfth Corps from the Army of the Potomac, General Hooker to be placed in command of both . . .

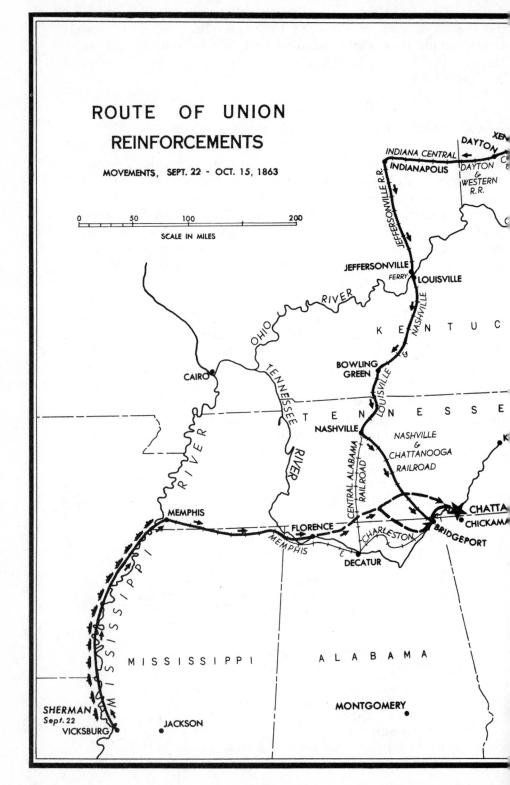

ROUTE OF UNION
REINFORCEMENTS

MOVEMENTS, SEPT. 22 - OCT. 15, 1863

0   50   100   200
SCALE IN MILES

DAYTON   XEN
INDIANA CENTRAL   C.
INDIANAPOLIS   DAYTON
&
WESTERN
R.R.

JEFFERSONVILLE R.R.

JEFFERSONVILLE   FERRY   LOUISVILLE

OHIO   RIVER

K E N T U C

NASHVILLE

CAIRO

BOWLING
GREEN

LOUISVILLE

TENNESSEE

T E N   N E S S E

NASHVILLE   K

NASHVILLE
&
CHATTANOOGA
RAILROAD

CENTRAL ALABAMA RAILROAD

RIVER

MEMPHIS

FLORENCE   CHATTA
CHICKAMA
CHARLESTON   BRIDGEPORT
MEMPHIS   &
DECATUR

MISSISSIPPI

M I S S I S S I P P I   A L A B A M A

MONTGOMERY

SHERMAN
Sept. 22
VICKSBURG   JACKSON

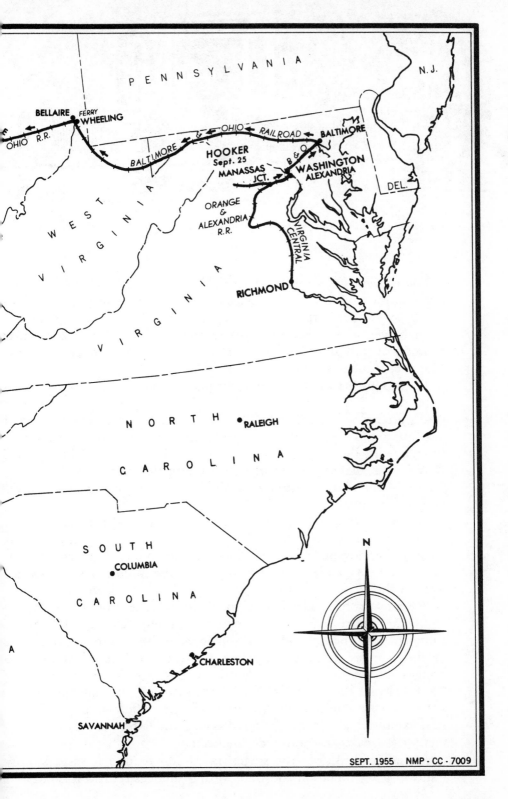

Chattanooga headquarters of General Rosecrans during the siege. Courtesy National Archives.

The movement of the Eleventh and Twelfth Army Corps from the Army of the Potomac to Tennessee eclipsed all other such troop movements by rail up to that time. It represented a high degree of cooperation between the railroads and the government and was a singular triumph of skill and planning. It also shows the great importance the War Department attached to the Chattanooga campaign.

The troops began to entrain at Manassas Junction and Bealton Station, Va., on September 25, and 5 days later on September 30 the first trains arrived at Bridgeport, Ala. The route traveled was by way of Washington, D. C.; Baltimore, Md.; Bellaire and Columbus, Ohio; Indianapolis, Ind.; Louisville, Ky.; Nashville, Tenn.; and Bridgeport, Ala. Several major railroad lines, including the Baltimore and Ohio, Central Ohio, Louisville and Nashville, and Nashville and Chattanooga were involved.

Not all of the troops, however, made such good time as the first trains, and for the majority of the infantry the trip consumed about 9 days. The movement of the artillery, horses, mules, baggage, and impedimenta was somewhat slower, but by the middle of October, all were in the vicinity of Bridgeport ready to help break the siege.

These two corps under Maj. Gen. Joseph Hooker, comprising 20,000 troops and more than 3,000 horses and mules, traveled 1,157 miles. Differences in the railroad gauges hampered the movement, but most of the changes in gauge occurred at river crossings which had no bridges and the troops had to detrain at these points anyway.

Confederate cavalry raids, bent on destroying the railroad bridges and otherwise interfering with the reinforcing effort, imposed a more serious difficulty, but, except for delaying the latter part of the movement a few days, the raids were ineffective.

At the beginning of the siege, the Union Army had large supply trains in good condition and transporting supplies seemed feasible. But early in October rain began to fall and the roads became almost impassable. To make the situation more critical Bragg sent Wheeler to harass and destroy the Union supply trains as they moved over Walden's Ridge on their trips to and from Bridgeport. Wheeler destroyed hundreds of wagons and animals and it was not long before the Union soldier received less and less food. Wagon horses and mules and artillery horses were on a starvation diet and many died each day.

Command of the two hostile armies had undergone a considerable change during the siege period. Grant received orders to meet "an officer of the War Department" at Louisville, Ky. He proceeded by rail to Indianapolis, Ind., and just as his train left the depot there, en route to Louisville, it was stopped. A message informed Grant that Secretary of War Stanton was coming into the station and wished to see him. This was the "officer" from the War Department who gave Grant command of the newly organized Military Division of the Mississippi. Thomas replaced Rosecrans. McCook and Crittenden had previously been relieved of their commands and their corps consolidated into the Fourth Corps under command of Granger. Stanton accompanied Grant to Louisville and there the two spent a day reviewing the situation.

In Bragg's camp, Polk was relieved of his command, and Lt. Gen. William J. Hardee rejoined the army. Bragg's army was reorganized into three corps commanded by Longstreet, Hardee, and Breckinridge.

When Grant reached Chattanooga on October 23 he found a plan already drawn up to open a new supply line for the besieged army. This plan of necessity was conditioned upon the terrain and the configuration of the river between Bridgeport, the railhead and base of supplies for the Union Army, and Chattanooga. (After the Tennessee River passes the city it flows southward for some 2 miles until it strikes Lookout Mountain where, after a short westerly course, it

Entrenchments of Thomas' Corps, Army of the Cumberland in front of Chattanooga. Lookout Mountain in distance. From *Battles and Leaders of the Civil War.*

curves northward. This elongated loop of the river is called Moccasin Bend.)

The plan called for 1,500 men on pontoons to float down the river from Chattanooga during the night of October 26–27 while another force marched across Moccasin Point to support the landings of the river-borne troops. Grant ordered the plan executed. The pontoon-borne troops quickly disembarked upon striking the west bank at Brown's Ferry, drove off the Confederate pickets, and threw up breast-works. The troops marching across the neck of land came up to the east side of the ferry, joined this group, and constructed a pontoon bridge.

Hooker's advance from Bridgeport coincided with this action. He marched by the road along Raccoon Mountain into Lookout Valley. There he met the advance post of a Confederate brigade and drove it back. Maj. Gen. O. O. Howard's Eleventh Corps moved to within 2 miles of Brown's Ferry, while Brig. Gen. John W. Geary of the Twelfth Corps remained at Wauhatchie to guard the road to Kelley's Ferry.

The Confederates made a night attack against Geary which the latter repulsed, but both sides lost heavily. After this action, the short line of communication with Bridgeport by way of Brown's and Kelley's Ferries was held by Hooker without further trouble.

With the successful seizure of Brown's Ferry and construction of a pontoon bridge across the Tennessee River there, and Hooker's equally successful advance from Bridgeport and seizure of the south side of the river at Raccoon Mountain and in Lookout Valley, the way was finally clear for the Union Army to reopen a short line of supply and communication between Chattanooga and Bridgeport, the rail end of its supply line. This "Cracker Line" ran by boat up the Tennessee River from Bridgeport to Kelley's Ferry. Above Kelley's Ferry, the swift current made the stream unnavigable at certain points to boats then available. Accordingly, at Kelley's Ferry, the "Cracker Line" left the river and crossed Raccoon Mountain by road to Brown's Ferry. There it crossed the river on the pontoon bridge, thence across Moccasin Point, and finally across the river once more into Chattanooga.

Early in November, Bragg ordered Longstreet to march against Burnside in East Tennessee with Maj. Gen. Lafayette McLaw's and Maj. Gen. John B. Hood's Divisions of infantry, Col. E. Porter Alexander's and Maj. A. Leyden's battalions of artillery, and five brigades of cavalry under Maj. Gen. Joseph Wheeler—about 15,000 men in all. This movement caused great anxiety in Washington and the authorities urged Grant to act promptly to assist Burnside. Grant felt that the quickest way to aid him was to attack Bragg and force the latter to recall Longstreet. On November 7, Thomas received Grant's order to attack Bragg's right. Thomas replied that he was unable to move a single piece of artillery because of the poor condition of the horses and mules. They were not strong enough to pull artillery pieces. In these circumstances, Grant could only answer Washington dispatches, urge Sherman forward, and encourage Burnside to hold on.

Lifting the Siege—The Battle of Chattanooga

With the Confederate Army in front of Chattanooga divided into two corps, Hardee on the right and Breckinridge on the left on Missionary Ridge, and General Stevenson with a small force occupying Lookout Mountain, Bragg waited.

Grant's plan of battle was for Sherman with his four divisions to cross the Tennessee River at Brown's Ferry and march behind Stringer's Ridge, concealed from the eyes of the Confederates, and take a position near the North Chickamauga Creek. He was to recross the river by pontoon bridge at the mouth of the South Chickamauga Creek, strike the north end of Missionary Ridge and capture it as far as the railroad tunnel. Thomas was to move his Army of the Cumberland to the left, and connect with Sherman. This united force was to sweep the Confederates southward off Missionary Ridge and away from their base of supplies at Chickamauga Station. Howard's Corps was to act as a general reserve for this force. Hooker, with the Twelfth Corps and Brig. Gen. Charles Cruft's Division (Fourth Corps), was to hold Lookout Valley. Col. Eli Long's Cavalry was to cover Sherman's left and when no longer needed for this task was to strike Bragg's communications. This original plan, however, was changed several times to fit the situation.

The rains that hampered movement of Union supplies also delayed Sherman's movement across the Tennessee. High water broke the bridge at Brown's Ferry and Osterhaus' Division could not cross the river. Subsequently it received orders to join Hooker in Lookout Valley.

On November 22, Grant received word that Bragg was withdrawing his army; actually the movement reported was Buckner leaving to reinforce Longstreet. To "test the truth" of the report, Grant changed his plans and ordered Thomas to make a demonstration to his front on the 23rd. This began the battles of Chattanooga.

ORCHARD KNOB. The Union Army of the Cumberland had made its positions very strong during the time it was besieged by Bragg's army. One of its strong points was Fort Wood on an elevated point east of the town. Thomas, according to instructions, sent Maj. Gen. Philip H.

TABLE 3.—*Union Army at Chattanooga*
MAJ. GEN. ULYSSES S. GRANT

Army of the Cumberland— MAJ. GEN. GEORGE H. THOMAS

    Fourth Army Corps—MAJ. GEN. GORDON GRANGER
        1st Division—Brig. Gen. Charles Cruft
        2d Division—Maj. Gen. Philip H. Sheridan
        3d Division—Brig. Gen. Thomas J. Wood

    Fourteenth Army Corps—MAJ. GEN. J. M. PALMER
        1st Division—Brig. Gen. Richard W. Johnson
        2d Division—Brig. Gen. J. C. Davis
        3d Division—Brig. Gen. Absalom Baird

    Engineer Troops—BRIG. GEN. WILLIAM F. SMITH

    Artillery Reserve—BRIG. GEN. J. M. BRANNAN
        1st Division—Col. James Barnett
        2d Division

    Cavalry
        2d Division
        —2d Brigade—Col. Eli Long

    Post of Chattanooga—COL. JOHN G. PARKHURST

Detachment from the Army of the Potomac—MAJ. GEN. JOSEPH HOOKER

    Eleventh Army Corps—MAJ. GEN. O. O. HOWARD
        2d Division—Brig. Gen. Adolph von Steinwehr
        3d Division—Maj. Gen. Carl Schurz

    Twelfth Army Corps—MAJ. GEN. HENRY W. SLOCUM
        2d Division—Brig. Gen. John W. Geary

Army of the Tennessee—MAJ. GEN. WILLIAM T. SHERMAN

    Fifteenth Corps—MAJ. GEN. FRANK P. BLAIR, JR.
        1st Division—Brig. Gen. Peter J. Osterhaus
        2d Division—Brig. Gen. Morgan L. Smith
        4th Division—Brig. Gen. Hugh Ewing

    Seventeenth Army Corps
        2d Division—Brig. Gen. John E. Smith

Sheridan's and Brig. Gen. T. J. Wood's divisions to level ground at Fort Wood and there formed them in line—Wood on the left, Sheridan on the right, with Brig. Gen. Absalom Baird supporting Sheridan. Brig. Gen. R. W. Johnson's troops held the trenches, and Maj. Gen. O. O. Howard's Corps, which had crossed from the north bank of the river, acted as the reserve.

At 2 p. m. on November 23, the lines of blue moved forward, driving the Confederate outposts and their supports back to the base of Missionary Ridge, and captured Orchard Knob, a low hill a little more than a mile in front of the ridge. The Union forces occupied the

TABLE 4.—*Confederate Army at Chattanooga*
GEN. BRAXTON BRAGG

Hardee's Corps—LT. GEN. WILLIAM J. HARDEE
Cheatham's Division—Brig. Gen. John K. Jackson
Stevenson's Division—Maj. Gen. Carter L. Stevenson
Cleburne's Division—Maj. Gen. P. R. Cleburne
Walker's Division—Brig. Gen. States R. Gist

Breckinridge's Corps—MAJ. GEN. JOHN C. BRECKINRIDGE
Hindman's Division—Brig. Gen. J. Patton Anderson
Breckinridge's Division—Brig. Gen. William B. Bate
Stewart's Division—Maj. Gen. Ambrose P. Stewart
Reserve Artillery
Robertson's Battalion—Capt. Felix H. Robertson
Williams' Battalion—Maj. S. C. Williams

captured entrenchments and erected a battery on Orchard Knob. Except for occasional artillery firing, the fighting ended for the day.

SHERMAN MOVES. During the night of November 23-24, Sherman began to carry out his role in the drama. He selected Brig. Gen. Giles A. Smith's brigade to man the pontoon boats, concealed in North Chickamauga Creek, to cross the Tennessee River and secure a bridgehead near the mouth of the South Chickamauga Creek. During the hours of darkness the brigade landed at its designated place. A few soldiers stopped at the mouth of the creek, surprising and capturing the pickets there. The remaining troops landed and prepared to build bridges across the Tennessee River and South Chickamauga Creek. By early afternoon they had finished the bridge across the river, and Sherman's forces were across and ready to attack. Brig. Gen. Jefferson C. Davis' Division (Fourteenth Corps), which had guarded the pontoons, also crossed and became part of Sherman's force.

Sherman attacked and seized the north end of Missionary Ridge at 4 p. m. against only Confederate outpost opposition. To his surprise, Sherman found a deep and wide ravine separating the north end of the ridge from Tunnel Hill immediately southward, his real objective. Cleburne's Division of Confederate troops had hurried to Tunnel Hill only an hour or two before Sherman seized the north end of Missionary Ridge, and they were busily engaged entrenching there when Sherman arrived across the ravine from them. Sherman did not attack Tunnel Hill that afternoon, but entrenched where he was.

THE BATTLE ABOVE THE CLOUDS, NOVEMBER 24. While operations were in progress, east of Chattanooga, Hooker moved into action west of the town. The failure of Osterhaus' Division to join Sherman resulted in another change of orders. A new plan for Hooker to take

Lookout Mountain and descend into Chattanooga Valley replaced the original one of having him merely hold Lookout Valley and the route to Bridgeport. Hooker had three divisions in his force commanded by Brigadier Generals Peter J. Osterhaus, John W. Geary, and Charles Cruft, each from a different army corps. Geary was on the right at Wauhatchie, Cruft in the center, and Osterhaus near Brown's Ferry. It

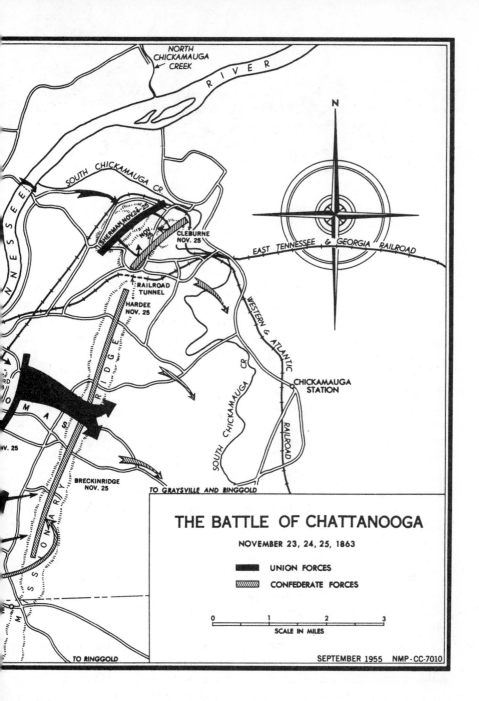

North Chickamauga Creek

RIVER

NORTH
CHICKAMAUGA
CREEK

TENNESSEE

SOUTH CHICKAMAUGA CR.

SHERMAN NOV. 24-25

NOV. 25

CLEBURNE
NOV. 25

EAST TENNESSEE & GEORGIA RAILROAD

N

RAILROAD
TUNNEL

HARDEE
NOV. 25

RIDGE

MISSIONARY

WESTERN & ATLANTIC

SOUTH CHICKAMAUGA CR.

CHICKAMAUGA
STATION

RAILROAD

NOV. 25

BRECKINRIDGE
NOV. 25

TO GRAYSVILLE AND RINGGOLD

MISSIONARY RIDGE

TO RINGGOLD

THE BATTLE OF CHATTANOOGA

NOVEMBER 23, 24, 25, 1863

UNION FORCES

CONFEDERATE FORCES

0   1   2   3
SCALE IN MILES

SEPTEMBER 1955   NMP·CC-7010

was a unique team. One who was present wrote, "We were all strangers, no one division ever having seen either of the others."

The terrain that confronted Hooker's command was rugged, steep, heavily timbered, and topped by a rocky cliff. At the northern end, at the cliff base and halfway up the mountain, was a bench of nearly level land. On it stood the Cravens Farm. At 8 a. m. on November 24 Hooker sent

Hazen's men landing from pontoon boats at Brown's Ferry, Tennessee River. *Theodore R. Davis wartime sketch.* From *Battles and Leaders of the Civil War.*

Geary's Division, supported by a brigade from Cruft's Division, to effect a crossing of Lookout Creek. The troops accomplished this with little opposition and Geary climbed the mountain until the head of his column reached the cliff. The division then moved to the left and proceeded northward toward the point of the mountain.

While Geary climbed the mountain, Cruft, with his force, moved farther down the valley toward the Tennessee River and seized a bridge over the creek. Osterhaus's Division then crossed the stream at that point in the face of sharp skirmishing with Confederate defenders before the latter retreated up the mountain. The three Union divisions soon joined on a common line and, supported by Union batteries on Moccasin Point, steadily drove Walthall's Confederate brigade around the point of Lookout Mountain to the Cravens farmhouse. By noon, Hooker's forces were in possession of the farm but the Confederates made a stand beyond the Cravens house within prepared defense works, and were joined there by two brigades from the top of the mountain. Fog which covered the mountainside most of the morning became so heavy that by 2 p. m. it was almost impossible to see. This factor, plus a shortage of ammunition, caused Hooker to halt and consolidate his position. Later in the afternoon, Carlin's brigade arrived with a resupply of ammunition.

During the night, General Stevenson withdrew the Confederate forces from Lookout Mountain and marched them to Missionary Ridge where they joined their comrades holding that sector of the line.

"The Battle Above the Clouds" was fought on the bench of land surrounding the Cravens house. There was no fighting on top the mountain. The romantic name given in later years to this action on the Union right was the result of the fog and mist which shrouded the mountain that day from observers below. It was not until the next morning that the 8th Kentucky Volunteers planted the Stars and Stripes on top of the bluff.

Lookout Mountain from Union works in Chattanooga. From *Harper's Pictorial History of the Great Rebellion.*

MISSIONARY RIDGE, NOVEMBER 25. The decisive blow of the battle was at hand. Grant's orders for the morning of November 25 were as follows: "Sherman was directed to attack at daylight. Hooker was ordered to move at the same hour, and endeavor to intercept the enemy's retreat, if he still remained; if he had gone, then to move directly to Rossville and operate against the left and rear of the force on Missionary Ridge. Thomas was not to move until Hooker had reached Missionary Ridge."

Gen. Ulysses S. Grant on Lookout Mountain, 1863. Grant is in the lower left corner. Courtesy National Archives.

Missionary Ridge from a Union trench. From Elson, *The Civil War Through the Camera.*

Sherman began his attack, as directed, just after sunrise. His troops attacked Cleburne's Division frontally, but without success. All night the Confederates had worked at strengthening their position on Tunnel Hill which now formed the Confederate right. These field works gave good protection to Cleburne's men from enemy fire. The stubbornly fighting Confederates held their positions against repeated attacks by superior numbers. This fight continued until 3 p. m., and is a notable example of the value to a greatly outnumbered defending force of field works on a good position. Some Union troops did make a lodgment on the slopes of Tunnel Hill in the afternoon, but a Confederate charge drove them off. Cleburne's soldiers held the hill.

In the meantime, Hooker was in trouble—not with the enemy, but with Chattanooga Creek. He started for Rossville bright and early to get into position to strike Bragg's left. Stevenson's men, who had evacuated Lookout Mountain during the night, had burned the bridge across Chattanooga Creek and had done all they could to obstruct the roads that Hooker needed to march to Rossville. Hooker lost 3 hours building a bridge across the creek and it was late afternoon before his men took their places on Missionary Ridge.

From his post on Orchard Knob, Grant realized that Sherman's attacks had failed to gain their objective and that Hooker had been delayed in reaching his assigned position. To relieve some of the pressure on Sherman, Grant ordered Thomas to move out against the Confederate center on Missionary Ridge.

The ridge that lay before the Union troops was rough and steep. It rose from 200 to 400 feet higher than the level ground at its base. Its steep slopes were broken by ravines, strewn with boulders, and dotted with stumps, the latter reminders of recently felled timber. The first line of Confederate breastworks was at the foot of the ridge. Some unfinished works had been built half-way up the slope. Finally, a third line of works was built on the natural, instead of the military, crest of the hill. Thus, Confederate fire from the crest could not cover some of the ravine approaches.

Four Union divisions—Baird, Wood, Sheridan, and R. W. Johnson, from left to right—started toward the ridge. The hard charging Union soldiers soon overwhelmed the gray defenders in the rifle pits at the base of the ridge. Scarcely halting, and generally without orders to continue, the men in blue charged up the ridge. They followed the retreating Confederates so closely from the rifle pits that the Confederates on the crest in many places hesitated to fire for fear of hitting their own men. It was not long before units of the Army of the Cumberland pierced the Confederate line in several places and sent Bragg's veterans reeling in retreat down the east slope of the ridge toward Chickamauga Creek. Sheridan pushed forward in pursuit of the retreating army, capturing men, artillery, and equipment. Even though the Confederate center had disintegrated, Hardee held his position on the Confederate right until darkness, and then began his withdrawal with Cleburne's Division covering the retreat. Bragg's army crossed Chickamauga Creek during the night, carrying out a surprisingly successful retreat.

During the evening of the 25th, Grant issued orders to Thomas and Sherman to pursue Bragg. The next morning, Sherman advanced by way of Chickamauga Station, and Thomas' troops marched on the Rossville Road toward Graysville and Ringgold. In the vicinity of

A skirmish line and regimental line behind it—Union troops drilling at Chattanooga, circa January 1864. This gives a conception of how the soldiers of the Civil War ordinarily fought. A skirmish line moved ahead of the main regimental line, which charged upon order. The Union attack on Missionary Ridge must have looked something like this to watching Confederate soldiers. From Miller's, *Photographic History of the Civil War.*

Ringgold, Cleburne's Confederates held a strong position on Taylor's Ridge covering Bragg's retreat. Cleburne's men repulsed a Union attack, inflicting heavy casualties, until Bragg's army had successfully withdrawn southward, and then they followed. Union troops then occupied Taylor's Ridge. There the pursuit stopped.

This decisive Union victory raised the siege of Chattanooga.

The following tabulation of strength and casualties at the Battle of Chattanooga is based on Livermore's studies:

Army	Total Strength	Total Casualties	Killed	Wounded	Missing	Percent Casualties
Union	56,360	5,824	753	4,722	349	10
Confederate	46,165	6,667	361	2,160	4,146	14

Relief of Knoxville

Meanwhile, in East Tennessee, Burnside attempted to hold Longstreet in check by abandoning territory and skirmishing when necessary, but avoiding any serious fight. This took Longstreet farther away from Chattanooga and lessened his opportunity to assist Bragg. Burnside gained precious time by using these tactics. Grant's plan was to "whip" Bragg and then help Burnside.

After Missionary Ridge, with Bragg in full retreat, Thomas prepared to send Granger's Corps and detachments from other commands, about 20,000 men altogether, toward Knoxville. In addition, Sherman was to march along the Hiwassee River to protect Granger's flank. Grant reports that upon "Returning from the front on the 28th, I found that Granger had not yet got off . . . I therefore determined . . . to send

Gen. Joseph Hooker and his staff. Hooker is sixth from the right. Courtesy National Archives.

Steamboat with supplies for Union Army being warped up narrows of Tennessee River between Bridgeport, Ala. and Chattanooga. Courtesy *National Archives.*

him [Sherman] with his command, and orders . . . were sent him at Calhoun to assume command of the troops with Granger, in addition to those with him, and proceed, with all possible dispatch, to the relief of Burnside."

Skirmishing was more or less continuous around Knoxville. Burnside followed the original plan of buying time by giving up ground and fell back toward Knoxville, withdrawing into the city during the night of November 16–17. Longstreet drew up before the city the next day, and on the 29th made his initial attack against the Union position at Fort Sanders. The assault was repulsed and before it could be renewed Longstreet received word of Bragg's defeat on Missionary Ridge. The Confederate commander deemed it necessary to maintain a threatening position before Knoxville until the approaching Union relief columns were but a day's march distant. On December 4, Longstreet began his retreat toward Virginia. Sherman arrived on the 6th, and preparations for the pursuit of Longstreet were soon under way. Burnside's command moved out in pursuit of Longstreet's force; Granger's Corps became the garrison of Knoxville; and Sherman's command returned to Chattanooga.

Effects of the Battle of Chattanooga

The battles around Chattanooga must be considered as ending in one of the most complete victories of the war. Bragg's army was defeated, men and material captured, and the Confederates driven south. The mountainous defense line which the Confederacy hoped to hold had been pierced and large sections of it were in Union control. Chattanooga, the railroad center, was now in Union hands and the interior line of communication from this section of the Confederacy to Richmond, by way of Knoxville, was destined to remain in Union control for the remainder of the war. Not only Chattanooga, but Knoxville and the rich, food-producing East Tennessee section was lost to the Confederacy. With this came relief for the Union sympathizers in East Tennessee. Virtually all of Tennessee was now under Northern control.

The fortunes of war brought changes to both commanders. Bragg asked to be relieved from his command and went to Richmond to become military advisor to Jefferson Davis. President Lincoln promoted Grant, in March 1864, to command of all Union armies in the field. Grant then left Chattanooga for the East, to lead the attack against General Lee in Virginia.

The War After Chattanooga

In the spring of 1864, the Union armies began to move into the heart of the Confederacy. Grant attached himself to the Army of the Potomac (General Meade) and began operations against Lee; Sherman moved against Gen. Joseph E. Johnston in Georgia.

The Army of the Potomac launched a campaign against Richmond. In the bitter battles of the Wilderness and Spotsylvania Court House, in May 1864, Grant reduced Lee's offensive power. After being repulsed at Cold Harbor, Grant moved against Petersburg and a 10-month siege finally forced Lee to evacuate the city. Lee moved westward to Appomattox Court House where on April 9, 1865, Grant forced him to surrender.

While Lee and Grant fought it out in Virginia, Sherman, using Chattanooga for his base of supplies, conducted a strenuous campaign against the Army of Tennessee, first under Johnston and then Hood, finally entering Atlanta on September 2. In November, Sherman began his famous "march to the sea," reaching Savannah in late December. From there he struck northward through the Carolinas and forced the surrender of Joseph E. Johnston's army on April 26. By June all isolated Confederate forces had laid down their arms.

Brotherton House, scene of Confederate breakthrough, Chickamauga Battlefield.
Courtesy Chattanoogans, Inc.

Union monuments along Battleline Road, Chickamauga Battlefield.

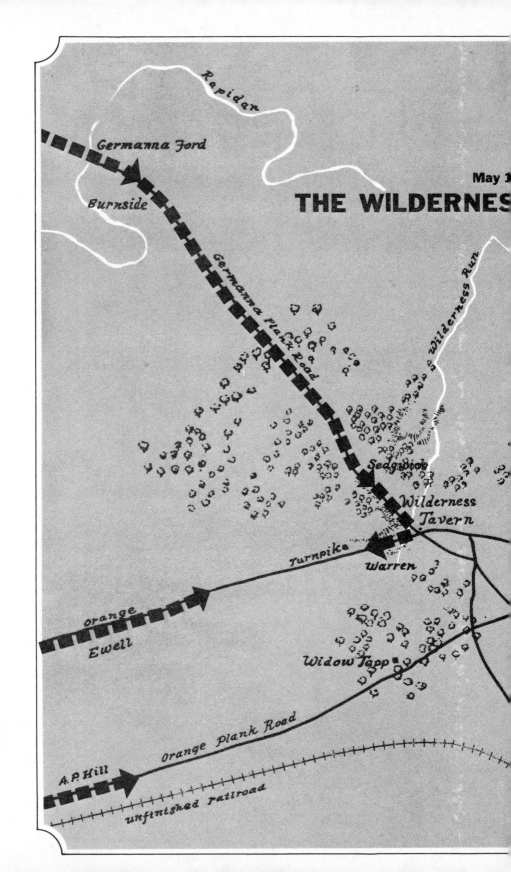

THE WILDERNES

May 1

Rapidan

Germanna Ford

Burnside

Germanna Plank Road

Wilderness Run

Sedgwick

Wilderness Tavern

Turnpike

Warren

Orange

Ewell

Widow Tapp

Orange Plank Road

A. P. Hill

unfinished railroad

Ulysses S. Grant

Hancock

CHAPTER XII

Battles of
The Wilderness
and Spotsylvania

Death hung in the air

IN MARCH 1864 President Lincoln appointed Gen. Ulysses
S. Grant commanding general of all the Union armies. Said
Grant:

> In the east the opposing forces stood in substantially
> the same relations toward each other as three years be-
> fore, or when the war began; they were both between
> the Federal and Confederate Capitals. Battles had been
> fought of as great severity as had ever been known in
> war . . . from the James River to Gettysburg, with in-
> decisive results.

He hoped to change this situation by putting pressure on all
Confederate armies at the same time, something that had never
been done before.

Lee's strategy had always been to "risk some points in order
to have a sufficient force concentrated, with the hope of dealing
a successful blow when opportunity favors." He believed "as
the enemy cannot attack all points at one time . . . the troops
could be concentrated . . . where an assault should be made."
With its interior, or shorter, lines of communication the South
could so concentrate its forces.

This is exactly what Grant realized and wished to prevent.
The way to prevent the Confederates from concentrating, as he saw
it, was to put and keep pressure on all points at all times, so that
the South would be unable to continue its thus successful strategy.

w Homer's painting
ts the vague nature of
nting in the Wilderness,
the thickets broke up
:tlelines and the
, more often than
mained unseen.

ONCE MORE
INTO THE
FOREST

Grant's plan called for Gen. Benjamin Butler to march up the
south side of the James River and attack Petersburg or Richmond,
or both, and for Gen. Franz Sigel to push down the Shenandoah
Valley driving Gen. Jubal Early before him, thereby protecting
Washington. Gen. Nathaniel Banks in New Orleans would
march on Mobile; Gen. William T. Sherman would cut across
Georgia driving Gen. Joseph E. Johnston before him, take
Atlanta, and if necessary swing north to Richmond; Meade's

353

Army of the Potomac, with Grant actually in command, was to push Lee's Army of Northern Virginia and capture Richmond. As Grant stated: "To get possession of Lee's Army was the first great object. With the capture of his army Richmond would necessarily follow."

Lee was well aware of Grant's determination. He wrote to Jefferson Davis:

> The importance of this campaign to the administration of Mr. Lincoln and to General Grant leaves no doubt that every effort and every sacrifice will be made to secure its success.

He realized that he had to destroy Grant's army before he got to the James River. "If he gets there it will become a siege, and then it will be a mere question of time." To accomplish this, his strategy was to inflict such heavy losses on Grant that either he would abandon the campaign or the North would become tired of so costly a struggle and not reelect Lincoln.

The campaign began on May 4 when the Army of the Potomac crossed the Rapidan at Ely's and Germanna Fords and headed into the Wilderness. Grant wanted to turn Lee's flank and get him out from behind his fortifications at Mine Run, farther up the river, so he risked battle in the Wilderness even though he could not use his preponderance of forces to best advantage.

That night Gen. Gouverneur Warren's V and Sedgwick's VI Corps encamped at a strategic crossroads near the Wilderness Tavern. Here the Germanna Plank Road leading south crossed the Orange Turnpike, running east and west. South of the turnpike, but before it met the Orange Plank Road, the continuation of the Germanna Road crossed Brock Road. Hancock's II Corps camped around the crossroads at Chancellorsville, where the Ely's Ford Road met the turnpike. Burnside's IX Corps was still north of the river.

A line of James Wadsworth's Union division goes into action on May 6. Waud wrote on the drawing that 'it was near this spot that the stout old general, much admired by his troops, was killed.

Many of the men remembered later that a sad silence settled over the army that night. The cry of the whippoorwill echoed through the deep shadows. Bones of the unburied dead from the Chancellorsville battle just over a year before gave a gruesome air to the place and sapped the morale of the new men in the blue ranks. Around the campfires in the stillness of the woods, even the veterans were unusually quiet, haunted by memories and premonitions. One recalled that they all seemed to have "a sense of ominous dread which many of us found almost impossible to shake off." Under soft stars the pickets near the Wilderness Tavern heard a rumbling far off to the west and guessed that the Confederates were moving somewhere in the night to meet them.

They guessed right. Because of the size of the Federal forces, Lee did not contest the crossing of the Rapidan. Instead, he planned to strike Grant's right flank in the area of the Wilderness where the Federal artillery would be practically disabled and he could use his smaller force to best advantage.

At the first streaks of dawn the Federal army was on the move. Hancock marched south from Chancellorsville and then angled slightly west to unite with Warren, who then moved south from Wilderness Tavern, followed by Sedgwick. Warren wisely took the precaution of leaving Gen. Charles Griffin's division on the turnpike to guard his right flank while he started his other two divisions south

As Griffin's men moved west the air became still and sultry, the dry underbrush crackling beneath their feet. From beyond the trees in their front came the dull popping of the skirmishers' guns. Yellow slits of light began to blink along the regimental lines and little balls of smoke, gray and compact, floated upward in the stifling air. Minie balls buzzed among the branches and slapped into the trees. Leaves and pine needles showered down like the first splatter of a sudden summer storm. The whirlwind of battle fast approached.

The Federals ran into Gen. Richard Ewell's corps advancing east on the turnpike, the first of Lee's force to make contact.

As the troops on both sides spread north and south of the turnpike, they disappeared into the twilight gloom of the dense foliage among the gnarled and twisted tree trunks. Soon the woods echoed to the roar of cannon, the crack of musketry, the angry, confused shouts of men trying desperately to kill each other.

When Grant realized that this was more than just a Confederate reconnoitering force on his flank, he quickly suspended the movement south. Warren's other two divisions were ordered back and went into line south of the turnpike on Griffin's left, and Sedgwick was moved north of the turnpike on Griffin's right. Hancock was to swing west and hold the strategic Orange Plank and Brock crossroads, where only a thin line of cavalry patrolled it. But when Lee sent A. P. Hill's corps down the Orange Plank Road, quickly driving off the Federal cavalry, Grant realized Hancock could not get there in time, so Gen. George Getty's division of Sedgwick's corps was rushed over to fill the gap until Hancock could come up.

In this hasty sketch by Waud Francis Barlow's Union division pushes forward into smoke-filled underbrush on May 6, 1864. Some of the wounded were carried to safety, as Waud depicts below. Others were consumed by the flames.

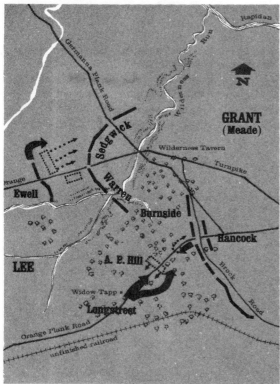

The Battle of the Wilderness, May 6, 1864.

Fighting near the junction
of the Orange Plank and
Brock Roads, a line of
Winfield Hancock's VI
Corps looses a volley in
the above sketch by
Edwin Forbes. Below,
a supply wagon brings
ammunition to troops of
Gouverneur Warren's V
Corps in the Wilderness.

THE
FLAMING
WILDERNESS

During the day fighting raged furiously all along the line,
from south of the Orange Plank Road to north of the turnpike—
fighting such as these two armies had never seen before and
would never see again. Troops could not maneuver in the wild
country, battlelines broke into tiny fragments, nobody could see
anything at all. Line officers guessed at the progress of the battle
by the sound of the musketry. Regiments, brigades, and even
divisions became inextricably mixed. Yet, in fighting as vicious
as any in the whole war, neither side gave an inch. Here and
there the dry underbrush caught fire, adding to the horror and
confusion, and many of the wounded burned to death in the
flaming Wilderness.

In the hot, still air the thick smoke clung to the ground before
lifting, and through it muskets flashed and crackled as men fired
blindly. The noise roared to a crescendo that left them dazed.
Regimental and company commanders lost communication and
control in the dense forest, amid the underbrush, swamps, creeks,
smoke, flames, and noise. In some places even companies had
to advance or retreat in single file, never knowing who or what
was on their left or right.

As the sunset faded, darkness finally settled like a gently re-
straining hand over the horror and confusion on the field. Mo-
tionless forms covered the ground in grotesque positions, as if
carelessly heaved there. That night, in the flickering light of
candles and lanterns, stretcher bearers worked to carry in the
wounded and dying.

The next morning it began all over again. Hancock had reached the Brock Road late the previous afternoon, just in time to save Getty's division from being driven off by A. P. Hill, and now was firmly entrenched along it. When Burnside's IX Corps came up, Grant used it to try to fill the gap between Hancock's right and Warren's left. The entire army was now committed to action, and Grant ordered Hancock to drive Hill back and roll up Lee's right flank before Longstreet's corps could arrive. Sedgwick and Warren were to keep pressure on Ewell to prevent Lee from shifting forces from left to right to help Hill.

Hill's men had fought all the previous day and were trying to straighten out their lines that morning when Hancock's relatively fresh troops hit them and drove them west along the Orange Plank Road. About 2 miles west of the crossroads was a meager little clearing in the woods around the Widow Tapp farm. Here stood Lee himself among some parked guns trying to rally the men. Another mile west and the Federals would be around his right flank and among his supply trains, and the whole Army of Northern Virginia would be in grave danger.

But as Hancock's men emerged from the woods into the Tapp clearing, the massed Confederate cannon blasted them back. Before they could regroup for another advance, Longstreet's troops appeared dramatically on the field at the most crucial moment of the battle for Lee. The furious fighting continued all day, but Longstreet had stopped Hancock's advance. By swinging south of the Plank Road he had overlapped the Federal left, and forced Hancock to withdraw behind his works along the Brock Road. Confederate attempts to capture these works failed, and, in the process of reconnoitering, Longstreet was wounded. Gen. A. H. Anderson then assumed command of the corps.

As night came on, it was evident to both Lee and Grant that the two armies were now entrenched so strongly that attack by either side could be suicidal. The struggle in the Wilderness was over. The Federals lost 15,387 out of 118,000 in killed, wounded, and missing; the Confederates 11,400 out of 62,000.

Grant pounds southward

THE FIGHT FOR THE SALIENT

INSTEAD of retreating to lick his wounds as other Federal commanders had done, Grant again decided to move around Lee's right flank by sliding leftward and southward. South and slightly east of the Wilderness area was another strategic crossroads at the village of Spotsylvania Court House. The village itself was just a sleepy hamlet, a handful of houses scattered about a country crossroads, but Federal possession would seriously endanger the Confederate line of communication to Richmond.

During the night of May 7, Warren was ordered to pull out of line and proceed toward Spotsylvania Court House by way of the Brock Road, passing behind Burnside's and Hancock's corps. Sedgwick would follow Warren by way of Chancellorsville and the Piney Branch Church Road to where it met the Brock Road. Burnside would proceed farther east and take the Fredericksburg-Spotsylvania Court House Road. When the rest of the army had moved, Hancock would follow Warren on the Brock Road. The cavalry had been ordered to clear the way.

In the blackness of the night the men stumbled along the unfamiliar country roads, falling into ditches, tripping over underbrush, floundering in swamps, walking into bushes and limbs of trees. Some fell asleep marching; imagination played havoc as mirages appeared before tired eyes; a clump of trees became a group of the enemy, a runaway horse, a cavalry charge. Faces of lost buddies seemed to stare out between the silent trees. "It is no small tax upon one's endurance to remain marching all night," one veteran recalled. "During the day there is always something to attract the attention and amuse, but at night there is nothing."

Warren reached Todd's Tavern on the Brock Road about 3 a.m., but here he was halted by Confederate and Union cavalry blocking the road. The delay enabled Anderson's corps to take up an entrenched position on the high ground, about a mile and a half northwest of the vital crossroads. Warren attacked him about 8 o'clock but was beaten back. Later in the day Sedgwick came up and formed on Warren's left, while Ewell formed on Anderson's right just in time to repulse another Federal attack. Then Hill's corps, now under Early because of Hill's illness, formed on Ewell's right, and Hancock came into line on Warren's right.

That night Grant ordered his cavalry, under Gen. Philip Sheridan, to make a raid around Lee's army to disrupt his communications with Richmond, and then to proceed south to reprovision his force from Butler's army south of the James River. Grant believed Lee would be forced to send Stuart's cavalry after Sheridan, and this in effect would protect the Union supply trains from Confederate cavalry raids. Lee did send Stuart after Sheridan, and in a later engagement of the two cavalry forces at Yellow Tavern, on the outskirts of Richmond, Stuart was killed.

The next day, May 9, Grant, misled by reports that Lee was withdrawing from the Federal right, ordered Hancock across the Po River to take Lee in flank and rear. Before Hancock could make contact, however, the mistake was realized, and he was recalled. In recrossing the river he was attacked by Early who had marched from the Confederate right to block his advance. Hancock extricated himself from the dangerous position and went into line again on the left of the VI Corps, now under Gen. Horatio Wright. Sedgwick had been killed by a Confederate sharpshooter. Burnside held the left of the Union army, next to Hancock. Then came Wright and Warren holding the right flank.

Lee had Anderson on his left opposite Warren and Wright. Ewell was in front of Hancock, and Early on the right facing Burnside. All were strongly entrenched. There was one weak spot in the line, however. Ewell's entrenchments jutted out in a U-shaped salient beyond the rest of the lines. It was nearly a mile deep and half a mile wide. The "Mule Shoe," as the Confederates called it, made an inviting target.

On May 10 Col. Emory Upton, of Wright's corps, attacked the west side of the salient with 12 picked regiments. He ordered the assault made with four lines of three regiments each. When the first line reached the salient, they planned to fan out left and right to take the Confederate troops in flank, while the remaining regiments went straight ahead to stop any reinforcements that might be sent up. After some brief, but desperate, hand-to-hand fighting, the attack succeeded, but when the expected support from Gen. Gershom Mott's division of Hancock's corps failed to appear, the Federals were forced to withdraw.

Upton's plan had worked, however, and Grant now decided to use the same tactics on a larger scale. Hancock was ordered to break the salient at its weakest point, the apex, supported by Burnside and Wright attacking the east and west sides. Warren would keep pressure on Anderson in his front, at the same time

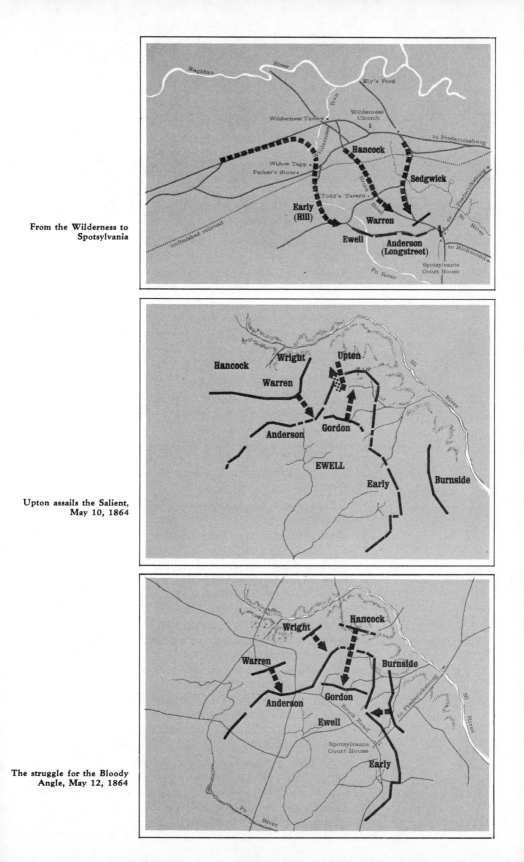

From the Wilderness to
Spotsylvania

Upton assails the Salient,
May 10, 1864

The struggle for the Bloody
Angle, May 12, 1864

holding himself ready to support the other corps if need
Again, as in the Wilderness, the whole army was committed
action.

In the predawn darkness of May 12, rain set in, wrapp
the area in a sullen mist. The drops ticked off the leaves mor
onously as Hancock's men formed for the attack, stumbl
through the dark, the rain, and the mud.

Their noisy approach alerted the Confederate pickets that t
would be no small attack. Ewell knew that the apex of
salient was his weakest point and had placed 22 guns the
But Lee, misled by a report that Grant was moving around
right flank again, ordered the guns to the rear to be ready
move quickly if necessary. Now they were frantically gallop
up to the front again, arriving just in time for 20 of them to
captured without firing a shot.

In the early morning rain, the massed Federal column
the apex of the salient and broke through, capturing over 3,0
Confederates, while Burnside and Wright assaulted the sic
The blue-clad troops poured through the gap. But, instead
fanning out to the left and right to widen the breach and ena
Burnside and Wright to come through, they went straight ahe
Again, as in the Wilderness, Lee appeared on the field to ra
his men in this critical moment. If the assault succeeded,
Army of Northern Virginia might be cut in two. But the tim
arrival of reserves from Early's corps stopped the advance, a
the Federals were driven back to the captured trenches. T
heavy fighting raged all day and into the night as Lee vai
sought to recover the position. Although he failed in this
tempt, the Confederates did hold until Lee could build n
works at the base of the Mule Shoe to straighten his line.

A few hundred yards west of the apex the Confederate trenc
made a slight bend to the south. Here the men of Wright's co
came face to face with Ewell's veterans in brutal hand-to-ha
fighting. Clubbed muskets and bayonets were used freely, as
rain came down in sheets and the trenches ran red with blo
In some places the wounded and dying of both sides were tra
pled into the mud in the frantic fighting. "The flags of bo
armies waved at the same moment over the same breastwork

Forbes drawing at
diers of Hancock's
s clear a field of fire
e Brock Road on
1864, a position
d only with hard
and heavy losses.
vs later his Union
massed for the dawn
n Lee's salient
. The fighting there
e of the toughest
ntire war. At one
rote Hancock, the
delines were so close
Confederate flags
one side of the
ments while ours
the other, only
d by the parapet, the
s firing into each
faces.' The Confed-
low lies at the foot
ricade he had
d during Ewell's
n the Union right
19.

one soldier noted, "while beneath them Federal and Confederate endeavored to drive home the bayonet through the interstices of the logs. The fire was so intense, that in one instance an oak tree, nearly two feet in diameter, was cut through by bullets. . . ." Since that day this area has been known as the "Bloody Angle."

During the night Lee's men withdrew to their new line at the base of the salient. Then a tragic silence settled over the field. In the dark woods, surgeons were busy amputating by the eerie glow of lanterns. The very air was sick and troubled. The night was deep with grief.

A comparative lull settled over the area for the next several days as Grant continued to maneuver his left farther eastward and southward. On May 18 Hancock made a last attempt to break Ewell's new line, but this time the attack was blasted by 30 massed cannon and beaten back before it even reached the Confederate position. The next day Ewell tried to find a weak spot on the Federal right flank but was quickly repulsed. The battle of Spotsylvania Court House was over. Union losses in killed, wounded, and missing were 17,555; Confederate losses are unknown.

ANOTHER MARCH

As in the Wilderness, there had been no victory and no defeat, only mud, blood, and death. But one fact was becoming clear: Grant would not turn back under any circumstances. Despite his heavier losses, he was slowly but methodically destroying Lee's ability to wage offensive war. Death, disease, and desertion were slowly dissolving the proud Army of Northern Virginia.

So, 2 days later, the armies marched away from the fields of Spotsylvania. Yet for the men of Lee and Grant, now grappling southward in a twilight struggle, even more glory and agony lay ahead. Another year's fighting at Cold Harbor, Richmond, and Petersburg would follow before peace drifted in with the spring-tide of 1865 at a dusty village called Appomattox Court house.

Federal trenches at Cold Harbor.   From a contemporary sketch.

Federal coehorn mortars at Cold Harbor.   From a contemporary sketch.

CHAPTER XIII

The Final Struggle for Richmond

THE FINAL STRUGGLE FOR
RICHMOND, 1864–65

Lincoln's New Commander

In March 1864 President Lincoln appointed Gen. Ulysses S. Grant as commanding general of all the Union armies. Said Grant: "In the east the opposing forces stood in substantially the same relations toward each other as three years before, or when the war began; they were both between the Federal and Confederate Capitals. Battles had been fought of as great severity as had ever been known in war * * * from the James River to Gettysburg, with indecisive results." He hoped to change this situation by putting pressure on all Confederate armies at the same time, something that had never been done before.

Grant's plan called for Gen. Benjamin F. Butler to march up the south side of the James and attack Petersburg or Richmond or both; Gen. Franz Sigel to push down the Shenandoah Valley driving Gen. Jubal Early before him, thereby protecting Washington; Gen. Nathaniel Banks in New Orleans to march on Mobile; Gen. William T. Sherman to cut across Georgia driving Johnston before him, take Atlanta, and if necessary swing north to Richmond; Meade's Army of the Potomac, with Grant in command, to push Lee's Army of Northern Virginia and capture Richmond. As Grant stated: "Lee, with the Capital of the Confederacy, was the main end to which all were working."

Lee's objective now was to stop Grant and protect Richmond. Said Lee: "We must destroy this army of Grant's before he gets to the James River. If he gets there it will become a siege, and then it will be a mere question of time."

The campaign started in the spring of 1864 when the Army of the Potomac crossed the Rapidan River and the Army of Northern Virginia blocked its path at the Wilderness. After a particularly vicious and costly battle, Grant instead of retreating to lick his wounds as other Federal commanders had done, executed a left flank movement, still heading south and trying to get between Lee and Richmond. A few days later the two armies clashed again at Spotsylvania in a series of grim battles, but still indecisive as far as major objectives were concerned. Although Grant's losses were staggering, he was slowly but methodically destroying Lee's ability to wage offensive war.

Gen. Ulysses S. Grant.   From a contemporary sketch.

Again Grant executed a left flank movement to get around Lee, and then by a series of flanking marches, which the Confederate soldiers called the "sidling movement," and the Union soldiers the "jughandle" movement, Grant gradually worked his way down to Cold Harbor.

Cold Harbor

Where and what was Cold Harbor? Cold Harbor was a seedy-looking tavern, squatting by a dusty crossroads 8 miles from Richmond, on the flat, featureless plain, intersected by hundreds of small

Cold Harbor Tavern.   From a photograph taken in 1885 as it appears in *Battles and Leaders of the Civil War.*

creeks, gullies, and swamps, that is characteristic of the land between the Pamunkey and the Chickahominy Rivers.   There wasn't
a harbor for miles and it was anything but cold.   It was the only
Cold Harbor in the United States, although there were many Cold
Harbors on the stagecoach routes along the Thames River in England.   The name indicated a place to get a bed for the night and
something cold to drink, but not hot meals.

But these dusty crossroads were strategically important if Grant
was to attack Richmond, and both Lee and Grant realized it.   Also,
it was Grant's last chance to continue his strategy of trying to get
between Lee and Richmond—any more flanking movements and Lee
would be in the entrenchments around the Confederate Capital
where Grant did not want to fight him.   As Grant stated: "Richmond was fortified and entrenched so perfectly that one man inside
to defend was more than equal to five outside besieging or assaulting."

It is significant that Lee also did not want to fight in the entrenchments around Richmond.   There he would be on the defensive, and
in such a position could not possibly destroy Grant's army.   So both
commanders were willing for the test.

And what of the lowly foot-soldier, the unsung hero in the ranks,
the poor bloody infantryman?   Was he ready for the awful test?

Confederate camp.   From a contemporary sketch.

To the average soldier, this whole campaign was fast becoming just a series of hazy, indistinct recollections, like the fragments of a half-forgotten dream: Long columns of sweat-soaked soldiers marching over hills and rivers and swamps, across ploughed fields and corn fields, down endless dusty roads through dark, lonely woods; 30 days of marching by night and fighting by day, until it must have seemed to them that the only things left in life were stupefying fatigue, merciless heat, choking dust, smoke and noise, mud and blood.

In the Union ranks many of the men began to find out for the first time what hunger really was. They had moved so fast and so often the ration wagons were left far behind. Hardtack was selling for a dollar apiece—if you could find a seller. And here at Cold Harbor the soldiers wrote their names and regiments on pieces of paper and pinned or sewed them to the inside of their dirty blouses, with the forlorn hope that if and when they were killed someone might take the time to find out who they were.

To Lee's barefoot, ragged veterans, hunger had been a constant companion for a long time, but at Cold Harbor they approached starvation. A Confederate sergeant recorded in his diary: "When we reached Cold Harbor the command to which I belonged had been marching almost continuously day and night for more than fifty hours without food, and for the first time we knew what actual starvation was." When scurvy appeared among the men, owing primarily to a lack of fresh vegetables, Lee advised them to eat the roots of the sassafras and wild grape, if they could find any.

In the race for initial possession of the crossroads at Cold Harbor, Lee's cavalry won by a few hours. But in the afternoon of May 31 Gen. Philip Sheridan's cavalry drove them out and held the crossroads until relieved by the Federal VI Corps under Gen. Horatio Wright. Most of Sheridan's troopers were armed with the new Spencer repeating carbine, which made dismounted cavalrymen effective infantry.

The next morning, June 1, Lee threw Gen. Richard Anderson's corps (Longstreet's old corps—Longstreet having been wounded in the Wilderness) against the Federal VI Corps in a bold attempt to sieze the crossroads and roll up Grant's left flank before he could reinforce it, but Anderson was repulsed. Grant then moved the XVIII Corps under "Baldy" Smith, which he had borrowed from Butler's army bottled up on the south side of the James, over to the right of the VI Corps. That afternoon they attacked Anderson, now supported by Gen. Robert Hoke's division.

The assault failed to break the Confederate line, but it did bend it back in several places. Grant believed that with a greater concentration a breakthrough could be achieved. Consequently, he ordered the II Corps under Gen. Winfield Hancock over to the left of the VI Corps, between it and the Chickahominy River, and planned an all out attack by the three corps for the morning of June 2.

Anticipating the move, Lee put A. P. Hill, supported by Gen. John Breckinridge's division, over to his right between Anderson and the Chickahominy and waited.

The expected attack failed to materialize, however. Hancock got lost in the woods and swamps moving to his assigned position, and after an all-night forced march the men were too exhausted to mount an attack. Any chance the assault might have had for success was now gone. The delay was fortunate for Lee because Breckinridge also got lost and was not in position to support Hill on the morning of June 2. The attack was then ordered for that afternoon but again postponed until 4:30 the morning of June 3. And each corps commander received a telegram from Grant's headquarters that read: "Corps Commanders will employ the interim in making examinations of the ground in their front and perfecting arrangements for the assault."

Lee's veterans took advantage of this fatal 24-hour delay to entrench themselves quickly and effectively, using every creek, gully, ravine, and swamp in such fashion that all approaches to their positions could be covered with a murderous fire. A newspaper reporter present at Cold Harbor wrote a vivid description of those entrenchments. "They are intricate, zig-zagged lines within lines, lines protecting flanks of lines, lines built to enfilade opposing lines * * * works within works and works outside works, each laid out with some definite design."

Lee needed this strong position; he would fight at Cold Harbor without a reserve. He wrote to Jefferson Davis: "If I shorten my lines to provide a reserve, he will turn me; if I weaken my lines to provide a reserve, he will break them."

Grant's battle plan was relatively uncomplicated. It was, essentially, a simple, frontal assault. Hancock's II Corps and Wright's VI Corps, between the Chickahominy and the Cold Harbor road (now State Route 156), together with Smith's XVIII Corps north of the road, were to attack all out and break the Confederate lines. Gen. Gouverneur Warren's V Corps, north of the XVIII, was to be held in reserve, while Burnside's IX Corps, on Grant's extreme right, was not to enter the fight unless Lee weakened his line in that sector, then it would attack, supported by the V Corps. Lee did not weaken any part of his line, so these two corps were not engaged to any appreciable extent. Thus the battle actually took place on approximately a 2½-mile front, although the armies stretched for 6 miles from south to north, with the Union army facing west. Grant's total strength was over 100,000 men, but less than 50,000 were actually engaged in the struggle.

Lee now had A. P. Hill, supported by Breckinridge, on his south flank next to the Chickahominy opposite Hancock and Wright. Hoke's division straddled the Cold Harbor road with Gen. Joseph Kershaw's division just north of Hoke, then Anderson and Gen. Richard Ewell's corps. Lee's total strength consisted of less than 60,000 men, but only about half were involved in the action of June 3.

It rained all night the night of June 2. Toward morning the heavy rain died to a soft, sticky mist that held the area in clammy fingers. The first gray streaks of dawn warned of the approach of a scorching sun that would turn the rain-soaked plain, with its myriad streams and swamps, into a steaming cauldron. Promptly at 4:30 the three corps jumped off to the attack, knowing nothing of the strength of the Confederate positions they would have to face. The corps commanders had ignored Grant's telegraphed order of the previous afternoon and no proper reconnaissance was made.

The average soldier saw little in any battle in the Civil War, and even less at Cold Harbor because of the terrain. But as the first yellow rays of the sun shifted the gray mists, most of the Union soldiers could see the main line of Confederate entrenchments across the open spaces in front of them—a tracing of raw earth that had been turned up like a huge furrow, along a line of uneven ridges, looking empty but strangely ominous. Here and there bright regimental colors perched insolently on the dirt hills.

Suddenly, it seemed, the line was dotted with black slouch hats and glistening bayonets. Yellow sheets of flame flashed from end to end, then disappeared in a heavy cloud of smoke. Regiment after regiment exploded into action with a metallic roar. Gigantic crashes of artillery split the air. Shells screamed overhead like a pack of banshees, exploding in clouds of earth, horses, and men. The noise roared to a crescendo with a volume of sound that left the men dazed and confused. One veteran said it was more like a volcanic blast than a battle.

It was over in less than 30 minutes, but 7,000 killed and wounded Union soldiers were left lying in the sun between the trenches. Said one general sadly: "In that little period more men fell bleeding as they advanced than in any other like period of time throughout the war."

Those not already killed or wounded threw themselves on the ground and desperately heaved up little mounds of earth in front of them with bayonets, spoons, cups, and broken canteens. They could neither advance nor retreat—nothing standing could live long in that hail of lead and iron. They just dug in and stayed there.

A peculiar thing about the battle came to light afterwards. The three corps commanders sent identical telegrams to Grant's headquarters, each accusing the other of not supporting him in the attack. Later it was discovered what had actually happened. Hancock, on the left, had veered to his left because of the heavy fire from there and the peculiarities of the terrain. Wright, in the center, had gone straight ahead. And Smith, on the right, bore off to his right because of swamps and ravines. So the farther they advanced the more separated they became and the more their flanks were left open to a deadly crossfire.

No other major assault was attempted by either army, although the troops stayed in the hot, filthy trenches until June 12, with constant, nerve-wracking sharpshooting and skirmishing. From June 1 to 12 the Union losses totaled 12,700; Confederate losses are estimated at between 1,500 and 2,000.

Cold Harbor proved to be Lee's last major victory in the field, and although it was a military zero so far as Grant was concerned, it turned out to be one of the most important and significant battles fought during the Civil War. The results of this battle changed the course of the war in the east from a war of maneuver to a war of siege. It also influenced the strategy and tactics of future wars

Looking for a friend at Cold Harbor.   From a contemporary sketch.

by showing that well-selected, well-manned entrenchments, adequately supported by artillery, were practically impregnable to frontal assaults.

On June 5, Grant decided to bypass Richmond, cross the James and attack Petersburg, an important railway center 25 miles south of the Confederate Capital. This would still keep Lee's army pinned down, and if successful would cut communications between Richmond and the rest of the Confederacy.

On June 6 he withdrew Warren's V Corps from the lines and used it to secure the passages across the Chickahominy and down to the James. On June 7 he sent Sheridan, with two divisions of cavalry, back into the Shenandoah Valley against Early. To counter this, Lee was forced to send Gen. Wade Hampton's cavalry after Sheridan, which in effect left Lee without adequate cavalry. During the night of June 12 Grant secretly moved all the troops out of the trenches at Cold Harbor, without Lee's being aware of the move until the following morning, and by June 16 the Army of the Potomac of over 100,000 men, 5,000 wagons, 2,800 head of cattle, and 25,000 horses and mules, were all safely across the James River. Richmond was saved for another 10 months.

Pontoon bridge across the James.   Courtesy, National Archives.

Fort Harrison

In the pre-dawn darkness of September 29, Grant quietly slipped Gen. David Birney's X Corps and Gen. Edward Ord's XVIII Corps back across the James in a surprise move against the outer defenses of Richmond.   The primary purpose was to prevent Lee from re-enforcing Early in the Shenandoah Valley.   If, however, any weakness was discovered it could be exploited fully, and it might force Lee to weaken some part of the Petersburg line.

Shortly after daybreak Gen. George Stannard's division of the XVIII Corps successfully stormed heavily armed but badly under-manned Fort Harrison on the Varina road.   Gen. Hiram Burnham, commanding the leading brigade, was killed in the assault and the Union forces renamed the captured fort for him.   A mile and a half farther north, Gen. Adelbert Ames' division of the X Corps was repulsed in a similar attack on another fortification, Fort Gilmer, on the New Market road.

General Lee regarded the loss of Fort Harrison as serious enough to demand his personal attention.   The next day, with re-enforce-

Members of the 1st Connecticut Artillery at Fort Brady, 1864. Courtesy, Library of Congress.

ments rushed from Petersburg, he directed several vigorous assaults against the fort. However, the Union forces had closed in the rear and strengthened it, and, armed with new repeating rifles, successfully beat back the attacks and inflected heavy losses on the Confederates.

The fall of Fort Harrison forced Lee to draw back that part of his outer line and to build new entrenchments to compensate for the loss. It also forced him to extend his line north of the James, thus weakening his already dangerously undermanned defenses in front of Petersburg. The Union forces, to protect their position further and to neutralize Confederate gunboats, constructed Fort Brady a few miles south of Fort Burnham (Harrison) on a high bluff overlooking the James River.

No further serious efforts were made to enter Richmond from the north side of the James, and the two armies faced each other in these respective positions until Grant finally broke Lee's lines at Petersburg on April 1, 1865, forcing the Confederates to abandon Richmond.

Spring came gently to Richmond that year of 1865. The winter had been long and hard. After a cold, wet March, Sunday, April 2, dawned mild and pleasant. The green buds on the trees and the bright new grass put the breath of seedtime in the air; sap flowed warm in the lilac and the magnolia. Under a rich blue sky the people strolled leisurely to church amid the cheerful music of the bells and the soft murmur of the James River falls.

In St. Paul's Episcopal Church, at the corner of Ninth and Grace streets, Jefferson Davis sat in the family pew listening to the sermon. The sexton walked up the aisle and handed him a message from General Lee.

"I advise that all preparation be made for leaving Richmond tonight."

Davis arose quietly and left the church, walked a block down Ninth street to his office in the War Department and gave the necessary orders for evacuation.

Late in the afternoon the official order was posted—then pandemonium reigned. Trunks, boxes, bundles of every description were piled on the sidewalks and in the streets. Wagons, carts, buggies, anything that had wheels and could move, were loaded and raced through the city to fight their way across Mayo's Bridge in the mad rush to cross the James and flee south.

A frantic mob trampled each other without mercy and jammed the streets leading to the railroad stations, only to be turned back by soldiers' bayonets. The few trains that would manage to leave were reserved for government officials, archives, the treasury, and military personnel.

Early in the evening the character of the crowds began to change. From a city of less than 38,000 before the war, Richmond now had over 100,000 people jammed into every available nook and cranny. They had come by the thousands to work for the various government departments and in the munitions factories. Refugees from the many battles fought in Virginia had poured in, as well as the sick and wounded, followed inevitably by deserters, spies, criminals, gamblers, speculators, and derelicts of every kind.

And now the cheap hotels, saloons, and gambling dens began to empty their customers into the streets, many of them half drunk.

All semblance of law and order disappeared. When the guards at the State penitentiary fled, the prisoners broke loose to roam the city at will. The provost guard took the prisoners of war from Libby Prison down the river to be exchanged. This left only the Local Defense Brigade, consisting of government and munitions workers. But most of them were required in government buildings to pack and burn records; some guarded the railroad depots, while others were engaged in destruction assignments. The order had been given to burn all tobacco and cotton that could not be removed by tossing flaming balls of tar into the warehouses along the riverfront.

In the meantime, Mayor Mayo and the city council had appointed a committee in each ward to see that all liquor was destroyed, and shortly after midnight they set to work. Casks and barrels of the finest southern bourbons were rolled to the curbs, the tops smashed open and left to drain.

Like flies around honey, the mobs swarmed and fought their way into the streets where the whiskey flowed like water. Men, women, and children, clawing and screaming, scooped it up with bare hands, or used pails, cups, basins, bottles, anything that would hold the amber liquid. They used rags on sticks dipped in whiskey for torches, and went howling through the city in search of food and plunder like a pack of mad wolves, looting, killing, burning.

The soft night sky became pink, then turned a dull red. The blaze from the Shockhoe Warehouse at Thirteenth and Cary streets, where 10,000 hogsheads of tobacco was put to the torch, flew skyward as if shot from a huge blowtorch. The flames quickly spread to the Franklin Paper Mills and the Gallego Flour Mills, 10 stories high. Higher and higher they soared, and then widened until it seemed a red hot sea of fire would engulf the whole city.

Evacuation of Richmond. From a contemporary engraving.

A faint hot breeze began to stir from the southeast, scattering burning embers through the streets and alleys and houses. Powder magazines and arsenals let go with a whooshing boom. Thousands of bullets and shells tore through buildings and ploughed up the streets. Shells exploded high in the smoke cascading a metal spray over the area, followed by the rattle of bursting cartridges in one great metallic roar. Just before daybreak a deafening explosion from the James River signalled the destruction of the Confederate warships and the Navy Yard.

Richmond was now one vast inferno of flame, noise, smoke, and trembling earth. The roaring fire swept northwestward from the riverfront, hungrily devouring the two railroad depots, all the banks, flour and paper mills, and hotels, warehouses, stores, and houses by the hundreds.

About dawn a large crowd gathered in front of the huge government commissary at Fourteenth and Cary streets, on the eastern edge of the fire. The doors were thrown open and the government clerks began an orderly distribution of the supplies. Then the drunken mob joined the crowd.

Barrels of hams, bacon, flour, molasses, sugar, coffee, and tea were rolled into the streets or thrown from windows. Women ran screaming through the flames waving sides of bacon and whole hams. Wheelbarrows were filled and trundled away. When the building finally caught fire from the whiskey torches, the mob swarmed into other sections of the doomed city where the few remaining clothing, jewelry, and furniture stores were ruthlessly looted and burned. A casket factory was broken into, the caskets loaded with plunder and carried through the streets, and the fiendish rabble roared on unchecked.

As the drunken night reeled into morning the few remaining regiments of General Kershaw's brigade, which had been guarding the lines east of Richmond, galloped into the city on their way south to join Lee in his retreat to Appomattox. They had to fight their way through the howling mob to reach Mayo's Bridge. As the rearguard clattered over, Gen. M. W. Gary shouted, "All over, good-bye; blow her to hell."

The barrels of tar placed along the bridge were promptly put to the torch. Soon tall flames shot high into the air, and with the two railroad bridges already burning, the three high-arched structures were like blazing arrows pointing to the very gates of hell.

Then down Osborne Turnpike and into Main Street trotted the Fourth Massachusetts cavalry. When the smoke and heat blocked their path, they turned into Fourteenth Street past fire engines blazing in the street and proceeded up the hill to Capitol Square, where a tragic scene awaited them.

Richmond burns. From a contemporary sketch.

Like a green oasis in a veritable desert of fire and destruction, the sloping lawn around the Capitol was jammed with frightened people seeking safety from the flames. Family groups, trying desperately to stay together, huddled under the linden trees for protection from the burning sparks. Piles of furniture were scattered in every direction—beds, chairs, settees, paintings, silverware, gilt-framed mirrors—the few possessions left, the family heirlooms, the treasures faithfully passed down from generation to generation. In the background the massive white columns of the Capitol, designed by Thomas Jefferson as a replica of the famous Maison Carée at Nimes, stood guard over the huddled masses below.

The soldiers in blue quickly dispersed the mobs at bayonet point. Guards were immediately placed to prevent further looting. The fire was contained by blowing up buildings in its path to create a fire-lane, leaving the main part to burn itself out. By nightfall everything was under control, but most of the business and industrial section of the city was gone.

The stars shone down that night on the smouldering ruins of more than 700 buildings. Gaunt chimneys stood naked against the black velvet sky. A Federal officer, picking his way through thousands of pieces of white granite columns and marble facades that littered the streets to inspect the guard, noted that the silence of death brooded over the city. Occasionally a shell exploded somewhere in the ruins. Then it was quiet again.

A week later Lee surrendered to Grant at Appomattox Court House, Va. The war was over.

Richmond after the war. Courtesy, Library of Congress.

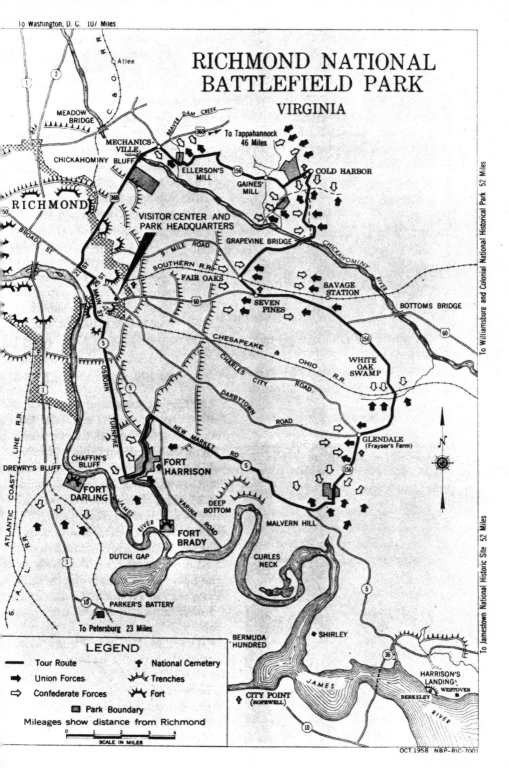

Richmond National Battlefield Park.

Union soldiers on Sycamor Street in Petersburg, April 1865. For these men, baski in the aftermath of a successful campaign, the war is almost over. To the west, General Sheridan's cavalry is racing to cut off the retreating Southern arm "If the thing is pressed," Sheridan tells Grant, "I thi Lee will surrender." Says Lincoln: "Let the thing be pressed."

CHAPTER XIV

The Campaign for Petersburg

PROLOGUE

By June 1864, when the siege of Petersburg began, the Civil War had lain heavily on both the North and the South for more than 3 years. Most of the fighting in the East during this period had taken place on the rolling Virginia countryside between the opposing capitals of Washington and Richmond, only 110 miles apart, and all of it had failed to end the war and bring peace to the land. Various generals had been placed in command of the Union's mighty Army of the Potomac and had faced Gen. Robert E. Lee's Army of Northern Virginia. So far not one had succeeded in destroying Lee's army or in capturing Richmond.

Perhaps Maj. Gen. George B. McClellan had come the closest to success when, in the late spring and early summer of 1862, his Northern troops had threatened the Confederate capital, only to be repulsed on its outskirts. The other Northern commanders who followed McClellan—Pope, Burnside, Hooker, and Meade—were less successful. Lee had met and turned aside their drives.

After 36 months of bitter conflict the war in the East seemed, to many observers, to be far from a final settlement. The failure of Union forces to deliver a decisive blow against the Army of Northern Virginia was a source of growing concern in Washington. The Confederacy, for its part, was no more successful in settling the issue. Attempted invasions of the Northern States by Lee were turned back at Antietam in September 1862 and at Gettysburg in July 1863.

Farther west the picture was brighter for Northern hopes. In the same month as the Battle of Gettysburg the Confederate stronghold of Vicksburg, Miss., fell into Union hands. A few days later, Port Hudson, La., the last remaining stronghold of the Confederacy on the banks of the Mississippi River, surrendered. Later in 1863, the Union capture of Chattanooga, Tenn., threw open the gateway to Georgia.

Strategically, despite the stalemate in Virginia, the beginning of 1864 found the Northern armies in a stronger position than the Confederate military forces. Not only was there a distinct possibility that the Southern States east of the Mississippi could be split into two parts, but the greater resources at the command of the Lincoln ad

From the Rapidan River to the James, Lt. Gen. Ulysses S. Grant (above), commanding the armies of the United States, found all his efforts to capture Richmond and destroy the Confederacy blocked by Gen. Robert E. Lee (left) and his Army of Northern Virginia. Finally, Grant turned his attention to Petersburg.

ministration were beginning to count more heavily with each passing day. All that seemed to be needed to end the war was an able Union commander who could marshal the mighty resources of his country for a last tremendous blow at the South.

Such a man was found in Maj. Gen. Ulysses S. Grant, the victor at Vicksburg and Missionary Ridge, who was brought east and, on March 9, 1864, commissioned lieutenant general to be responsible for all the Union armies. Unlike his predecessor, Henry W. Halleck, Grant decided not to remain in Washington but chose instead to accompany the Army of the Potomac, where he would provide general direction to the military operations but leave the execution of them to that army's commander, Maj. Gen. George G. Meade.

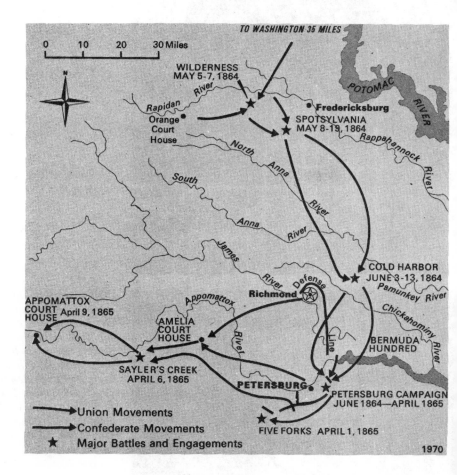

Maj. Gen. George G. Meade commanded the Army of the Potomac during the 1864–65 Virginia campaign. With General Grant actively directing most of the military operations, Meade was in the awkward position of serving much like a corps commander in his own army. He nevertheless functioned well in this difficult situation.

UNION STRATEGY 1864

To accomplish the conquest of the Confederacy, the Northern plan called for a huge two-pronged attack. Maj. Gen. William T. Sherman, in command of the southern prong, was assigned the task of destroying Gen. Joseph E. Johnston's Confederate Army of Tennessee, capturing Atlanta, marching to the sea, and then turning north to effect a junction with Grant.

It was the upper arm of the movement which was directly concerned with Richmond and Petersburg. This was composed of two armies: the Army of the Potomac and the Army of the James. It was the task of these armies to capture Richmond, crush the Army of Northern Virginia, and march south toward Sherman.

The story of the Army of the James in the early phase of the offensive can be briefly told. Maj. Gen. Benjamin F. Butler was ordered to advance upon Richmond from the southeast and threaten communications between the Confederate capital and the Southern States. With some 40,000 Union troops, the advance was begun. City Point, located at the junction of the James and Appomattox Rivers and soon to be the supply center for the attack on Petersburg, was captured on May 4, 1864. Within 2 weeks, however, a numerically inferior Confederate force shut up the Army of the James, "as if it had been in a bottle strongly corked," in Bermuda Hundred, a loop formed by the winding James and Appomattox Rivers. Here Butler waited, while north of him the Army of the Potomac and the Army of Northern Virginia engaged in a series of bloody battles.

The Battle of the Wilderness, May 5–7, 1864, began what proved to be the start of the final campaign against the Army of Northern Virginia. Here Meade's Army of the Potomac, numbering approximately 118,000 troops, fought the Confederate defenders of Richmond. Lee had about 62,000 men with him, while an additional 30,000 under Gen. P. G. T. Beauregard held the Richmond-Petersburg area. The battle resulted in a fearful loss of men on both sides, although the armies remained intact. This was followed by a series of fierce engagements around Spotsylvania Court House from May 8 to 21.

Failing to destroy the Army of Northern Virginia in these battles, Grant moved the Army of the Potomac to the east of Richmond. It was his hope that he would outflank the Confederate defenders by persistent night marches. Lee was not to be so easily outguessed, however. After minor battles at the North Anna River (May 23) and Totopotomoy Creek (May 29), Grant arrived at Cold Harbor, about 8 miles northeast of Richmond, but Lee's army still stood between him and that city. On June 3, 2 days after he arrived at Cold Harbor, Grant ordered a direct frontal assault against the Confederate lines. He was repulsed with heavy losses— about 7,000 men. "I have always regretted that the last assault at Cold Harbor was ever made," Grant would write many years later.

By the end of the first month of Grant's campaign, both sides had suffered heavy casualties, but the North's ability to refill its depleted ranks was greater than the South's. Lee's offensive strength had been sapped. From the Battle of Spotsylvania Court House until the end of the war, except for counterattacks and the lunge at Fort Stedman during the siege of Petersburg, the Army of Northern Virginia was a defensive weapon only.

After Cold Harbor, Grant decided to turn quickly to the south of Richmond and isolate the city and the defending troops by attacking Petersburg and cutting the railroads that supplied them. Lee knew he could not allow this to happen. "We must destroy this army of Grant's before he gets to James River," he told one of his generals. "If he gets there, it will become a siege, and then it will be a mere question of time."

STRATEGIC PETERSBURG

According to the United States census of 1860, Petersburg was a city of 18,266 people. It was situated on the southern bank of the Appomattox River about 8 miles from City Point, where the Appomattox joins the James, and 23 miles south of Richmond. As the war progressed and the territory to the north and east was shut off, Richmond became increasingly dependent on Petersburg for supplies. Through it passed a constant stream of war materials and necessities of life from the South to sustain the straining war effort. In short, Petersburg was a road and rail center of vital importance to the Confederacy, and its capture would almost certainly lead to the abandonment of Richmond.

The transportation vehicles of the 1860's did not require the wide, straight highways of the present. However, several good roads came into the city from the east, south, and west where they joined with the Richmond Turnpike. Along these roads passed supply wagons, couriers, and, on occasion, troops on their way to repel the foe. Several were built of logs laid across the road to form a hard surface. Because of this they were called "plank roads." Two of the most important arteries of traffic into Petersburg were the Jerusalem Plank Road, connecting Petersburg with Jerusalem (now Courtland),

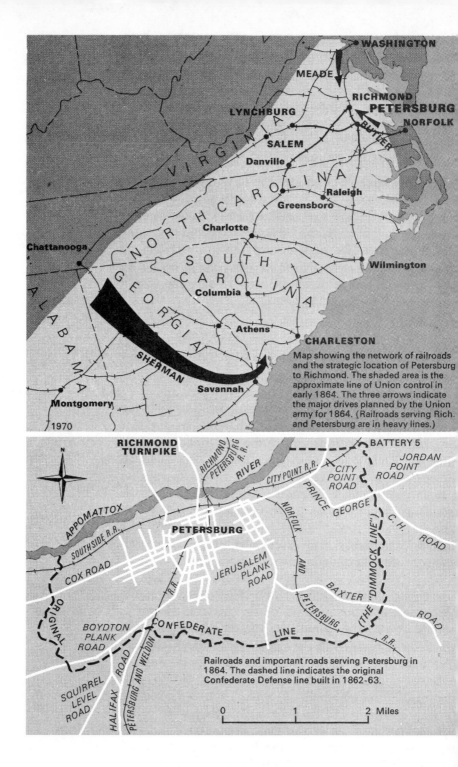

WASHINGTON

MEADE

RICHMOND
PETERSBURG
NORFOLK
BUTLER

LYNCHBURG

SALEM

Danville

V I R G I N I A

N O R T H   C A R O L I N A

Raleigh

Greensboro

Charlotte

Chattanooga

G E O R G I A

S O U T H
C A R O L I N A

Columbia

Wilmington

Athens

CHARLESTON

SHERMAN

A L A B A M A

Montgomery

Savannah

1970

Map showing the network of railroads
and the strategic location of Petersburg
to Richmond. The shaded area is the
approximate line of Union control in
early 1864. The three arrows indicate
the major drives planned by the Union
army for 1864. (Railroads serving Rich.
and Petersburg are in heavy lines.)

RICHMOND
TURNPIKE

BATTERY 5

JORDAN
POINT
ROAD

RICHMOND
PETERSBURG R.R.

RIVER

CITY POINT R.R.

CITY
POINT
ROAD

PRINCE

GEORGE

C. H.

ROAD

APPOMATTOX

N

PETERSBURG

SOUTHSIDE R.R.

COX ROAD

NORFOLK

AND

JERUSALEM
PLANK
ROAD

PETERSBURG

BAXTER

(THE "DIMMOCK LINE")

R.R.

ROAD

ORIGINAL

BOYDTON
PLANK
ROAD

CONFEDERATE

LINE

R.R.

SQUIRREL
LEVEL
ROAD

HALIFAX
ROAD

PETERSBURG AND WELDON

Railroads and important roads serving Petersburg in
1864. The dashed line indicates the original
Confederate Defense line built in 1862-63.

0   1   2 Miles

a., and the Boydton Plank Road which led south through Dinwiddie Court House. Among others of importance were the City Point, Prince George Court House, Baxter, Halifax, Jordon Point, Squirrel Level, and Cox Roads.

It was the railroads more than the highways, however, which gave to Petersburg a significance out of all proportion to its size. Tracks radiated from the city in all directions. The Richmond and Petersburg Railroad left the city to the north; the Southside Railroad ran west to Lynchburg; the Petersburg and Weldon Railroad led south to North Carolina; the Norfolk and Petersburg Railroad passed through a ravine east of the city before turning southeast toward Norfolk; and the Petersburg and City Point Railroad struck out for the hamlet of City Point, situated at the junction of the James and Appomattox Rivers about 8 miles away.

Because of its proximity, Petersburg became a part of the transportation system of the Confederate capital, serving as a major point of transfer to the larger metropolis for products and materials from the vast regions to the south and southwest. By June 1864, all but one railroad from the south and west into Richmond—the Richmond and Danville Railroad—passed through Petersburg. As other lines of supply were cut off or threatened, the dependence of Richmond upon Petersburg increased and made the security of that city a matter of vital concern.

In the spring of 1862, McClellan's Peninsular Campaign had threatened Richmond from the east and southeast, making that city's defenders acutely aware of the need for a system of fortifications around Petersburg. In August a defense line was begun, and work continued until its completion about a year later. Capt. Charles H. Dimock, a Northerner by birth, was in charge of it under the direction of the Engineer Bureau, Confederate States Army, and the line so constructed became unofficially known as the "Dimmock Line."

When finished, the chain of breastworks and artillery emplacements around Petersburg was 10 miles long, beginning and ending on the Appomattox River and protecting all but the northern approaches to the city. The

55 artillery batteries were consecutively numbered fro
east to west. Although natural terrain features were ut
lized whenever possible, some glaring weaknesses e
isted, such as the deep ravine between Batteries 7 and
which could provide a means of penetration by an a
tacking force. The very length and size of the fortifica
tions proved to be a disadvantage. It meant that a larg
number of troops would be necessary to defend the lin
than General Beauregard, charged with this heavy re
sponsibility, had present for duty. Col. Alfred Roma
an aide-de-camp to Beauregard, estimated that the lor
"Dimmock Line" would require more than 10 times a
many men to defend it as were available.

On several occasions raids were made on the railroa
south and west of Petersburg. The most serious of thes
occurred on June 9, 1864, when 3,000 infantry an
1,300 cavalry appeared in force along the eastern an
southeastern sector of the Dimmock Line. The infantr
contented itself with a menacing demonstration, bu
the cavalry attacked up the Jerusalem Plank Road. Aft
breaking through the defenses, the horse soldiers wer
checked by regular Southern army units assisted by
hastily summoned home guard of old men and youth
The damage done by such raids was quickly patched u
but they were a constant nuisance to the city's transpo
tation lines. To shut off permanently the supplies th
streamed along the railroads, the Union forces wou
have to take permanent physical possession of them.

BATTLE OF PETERSBURG

After the Battle of Cold Harbor on June 3, Grant ha
abandoned, for a time at least, his plan to capture Ric
mond by direct assault. With characteristic zeal he ha
ordered Meade to move the Army of the Potom
across the James River and to invest the more souther
city. On June 14, Grant and Butler conferred at Be
muda Hundred. At that time, orders were given for th
attack on Petersburg.

The first of the Northern forces to arrive on the scene
battle was the XVIII Corps of the Army of the Jame
which had fought at Cold Harbor. Early in the mornin
of June 15, these troops, commanded by Maj. Gen. W

F. "Baldy" Smith, crossed from Bermuda Hundred to
the south side of the Appomattox by means of a pontoon
bridge at Broadway Landing. Eighteen thousand Union
soldiers were on their way to face less than 4,000 under
Beauregard. Throughout the day they approached the
city and assembled for the attack.

There was skirmishing throughout the afternoon as the
Federals drove in the Confederate pickets, and shortly
after 7 p.m. on June 15 the XVIII Corps launched a
fierce attack on the Dimmock Line. Among the first
points to fall was Battery 5, one of the strongest of the
Confederate positions. Within a few hours Beauregard

*Gen. P. G. T. Beauregard,
Confederate commander at
Petersburg during the early
days of the campaign,
defended the "Dimmock
Line" against the Federal
assaults of June 15–18, 1864.
When Lee arrived to direct
operations, Beauregard's
troops were merged with the
Army of Northern Virginia.*

393

had lost not only Battery 5 but all the line for more tha
a mile south. The defenders withdrew and threw up
hasty entrenchment behind Harrison's Creek, well to th
rear of the captured section of the line. While th
Confederate retreat was taking place, the Union I
Corps, commanded by Maj. Gen. Winfield S. Hancocl
arrived to reinforce the Federal columns.

The appearance on the field of the II Corps was a
ominous sign for the Confederates. While the initial a
tacks were taking place on June 15, the Army of th
Potomac had been busily engaged in crossing the Jame
River farther to the east. The number of Union troop
south of the river was increasing hourly, until by mid
night of June 16 at least 70,000 had crossed.

Darkness ended the fighting on June 15, but early th
next day the attacks were renewed. More of the defens
line south of the portion captured the previous day
now gave way. In response to repeated entreaties fror
Beauregard throughout June 15 and 16, Lee ordere
more divisions to the support of Petersburg, necessita
ing the draining of precious reserves from the Richmon
lines. By dawn of that second day, Beauregard coul
muster about 14,000 men to face the enemy. Thus, th
center of attention rapidly shifted from Richmond t
Petersburg, which had so recently seemed of but sec
ondary importance.

1. *Broadway Landing on the Appomattox River where Maj. Gen. W. F. "Baldy" Smith's XVIII Corps of the Army of the James crossed on June 15, 1864. It was later used as an ordnance depot by the Union Army.*
2. *Pontoon bridge at Broadway Landing constructed by Federal soldiers in 1864.*
3. *Confederate Battery 5, shown here under Federal occupation 6 days after its capture, was one of the first points on Petersburg's outer defense lines to fall to the XVIII Corps during the June 15 attack.*

The third day of battle was practically a repetition
that of the preceding day. Again the Northern forc
attacked the Confederate troops, concentrating their
forts to the south of the positions captured earli
Again the Confederates were forced to draw back.
decisive breakthrough of the opposing line was now a
ticipated by the assaulting forces. About 12:30 a.n
June 18, Beauregard ordered his troops to begin a wit
drawal to new positions about a mile closer to the ci
Throughout the early morning hours of that day Bea
regard had his men busily engaged in the constructi
of this defense line. Colonel Roman later recalled th
"without a moment's rest the digging of the trenches w
begun, with such utensils as had been hastily collect

A section of the Confederate defense lines around Petersburg. Note the use of wickerware (gabions), sharpened stakes (fraises), and branches (abatis) to protect the position.

Petersburg, many of the men using their bayonets, their knives, and even their tin cans, to assist in the rapid execution of the work."

A general assault by the Union forces was ordered for 4 p.m. on June 18. When the attack began it was soon discovered that the ranks of the enemy had not been broken nor had the city fallen into Northern hands. The area where the left flank of the Dimmock Line anchored on the Appomattox was empty, except for a thin line of skirmishers who were gradually forced back. The Northern troops came on, crossing the Norfolk and Petersburg Railroad west of where the defenders had constructed their new line and continuing on until they were brought face to face with the muzzles of Confederate guns. Meanwhile, elements of Lee's command continued pouring in to aid their comrades, and Lee came down from his temporary headquarters near Chester, Va., to personally direct the defense operations.

Throughout that June Saturday, brisk action occurred on the new Petersburg front. The major Union drive, involving elements of five corps, came about 4 p.m. Artillery hammered the Confederates. Infantry charged only to be hurled back. During the course of one of these futile drives, the 1st Maine Heavy Artillery reportedly suffered the most severe losses of any regiment in a single engagement of the entire war. This unit, 850 strong, charged from the concealment of the Prince George Court House Road north of where Fort Stedman was soon to stand. Met by a heavy crossfire, it withdrew in less than one-half hour, with 632 casualties

As on the previous days, fighting ended with the coming of darkness. Grant's attempt to capture Petersburg had failed, with a loss of 10,000 men; but his efforts could not be considered entirely wasted. Two of the railroads leading into the city had been cut, and several roads were in Union hands. Behind the Northern troops was City Point, which Grant speedily converted into a huge supply base.

The major result of the opening 4 days of combat, however, was the failure of the Federal forces to break the Confederate defense line. First Beauregard, and then Lee, had held against heavy odds. They had been pushed back closer to their base—but they had held. Possibly if Smith had advanced his XVIII Corps farther into the defenses on the opening night, or if Hancock's II Corps had arrived earlier, Petersburg would have fallen on June 15 or 16. But these had not happened, and now 47,000 to 51,000 Confederates would settle down to defend the city against 111,000 to 113,000 Union besiegers.

The defenses of Richmond now ran from White Oak Swamp, east of that city, south to Jerusalem Plank Road, 26 miles away. The fate of the Army of Northern Virginia—of the Confederate capital itself—would depend upon the outcome of the drive against Petersburg.

The Union Army, having failed in its initial attack on Petersburg, was now committed to doing something further to effect its capture. From June 19 to July 9, the Union forces were engaged in three kinds of activity. First, elements of the army were set to work consolidating the positions captured in the 4-day battle and constructing the devices needed for siege operations. Second, jabbing cavalry thrusts were made at the important supply routes into Petersburg. And third, they reconnoitered the Confederate defenses to determine a plan which would force Lee out of his lines.

A threatening movement toward the Weldon Railroad was promptly undertaken by the Northern troops. Three days after the failure to capture the city, two corps (the II and VI) began to push to the southwest of Grant's flank on the Jerusalem Plank Road. The following day, June 22, Confederate divisions led by Generals Cadmus M. Wilcox and William Mahone advanced from the defense line south of Petersburg and rolled by the Federals, capturing 1,700 prisoners, four cannons, and eight stands of colors.

FIRST UNION ATTEMPT TO ENCIRCLE PETERSBURG

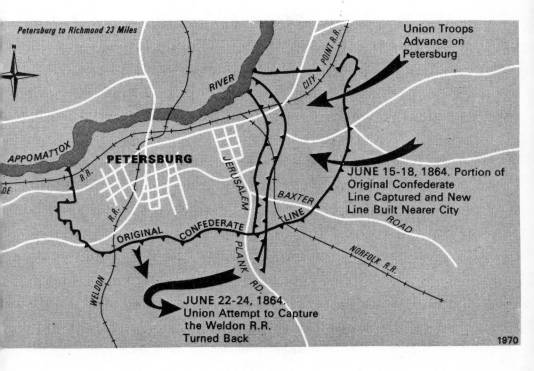

Petersburg to Richmond 23 Miles

Union Troops Advance on Petersburg

JUNE 15-18, 1864. Portion of Original Confederate Line Captured and New Line Built Nearer City

JUNE 22-24, 1864. Union Attempt to Capture the Weldon R.R. Turned Back

1970

The next morning saw the resumption of the adva
toward the Weldon Railroad. A Union patrol succee
in reaching the tracks on the 23d and promptly star
the work of destruction. Alarmed by the threat to
important supply line, the Confederates launchec
sharp attack that forced the withdrawal of the Un
forces from the vicinity of the railroad. However,
Union lines confronting Petersburg had been exten
across the Jerusalem Plank Road, thus cutting off its
to the city.

In itself, the Battle of Jerusalem Plank Road on J
22–24 was not too important militarily. The North co
quickly replace the loss of 2,300 men. The Weldon R
road, although its days were numbered, was still able
deliver supplies to Petersburg. But as an indication
Grant's tactics, it pointed the course of the campa
ahead. It marked the first of several attempts to enci

Destruction of Genl. Lees lines of c

ersburg, and the others to follow would not all be as ppointing to Northern hopes. In these repeated es to the west lay the essence of the basic plan to ture Petersburg.

July 9, the plan of operations decided upon by the ion high command was revealed in an order from ade's headquarters giving detailed instructions for building of fortifications and the development of ge tactics. It thus became apparent that the Union n was to reduce Petersburg by a process of attrition process that was to last for 9 months.

ere were still those in the attacking forces, however, o felt that, with a little imagination, the city could be en by direct assault. While most of the troops were ging siege lines, another smaller group had already un work on a unique plan which would, if successful, ke further encirclement unnecessary.

The Federal cavalry saw little battle action during the siege, but it did its share in destroying Lee's lines of communication. Combat artist Alfred R. Waud of Harper's Weekly made this sketch of Brig. Gen. James H. Wilson's troopers tearing up part of the Weldon Railroad, south of Petersburg, during their June 1864 raid.

401

The "Dictator," also called "The Petersburg Express," was a 17,000-pound, 13-inch Federal seacoast mortar mounted on a reinforced railroad car. During the early part of the siege, this huge weapon fired 200-pound explosive shells into Petersburg, 2½ miles away, from a curved section of the Petersburg and City Point Railroad. On July 30, 1864, it was part of the artillery support for Union troops during the Battle of the Crater.

1

2

1. The men who commanded the "Dictator"—Col. H. L. Abbot (the man on the left in front) and officers of the 1st Connecticut Heavy Artillery. Next to Abbot is Maj. Gen. Henry J. Hunt, in charge of all artillery operations on the Petersburg front.

2. The "Dictator" in permanent position near Union Battery IV, formerly Confederate Battery 5.

3. A 13-inch seacoast mortar on display at Petersburg National Battlefield today, on the site where the "Dictator" stood during most of the siege.

BATTLE OF THE CRATER

At several places east of the city the opposing lines wer
extremely close together. One of these locations was
front of Pegram's (sometimes called Elliott's) Salient,
Confederate strong point near old Blandford Churc
Here the Confederate position on Cemetery Hill and t
Union picket line were less than 400 feet apart. Becau
of the proximity of the Union line, Pegram's Salient w
well fortified. Behind earthen embankments was a ba
tery of four guns, and two veteran South Carolina infa
try regiments were stationed on either side. Behind the
were other defensive works; before them the grou
sloped gently downward toward the Union advance lin

This forward Union line was built on the crest of
ravine which had been crossed on June 18. Through t
ravine, and between the sentry line and the main lin
lay the roadbed of the Norfolk and Petersburg Railroa
The front in this sector was manned by Maj. Ge
Ambrose E. Burnside's IX Corps. Among the ma
units which composed this corps was the 48th Regime
Pennsylvania Veteran Volunteer Infantry. A large pr
portion of this regiment was made up of onetime co
miners, and it apparently occurred to one or more
them that Pegram's Salient would provide an excelle
place to use their civilian knowhow. Lt. Col. Hen
Pleasants, the commanding officer of the 48th and
mining engineer by profession, overheard one of t
enlisted men mutter, "We could blow that damned fo
out of existence if we could run a mine shaft under it
From this and similar remarks came the germ of the id
for a Union mine.

The 48th Regiment proposed to dig a long gallery fro
the bottom of the ravine behind their picket line to
point beneath the Confederate battery at Pegram's Sa
ent, blow up the position by powder placed in the end
the tunnel, and then send a strong body of troops throu
the gap created in the enemy's line by the explosio
They saw as the reward for their effort the capitulati
of Petersburg and, perhaps, the end of the war.

After obtaining the permission of Burnside and Gran
Pleasants and his men commenced digging their mi
shaft on June 25. The lack of proper equipment made
necessary to improvise tools and apparatus with whi

Lt. Col. Henry Pleasants,
onetime mining engineer and
the commanding officer of the
48th Pennsylvania Regiment
which dug the tunnel
under the Confederate line.

to excavate. Mining picks were created by straightening army picks. Cracker boxes were converted into hand-barrows in which the dirt was removed from the end of the tunnel. A sawmill changed a bridge into timber necessary for shoring up the mine. Pleasants estimated the tunnel's direction and depth by means of a theodolite sent him from Washington. The instrument, although outmoded, served its purpose well: the mine shaft hit exactly beneath the salient at which it was aimed.

One of the most remarkable features of the gallery was the method devised to supply the diggers at the end with fresh air. The longer the tunnel grew, the more serious the problem of ventilation became. It had been considered impossible to dig a tunnel for any considerable distance without spacing shafts at regular intervals in

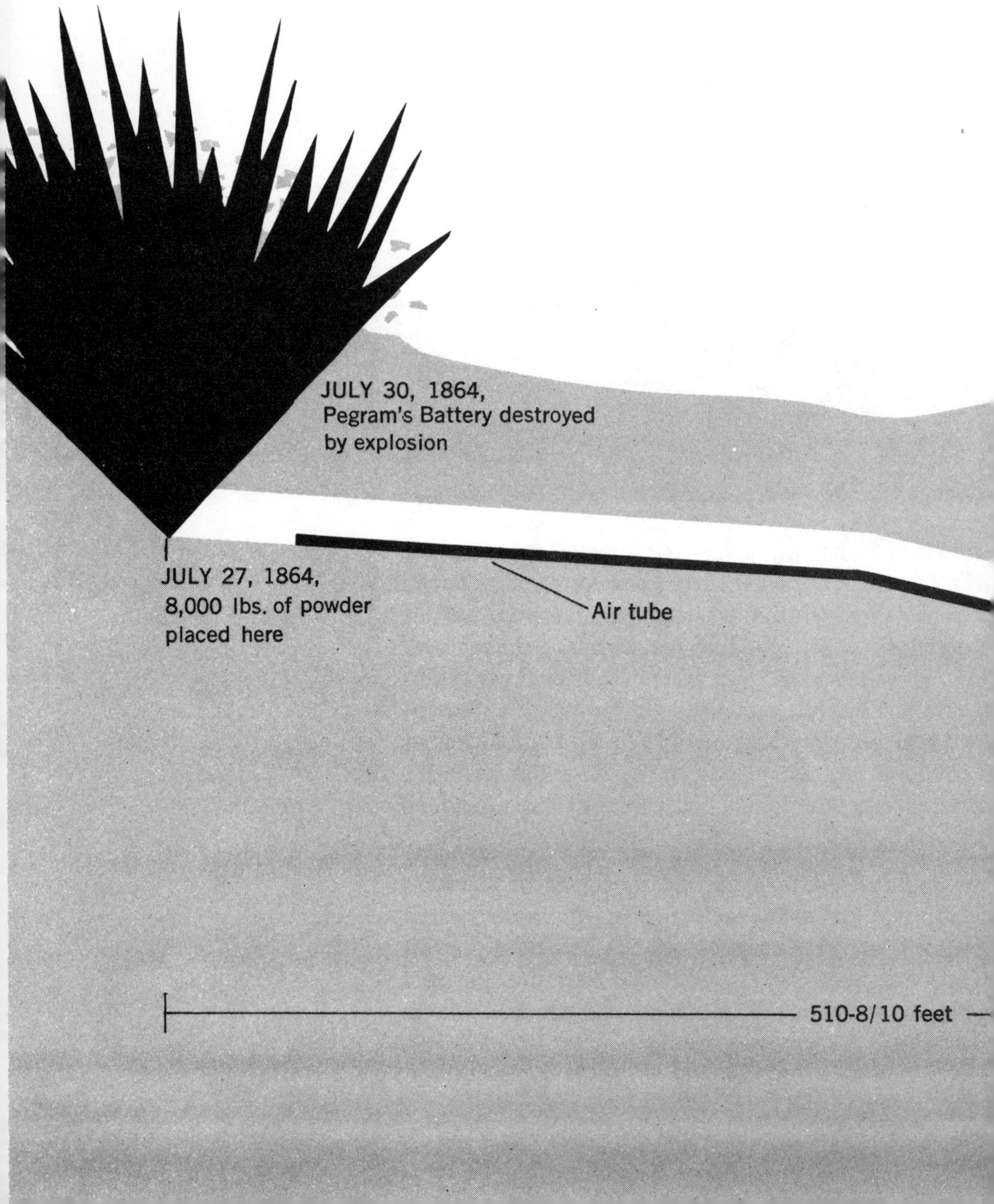

JULY 30, 1864,
Pegram's Battery destroyed
by explosion

JULY 27, 1864,
8,000 lbs. of powder
placed here

Air tube

510-8/10 feet

Cross-section view of the Federal tunnel under the Confederate line. Colonel Pleasants later recalled that "General Burnside told me that General Meade and Major Duane, chief engineer of the Army of the Potomac, said the thing could not be done—that it was all clap-trap and nonsense; that such a length of mine had never been excavated in military operations, and could not be; that I would either get the men smothered, for want of air, or crushed by the falling of the earth; or the enemy would find it out and it would amount to nothing."

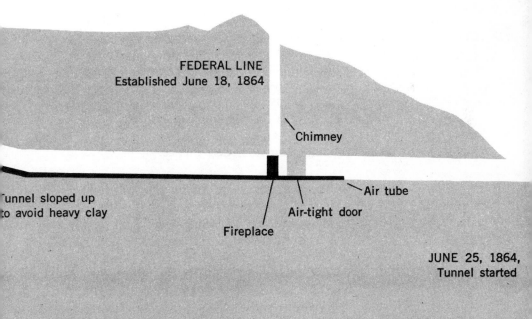

FEDERAL LINE
Established June 18, 1864

Chimney

Tunnel sloped up
to avoid heavy clay

Air tube

Air-tight door

Fireplace

JUNE 25, 1864,
Tunnel started

order to replace the polluted air with a fresh supply. This problem had been solved by the application of the simple physical principle that warm air rises. Behind the Union picket line and to the right of the mine gallery, although connected with it, the miners dug a ventilating chimney. Between the chimney and the mine entrance they erected an airtight canvas door. Through that door and along the floor of the gallery they laid a square wooden pipe. A fire was then built at the bottom of the ventilating shaft. As the fire warmed the air it went up the chimney. The draft thus created drew the bad air from the end of the tunnel where the men were digging. As this went out, fresh air was drawn in through the wooden pipe to replace it.

Work on the tunnel continued steadily from June 25, and by July 17 the diggers were nearly 511 feet from the entrance and directly beneath the battery in Pegram's Salient. The Confederates had learned of the mine by this time and had dug several countermines behind their own lines in an effort to locate the Union gallery. Two were very close, being dug on either side of where the Pennsylvanians were at work. Although digging in the countermines continued throughout July, Confederate fears seemed to lessen during the same period. There were many reasons for this, one being the failure of their tunnels to strike any Union construction. Another major reason, undoubtedly, was a belief held by many that it was impossible to ventilate a shaft of any length over 400 feet without constructing air shafts along it, and so far no air shafts could be seen between the Union and Confederate lines.

The next step in the Union plan was to burrow out into lateral galleries at the end of the long shaft. Accordingly, on July 18, work was begun on these branches which extended to the right and left, paralleling the Confederate fortifications above. When completed, these added another 75 feet to the total length of the tunnel which now reached 586 feet into the earth. It was about 20 feet from the floor of the tunnel to the enemy works above. The average internal dimensions of the shaft were 5 feet high, with a base 4½ feet wide tapering to 2 feet at the top.

Digging was finally completed on July 23. Four days later the task of charging the mine with black powder was accomplished. Three hundred and twenty kegs of powder weighing about 25 pounds each were arranged in the two lateral galleries in eight magazines. The total charge was 8,000 pounds. The powder was sandbagged to direct the force of the explosion upward and the fuses were spliced together to form a 98-foot line.

Meanwhile, preparations for the large-scale attack which was to follow the explosion of the mine had been carried out. Burnside wanted his IX Corps to lead the attack, spearheaded by a fresh, 4,300-man Negro division, and pressed his wishes on Meade. Both Meade and Grant approved the request, but refused to allow the black troops to lead the assault for fear that, if the attack failed, the Union commanders could be accused of wanting to get rid of the only Negro troops then with the Army of the Potomac. Burnside did not learn of this decision until the day before the assault, July 29, and he was forced to change his plans at the last moment. Three white divisions would make the initial charge, with the black division in reserve. Burnside had the commanding generals of these three divisions draw straws to see which would lead. Brig. Gen. James F. Ledlie of the 1st Division won the draw.

Despite these 11th-hour changes, a plan of battle had been evolved. During the night of July 29–30, the bulk of the IX Corps was assembled in the ravine behind the mine entrance and in the two approach trenches leading to the picket line. Troops from other Union corps were marshalled as reinforcements. Artillerymen, manning 110 guns and 54 mortars, were alerted to begin shelling the Confederate line. To assist the attack, Grant sent a cavalry and infantry force north of the James to threaten the Richmond defenses and destroy whatever they could of the Virginia Central Railroad. The object was to draw as many of Lee's soldiers away from Petersburg as possible. And it worked. When the assault came, only 18,000 Confederates were left to guard the city.

At 3:15 a.m., July 30, Pleasants lit the powder fuse and mounted the parapet to see the results of his regiment's work. The explosion was expected at 3:30 a.m. Time passed slowly and the men, huddled behind the lines, grew more apprehensive. By 4:15 there could be no doubt that something had gone wrong. Two volunteers from the 48th Regiment (Lt. Jacob Douty and Sgt Harry Reese) crawled into the tunnel and found that the fuse had burned out at a splice. They relighted it and scrambled to safety. Finally, at 4:40 a.m., the earth trembled, and with one great roar, men, equipment, and debris were hurled high into the air. At least 278 Confederate troops were killed or wounded in the tremendous blast, and two of the four guns in the battery were destroyed beyond repair. The crater torn by the powder was at least 170 feet long, 60 to 80 feet wide and 30 feet deep.

The awesome spectacle of the mine explosion caused a delay in the Union charge following the explosion. Removal of obstructions between the lines caused further delay. Soon, however, an advance was made to the crater, where many of the attacking force paused to seek shelter on its steep slopes or to look at the havoc caused by the mine. The hard-pressed Confederates rallied quickly and soon were pouring shells and minié balls into their opponents. Union reinforcements poured into the breach; but, instead of going forward, they either joined their comrades in the crater or branched out to the immediate right and left along the lines. By 8:30 that morning a large part of the IX Corps had been poured into the captured enemy salient. More than 15,000 troops now milled in and about the crater.

By prompt action and determined effort the Confederates had prevented a breakthrough. The attention of three batteries was soon directed on the bluecoats at the crater. Artillery hammered with shot and shell the huddled groups of increasingly demoralized men. In addition, mortars brought to within 50 yards of the crater dropped shells on the soldiers with deadly effect.

Successful as these devices were in halting the Union advance, Lee was aware that an infantry charge would be necessary to dislodge the enemy. By 6 a.m. an order had gone out to Brig Gen. William Mahone to move two brigades of his division from the lines south of Peters-

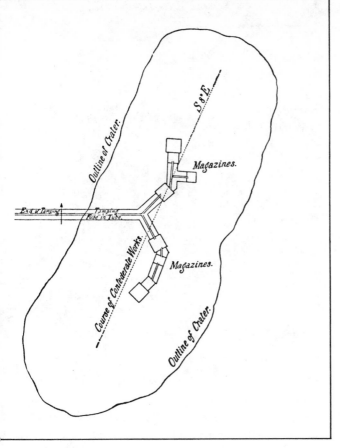

Colonel Pleasants' sketch of the Crater.

urg to the defense of the threatened position; Mahone had anticipated the order and already had his troops in motion. Then Lee joined Beauregard in observing the battle from the Gee house, 500 yards to the rear of the scene of action.

n spite of the Confederate resistance, part of the Northern black division and other regiments had, by 8 a.m., advanced a short distance beyond their companions at the crater. Shortly thereafter, Mahone's lead Confederate brigade arrived on the scene. The men filed into a ravine about 200 yards northwest of the crater and between it and Petersburg. No sooner had they entered this protected position than, perceiving the danger to their lines, they charged across the open field into the mass of Federal soldiers. Although outnumbered, they

forced the Northerners to flee back to the comparati
shelter of the crater. Then they swept on to regain
portion of the line north of the Union-held positic

By 10:30 another of Mahone's brigades had reached t
point of danger, and it charged the Union troops hol
ing the crater, only to be repulsed. Meanwhile, the lot
the Northern soldiers was rapidly becoming unbearab
Confederate artillery continued to beat upon them. T
closely packed troops (dead, dying, and living indiscri
inately mixed) lacked shade from the blazing sun, foo
water and, above all, competent leadership. Meade h
ordered their withdrawal more than an hour before t
second Confederate charge, but Burnside delayed t
transmission of the order till after midday. Many m
had chosen to run the gantlet of fire back to their o
lines, but others remained clinging to the protect
sides of the crater.

The last scene in the battle occurred shortly after 1 p.

To many soldiers, the explosion of the mine and the bitter Battle of the Crater that followed were the most memorable events of the siege. Artist A. R. Waud sketched the explosion from the Union lines.

hone had called up a third brigade, and an attack arheaded by the fresh unit succeeded in gaining the les of the crater. Some of the Union men, overcome a exhaustion and realizing the helplessness of their ation, surrendered; but others continued to fight. At point where resistance centered, the Confederates their hats on ramrods and lifted them over the rim he crater. The caps were promptly torn to shreds by olley of minié balls. Before their foe could reload, hone's forces jumped into the crater where a desper-struggle with bayonets, rifle butts, and fists ensued.

In it was all over. The Union army had lost more n 4,000 men killed, wounded, or captured, as against ut 1,500 for the Confederates. Again, as on June -18, a frontal assault had failed to take the Confeder-stronghold, even though Union numerical strength atly exceeded that of the Confederates. At the tle's close Grant had more than 83,000 men south the Appomattox River; Lee had about 22,000.

FIGHT FOR THE WELDON RAILROAD

Grant, if he reviewed the fruits of his campaign shortly after July 30, could not have felt much comfort. Three hammering blows delivered against Petersburg had failed. Moreover, two important railroads still connected the city with the South. Lee, despite his numerically inferior numbers, was still able to maintain a long line of defenses around Petersburg and Richmond. Farther south, the Union outlook was brighter. Ten days before the Battle of the Crater, final operations against Atlanta had been begun by Sherman. On September 2 it was to fall, and the march to the sea followed in 10 weeks.

Yet it was equally certain that Grant had accomplished an important objective. By committing Lee's weakened but still potent Army of Northern Virginia to a defensive position in the area adjacent to Richmond, he was immobilizing the South's most powerful striking force. Moreover, the Union failure at the crater decided the future direction of the campaign to capture Petersburg. All Grant's energy now turned to extending his siege lines around the city and cutting Lee's supply lines in an attempt to force him out of his defenses.

The first step taken in this direction after July 30 was a strong effort to capture the Weldon Railroad, which the Confederates had so nearly lost in June. On August 16, Maj. Gen. Gouverneur K. Warren, Union V Corps commander, received orders to attack, occupy, and hold the Weldon Railroad 3 miles below the city.

The seizure of the objective was quickly accomplished on August 18, the opening day of battle. More than a mile of track near Globe Tavern, an old colonial inn, was soon in Union hands. Then Warren marched most of his troops northward toward the city. They were in unfamiliar and heavily wooded terrain where they were assailed by two Confederate brigades led by Maj. Gen. Henry Heth. The Union troops were forced to fall back a short distance and entrench. Here the V Corps was reinforced by the IX Corps.

On the afternoon of the 19th, five brigades of Lt. Gen. A. P. Hill's Corps struck the Union infantry. Three of the brigades under Mahone managed to slip in behind their opponents by taking advantage of the concealment offered. by the heavy growth of trees. They inflicted

Globe Tavern, near the Weldon Railroad. During the Battle for the Weldon Railroad, August 18–21, 1864, this building was headquarters for Maj. Gen. Gouverneur K. Warren's V Corps.

rious losses and captured 2,500 prisoners. By nightll, Warren had been forced back one-half mile nearer is new headquarters at Globe Tavern.

ugust 20 was marked by comparative inactivity, alough there was some skirmishing in the morning. hroughout the following day A. P. Hill, who had reived reinforcements, threw his men at the Union ositons around the tavern. The attacks were in vain, r the new Union lines held. General Lee arrived with ore infantry brigades during the afternoon, but after iscussing the situation with his generals, he determined ot to renew the attack. By the end of the day Lee ealized that the upper portion of the Weldon Railroad ad been lost and that any attempt to regain it would be needless sacrifice of manpower.

Cattle Raid
+ R. Waud

One sentence from a dispatch sent by Lee to th
Confederate Secretary of War on August 22 shows th
seriousness of the loss of the railroad: "Our supply
corn is exhausted today, and I am informed that th
small reserve in Richmond is consumed." For a time th
Confederate government was able to utilize the Weldo
Railroad as far as Stony Creek, 20 miles below Peter:
burg, where supplies were transferred to wagons an
hauled around the left of the Northern army to Peter:
burg and Richmond. In December the railroad line wa
destroyed below Stony Creek and henceforth the bele:
guered cities had only two direct rail communicatio
with the South—the Richmond and Danville Railroa
out of Richmond and the Southside from Petersburg.

On August 25, 2 days after the fighting at Globe Taver
had ended, the Confederates scored a minor victor
with a surprise attack. Their blow was aimed at Har
cock's II Corps busily engaged in destroying railroa
tracks at Reams Station, nearly 5 miles below Glob

Petersburg's hungry defenders were delighted when Maj. Gen. Wade Hampton's Confederate horsemen rustled more than 2,000 cattle from the Union army in September 1864. Alfred Waud sketched the raid for Harper's Weekly.

avern. The II Corps, containing large numbers of inexperienced recruits, was badly beaten and more than ,700 were taken prisoner. The Southern victory was nortlived, for the destruction of their rail communications was continued. The best that Lee could hope for in ne future would be to stem the Federal advance.

n mid-September, Maj. Gen. Wade Hampton, cavalry nmmander of the Army of Northern Virginia since J. . B. Stuart's death in May, led a remarkable raid of 000 mounted troops around the rear of the Union my, now numbering 80,000. He succeeded in returng to Petersburg on September 17 with about 2,400 ead of cattle and more than 300 prisoners, while suffer-g losses of only 61 men in two engagements with the nemy. Although this raised the morale of the Confedates, it did not change the course of the campaign. The on band being forged outside their city was a reality, d Grant, a tenacious man, had not loosened his grip.

1

5

1. *Federal soldiers in the trenches before Petersburg. By 1864, most of the men of the Armies of the Potomac and the James were veteran combat soldiers, but the strain of siege warfare eventually affected even the most hardened of them. "It was hell itself," one soldier recalled, "and it is wondrous to me that so many of us survived the event."*

2. *Constructing gabions for the attack on Petersburg. When filled with earth, these cylindrical, basket-like objects offered strong protection against enemy fire.*

3. *Federal pickets in front of Union Fort Sedgwick, opposite Confederate Fort Mahone. Note how the gabions are being used.*

4. *Rifled siege guns in Union Battery IV. Fire from this battery helped to seal off the Confederate breakthrough at Fort Stedman in March 1865.*

5. *Capt. James H. Cooper's Battery, 1st Pennsylvania Light Artillery, V Corps. While the men were standing to their guns to have this picture taken, a Confederate battery, thinking the Federals were preparing to fire, opened up on them. The famous Civil War photographer Mathew B. Brady is standing with hands in pocket beside the trail of the second gun.*

421

UNION ENCIRCLE- MENT CONTINUES

The relentless westerly advance of the besieging force was soon resumed after the capture of the Weldon Railroad in August. Constant skirmishing occurred between the lines until, in late September, Grant struck again.

The Battle of Peebles' Farm, September 29 to October 1, was really the second section of a two-part struggle. The first took place closer to Richmond and was directed at Fort Harrison, a strongly fortified point on the outer defense line of the Confederate capital. Fort Harrison was approximately midway between Richmond and Petersburg. On the morning of September 29, Union troops advanced and captured the fort and held it the next day against a counterattack by the former occupants. At the same time, Meade was moving toward a further encirclement of Petersburg with more than 20,000 troops. The direction of his attack was northwest toward Confederate earthworks along the Squirrel Level Road. The ultimate goal was the capture of the Southside Railroad.

Fighting began on the 29th as the Federal vanguard approached the Confederates in the vicinity of Peebles' farm. The engagement increased in fury on the 30th and continued into the next day. When the smoke of battle had blown away on October 2, Meade had extended the Union left flank 3 miles farther west and had secured the ground on which Fort Fisher would soon be built. (This fort was to be the Union's biggest and was one of the largest earthern forts in Civil War history.) He was, however, stopped short of the coveted Southside Railroad. Against the gain in territory the Union army had suffered a loss of more than 1,300 prisoners to the Confederacy and more than 650 killed and wounded. The Southerners found that their lines, while unbroken, were again extended. Each extension meant a thinner Confederate defense line.

For a period of about 3 weeks after the Battle of Peebles' Farm, the shovel and pick again replaced the rifle-musket as the principal tools for soldiers on both sides. Forts were built, breastworks dug, and gabions constructed. Then, on October 27, the Union troops moved again. This time they turned toward the Boydton Plank Road and a stream known as Hatcher's Run, 12

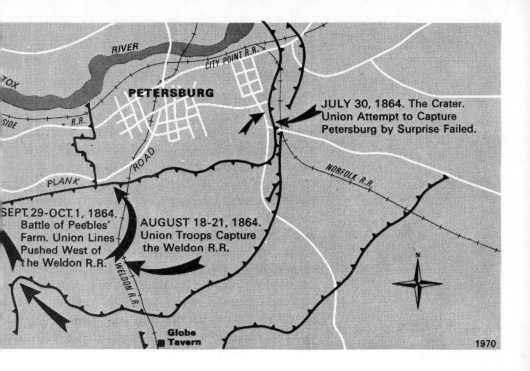

PETERSBURG

RIVER

CITY POINT R.R.

TOX

SIDE

R.R.

JULY 30, 1864. The Crater.
Union Attempt to Capture
Petersburg by Surprise Failed.

ROAD

NORFOLK R.R.

PLANK

SEPT. 29-OCT. 1, 1864.
Battle of Peebles'
Farm. Union Lines
Pushed West of
the Weldon R.R.

AUGUST 18-21, 1864.
Union Troops Capture
the Weldon R.R.

WELDON R.R.

N

Globe
Tavern

1970

iles southwest of Petersburg. Again Grant's objective
as Lee's vital supply line—the Southside Railroad.

he general plan of operations was nearly the same as
at used at Peebles' farm. Butler's Army of the James
as ordered to threaten attack in front of Richmond.
leanwhile, at the left of the Union line, nearly 43,000
fantry and cavalry of the Army of the Potomac started
r the Boydton Plank Road. The columns made rapid
ogress, driving the enemy outposts ahead of them and
lvancing until they neared Burgess' Mill where the
oydton Plank Road crossed Hatcher's Run.

ear Burgess' Mill, heavy Confederate opposition was
et and a spirited engagement took place. The failure of
nion Generals Hancock of the II Corps and Warren of
e V Corps to coordinate the efforts of their respective
lumns, coupled with a slashing thrust by Heth's infan-
y and dogged resistance by Hampton's cavalry and

horse-artillery, resulted in a speedy Northern withdrawal. The Boydton Plank Road, for a time at least, remained in Southern hands, and Grant's encircling movement to cut Lee's railroad was checked.

The approach of winter made any large-scale effort by either side less probable, although daily skirmishes and tightening of the siege lines continued. The slackening of hostile action was used to good advantage by Union and Confederate alike, as it had been in the previous respites between battles, in the strengthening of the battlelines and efforts to develop some rudimentary comforts in the cheerless camps. Throughout the last 2 months of 1864 and the 1st month of the new year there were no strong efforts by either side before Petersburg; picket duty, sniping, and patrolling prevailed. The only action out of the trenches was the Hicksford Raid in December when a strong Union force destroyed the Weldon Railroad as far as Hicksford, about 40 miles south of Petersburg. Lee now had a 35-mile front, with the left resting on the Williamsburg Road east of Richmond and the right on Hatcher's Run southwest of Petersburg. To hold this long line he had in December an effective troop strength of only 66,533. Facing these undernourished and ragged soldiers were, according to official Union returns of the same month, 110,364 well-fed and equipped Federals.

The picture throughout the rest of the South was no more reassuring to Confederate sympathizers. In the Shenandoah Valley, northwest of Richmond, Maj. Gen. Philip H. Sheridan's army had finally crushed Lt. Gen. Jubal A. Early's Southern forces at Cedar Creek on October 19 and was destroying the scattered resistance that remained. Far to the southwest, Sherman had captured Atlanta, Ga., in September, and Savannah had surrendered on December 21. As the new year dawned, his army was prepared to march north toward Grant. To complete the gloomy Southern prospects, Fort Fisher, guardian bastion of Wilmington, N.C., the last of the Confederacy's Atlantic coast ports to remain open, was under fatal bombardment by mid-January.

In late January, President Jefferson Davis, hoping that peace might be made with the Union, agreed to send commissioners to meet with President Lincoln. The

Not everyone was shooting all the time. Often only handpicked sharpshooters traded shots from the trenches and tried to pick off each other's artillerymen. An artist caught these men of the Federal XVIII Corps at their daily, deadly business.

Peace Commissioners, on January 31, 1865, crossed over to the Union lines at Petersburg. Soldiers of both armies, suspecting their mission, cheered as the commissioners slowly walked over the scarred earth of the crater battlefield. At Hampton Roads they met Lincoln, but the "Peace Conference" ended in failure; Davis' insistence on Southern independence as a condition for peace brought about the impasse. The war continued.

The Battle of Hatcher's Run on February 5–7, 1865 was the result of a further drive by the Federals in their attempt to encircle Petersburg. Two Union corps (the II and V), reinforced by a cavalry division and elements of the VI Corps, advanced across Hatcher's Run. Their immediate objective was the Boydton Plank Road.

As had happened before, the Confederates quickly moved out to engage the Union columns. On the afternoon of the 5th, and again the next day, the Southerners counterattacked. While many Confederate units displayed their customary élan, others did not. There were several reasons for this: the inferior numbers of the Southern army, the extremely bad weather which made a Union attack appear unlikely, the ravages of cold on badly equipped and poorly uniformed men, and, most important, the breakdown of the food supply system.

The only Federal units to reach the Boydton Plank Road belonged to the cavalry, but in view of the Confederate response and the discovery that General Lee was not utilizing this road to supply his army, they were recalled. Consequently, no effort was made to hold the Boydton Plank Road, but the Federals did occupy and fortify the newly extended line to Hatcher's Run at a point 3 miles below Burgess' Mill. Thus, again the Union lines had been pushed to the west, and, as before, Lee was forced to lengthen his defenses. The Petersburg-Richmond front, with its recent extension, now stretched over 37 miles, and the army holding it had dwindled through casualties and desertion to slightly more than 56,000 on March 1, 1865.

The Battle of Hatcher's Run was another fight in the constant movement of the Union Army to the west after June 18, 1864. In its relentless extension around Petersburg

One of the most impressive oddities of the siege was Poplar Grove Church, built about February 1865 by the 50th New York Engineers to while away their leisure hours. It could seat 225 men and was used for recreational and religious purposes until the regiment moved away to take part in the pursuit of Lee. The building was dismantled in 1868. Today, Poplar Grove Cemetery is on the site.

burg, which continued day by day with the addition of a few more feet or yards of picket line and rifle-pits, there had occurred five important thrusts aimed by the Northern leaders at encircling the city. They included two attacks on the Weldon Railroad, in June and August 1864; Peebles' Farm, in September and October; Boydton Plank Road, in October; and, finally, the move to Hatcher's Run in February 1865. They met with varying degrees of success, but still the Union noose was not drawn tightly enough.

The enlisted men of both armies, however, remained largely unaware of the strategy of their commanders. Their daily existence during the campaign took on a marked flavor, different in many respects from the more dashing engagements which preceded it. Too often war is a combination of bloodshed and boredom, and Petersburg, unlike most other military operations of the Civil War, had more than its share of the latter. The Petersburg episode—assault and resistance—dragged on to become the longest unbroken campaign against a single American city in the history of the United States. The romantic and heroic exploits were relatively few, and between them came long stretches of uninspiring and backbreaking routine.

The men of both sides had much in common, despite the bitterness with which they fought. In battle they were enemies, but in camp they were on the same common level. Stripped of the emotional tension and exhilaration of combat they all appear as bored, war-weary homesick men. The greater part of their time was primarily utilized by digging and constructing fortifications, performing sentry and picket duty, and striving to speed up the long succession of days. They lived in rude improvised shelters, often made of mud and log walls with tent roofs. Chimneys were made of mud and barrels. There was some friendly interchange of words and gifts between the lines, but enmity was more rampant than brotherly regard. Off duty, the amusements and pastimes of the soldiers were simple and few—limited in most cases to their ability to improvise them. The most striking difference between the armies as the Petersburg campaign lengthened was that, while the

In late 1864, with food and supplies dwindling, desertion in the Confederate ranks became a major problem. This Southern cavalryman, completely discouraged and in rags, was one of those who crossed the lines to surrender. By early 1865, more than 2,000 Confederates had followed his example. One Union officer concluded that "if we stay here, the Johnnies will all come over before the 4th of July."

During the Civil War, a handful of "special artists" followed the Federal armies to supply glimpses of soldier life to news- and picture-hungry readers of such popular publications as the New York Illustrated News, Harper's Weekly, and Frank Leslie's Illustrated Newspaper. Artists Edwin Forbes and the Waud brothers, Alfred and William, caught these scenes during the siege of Petersburg.

1. Pickets trading between the lines. At quiet moments, opposing pickets sometimes met between the lines to trade coffee, tobacco, newspapers, and trinkets.

2. The wagon camp at night. Necessary but thankless was the task of the teamsters, those thousands of soldiers and civilians who drove the supply wagons from the railroads and ships to the front line. Theirs may have been a relatively safe job, but a bone-wearying one.

3. Pennsylvania soldiers voting, 1864. Volunteers considered themselves citizens first, soldiers second. These men, and thousands like them, took time out from their deadly work to vote in the Presidential election, doubtless, as the campaign song ran, "For Lincoln and Liberty, too."

4. Bivouac in the rifle-pits. Life in the infantry line was anything but pleasant: steaming, stinking mud in summer, frozen muck in winter. These soldiers of the V Corps built wood-and-canvas "shebangs" over their trenches as protection against the elements.

Northerners suffered most from boredom, the Confed
ates were plagued by the demoralizing effects of hung

The Petersburg campaign was grim business. Amu
ments could lighten the heart for only a brief time
best. Ever present were the mud and disease which f
lowed every Civil War camp. Both opposing forces
the chill of winter and the penetrating rain. The disco

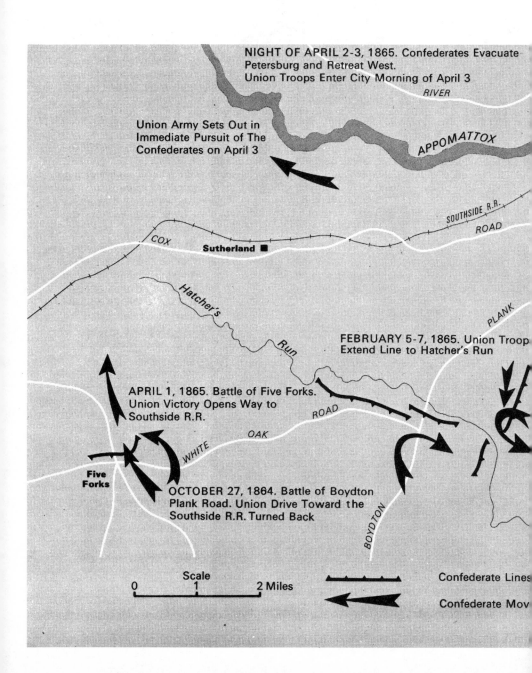

NIGHT OF APRIL 2-3, 1865. Confederates Evacuate
Petersburg and Retreat West.
Union Troops Enter City Morning of April 3

RIVER

Union Army Sets Out in
Immediate Pursuit of The
Confederates on April 3

APPOMATTOX

SOUTHSIDE R.R.

ROAD

COX

Sutherland ■

Hatcher's

Run

PLANK

FEBRUARY 5-7, 1865. Union Troop
Extend Line to Hatcher's Run

APRIL 1, 1865. Battle of Five Forks.
Union Victory Opens Way to
Southside R.R.

ROAD

OAK

WHITE

Five
Forks

OCTOBER 27, 1864. Battle of Boydton
Plank Road. Union Drive Toward the
Southside R.R. Turned Back

BOYDTON

Scale
0   1   2 Miles

Confederate Lines

Confederate Mov

gement of the homesick, who never knew when, or if, they would return to their homes, was a hardship not peculiar to any rank. However, when spring came to warm the air, there was a difference between the two opposing armies. It was more than a numerical superiority. Then the Union soldiers felt confidence, while the Southern veterans, ill-clothed, ill-fed, and nearly surrounded, knew only despair.

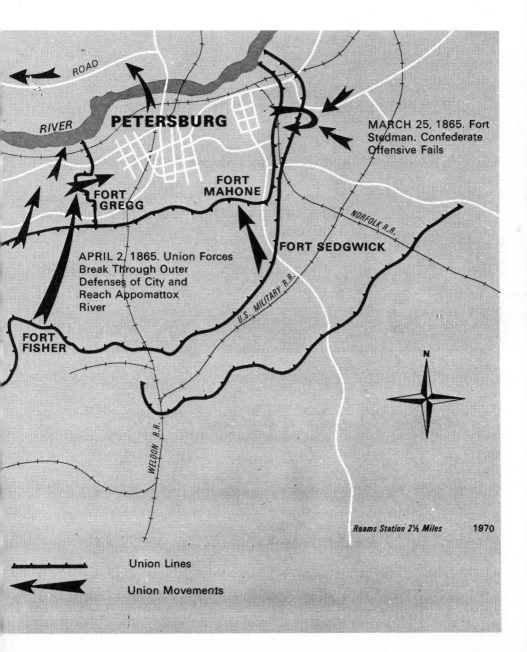

ROAD

RIVER

PETERSBURG

MARCH 25, 1865. Fort Stedman. Confederate Offensive Fails

FORT GREGG

FORT MAHONE

NORFOLK R.R.

FORT SEDGWICK

APRIL 2, 1865. Union Forces Break Through Outer Defenses of City and Reach Appomattox River

U.S. MILITARY R.R.

FORT FISHER

N

WELDON R.R.

Reams Station 2½ Miles   1970

Union Lines

Union Movements

From June 1864 until April 1865, City Point was the "busiest place in Dixie." While Lee's outnumbered Confederates fought and starved behind their slowly crumbling defenses at Petersburg, here, just 8 miles away, Grant built up one of the largest supply depots of the Civil War which, during the 10 months of its existence, kept his army the best-fed, best-clothed, and best-munitioned in the field.

1

2

3

4

5

Explosion at City Point

1–4. Scenes at City Point, Va., showing some of the supplies and munitions destined for Grant's army. An Episcopal bishop from Atlanta, visiting Grant at City Point, was awed by the abundance of military stores that he saw—"not merely profusion, but extravagance; wagons, tents, artillery, ad libitum. Soldiers provided with everything."
5. On August 9, 1864, a Confederate spy slipped a time bomb on board one of the ammunition barges tied up at City Point. The bomb's explosion, sketched by A. R. Waud, killed or wounded 200 people and demolished more than 600 feet of warehouses and about 180 feet of wharf. Grant himself was shaken up by the blast, and one of his staff members was wounded.

LEE'S LAST GAMBLE

By mid-March 1865 the climax of the campaign, and of the war, was close at hand. Lee's forces in both Richmond and Petersburg had dwindled to about 55,000. Grant, on the other hand, had available, or within easy march, at least 150,000. Moreover, Sheridan, having destroyed the remnants of Early's forces at Waynesboro, Va., on March 2, had cleared the Shenandoah Valley of Confederates and was now free to rejoin Grant before Petersburg.

Everywhere Lee turned, the military situation was black. Union forces under Sherman, driving the Confederates before them, had turned north from Savannah and were now hammering Johnston's forces in North Carolina. With President Jefferson Davis' consent, Lee sent a letter to General Grant on March 2 suggesting an interview. In the early morning hours of the second day following the dispatch of the letter, Lee and Maj. Gen. John B. Gordon discussed the three possible solutions to the problem which perplexed them: (1) Try to negotiate satisfactory peace terms. (This had already been acted upon in Lee's note to Grant.) (2) Retreat from Richmond and Petersburg and unite with Johnston for a final stand. (3) Attack Grant in order to facilitate retreat.

There followed a series of interviews with Confederate government officials in Richmond. Each of the plans was analyzed. The first was quickly dropped when Grant made it clear that he was not empowered to negotiate. Nor was the second proposal, that of retreat, deemed advisable by President Davis who wished to strike one more blow before surrendering his capital. This left only the third alternative—to attack.

Before settling on a definite course of action, however, Lee ordered General Gordon to make a reconnaissance of the Federal lines around Petersburg to see if they could be broken anywhere. Gordon soon reported that the best place for an attack was at Fort Stedman, a Union work located near the City Point and Petersburg Railroad and only 150 yards to the east of a strongly fortified Confederate position named Colquitt's Salient. Lee agreed with Gordon's assessment and, on the night of March 23, told Gordon to make preparations for an attack on the fort.

In Petersburg, sometime in the autumn of 1864, Lee was photographed on his horse Traveller for the first time. Although determined to fight on until all hope was gone, already Lee knew the war was going badly and that his tired, hungry, dirty, and cold soldiers could not hold out for long against Grant's growing might.

About one-half of the besieged army would be used to charge the Union line in the vicinity of Fort Stedman. It was hoped that this would cause Grant to shorten his front by withdrawing his left flank to protect his endangered right. Then Lee could detach a portion of the Confederate army to send to the aid of Johnston as, with shorter lines, he would not need as many men in Petersburg. Should the attack fail, he would attempt to retreat with all his forces for a final stand with Johnston. This would be the last desperate gamble of the Army of Northern Virginia.

The details for the attack were worked out by Gordon. During the night preceding the assault, the obstructions before the Confederate lines were to be removed and the Union pickets overcome as quietly as possible. A group of 50 men were to remove the chevaux-de-frise and abatis protecting Fort Stedman; then three companies of 100 men each were to charge and capture the fort. When Stedman was safely in Confederate hands, these men were to pretend they were Union troops and, forming into three columns, were to rush to the rear to capture other positions.

The next step was to send a division of infantry to gain possession of the siege lines north and south of the fallen bastion. When the breach had been sufficiently widened, Southern cavalry were to rush through and destroy telegraphic communication with Grant's headquarters at City Point. They were also ordered to cut the military railroad. Additional reserves were to follow the cavalry.

The attack was scheduled for the morning of March 25. The 50 axmen and the 300 soldiers who were to make up the advance columns were given strips of white cloth to wear across their chests to tell friend from foe. The officers in charge were given the names of Union officers known to be in the vicinity and were told to shout their assumed names if challenged. Beginning about 3 a.m., Confederates professing to be deserters crossed to the Union pickets offering to surrender. Their purpose: to be near at hand to overwhelm the unsuspecting pickets when the attack began.

At 4 a.m. Gordon gave the signal, and the Confederates sprang forward. At first the attack went as planned. Blue-clad pickets were silenced so effectively that not a shot was fired. Union obstructions were quickly hewn down by the axmen, and the small vanguard of 300 swept through Battery No. X which stood immediately north of Fort Stedman. They then rushed into the fort; the occupants were completely surprised and many surrendered without a fight. Battery XI to the south of Fort Stedman was also soon in Confederate hands. Union resistance in this early stage was ineffective, although Battery XI was recaptured for a short time.

More Confederates pressed into the torn line. While three columns set out in the general direction of City Point and along the Prince George Court House Road behind Stedman, other infantry units moved north and south along the Federal emplacements. To the north, they captured the fortifications as far as Battery IX where they were stopped by the Union defenders; to the south, they progressed as far as the ramparts of Fort Haskell. A desperate struggle ensued, but here, too, the

Maj. Gen. John B. Gordon planned and led the March 25 attack on Fort Stedman, one of the most advanced works on the Union line.

441

Northerners refused to yield. Despite these checks, the Confederates were now in possession of almost 1 mile of the Union line.

In the center of the Confederate attack, the three small columns quickly advanced as far as Harrison's Creek— a small stream which winds its way north to the Appomattox River 650 yards behind Fort Stedman. One of the columns succeeded in crossing the stream and continuing toward a small Union artillery post on the site of what had been Confederate Battery 8 (renamed Fort Friend by the Federals), but canister from the post forced the column back to the creek. Confusion took hold of the Confederates who were unable to locate the positions they had been ordered to capture behind the Union line. Artillery fire from Northern guns on a ridge to the east held them on the banks of Harrison's Creek. By 6 a.m. their forward momentum had been checked.

Union infantry then charged from the ridge to attack the Southerners. The forces joined battle along Harrison's Creek and the Confederates were soon forced back to Fort Stedman. For a brief time they held their newly captured positions. At 7:30 a.m. Brig. Gen. John F. Hartranft advanced on them with a division of Northern

troops. Heavy small-arms and artillery fire on Gordon's men threatened them with annihilation unless they retired to their own lines. About 8 a.m., Gordon received an order from Lee to withdraw his men. The order was quickly dispatched across the open fields to the soldiers in the captured Union works. By now, however, the line of retreat was raked by a vicious crossfire and many Confederates preferred surrender to withdrawal. About the same time Gordon was starting back, Hartranft ordered his division of Pennsylvania troops to recapture Fort Stedman. Within a few moments the Union line was completely restored and the forlorn Southern hope of a successful disruption of Northern communications, followed by secret withdrawal from the city, was lost. Equally bad, if not worse, to the Confederates was the loss of more than 4,000 killed, wounded, and captured as compared to the Union casualties of less than 1,500.

Of the three Confederate plans of action before the Battle of Fort Stedman, now only the second—retreat —was possible. The situation demanded immediate action, for, even as Gordon had been preparing on March 24 to launch his attack, Grant had been engaged in planning more difficulties for the harassed defenders of Petersburg.

Advancing from Colquitt's Salient (far left), Gordon's men captured Fort Stedman (left) but were driven out by a murderous crossfire from Federal artillery. In the assault, some 4,000 Confederates were killed, wounded, or captured.

FIVE FORKS: BEGINNING OF THE END

The coming of better weather heralded the opportunity for the final blows against the city. Grant, who was now passing some of the most anxious moments of his life, planned that this effort should be concentrated on the extreme right of the long Confederate line which protected Richmond and Petersburg. This meant that hostilities would soon commence somewhere west of Hatcher's Run, perhaps in the neighborhood of Dinwiddie Court House or a road junction called Five Forks which lay 17 miles southwest of Petersburg. On March 24, Grant ordered the II and IX Corps and three divisions of the Army of the James to the extreme left of the Union lines facing Lee. This resulted in a strong concentration northeast of Hatcher's Run. Two days later Sheridan arrived at City Point, fresh from his victorious campaign in the Shenandoah Valley, and was ordered to join his troops to those concentrated on the left. Finally, it began to appear that the Army of Northern Virginia was to be encircled.

Meanwhile, Lee was waiting only until he collected supplies and rations to last his men for a week and until the roads were passable before leaving to join Johnston. He hoped to leave on or about April 10. The information he received about the rapid accumulation of Union forces opposite his lightly held right was very disturbing, for, if it was true, the Federals not only threatened to cut off his retreat to the west and south, but they also posed a serious danger to the Southside Railroad—the last remaining communication link between Petersburg and the South, which continued to deliver a trickle of supplies to the city.

On March 29 the Union troops moved out. Sheridan's cavalry crossed the Rowanty Creek and occupied Dinwiddie Court House, while the II and V Corps crossed Hatcher's Run. In moving into position on the left of the II Corps, Warren's V Corps soldiers encountered heavy resistance north of Gravelly Run. While Sheridan was marshaling his troops around Dinwiddie, Lee issued orders on March 29 which sent Maj. Gens. George E. Pickett and Fitzhugh Lee to the Confederate right near Five Forks, far beyond Petersburg.

Sheridan was prepared to move against the Confeder-

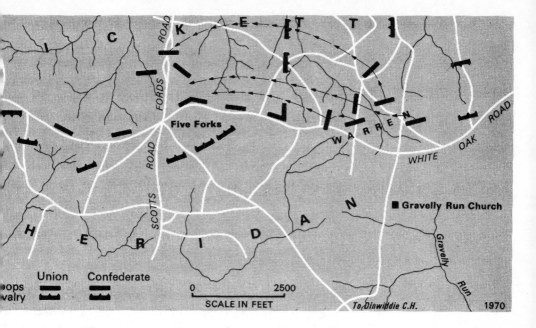

Union   Confederate

Five Forks

Gravelly Run Church

WHITE   OAK   ROAD

Gravelly Run

SCALE IN FEET

0   2500

To Dinwiddie C.H.   1970

ates with his cavalry on March 30, but heavy rains lasting from the evening of March 29 until the morning of the 31st made a large-scale movement impracticable over the muddy roads. On the last day of the month, part of Sheridan's forces which has pushed northwest toward Five Forks was attacked by Southern forces which succeeded in driving them back to Dinwiddie Court House, where Sheridan had a fresh division. Pickett then found his men badly outnumbered and withdrew them to Five Forks without pressing the advantage he had gained. This incident, called the Battle of Dinwiddie Court House, was a minor Confederate victory, although Sheridan's men were neither demoralized nor disorganized by the attack, and Robert E. Lee could find small comfort in the situation.

Meanwhile, there had been a savage clash on White Oak Road between Warren's V Corps and Maj. Gen. Bushrod Johnson's Confederate division. The Confederates at first swept all before them, but in the end numbers told and they were compelled to withdraw behind their breastworks.

The Confederates had been able to concentrate on their extreme right in the vicinity of Five Forks only about 10,000 cold and hungry soldiers to meet the expected Union drive to turn their right flank. Massed against this force commanded by Pickett were about 10,000 Northern cavalry and 12,000 infantry. The desperate urgency of General Lee's fears was indicated in the dispatch he sent to Pickett early on April 1, the day of the struggle for Five Forks: *"Hold Five Forks at all hazards.* Protect road to Ford's Depot and prevent Union forces from striking the south-side railroad. Regret exceedingly your forced withdrawal, and your inability to hold the advantage you had gained."

Throughout April 1, Pickett's troops worked unceasingly, erecting barricades of logs and earth around Five Forks. About 4 p.m., with only 2 hours of daylight remaining, Sheridan's cavalry and Warren's infantry attacked. While the cavalry occupied the attention of the Confederate defenders along White Oak Road, divisions of infantrymen from the V Corps moved to the left of Pickett's troops and, after crossing the White Oak Road which connected Five Forks with Petersburg, hit them on the weakly held left flank. Lacking sufficient artillery support, infantry reserves, and the presence of their commander, the Southerners were quickly overcome. Realizing that their position was no longer tenable, portions of the Confederate troops tried to retreat to Petersburg, but the avenue of escape had been cut by the Union advance across the White Oak Road.

By dusk, the Battle of Five Forks had ended. Union troops were in possession of the disputed area. They had cut off and captured more than 3,200 prisoners, while suffering a loss of probably less than 1,000.

Now the besieging forces were in position for the first time to accomplish Grant's objective of cutting Lee's supply lines and breaking through his fortifications. The western end of Lee's mobile defenses had crumbled.

Those Confederates who had survived the Battle of Five Forks had fallen back to the Southside Railroad where

When Maj. Gen. Philip H. Sheridan (above) sent cavalry and infantry crashing into the Confederate right flank at Five Forks on April 1, 1865, the Southern commander, Maj. Gen. George E. Pickett (left), was at a shad bake in the rear. By the time Pickett returned to his command, both it and the defense line had crumbled. Suddenly, Petersburg was no longer tenable. "It has happened as I told them in Richmond it would happen," said Lee. "The line has been stretched until it is broken."

447

they rallied for a stand, but darkness had prevented a Union pursuit. Grant's troops were within striking distance of the rail line, located less than 3 miles from Five Forks. Lee now knew that Petersburg and Richmond must be evacuated without delay or the Army of Northern Virginia would be completely cut off from outside help and all possible escape routes would be gone.

The problem of assigning a proper significance to Five Forks is a difficult one. It is now known that Lee and the Confederate government officials were on the verge of abandoning their capital. In June of the previous year the Southside Railroad had been a most important objective of the invading army, but the plight of Lee's army had grown so desperate during the intervening months that whether the railroad remained open or not mattered little. Grant, of course, did not know this as a positive fact, although the uncomfortable situation of his opponents was something of which he was doubtless aware. The real importance of Five Forks lay in the probability that, by making it more difficult for Lee to escape, it brought the inevitable a little closer. Lt Col. Horace Porter, of Grant's staff, was positive more than 30 years later that news of Sheridan's success prompted the Union commander in chief to issue the orders for the attack that carried the city.

FALL OF PETERSBURG AND RICHMOND

Continuously throughout the night following the Battle of Five Forks, the Union artillery played upon the Confederate earthworks and dropped shells into the city. Troops were prepared for a general assault ordered for the following dawn. At 4:40 a.m., April 2, 1865, a frontal attack began with the sound of a signal gun from Fort Fisher. A heavy ground fog added to the confusion as the Federals drove in the Confederate pickets, cut away the abatis, and stormed over the works.

The story of the fighting along the Petersburg front on that spring Sunday is one of Union success over stout Confederate resistance. Maj. Gen. Horatio G. Wright's Union VI Corps broke through the works defended by troops of A. P. Hill's Corps and rolled up the Confederate line to right and left, while several regiment ushed on toward the Southside Railroad. Other elements of Grant's army swept away the remnants of the Confederate lines along Hatcher's Run. General Hill was killed early in the day by a Union soldier near the Boydton Plank Road while on the way to rally his men at Hatcher's Run.

The desperateness of the Southern position was shown when, about 10 a.m., Lee telegraphed President Davis to inform him of the turn of events at Petersburg. The message read: "I advise that all preparations be made for leaving Richmond tonight." Davis received the message while attending Sunday services at St. Paul's Church. He left immediately, destroying the calm of worship, to prepare for evacuating the capital. The flight of the Confederate government was promptly begun.

By midday the entire outer line to the west of Petersburg had been captured, with the exception of Fort Gregg. The city was now completely surrounded except to the north. The left of the Union line finally rested on the bank of the Appomattox River after months of strenuous effort.

It now became apparent to Lee that he must hold an inner line west of Petersburg until nightfall, when it would be possible for him to retreat from the city. While gray-clad troops were forming along this line built on the banks of Old Indian Town Creek, the defenders of Fort Gregg put up a stubborn delaying action against the Northern advance. Approximately 300 men and two pieces of artillery met an onslaught of 5,000 Northerners. The outcome of the struggle was determined by the numbers in the attacking force, but the capture of Fort Gregg occurred only after bitter hand-to-hand combat. The purpose of the defense had been accomplished, however, for a thin but sturdy line running behind them from Battery 45 to the Appomattox River had been manned. Temporarily, at least, street fighting within Petersburg had been avoided.

Blows directed at other points, such as Fort Mahone on the Jerusalem Plank Road, were slowed after troops of Maj. Gen. John G. Parke's IX Corps had captured 12 guns and 400 yards of the Confederate line to the right and left of the road. Desperate counterattacks by

Gordon's Confederates kept the Federals from exploiting this breakthrough. Yet there was no doubt in the minds of Lee and other Southern leaders that all hope of retaining Petersburg and Richmond was gone. It was obvious that, if the lines held the Union army in check on April 2, they must be surrendered on the morrow. The object was to delay until evening, when retreat would be possible.

The close of the day found the weary Confederates concentrating within Petersburg and making all possible plans to withdraw. Lee had issued the necessary instructions at 5 o'clock that afternoon. By 8 p.m. the retreat was under way, the artillery preceding the infantry across the Appomattox River. Amelia Court House, 40 miles to the west, was designated as the assembly point for the troops from Petersburg and Richmond.

Grant had ordered the assault on Petersburg to be renewed early on April 3. It was discovered at 3 a.m. that the Southern earthworks had been abandoned; an attack was not necessary. Union troops took possession of the city shortly after 4 o'clock in the morning. Richmond officially surrendered 4 hours later.

President Lincoln, who had been in the vicinity of Petersburg for more than a week, came from army headquarters at City Point that same day for a brief visit with Grant. They talked quietly on the porch of a private house for 1½ hours before the President returned to City Point. Grant, with all of his army, except the detachments necessary to police Petersburg and Richmond and to protect City Point, set out in pursuit of Lee. He left Maj. Gen. George L. Hartsuff in command at Petersburg.

Petersburg had fallen, but it was at a heavy price. In the absence of complete records, the exact casualties will never be known, but in the 10-month campaign at least 42,000 Union soldiers had been killed, wounded, and captured, while the Confederates had suffered losses of more than 28,000. Although the northern forces had lost more men than their opponents, they had been able to replenish them more readily. Moreover, Grant had been prepared to utilize the greater resources at his disposal, and the Petersburg campaign had been turned

Deserted Confederate huts on the abandoned Petersburg line.

im into a form of relentless attrition which the
ern army had not been able to stand. The result
een the capture of Petersburg and Richmond, but
important, it had led to the flight of the remnants
once mighty Army of Northern Virginia.

e Sunday following the evacuation of Petersburg
Richmond, Lee's troops were cut off at Appomattox
t House, destroying any hopes they might have had
niting with Johnston in North Carolina. In this
Virginia town nearly 100 miles west of Peters-
the Army of Northern Virginia, now numbering
more than 28,000, surrendered to the Union
s. Within a week of the fall of Petersburg the major
ng force of the Confederacy had capitulated. Gen-
ohnston surrendered his army to General Sherman
rth Carolina on April 26. By early June 1865,
onfederate forces had been surrendered, and the
War was over.

National Archives

CHAPTER XV

The Atlanta Campaign

SPRING 1864

One of the most important military campaigns of the American Civil War was fought in northwestern Georgia during the spring and summer of 1864 between Northern forces under Maj. Gen. William T. Sherman and Confederates commanded first by Gen. Joseph E. Johnston and then by Gen. John B. Hood. This campaign resulted in the capture of Atlanta by the Unionists, prepared the way for Sherman's "March to the Sea," and, in the opinion of many historians, made inevitable the reelection of Abraham Lincoln and the consequent determination of the North to see the war through to final victory rather than accept a compromise with secession and slavery.

Spring 1864 marked the beginning of the war's fourth year. In the eastern theater, 3 years of fighting had led to a virtual stalemate, with the opposing armies hovering between Washington and Richmond—about where they had been when the war began in 1861. However, the situation was quite different in the vast area between the Appalachian Mountains and the Mississippi River, a region known in the 1860's as "the West." There in 1862 Federal armies had driven the Southerners out of Kentucky and much of Tennessee. In the following year the Northerners secured control of the Mississippi River and captured the important city of Chattanooga. By early 1864, Union armies were poised for what they hoped would be a quick campaign to dismember the Confederacy and end the war. This feeling was well illustrated by an Illinois soldier who wrote his sister on April 22, "I think we can lick the Rebs like a book when we start to do it & hope we will Clean Rebeldom out this summer so we will be able to quit the business."

To realize these hopes, Lt. Gen. Ulysses S. Grant, commander of the Northern armies, planned a simultaneous move on all fronts, with the greatest efforts devoted to Virginia, where he would personally direct operations, and to the region between the Tennessee and Chattahoochee Rivers, where the Federals would be led by Sherman and Maj. Gen. Nathaniel P. Banks. Grant hoped that Banks would move from New Orleans, seize Mobile, and advance northward toward Montgomery, while Sherman's force struck southward from Chattanooga. Had these plans succeeded, the Confederacy would have been reduced to a small area

Maj. Gen. William T. Sherman

along the coast of Georgia, the Carolinas, and Virginia. Confederate victories in Louisiana, however, made Banks' projected campaign infeasible, and Sherman's drive southward into Georgia, with Atlanta as the initial goal, became the major Union effort in the West.

Leaders on both sides had long recognized the importance of Atlanta, located a few miles south of the Chattahoochee and about 120 miles from Chattanooga. In 1864, only Richmond was more important to the South. Atlanta's four railroads were not only the best means of communication between the eastern and western parts of the Confederacy but they were also the major lines of supply for the Southern armies in Virginia and north Georgia. The city's hospitals cared for the sick and wounded and her factories produced many kinds of military goods. In the words of a Northern editor, Atlanta was "the great military depot of Rebeldom." In addition, the city's capture would give the Union armies a base from which they could strike further into Georgia to reach such vital manufacturing and administrative centers as Milledgeville, Macon, Augusta, and Columbus. All of these things were clear to the men who led the opposing armies.

William Tecumseh Sherman was a thin, nervous, active man, with a wild shock of reddish or light-brown hair. A 44-year-old native of Ohio, he had been graduated from the U.S. Military Academy in 1840 and, after several years' service in the Army, had resigned his commission to go into banking and later into education. The outbreak of war had found him serving as superintendent of a military college in Louisiana. He resigned this position and returned to the North, where he entered Federal service. Rising rapidly in the Army, he was chosen as supreme commander in the West in early 1864. His soldiers liked him and affectionately called him "Uncle Billy." An officer who was with him in 1864 described the Federal commander as "tall and lank, not very erect, with hair like a thatch, which he rubs up with his hands, a rusty beard trimmed close, a wrinkled face, prominent red nose, small bright eyes, coarse red hands . . . he smokes constantly." Sherman was also a dogged fighter unawed by obstacles that would have broken lesser men, and Grant knew he could be counted on to carry out his part of the grand strategical plan for 1864.

Sherman's assignment was to break up the Confederate army in north Georgia and "to get into the interior of the enemy's country as far as you can, inflicting all the damage you can against their war resources." To accomplish this mission, he had almost 100,000 men organized into three armies—the Army of the Cumberland, commanded by Maj. Gen. George H. Thomas; the Army of the Tennessee, commanded by Maj. Gen. James B. McPherson; and the Army of the Ohio, commanded by Maj. Gen. John M. Schofield. By early May, Sherman had assembled these troops around Chattanooga and was prepared to march with them into Georgia.

Opposed to Sherman's host was the Confederate Army of Tennessee, commanded by Gen. Joseph E. Johnston. Johnston was a Virginian and, like Sherman, a graduate of West Point (Class of 1829). He had served in the U.S. Army until Virginia seceded in the spring of 1861, when he resigned and entered Confederate service. In December 1863 he was named commander of the major Confederate force in the West and given the mission of defending the area against further Northern advance. Johnston had an almost uncanny ability to win the loyal support of his subordinates. An Arkansas officer who met the Southern commander in early 1864 noted in his diary: "General Johnston is about 50 years of age—is quite gray—and has a spare form, an intelligent face, and an expressive blue eye. He was very polite, raising his cap to me after the introduction."

Unfortunately for the Confederacy, Johnston was also secretive, stubborn when dealing with his superiors, petulant, and too prone to see difficulties rather than opportunities. He constantly worried about defeat and retreat, and was hesitant to act. In sum, he was a man whose personality prevented him from effectively utilizing his many abilities.

At the beginning of May, the 55,000 men of Johnston's army were concentrated around Dalton, Ga., 35 miles southeast of Chattanooga. The Southern force consisted of two infantry corps commanded by Lt. Gens. William J. Hardee and John Bell Hood, and a cavalry corps led by Maj. Gen. Joseph Wheeler. What Johnston would do with these troops was still very much in doubt. The Confederate government wanted him to march into Tennessee and reestablish Southern authority over that crucial

State. Johnston, however, believed that conditions for such an offensive were not favorable and that he should await Sherman's advance, defeat it, and then undertake to regain Tennessee. At the opening of the campaign in early May, this issue had not been settled. The lack of understanding and cooperation between the government in Richmond and the general in Georgia, illustrated by this incident, was to hamper Confederate efforts throughout the campaign.

Gen. Joseph E. Johnston

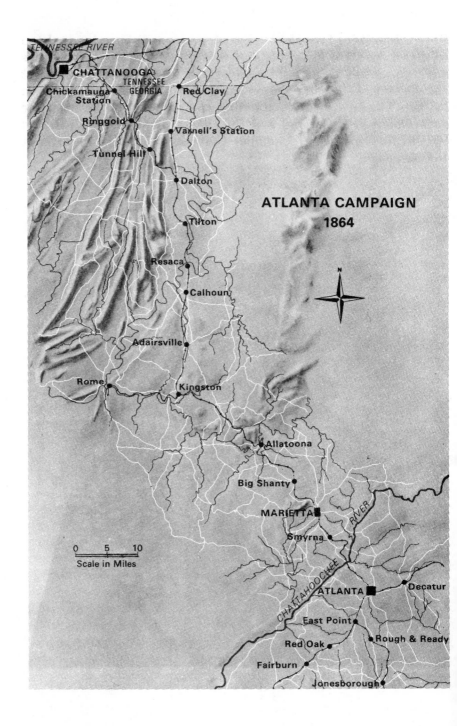

ATLANTA CAMPAIGN
1864

N

TENNESSEE RIVER

CHATTANOOGA
TENNESSEE
GEORGIA
Chickamauga
Station
Red Clay

Ringgold
Varnell's Station

Tunnel Hill

Dalton

Tilton

Resaca

Calhoun

Adairsville

Rome
Kingston

Allatoona

Big Shanty

MARIETTA

Smyrna

CHATTAHOOCHEE RIVER

0   5   10
Scale in Miles

ATLANTA
Decatur

East Point
Rough & Ready

Red Oak

Fairburn

Jonesborough

RESACA

Three major rivers—the Oostanaula, the Etowah, and the Chattahoochee—flow from northeast to southwest across northern Georgia, dividing the area into four distinct geographical regions. Between Chattanooga and the Oostanaula, several parallel mountain ridges slice across the State in such a manner as to hamper military movements. The most important of these was Rocky Face Ridge which ran from near the Oostanaula to a point several miles north of Dalton. This ridge rose high above the surrounding valleys and was the barrier between Johnston's army at Dalton and Sherman's forces at Chattanooga. There were three important gaps in this ridge: Mill Creek Gap west of Dalton, Dug Gap a few miles to the south, and Snake Creek Gap west of the little village of Resaca near the Oostanaula.

Dalton is on the eastern side of Rocky Face Ridge. The Western and Atlantic Railroad, which connected Chattanooga and Atlanta and served as the line of supply for both armies, crossed the Oostanaula near Resaca, ran north for 15 miles to Dalton, then turned westward to pass through Rocky Face Ridge at Mill Creek Gap, and continued on to Chattanooga. During the winter, the Confederates had fortified the area around Dalton to such an extent that they believed it to be secure against any attack. Johnston hoped that the Federals would assault his lines on Rocky Face Ridge, for he was confident that he could hurl the Northerners back with heavy loss.

Sherman, however, had no intention of smashing his army against what one of his soldiers called the "Georgian Gibralter." Northern scouts had found Snake Creek Gap unguarded and the Federal commander decided to send McPherson's Army of the Tennessee through this gap to seize the railroad near Resaca. Meanwhile, Thomas and Schofield would engage the Confederates at Dalton to prevent their sending men to oppose McPherson. Sherman hoped that when Johnston discovered his line of supply in Federal hands, he would fall back in disorder and his army could be routed by the Northerners. By May 6, the Federals were ready to begin the campaign. Sherman moved Thomas and Schofield toward Dalton while McPherson prepared to strike for Snake Creek Gap.

Maj. Gen. James B. McPherson

Johnston had not been idle. He had deployed his men in strong positions to block the expected advance. He had also requested reinforcements, and these were on the way. Some coastal garrisons had been withdrawn from their posts and were being sent to join Johnston. More important, though, was the large body of troops from Mississippi that was moving across Alabama toward Dalton. These men, numbering about 15,000, constituted the Army of Mississippi and were commanded by Lt. Gen. Leonidas Polk. A West Point graduate (1827), Polk had resigned from the Army to enter the Episcopal ministry. In 1861 he was Bishop of Louisiana and entered the Confederate service where he was known as the Bishop-General. When Polk joined Johnston the Confederate strength would be raised to about 70,000.

Before Polk arrived, however, Sherman sent Thomas and Schofield against Johnston's position. On May 7 and 8, there was heavy fighting all along the lines from the area north of Dalton south along Rocky Face Ridge to Dug Gap. The Federals made no real headway, but the demonstration served its purpose, for McPherson reached Snake Creek Gap on the evening of the 8th and found it open.

James Birdseye McPherson, who stood at Snake Creek Gap on

the morning of May 9 with an opportunity to strike Johnston a crippling blow, was one of the Civil War's most attractive leaders. Like Sherman, he was an Ohioan and a West Pointer (1853). In 1864 he was only 35 years old. His entire adult life had been spent in the Army, and in the Civil War his abilities had carried him from captain to major general in slightly more than a year's time. Both Sherman and Grant looked upon him as an outstanding leader—a belief shared by the Confederate editor who called McPherson "the most dangerous man in the whole Yankee army." He was handsome, with flowing hair and whiskers, and he had a special reason for wanting the war to end: when it was over

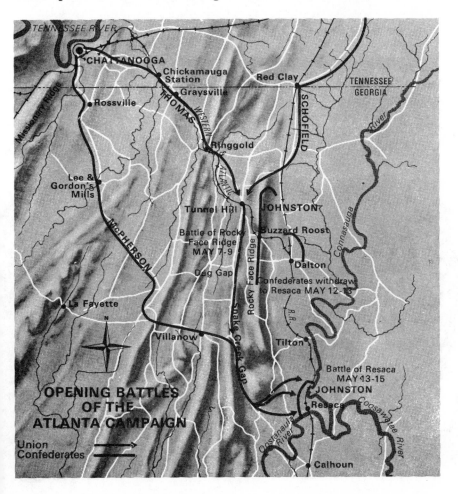

OPENING BATTLES
OF THE
ATLANTA CAMPAIGN

Union
Confederates

*For four long and bloody months, officers and men alike en-
dured the heat and mud of what must have been one of the
wettest seasons in the history of Georgia.*

he would be able to marry the beautiful girl who was waiting for him in Baltimore. He was courteous to men of all ranks, and his adoring soldiers remembered long afterwards his habit of riding in the fields to leave the roads open for them.

On May 9, while skirmishing continued about Dalton, McPherson led his army eastward, hoping to reach the railroad near Resaca and break Johnston's communications with Atlanta. Unknown to the Federals, there were some 4,000 Confederates in Resaca. These included the advance elements of Polk's army, as well as infantry and cavalry units assigned to guard the Oostanaula bridges and to protect the area.

The Northern advance met these Southerners near the town. McPherson, surprised at finding so large a force in his front, moved with great caution. Late in the afternoon, he became worried that Johnston might rush troops southward and cut him off from Sherman. This fear, and the fact that some of his men were without food, led him to break off the engagement and fall back to a position at Snake Creek Gap which he fortified that night.

In the following days, both armies shifted to the Resaca area. Sherman began by sending a division of Thomas' army to aid McPherson. Soon orders followed for almost all of the Federals to march southward, with only a small detachment left to watch Johnston. All day on the 11th the roads west of Rocky Face were crowded with troops, wagons, and guns. Although the march was slowed by a heavy rain, nightfall of the 12th found the Northern army concentrated at Snake Creek Gap. Johnston discovered the Federal move and during the night of May 12–13 ordered his men to Resaca where Polk's troops had been halted.

Skirmishing on the 13th developed the positions of the armies. Johnston had posted his men on the high ground north and west of Resaca. Polk's Corps (as the Army of Mississippi was called) held the Confederate left, Hardee's men occupied the center, and Hood was on the right, with his right flank curved back to the Conasauga River. The Federal advance, McPherson's army, had moved directly toward Resaca. When the advance was slowed, Thomas moved to the north and formed his army on McPherson's left. Schofield moved into position on Thomas' left.

The Battle of Resaca, fought May 13–15, was the first major engagement of the campaign. The 13th was spent in skirmishing and establishing the positions of the two armies. The 14th saw much heavy fighting. Sherman delivered a major attack against the right center of Johnston's line and was hurled back with a heavy loss. One Northerner described the Confederate fire as *"terrific and deadly."* Later, Hood made a determined assault on the Federal left and was prevented from winning a great victory when Union reinforcements were hurried to the scene from other sectors of the line. Late in the day, troops from McPherson's army made slight gains against the Confederate left. Fighting ceased at dark, although firing continued throughout the night. There was no time for the men to rest, however; both Johnston and Sherman kept their soldiers busy digging fortifications, caring for the wounded, moving to new positions, and preparing for the next day's battle.

The heaviest fighting on the 15th occurred at the northern end of the lines. There, both sides made attacks that achieved some local success but were inconclusive. Meanwhile, a Federal detachment had been sent down the Oostanaula to attempt a crossing. At Lay's Ferry, a few miles below Resaca, it got over the river and secured a position from which to strike eastward against Johnston's rail line. The Southern commander believed that this left him no choice but to retreat. Accordingly, during the night of May 15–16, the Confederates withdrew and crossed to the southern bank of the Oostanaula, burning the bridges behind them.

As is the case with many Civil War battles, no accurate casualty figures are available for the engagement at Resaca. Federal losses were probably about 3,500; Confederate casualties were approximately 2,600.

TO THE ETOWAH

South of the Oostanaula, steep ridges and heavy woods give way to gently rolling hills with only a light cover of vegetation. The area was almost without defensible terrain and thus afforded a great advantage to Sherman, whose larger forces would have more opportunities for maneuver than they had found in the mountainous region to the north.

Once across the Oostanaula, Johnston sought to make a stand and draw the Federals into a costly assault. He expected to find favorable terrain near Calhoun, but in this he was disappointed and during the night of May 16–17 he led the Confederates on southward toward Adairsville. The Federals followed—Sherman dividing his forces into three columns and advancing on a broad front. There were skirmishes all along the route during the 16th and 17th, but the main bodies were not engaged.

At Adairsville Johnston again hoped to find a position in which he could give battle, but there too the terrain was unsuitable for defense and the Confederate commander was forced to continue his retreat. As he fell back, however, Johnston devised a strategem that he hoped would lead to the destruction of a part of Sherman's forces. There were two roads leading south from Adairsville—one south to Kingston, the other southeast to Cassville. It seemed likely that Sherman would divide his armies so as to use both roads. This would give Johnston the opportunity to attack one column before the other could come to its aid.

When the Southerners abandoned Adairsville during the night of May 17–18, Johnston sent Hardee's Corps to Kingston while he fell back toward Cassville with the rest of his army. He hoped that Sherman would believe most of the Southerners to be in Kingston and concentrate the bulk of his forces there. Hardee would then hold off the Northerners at Kingston while Johnston, with Polk and Hood, destroyed the smaller Federal column at Cassville.

Sherman reacted as Johnston hoped, ordering McPherson and the bulk of Thomas' army toward Kingston while sending only Schofield and one corps of Thomas' army along the road to Cassville. On the morning of May 19, Johnston ordered Hood to march along a country road a mile or so east of the Adairsville-Cassville Road and form his corps for battle facing west. While

Polk attacked the head of the Federal column, Hood was to assail its left flank. As Hood was moving into position, he found Northern soldiers to the east. This was a source of great danger, for had Hood formed facing west, these Federals would have been in position to attack the exposed flank and rear of his corps. After a brief skirmish with the Northerners, Hood fell back to rejoin Polk. Johnston, believing that the opportunity for a successful battle had passed, ordered Hood and Polk to move to a new line east and south of Cassville, where they were joined by Hardee who had been pushed out of Kingston. Johnston formed his army on a ridge and hoped that Sherman would attack him there on May 20. As usual, the Southern commander was confident of repulsing the enemy.

That night the Confederate leaders held a council of war. Exactly what happened at the council is a matter of dispute. According to Johnston, Polk and Hood reported that their lines could not be held and urged that the army retreat. Believing that the fears of the corps commanders would be communicated to their men and thus weaken the army's confidence, Johnston yielded to these demands, even though he thought the position to be defensible. According to Hood, whose recollection of the council differs markedly from Johnston's, he and Polk told Johnston that the line could not be held against an attack but that it was a good position from which to move against the enemy. Johnston, however, was unwilling to risk an offensive battle and decided to fall back across the Etowah. No definite resolution of this dispute is possible, but most of the available evidence supports Hood's version of the conference. Certainly Johnston was not obligated to allow the advice of subordinates to overrule his own judgment. The responsibility for abandoning the Cassville position rests on the Southern commander.

During the night, the Confederates withdrew across the Etowah. As they fell back, their feelings were mixed. They had lost a very strong position at Dalton, and had fallen back from Resaca, Calhoun, and Adairsville. Now they were retreating again under cover of darkness. That morning as they prepared for battle, their spirits had been high. Now their disappointment was bitter. Although morale would revive in the next few days, many Southern soldiers would never again place as much confidence in Johnston's abilities as they once had.

By contrast, morale in the Federal ranks soared. In a short time of campaigning, the Northerners had "driven" their enemy from one position after another. Sherman was satisfied with the progress his armies had made and, after learning that the Confederates were south of the Etowah, he decided to give his men a short rest. On May 20, one of the Northern generals summarized the situation in a letter to his wife:

Thus far our campaign has succeeded though it must be confessed the rebels have retreated in very good order and their army is still unbroken. Our hard work is still before us. We are still 53 miles from Atlanta and have to pass over a rugged Country. We will have some bloody work before we enter that place.

After a council with Hood and Polk, Johnston abandoned the Cassville position.

NEW HOPE CHURCH

The region south of the Etowah was one of the wildest parts of north Georgia. The area was sparsely settled, hilly, heavily wooded, and, in 1864, little known and poorly mapped. Sherman expected to push through this region with little delay. On May 23 he wrote, "The Etowah is the Rubicon of Georgia. We are now all in motion like a vast hive of bees, and expect to swarm along the Chattahoochee in a few days." His optimism was ill-founded, for the rough terrain and heavy rains favored Johnston's smaller force and helped delay the Federal advance for 5 weeks.

Johnston posted his army around Allatoona Pass, a gap in the high hills south of the Etowah through which the railroad ran on its way southward to Marietta. He had again occupied a strong position hoping that Sherman would attack it. The Federal commander, however, aware of the natural strength of the terrain, was determined to avoid a direct assault and crossed the river to the west where the country was more open. Dallas, a small town about 14 miles south of the river and about the same distance west of the railroad, was the first objective.

The Northerners began their advance on the 23d. McPherson swung far to the west through Van Wert and then moved eastward toward Dallas. Thomas was in the center moving via Stilesboro and Burnt Hickory. Schofield was on the left, closest to the Etowah. The day was hot and the men suffered greatly from thirst. Nevertheless, the Federals made progress toward their objective and, on the 24th, were closing in on Dallas.

Confederate cavalry soon discovered Sherman's movement and Johnston took steps to meet it. By evening of the 24th, the Southerners held a line east of Dallas which ran from southwest to northeast. The key to the position was a crossroads at a Methodist church named New Hope. Hood's Corps held this part of the line. Polk and Hardee were to his left.

On May 25, some troops of Thomas' army ran up against Hood's line at New Hope Church. In a late afternoon battle fought under dark skies and rolling bursts of thunder, Thomas' men made a series of gallant assaults against the Southern line. The Federals met a withering hail of bullets and shells that quickly halted each advance. In this short engagement, Thomas

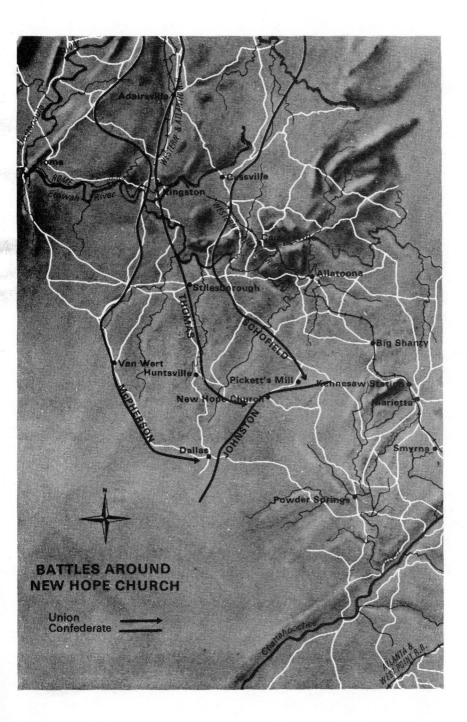

**BATTLES AROUND
NEW HOPE CHURCH**

Union
Confederate

473

lost about 1,500 men. The Confederates suffered little during the battle and were elated at their success.

Sunrise on the 26th found both commanders working to position their men in the woods east of Dallas. Except for skirmishing, there was little fighting during the day.

On the following day, Sherman attempted to defeat the right of the Southern line by a surprise attack. In a battle known as Pickett's Mill, the Northerners were hurled back with about 1,500 casualties. For the Federals, this engagement was one of the most desperate of the campaign. One company of the 41st Ohio Regiment lost 20 of its 22 men. The 49th Ohio carried slightly over 400 men into the battle and lost 203 of them. The commander of another regiment wrote that he lost a third of his men in the first few yards of the advance. "The rebel fire . . . swept the ground like a hailstorm," wrote another Unionist, adding, "this is surely not war it is butchery." A third Northerner noted in his diary that evening, "our men were slaughtered terribly 2 brigades of infantry were almost cut to pieces." The Southerners lost about 500 men.

Over the next few days fighting continued almost incessantly. Both sides made assaults with strongly reinforced skirmish lines, seeking to hold the enemy in position. This type of combat was very tiring on the men. One soldier wrote after a night battle, "O God, what a night. They may tell of hell and its awful fires, but the boys who went thru the fight at Dallas . . . are pretty well prepared for any event this side of eternity."

The days spent in the jungles near New Hope Church were among the most arduous of the war for the soldiers of both armies. In addition to the normal dangers of combat, the men had to undergo unusual physical hardships. Rain, heat, constant alarms, continuous sharpshooting, the stench of the dead, the screams of the wounded, and a serious shortage of food all added to the normal discomforts of life in the field. One Federal soldier described the time spent near Dallas as "Probably the most wretched week" of the campaign. Another wrote of it as "a wearisome waste of life and strength." A third Northerner, referring to an unsuccessful foray against the Confederate lines, wrote, "We have struck a hornet nest at the business end." So severe had the fighting been that Sherman's men would ever afterward refer to the struggle around New Hope Church as the "Battle of the Hell Hole."

When it became clear that no decisive battle would be fought at Dallas, Sherman gradually sidled eastward to regain the railroad. On June 3, advance elements of the Federal forces reached the little town of Acworth, and within a few days, almost all the Northern troops were in that general area. Sherman had outmaneuvered Johnston and bypassed the strong Confederate position at Allatoona, but he had not seriously weakened his opponent. Once again the Federal commander ordered a short halt to rest his troops and allow time to repair the railroad and for reinforcements to arrive.

KENNESAW MOUNTAIN

By June 10, Sherman was ready to resume the advance. The Southerners had taken up a line north of Marietta that ran from Brush Mountain on the east to Pine Mountain in the center to Lost Mountain on the west. McPherson moved against the right flank of this line, Thomas against the center, and Schofield against the left. Rain fell almost every day and hampered the Northern advance. For several days there was heavy skirmishing in which the Federals captured Pine Mountain and made gains at other points. Bishop-General Polk was killed on Pine Mountain by a Union artillery shell on June 14, when he foolishly exposed himself to enemy fire. Maj. Gen. William W. Loring commanded Polk's Corps for several weeks until a permanent replacement, Lt. Gen. Alexander P. Stewart, took command.

By the 16th, Schofield's advance had been so successful that the Southerners were forced to give up Lost Mountain. For several days, Johnston tried to hold a new line that ran west from Brush Mountain and then turned southward. This line was enfiladed by the Federal artillery, however, and during the night of June 18–19 the Confederates abandoned it and took up a new position extending along the crest of Kennesaw Mountain and off to the south. Hardee's Corps held the left of this line, Loring's was in the center, and Hood's was on the right.

When Sherman encountered this strong position, he extended his lines to the south to try to outflank Johnston. He moved most of McPherson's army to the area directly in front of Kennesaw Mountain and placed Thomas' army in line on McPherson's right with orders to extend to the right. In the days that followed, McPherson and Thomas were engaged in what amounted to a siege of the Southern position. Little progress could be made on the ground but the artillery on both sides was used in attempts to batter and weaken the enemy. Day after day, the big Union guns pounded the Southern line, their fire being answered by Confederate cannon high on Kennesaw Mountain.

Meanwhile, Sherman drew Schofield's army in from the Lost Mountain area and ordered it to move south on the Sandtown Road, which ran west of the Federal position toward the Chattahoochee. After a long and muddy march, Schofield's men reached

Nose's Creek at dark on June 19. On the following day, they crossed the swollen stream and drove the Southerners away. The bridge was rebuilt; on the 21st their advance was resumed. That same day, the right of Thomas' army established contact with Schofield near Powder Springs Road.

Johnston had seen the Federal right being extended and was aware of the dangers it presented to his line of communications. To meet this threat the Confederate commander shifted Hood's Corps from the right of his line to the left during the night of June 21–22. By early afternoon of the 22d, Hood's men were in position on Hardee's left.

Early on the 22d, the right of the Northern line resumed its advance. The XX Corps of Thomas' army moved east on Powder Springs Road, supported by some of Schofield's troops. By midafternoon, they reached the vicinity of Valentine Kolb's farm. The rest of Schofield's army continued down Sandtown Road to the Cheney farm, where it occupied a position overlooking Olley's Creek.

In the early part of the afternoon, the Federals captured several Southerners from whom they learned that Hood had moved to the Confederate left. From this they concluded that an attack upon the Federal line was imminent. Quickly the Northern commanders closed up their units and began to construct protecting works, using fence rails or whatever material was at hand. Skirmishers were thrown out, and they soon encountered an advancing line of Southerners. Just what brought about this attack is not clear. Perhaps the activities of the Northern skirmishers led the Confederates to think that the Federals were attacking. Hood may have believed that when the skirmishers fell back he had defeated an assault on his new position and decided to pursue the beaten enemy. At any rate, the Southern advance precipitated a battle at the Kolb farmhouse in which several Confederate attacks were hurled back by the Federals. Hood lost about 1,000 men. Northern casualties were about 300. After the battle, Hood fell back to his original position, extending the Southern line southward to Olley's Creek. For several days, there was relative calm along the lines which now ran from the railroad north of Marietta to Olley's Creek southwest of the town. Meanwhile, the rains ceased and the June sun began to dry the land.

Several days after the battle at Kolb's farm, Sherman decided on a change in tactics—he would make a direct assault on Johnston's lines. It was a bold decision that offered the possibility of a great victory. The Southern line was thinly held and a successful attack could lead to the isolation and destruction of a large part of Johnston's army. The Federal commander decided to strike the Confederates at three points: McPherson would assault the southern end of Kennesaw Mountain, Thomas would move against a salient known as the "Dead Angle" (on what is now called Cheatham's Hill) several miles to the south, and Schofield would push south on Sandtown Road and attempt to cross Olley's Creek. June 27 was set as the date for the assault, but Schofield was to begin demonstrations on the 26th to draw Southerners away from other portions of the line.

Early on the 27th, the Federals began to probe at various points along the Confederate trenches to distract the defenders. At 8 a.m. the Northern artillery opened a brief but heavy fire to prepare the way for the assaults. A few minutes later, the Federal infantry moved forward. McPherson's troops, advancing on both sides of Burnt Hickory Road, swept over the Southern outposts and moved rapidly across the broken ground toward the main Confederate trenches. Although their lines were disordered,

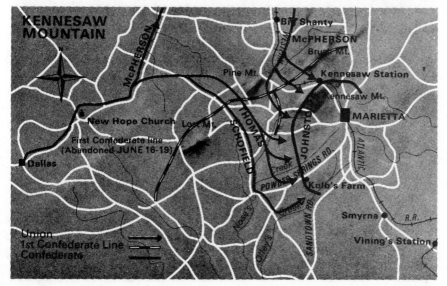

the blue-clad soldiers scrambled over rocks and fallen trees until they were finally halted by the heavy fire from their entrenched enemies. A few reached the Confederate line and were killed or captured while fighting in their opponents' works. Southerners on Little Kennesaw added to the Northerners' discomfort by rolling huge rocks down the mountainside at them. When the Union troops realized that their attack could not reach the Confederate lines, they broke off the engagement. Some were able to find protection in the advanced Confederate rifle-pits they had over-run and some managed to reach the positions from which they had begun the assault. A few were forced to seek shelter among the trees and large rocks on the slopes of the mountain where they remained until darkness offered a chance to return to their own lines.

To the south, Thomas fared no better. Two columns were di-rected against the Southern position—one at Cheatham's Hill, the other a short distance to the north. The Southerners expected no attack. Many of them were off duty and others were relaxing in the lines. The Federal artillery, however, alerted them to the danger and when Thomas' infantry started forward, the Confed-erates were ready.

As soon as the dense blue columns appeared in the cleared area between the lines, the Confederates opened what one Northerner called a "terrible" fire upon them. Men dropped rapidly but the columns continued up the long slope toward the Southern posi-tion. "The air," one Federal remembered, "seemed filled with bullets, giving one the sensation experienced when moving swiftly against a heavy rain or sleet storm." As the Union soldiers neared the crest of the ridge, they met the full fury of the defenders' fire. To one Federal it seemed as if the Confederate trenches were "veritable volcanoes . . . vomiting forth fire and smoke and rain-ing leaden hail in the face of the Union boys."

Most of the attackers never reached the Confederate line. Those who did were too few to overpower the defenders and were quickly killed or captured. For a few brief seconds, two Northern battle flags waved on the breastworks, but the bearers were soon shot down and within a short time the attack had failed.

As Thomas' left assaulting column struck that portion of the Southern line held by the consolidated 1st and 15th Arkansas

Regiments, the gunfire ignited the underbrush and many wounded Federals faced the terrifying prospect of being burned to death. In one of the notable acts of the war, Lt. Col. William H. Martin, commanding the Arkansans, jumped from his trenches waving a white handkerchief and shouting to the Northerners to come and get the wounded men. For a few minutes, fighting was suspended along that short stretch of the line and some of Martin's soldiers went to assist in moving their helpless enemies away from the flames. When the wounded had been removed to safety, the two sides resumed hostilities, but here too it was clear that the attack would not be able to break Johnston's lines.

At the Dead Angle, some of the attacking Northerners remained under the crest of the ridge within a few yards of the Confederate trenches. There they dug rifle pits of their own and started to burrow under the hill, hoping to fill the tunnel with gunpowder and blow up the salient. However, before this project had progressed very far, the Southerners abandoned the position and thus rendered the subterranean attack unnecessary.

While the attacks of McPherson and Thomas were being repulsed, Schofield was gaining a clear success at the extreme right of the Union line. On the 26th, one of his brigades crossed Olley's Creek north of Sandtown Road and, on the following day, cleared their opponents from the area, securing a position several miles to the south which placed the right of their line closer to the Chattahoochee than was the left of Johnston's army. From this position the Northerners could strike at the Confederate line of supply and perhaps cut Johnston off from all sources of help by breaking the railroad.

Exact casualty figures for the battles of June 27 are not available. However, the best estimates place Northern losses at about 3,000 men. The Southerners lost at least 750 killed, wounded, or captured.

Sherman has been criticized for ordering the frontal attack on Johnston's lines, but it now seems that his decision was not unwise. Had the assault succeeded, he would have won a great victory. As it was, he did not continue the attacks when it was clear that they would fail, and he had managed to secure a position from which he could easily pry Johnston out of the Kennesaw line.

Lt. Col. William H. Martin jumped from the trenches waving a white handkerchief and shouting to the Northerners to come and get the wounded men.

ACROSS THE CHATTAHOOCHEE

The success won by Schofield at Olley's Creek indicated the direction for the next Federal movement. Sherman quickly decided to shift troops to his right, knowing that such a move would force Johnston to choose between giving up the Kennesaw line or being cut off from Atlanta. Accordingly, he began to reinforce Schofield by moving McPherson from the left to the right. By the afternoon of July 2, Federal troops were pushing southward on Sandtown Road against only light opposition from small Confederate detachments.

Johnston was aware of what was happening—in fact, he had expected such a movement since the failure of the assault on the 27th. Believing that it would be unwise to stretch his lines further and realizing that the troops opposing the Federal advance could do no more than delay it, Johnston decided to abandon his Kennesaw Mountain position and fall back to a previously prepared line near Smyrna, 4 miles to the south. Accordingly, during the night of July 2–3, the Confederates filed out of their trenches around Marietta and marched southward.

When Sherman discovered that the Southerners were gone, he pushed forward in pursuit, hoping to strike while the enemy was retreating. In the late afternoon of the 3d, the Northerners reached the new Confederate line. The 4th was spent in skirmishing, but before a serious battle could develop, the Federal right secured a strategic position from which it threatened to slice in between Johnston's army and Atlanta. Again, the threat to his left forced Johnston to retreat. During the night of July 4–5, the Southerners fell back to a heavily fortified position on the north bank of the Chattahoochee.

On the 5th, the Federals pushed forward until they reached the new Southern line. Skirmishing that day convinced Sherman that the position was too strong to be carried by a headlong assault. He dispatched a cavalry force to seize Roswell, an important little manufacturing town about 16 miles upriver from Johnston's fortifications, and allowed his men a few days' rest while he planned the next move.

After carefully studying the situation, the Federal commander decided to attempt a crossing near the mouth of Soap Creek, above Johnston's right flank. On July 8, he moved Schofield's

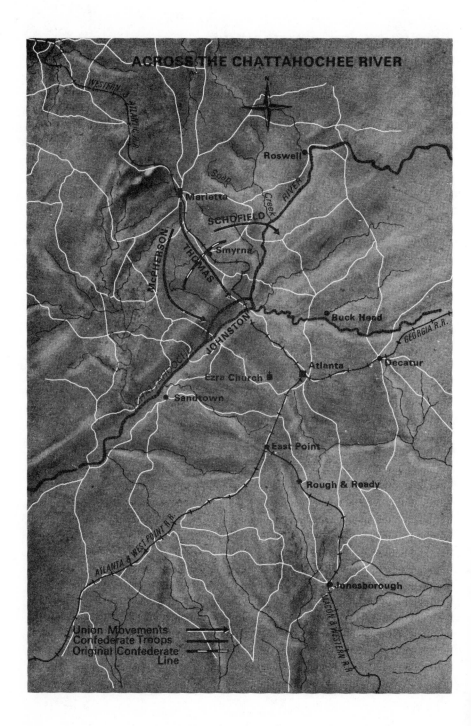

ACROSS THE CHATTAHOCHEE RIVER

Union Movements
Confederate Troops
Original Confederate
Line

Army of the Ohio into position for the crossing. In a brilliant movement, Schofield, utilizing pontoon boats and the ruins of a submerged fish dam, got over the river and drove away the small group of Southerners defending the area. Other troops were rushed across, bridges were built, trenches were dug, and by nightfall the Northerners held a secure bridgehead on the southern bank. On the following day, the Federal cavalry got over the river at Roswell. Sherman had successfully crossed the last major barrier between Chattanooga and Atlanta and had carried the fighting into the open country south of the Chattahoochee where the terrain would favor him.

During the night of July 9–10, Johnston retreated across the river and took up a position on the southern bank of Peachtree Creek only a few miles from Atlanta. The Confederate commander seems to have been optimistic at this time. Once again he believed that he had reached a position from which he could not be driven and he expected to fight the decisive battle of the campaign along Peachtree Creek.

Sherman, meanwhile, had decided upon his next step. He would swing north and east of Atlanta to cut Johnston off from Augusta and possible reinforcements from Virginia. McPherson was to strike eastward from Roswell to the Georgia Railroad at some point near Stone Mountain. As this force advanced, the rest of the Federals would move closer to the river. The line would thus become a great swinging movement, with McPherson on the far left, Schofield in the center as the pivot, and Thomas on the right along Peachtree Creek. This movement began on the 17th. The next day, McPherson reached the Georgia Railroad near Stone Mountain.

JOHNSTON REMOVED FROM COMMAND

The Confederate government had been displeased by Johnston's conduct of the campaign. President Jefferson Davis and other civilian officials had hoped that the Confederates would be able to regain Tennessee or at least to draw Sherman into a situation in which a severe defeat would be inflicted upon him. Instead, after 10 weeks of campaigning, Johnston was backed up against Atlanta and there was no assurance that he would even try to hold that important center. These circumstances led Davis to remove Johnston from command of the army and to replace him with John B. Hood, who was promoted to the temporary rank of full general.

Davis' replacement of Johnston with Hood is one of the most controversial acts of the war. Relations between the President and Johnston had not been friendly since a dispute over the general's rank in 1861. Disagreements over strategy and tactics as well as the personalities of the two men exacerbated matters in 1862 and 1863. During Johnston's tenure as commander of the Army of Tennessee, the situation became worse as communications between the two broke down almost completely. Davis promoted officers in the army without consulting Johnston, who maneuvered in the field without informing the government of his plans and operations in any meaningful detail.

Davis saw that Johnston had yielded much valuable territory to the enemy. Important officials in the government began to urge that the general be removed from command. On July 9, Davis sent his military adviser, Gen. Braxton Bragg, to report on the situation in Georgia. Bragg visited Johnston, learned nothing of the general's plans, and reported that it appeared the city would be abandoned. Other evidence brought to the President's attention—such as Johnston's suggestion that prisoners held in south Georgia be sent to safer points—seemed to confirm Bragg's assessment that Atlanta would not be defended. On July 16, Davis telegraphed Johnston: "I wish to hear from you as to present situation and your plan of operations so specifically as will enable me to anticipate events." The general's reply of the same date read in part:

As the enemy has double our numbers, we must be on the defensive. My plan of operations must, therefore, depend upon that of the enemy.

It is mainly to watch for an opportunity to fight to advantage. We are trying to put Atlanta in condition to be held for a day or two by the Georgia militia, that army movements may be freer and wider.

This vague reply did not satisfy Davis and on July 17 he issued the order that removed Johnston from command. In great haste, Johnston wrote out an order relinquishing his position and thanking the soldiers for their courage and devotion. By the afternoon of the 18th he had left Atlanta and the Army of Tennessee in the none-too-steady hands of John Bell Hood.

Much debate has swirled around Davis' decision. Johnston and his partisans have argued that the general's removal made inevitable the loss of Atlanta, the reelection of Lincoln, and the defeat of the Confederacy. They contend that had Johnston remained in command, the city would have been held, or that if it were surrendered, the army at least would not have been weakened and would have continued as an effective unit.

Hood and Davis maintained that Johnston's long retreat had demoralized the army, that Johnston would not have held Atlanta, and that the Confederacy's only chance for success lay in replacing Johnston with a bold commander who could strike Sherman a blow that would send the Northerners reeling back to Chattanooga.

Most historians have tended to accept Johnston's position. There can be no definite answer, of course, but it does seem that Johnston would have evacuated the city rather than lose a large portion of his army fighting for it. This would have saved the army but, coming after the long retreat from Dalton, might have so demoralized it that desertion and disgust would have ended its career as an effective fighting force. If the retention of Atlanta was essential to the life of the Confederacy, President Davis seems justified in his decision to remove Johnston. It was the Confederacy's misfortune that no bold, intelligent, and lucky general was available to take his place. But one thing was certain— with Hood leading the Southerners, the pattern of the campaign would change.

IN THE RANKS

Historians have long been in the habit of dealing with the past as if it were nothing more than the story of a small number of great men who moved about shaping the world as they saw fit. In reality, leaders are not long successful without followers—the great mass of the common people who do the work, bear the burdens, and suffer the consequences of their leaders' policies. The Civil War offers a unique opportunity to study the common people of America because during that conflict large numbers of people were directly involved in the great events of the times. For most of them, the war was the single most important event of their lives. Consequently they wrote about it in great detail in their letters and diaries and saved these documents after the conflict ended. It is therefore possible to see the Civil War armies as groups of humans, not masses of automata. The men who followed Sherman, Johnston, and Hood in 1864 left behind information that adds much to an understanding of the campaign.

Records kept by the Federal Government show that the typical Northern soldier was 5 feet 8¼ inches tall and weighed 143½ pounds. Doubtless the Southerners were of a similar stature. The same records also indicate that before the war 48 percent of the men had been farmers. Among the Confederates the percentage of farmers was more than half. Relatively few immigrants served in either western army—perhaps one-fifth to one-sixth of the men were of foreign birth. More than half the units in Sherman's armies were from Illinois, Indiana, and Ohio. Iowa, Kentucky, Missouri, and Wisconsin also furnished large contingents. Such Eastern States as New York, Connecticut, New Jersey, and Pennsylvania were represented, but their contributions were small. More than two-thirds of the units in the Southern army were from Tennessee, Alabama, Mississippi, and Georgia. Other States with significant numbers of troops in the Confederate ranks were Texas, Arkansas, and Louisiana. Alabama, Kentucky, Missouri, and Tennessee were represented by units on both sides. Most of the men in the armies that struggled for Atlanta had volunteered for military service in 1861 or 1862. By 1864 they had become veterans, inured to the hardships of military life. Nevertheless, they found the Atlanta Campaign a severe trial.

Unlike many Civil War military operations in which fighting occurred at infrequent intervals, the struggle for Atlanta was virtually a continuous battle. Sometimes, as at Resaca, almost all of the opposing forces were engaged; at other times, action was limited to the desultory firing of skirmishers. But only on rare occasions were the soldiers able to escape the sounds and dangers of combat.

The weather—whether a freak cold wave in mid-June, the unusually heavy rains of late May and June, or the normal heat of July and August—affected every man and often hampered troop movements as well. Frequently units on the march lost men who could not stand the pace. The soldiers would drop by the roadside until they had recovered their strength, then move on to overtake their comrades. For example, the heat on July 12 was so bad that only 50 of the men in an Illinois regiment could keep up on a 3-mile march. When the armies were in fortified positions, as they were at Kennesaw Mountain, the men often stretched blankets or brush across the trenches to protect themselves from the sun. On rainy days, fence rails or rocks in the trenches served to keep soldiers out of the water.

Clothing was also a problem. As a rule, Sherman's men were better supplied than their opponents, but the wool uniforms they wore were unsuited to the hot Georgia summer. The Confederates had almost no new clothing after the campaign began and their uniforms deteriorated rapidly. A Texan summed up their plight in early June when he wrote: "In this army one hole in the seat of the breeches indicates a captain, two holes a lieutenant, and the seat of the pants all out indicates that the individual is a private."

Rarely did the men of either army have a chance to wash and almost all of them were affected by body lice and other vermin. A sense of humor helped them to survive these trials—soldiers who were pinned down in a water-filled trench by enemy fire consoled themselves with the thought that they were at least drowning the lice. The Federals complained that the retreating Southerners infested the country with lice that attacked the advancing Northerners. Other pests included chiggers, ticks, snakes, scorpions, flies, and ants.

Soldiers in both armies suffered from a shortage of food and

By 1864 most of the men in the armies that struggled for Atlanta had become veterans, inured to the hardships of military life.

Soldiers in both armies had no scruples about supplementing their rations with whatever could be taken from surrounding farms and homes.

had no scruples about supplementing their rations with whatever could be taken from the surrounding farms and homes. Corn, pork, chickens, geese, hams, potatoes, apples, and onions disappeared as the armies moved through a neighborhood. Wild berries and fish were also eaten. Nevertheless, there were many times when food was in short supply. One Federal wrote, "most of the time we are on the move and cannot get such as is fit for a man to eat."

The Atlanta Campaign, like many of the later Civil War campaigns, saw the development of trench warfare on a large scale. Protecting works were built from loose rocks, fence rails, tombstones, or even the bodies of dead comrades. By the third or fourth week of the campaign, both sides had mastered the art of field fortification—a trench, with the dirt piled on the side toward the enemy and surmounted by a headlog under which were small openings for firing. Such works left "little but the eyes . . . exposed" to enemy fire. In front of the trenches the underbrush would be cleared away and young trees cut so they fell toward the foe. The trees were left partly attached to the stump so that they could not be dragged aside. Telegraph wire was sometimes strung between them to create further obstacles.

From behind their fortifications soldiers could pour out such a volume of fire that there was no chance for a successful massed attack—unless complete surprise could be achieved or overwhelming numbers brought against a weak part of the enemy's line. Much of the fighting was therefore done by small patrols and snipers, especially in heavily wooded country such as the area around New Hope Church and Kennesaw Mountain.

The soldier who died in battle could expect no elaborate funeral. Usually the armies were too busy to do more than bury the dead as quickly as possible and they would probably be put in a mass grave near the place where they had fallen. Later the bodies might be exhumed and moved to a cemetery where they would be listed as "unidentified" and reinterred in a numbered but nameless grave.

The soldier who was wounded or who was disabled by disease suffered greatly. As a rule, the Northerner who was sent to an army hospital fared better than his opponent because the Federals were better equipped and provisioned than the Confederates. Field hospitals treated men whose wounds were either very slight or too serious to permit further movement. Others were sent by wagon and rail to hospitals in the rear—Rome, Chattanooga, and Knoxville for the Federals; Atlanta and the small towns along the railroads south of that city for the Southerners.

Transportation in crowded hospital wagons over rutted roads or in slow hospital trains was an indescribable horror. The hospitals themselves were better but, by modern standards, uncomfortable and dirty. For painful operations, Northern soldiers often enjoyed the blessing of chloroform. Many Southerners, however, especially those in the hospitals in smaller towns, frequently endured major surgery without the benefit of any opiate except, perhaps, whiskey. In such cases the hospitals echoed with the screams of men undergoing amputations or such treatments as that calling for the use of nitric acid to burn gangrene out of their wounds.

No precise figures as to the number of men who were killed, wounded, or sick during the campaign are available. However, it is known that for the war as a whole, disease killed about twice as many men as did the weapons of the enemy. Sickness brought on by exposure and unsanitary camps undoubtedly accounted for

many lives among the soldiers in Georgia. Diseases that were especially common were smallpox, scurvy, dysentery, diarrhea (also known as "dierear" and the "Tennessee quick step"), and various types of fevers.

Religion provided a great source of comfort for many soldiers. Chaplains accompanied both armies but were too few to serve all the troops. Some chaplains preferred to spend the campaign in the rear where they would be safe, while others, of far more influence with the men, braved hardships and dangers with the units they served. At least three of the latter group were killed in battle during the campaign—either while helping the wounded or fighting in the ranks. When chaplains were not available the men sometimes organized and conducted their own religious services. On the other hand, many soldiers ignored religion altogether and continued such "sinful" practices as cursing, drinking, and gambling. Nevertheless, what one soldier called "the missionary influence of the enemy's cannon" and the constant presence of death and suffering led many to seek comfort in religion.

Throughout the campaign, when the armies were in a relatively stable situation, the men sometimes agreed not to shoot at one another. Instead, they would meet between the lines to talk, swim, drink, bathe, enjoy the sun, pick blackberries, exchange newspapers, swap Northern coffee for Southern tobacco, play cards, wrestle, eat, sing, rob the dead, and argue politics. Officers on both sides tried to prohibit this fraternization, but the men in the ranks had the good sense to ignore their orders. These informal truces would usually be respected by all, and when they were over, fighting would not resume until every man had gotten back to his own trenches. Much of the tragedy of the war was reflected in a letter written by a Wisconsin soldier on June 24:

We made a bargain with them that we would not fire on them if they would not fire on us, and they were as good as their word. It seems too bad that we have to fight men that we like. Now these Southern soldiers seem just like our own boys, only they are on the other side. They talk about their people at home, their mothers and fathers and their sweethearts, just as we do among ourselves.

However, regardless of the soldiers' feelings about each other during those times of truce, the war was being run by the generals and the generals said it must go on.

PEACHTREE CREEK

John Bell Hood, the new commander of the Confederate forces, found himself in a difficult position on the morning of July 18, 1864. Hood was young—only 33—and relatively inexperienced in handling large bodies of troops. After graduation from West Point (in the same class with the Federal generals McPherson and Schofield) he had served with the U.S. Army until the spring of 1861, when he resigned and cast his lot with the Confederacy. In the early years of the war Hood had risen rapidly in rank—a rise more than justified by his outstanding leadership at the brigade and division level.

Until the summer of 1863, Hood had been physically one of the most magnificent men in the Confederate Army. A woman who knew him in 1861 described him as "six feet two inches in height, with a broad, full chest, light hair and beard, blue eyes, with a peculiarly soft expression, commanding in appearance, dignified in deportment, gentlemanly and courteous to all." By the time he took command of the Army of Tennessee, Hood's appearance had undergone some changes. His left arm dangled uselessly at his side, smashed by a Federal bullet at Gettysburg in July 1863. His right leg was gone, cut away at the hip following a wound received at the Battle of Chickamauga in September 1863. Hood suffered great pain from these wounds, and no doubt he should have been retired from field command; but he was not the kind of man who could stay away from the army during a war.

After recovering from his second wound, he was sent to the Army of Tennessee as a corps commander and had served in that capacity until Davis selected him to succeed Johnston. He may have been taking a derivative of laudanum to ease his pain and some students of the war believe that this affected his judgment. Many soldiers in the army distrusted Hood's ability. Some officers resented his promotion over the heads of generals who had served with the army since the beginning of the war. Hood himself believed that the army had been demoralized by Johnston's long retreat and hence was unlikely to fight well.

Nor could the tactical situation have brought Hood any encouragement. Thomas' Army of the Cumberland was advancing southward directly toward Atlanta, while the armies of McPherson and Schofield were east of the city, advancing westward. Two

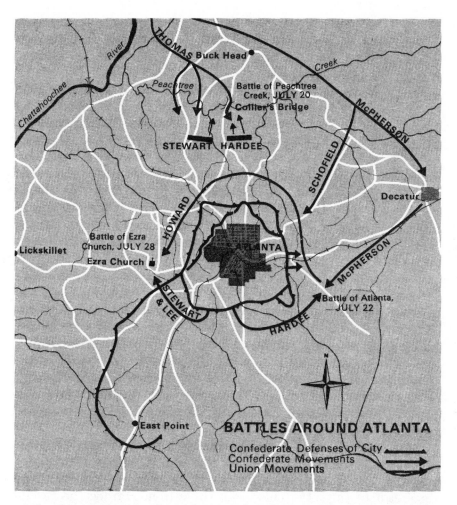

Battles Around Atlanta

Buck Head

Battle of Peachtree
Creek, JULY 20
Collier's Bridge

STEWART   HARDEE

Battle of Ezra
Church, JULY 28

Lickskillet

Ezra Church

SCHOFIELD

Decatur

Battle of Atlanta,
JULY 22

ATLANTA

STEWART
& LEE

HARDEE

HOWARD

THOMAS

McPHERSON

McPHERSON

East Point

BATTLES AROUND ATLANTA

Confederate Defenses of City
Confederate Movements
Union Movements

of the four railroads that connected Atlanta with the rest of the
Confederacy were in Federal hands. Unless Hood could keep the
remaining lines open, the city was doomed.

On July 19, the Army of the Cumberland crossed Peachtree
Creek, but as it advanced, it drifted toward the west. Thus by the
afternoon a gap had developed in the Northern line between
Thomas on the right and Schofield in the center. Hood decided to
concentrate the corps of Hardee and Stewart against Thomas.
The Confederate commander hoped to overwhelm the isolated
Army of the Cumberland before help could arrive from McPher-

son and Schofield. Hood relied upon his former corps, temporarily commanded by Maj. Gen. Benjamin F. Cheatham, and the cavalry to defend the area east of Atlanta. The attack on Thomas was set for 1 p.m., July 20.

Early in the morning of the 20th, while the Southerners were preparing to assail the right of the Federal line, the Northerners east of Atlanta moved west along the Georgia Railroad toward the city. Their progress was so rapid that Hood felt it necessary to shift his army to the right in an effort to strengthen the forces defending the eastern approaches to Atlanta. This movement led to such confusion in the Confederate ranks that the attack against Thomas was delayed for about 3 hours. When the Southerners were finally ready to strike, Thomas' men had had time to establish and partly fortify a position on the south side of Peachtree Creek.

What Hood had planned as a quick blow against an unprepared Northern army thus developed into a headlong assault against a partially fortified line. For several hours the Southerners threw themselves against the Federals. Most of the attacks were halted before they seriously threatened the Union position, but for a short while it appeared that some of Hardee's men would sweep around the left of Thomas' line and win a great victory. Hastily, Thomas assembled artillery batteries and directed their fire against the Southerners. Eventually the Confederates were driven back.

While fighting raged along Peachtree Creek, McPherson continued to push toward Atlanta from the east. By 6 p.m., Hood was forced to call upon Hardee for troops to reinforce the Southern lines east of the city. This order drew from Hardee the reserve division that he was preparing to throw into the assault against Thomas and forced him to abandon the attack. The first of Hood's efforts to cripple the Federal army had failed, although at the time some Southerners saw it as a blow that slowed Federal progress.

Northern casualties in the Battle of Peachtree Creek were reported at 1,600. Estimates of Southern losses (mostly from Federal sources) range from 2,500 to 10,000. It seems now that 4,700 is a reliable estimate of Confederate casualties.

Gen. John B. Hood

The battle later became a source of controversy between Hood and Hardee. Hood, smarting under the criticism of Joseph E. Johnston and others, blamed the failure to crush Thomas on Hardee. The corps commander, Hood charged, had failed to attack at the proper time and had not driven home the assault. Hardee, who had outranked Hood when they were both lieutenant generals and who may have been disgruntled at serving under his former junior, replied that the delay was caused by Hood's decision to shift the line to the right and that the assault had not been as vigorously executed as it normally would have been because Hood's late-afternoon order to send reinforcements to the right had deprived the attackers of the unit that was to deliver the final blow. Postwar commentators mostly favor Hardee and a careful examination of the evidence supports this view.

THE BATTLE OF ATLANTA

After the Battle of Peachtree Creek, attention shifted to the eastern side of the city. Hood determined to strike McPherson who, on July 20 and 21, had moved past Decatur and entrenched a line running north and south a few miles east of Atlanta. The Confederate commander realized that he might march troops around the left of McPherson's position and attack him from the flank and rear. He chose Hardee's Corps to be the flanking column and planned to have Cheatham's men attack the front of McPherson's army from the west while Hardee struck from the south and east. With luck, this sensible plan could result in the defeat of a large part of Sherman's forces.

Late on the 21st, Hardee's men withdrew from their advanced position north of Atlanta and by midnight they were marching out of the city. They were to move southward, then turn and swing eastward and northward. Meanwhile, the other Southerners fell back to shorter lines where, it was hoped, they would be able to hold off the Federals while Hardee outflanked them.

On the morning of July 22, Sherman found the Southerners gone from his immediate front and concluded that Atlanta had been abandoned. However, as his armies pushed forward, they discovered that the defenders had only fallen back to a new position. The Northern advance contracted the Federal lines and the XVI Corps of McPherson's army was crowded out of place. McPherson ordered it to move to his extreme left. Thus at the time Hardee was moving to that area, McPherson, by chance, was sending in reinforcements.

Hardee's march was long and hard. Poor roads, inept guides, and the July heat combined to delay the Southerners. It was not until noon that Hardee had his men in position, and at 1 p.m. he sent them forward. The Confederates made their way through heavy underbrush and emerged facing the Federal XVI Corps which had halted in a perfect position to meet the charge which broke upon them.

Poor coordination also weakened the force of the Confederate offensive. Cheatham's men, who assailed the XVII Corps, did not join the assault until about 3:30, by which time Hardee's attack had lost much of its force. Nevertheless, the fighting was severe. One Federal brigadier wrote of the attackers:

They burst forth from the woods in truly magnificent style in front of my right. . . . Hardly had the enemy made his appearance in my front when [the artillery] . . . opened on them a deadly fire, which rather staggered their line, yet on came the advancing rebels, and hotter grew the fire of . . . [our artillery]. At the same time the . . . infantry . . . opened on them with cool and deadly aim. Still on came the charging columns, more desperate than ever, those in front urged up by those in rear.

The first charge was driven back, but the Southerners returned to the attack again and again throughout the long afternoon. Several times they swarmed over the Federal positions, capturing men and cannon, but each time they were driven back. In one of the early charges, McPherson was killed by advancing Confederate skirmishers as he rode forward to rally his men. Finally, about 7 p.m., the Southerners abandoned the attack and fell back. Their losses have been estimated at about 8,000. Union casualties were reported at 3,722.

For the second time Hood had lashed out at his opponent and had been thrown back. Later he tried to shift the blame to Hardee whom he accused of failing to be in the proper place at the proper time. In post-war years, a bitter verbal battle raged over the question. Most present-day authorities feel that Hardee did all that could reasonably have been asked of him. His troops were worn from the battle on Peachtree Creek, the bad roads slowed his march, and the fateful positioning of the XVI Corps was a matter over which he had no control.

In the summer of 1864, however, many Confederates saw the battle as a splendid victory. One artilleryman wrote on July 23:

We gained a great victory yesterday of which I suppose you know [from newspapers] as much as I do. We left before much was accomplished but hear that our corps captured 3,500 prisoners and 22 pieces of artillery & the enemies killed & wounded amounted to twice our own.

EZRA CHURCH

For several days after the Battle of Atlanta, there was a lull in military activities around the city. Both sides were reorganizing. Sherman selected Maj. Gen. Oliver O. Howard to command the army that McPherson had led. On the Confederate side, Lt. Gen. Stephen D. Lee replaced Cheatham as commander of the corps that had originally been Hood's.

By July 26, Sherman had decided upon his next maneuver. His goal was the railroads south and west of Atlanta—the last links between that city and the rest of the Confederacy—and to reach them he would swing Howard's Army of the Tennessee around from his extreme left to his extreme right. The movement began that afternoon and by nightfall on the 27th, Howard's men were west of Atlanta. Early the following day the advance was resumed. The only effective opposition came from a small body of Confederate cavalry.

Hood was aware of Sherman's new maneuver and determined to block it by sending the corps of Lee and Stewart west along the road to the little settlement of Lickskillet. By noon the opposing forces were in the area of a meetinghouse known as Ezra Church, about 2½ miles west of Atlanta. The Confederates had been ordered to attack and prevent the Northerners from crossing the road, and Lee and Stewart sent their men forward in a series of assaults against the XV Corps. The Federals had not had time to entrench, but they had piled up barricades of logs and church benches, and these afforded some protection.

"Our skirmishers, overpowered by numbers, were compelled to fall back to the main line," wrote a Union officer,

followed at an interval of but a few paces by dense columns of the enemy, which, covered as they were by the undergrowth, advanced within forty or fifty paces of our lines, when a terrific and destructive fire was opened upon them, and was continued steadily until their advance was checked, at the distance of some twenty to thirty paces. Their lines were cut down, disordered, and driven back some distance, when they rallied and again came boldly forward to the charge, but under the murderous fire of our rifles were no more able to disorder or discompose our lines than before. They gained a little ground several times, only to lose it inch by inch, after the most terrible fighting on both sides. . . . After a very short interval, which did not amount to a cessation of the battle, new and largely augmented columns of the enemy came pouring in upon us, with the same results, however, as before, although their colors were planted within twenty paces.

For 4 or 5 hours the assaults continued, but the Confederates attacked piecemeal—separate units rushing forward—rather than striking a unified blow, and all their desperate courage was not enough to overcome this handicap. The Southern army is estimated to have suffered about 5,000 casualties in this battle. Federal losses were reported at 600.

504

THE MONTH OF AUGUST

Although he had inflicted heavy losses on the Southerners, Sherman seems to have become convinced that he would not be able to capture Atlanta by his customary tactics. Hood had constructed a line of trenches that ran from Atlanta southward to East Point, protecting the railroads. The Confederate fortifications were too strong to be attacked and too long to be encircled. Sherman brought up a battery of siege guns and shelled the city. The Southern artillery in Atlanta replied and for several weeks helpless citizens lived in their cellars and scurried about amid bursting shells as the artillery duels started fires and smashed buildings, killing soldiers and civilians indiscriminately.

The Federal commander also decided to try cavalry raids in the hope that his horsemen could reach the railroads below Atlanta and, by cutting them, force Hood to evacuate the city. Late in July, two expeditions were launched. One under Brig. Gen. George Stoneman was to swing to the east to McDonough, Lovejoy Station, and Macon, tearing up the railroad and destroying supplies as it went. These cavalrymen were then to strike southwest to Americus where they hoped to free the 30,000 Northerners held in the prisoner of war camp at Andersonville. The other expedition, under Brig. Gen. Edward M. McCook, was to operate to the west and join Stoneman in attacking the Confederate lines of communication south of Atlanta.

From the start both raids were badly managed. Much of the blame must rest upon Stoneman who chose to go directly to Macon rather than follow orders. The scattered Federals were faced by a well-handled Confederate force led by Wheeler. Except for Stoneman's column, the Northern horsemen were driven back to Sherman's lines after destroying some Confederate supplies. Stoneman reached the vicinity of Macon where on July 31 he was attacked by the Southerners and captured along with 500 of his men.

Somehow during these busy weeks, Sherman found time to write a letter to Miss Emily Hoffman of Baltimore, the fiancée of the dead McPherson. "I owe you heartfelt sympathy," he wrote, adding, "I yield to none of Earth but yourself the right to excell me in lamentations for our Dead Hero. Better the bride of McPherson dead than the wife of the richest Merchant of Baltimore." Sherman described the fallen leader of the Army of the Tennessee who had been a close friend as well as a trusted subordinate as "the impersonation of Knighthood" and added that "while Life lasts I will delight in the Memory of that bright particular star."

On August 10, Hood, perhaps thinking that the defeat of Stoneman and McCook had weakened Sherman's cavalry, struck out at his opponent's line of supply. He sent cavalry commander Wheeler with 4,000 men to destroy the railroad north of Marietta and to disrupt Sherman's communications with the North. Although Wheeler was able to make some temporary breaks in the line, he was unable to reduce substantially the flow of supplies to Sherman's armies. The Federal commander had built strong fortifications at the most strategic points on the railroad and his efficient repair crews quickly rebuilt those parts of the track that Wheeler could reach and damage. Eventually, the Confederate cavalry drifted into Tennessee and did not rejoin Hood until the campaign was over. Many students of the war regard Wheeler's mission as a mistake because the absence of the cavalry deprived Hood of the best means of keeping posted on Sherman's activities and thus proved fatal to the army at Atlanta.

Wheeler's departure led Sherman to send out a third cavalry expedition, commanded by Brig. Gen. Judson Kilpatrick. The Northerners reached the railroads below Atlanta and on August 18–20 succeeded in tearing up sections of the track. On the 20th they were driven away. Kilpatrick reported to Sherman that the railroad had been so thoroughly wrecked that it would take at least 10 days to repair it. However, on the following day, the Federals saw trains bringing supplies into the city from the south. Clearly the Northern cavalry was not strong enough to destroy Hood's lines of supply. New plans would have to be tried if the Unionists were to capture Atlanta.

Meanwhile, a curious kind of optimism was developing in the Southern ranks. Many Confederates did not see the hard battles of late July as defeats. Rather they viewed them as successful efforts to halt the progress of flanking columns that had threatened the city's lines of supply. One officer wrote on August 4 about the battles of Atlanta and Ezra Church: "General Hood watches his flanks closely and has twice whipped the flanking columns." When Sherman made no new efforts to flank the city and when the Northern cavalry raids were beaten off one after another, many men came to believe that Atlanta had been saved. In mid-August a Texan informed his homefolk that "affairs are brightening here. People and army seem more confident of success." At about the same time, a Mississippian wrote that "The enemy seems checked in his flanking operations on our left, as he has made no progress in that direction for the last four or five days." On August 28, an Alabamian wrote his wife that "It required hard fighting to check the enemy here after having pursued us so far."

At the very end of August there came exciting news for the Southerners. Sherman had fallen back! The Northerners were gone from in front of Atlanta! Many thought Wheeler's cavalry had cut off Sherman's supplies and that this had forced the Federal commander to lift the siege. Joyous Confederates swarmed out of the city to romp over the abandoned Northern trenches. "The scales have turned in favor of the South," wrote Capt. Thomas J. Key of Arkansas, "and the Abolitionists are moving to the rear."

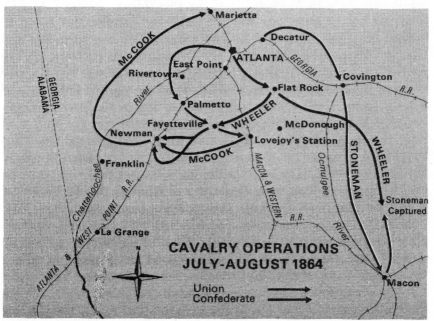

CAVALRY OPERATIONS
JULY-AUGUST 1864

Union
Confederate

JONESBOROUGH

Some Southerners suspected in 1864 what we now know—Sherman had not retreated. Rather, he had concluded that only his infantry could effectively break Hood's lines of supply and had resolved to move almost all of his force to the southwest of the city. The movement began on August 25. One corps was sent back to the Chattahoochee bridgehead to guard the railroad that connected Sherman with the North. The remaining Federal troops pulled out of their trenches and marched away to the west and south. By noon on the 28th, Howard's Army of the Tennessee had reached Fairburn, a small station on the Atlanta and West Point Railroad, 13 miles southwest of East Point. Later that afternoon, Thomas' troops occupied Red Oak, on the railroad 5 miles to the northeast. The Northerners spent the rest of the 28th and the 29th destroying the tracks. The rails were torn up, heated, and twisted so that they were useless. Only one railroad, the Macon and Western, running southeast from East Point to Macon, now remained in Confederate hands. Sherman soon moved to cut it.

By August 29, Hood had learned of the activities of the Federals at Fairburn. It was clear that the railroad to Macon would be Sherman's next objective and the Southern commander acted to defend that line. However, he badly misjudged the situation and thought that only two corps of Sherman's army were to the southwest. Late on August 30, Hood ordered Hardee to take two corps of the Southern army, move against the raiding column, and drive it away. Both armies were soon closing in on Jonesborough, 14 miles below East Point on the Macon railroad. By that evening, advance elements of the Union forces had crossed the Flint River and entrenched a position 1 mile west of Jonesborough. During the night, Hardee's Southerners moved into the town by rail; by morning they were deploying in front of the Federal line.

Hardee had his own corps (temporarily led by Maj. Gen. Patrick R. Cleburne) and Lee's. It took until mid-afternoon to complete preparations for an attack. The Confederates advanced about 3 p.m., their assault falling mostly on an entrenched salient on the east bank of the Flint held by the Army of the Tennessee. The attack was fierce but uncoordinated and failed to drive back the Northerners. When the fighting ceased that night, the relative positions of the armies were unchanged.

Meanwhile, Schofield's Army of the Ohio had managed to break the Macon railroad near Rough-and-Ready, a small station between Jonesborough and East Point. This movement led Hood to conclude that Sherman's main force was attacking Atlanta from the south. The Confederate commander, therefore, ordered Lee's Corps to leave Hardee at Jonesborough and move toward Atlanta to help defend the city. Lee began this movement at 2 a.m. the next morning.

At dawn on September 1, Sherman with almost all of his troops was south of Atlanta. The Federals were concentrating at Jonesborough where they had encountered the bulk of the Southern army on the preceding day and where it seemed a decisive battle would be fought. The Confederates were widely separated. Hood, with one corps, was in Atlanta; Hardee, with his corps, was at Jonesborough; and Lee, with the remaining corps, was near East Point.

At Jonesborough, Hardee had taken up a defensive position north and west of the town. During the afternoon he was attacked by the overwhelming force of Northerners concentrated there. Although suffering many casualties, especially in prisoners, Hardee's Corps fought well and held its position until night offered a chance to fall back to Lovejoy's Station, 7 miles to the south.

By this time Hood had realized what was happening and knew that Atlanta could not be held any longer. During the night of September 1–2, he evacuated the city. Supplies that could not be carried away were burned. Hood's forces moved far to the east of the city to pass around Jonesborough and join Hardee at Lovejoy's Station. On September 2, Mayor James M. Calhoun surrendered Atlanta to a party of Federal soldiers.

On the following day, Sherman sent a telegram to the authorities in Washington announcing that "Atlanta is ours, and fairly won." He added that he would not pursue the Confederates, who were then fortified at Lovejoy's Station, but would return to Atlanta so that his men could enjoy a brief respite from fighting. "Since May 5," he wrote, "we have been in one constant battle or skirmish, and need rest."

A few days later another Federal wrote from his camp near

Atlanta: "Here we will rest until further orders . . . . The campaign that commenced May 2 is now over, and we will rest here to recruit and prepare for a new campaign."

Some writers have been critical of Sherman's decision not to press after Hood's army. They maintain that the enemy force and not the city of Atlanta was the true objective of the Unionists. It may have been that Sherman's action was determined by the question of supplies or it may have been that his men were too exhausted for immediate operations south of the city. At any rate, the capture of Atlanta delighted and heartened Northerners. News of Sherman's victory was greeted with ringing bells and cannon fire all over the North.

EPILOGUE

Sherman soon turned Atlanta into an armed camp. Houses were torn down and the lumber used for fortifications or soldiers' huts. Civilians could not be fed by the army and were ordered out of the city with the choice of going north or south. In mid-September a truce was declared and the citizens who chose to remain in the Confederacy were transported by the Northerners to Rough-and-Ready, where they were handed over to Hood's men who conveyed them farther south.

After completion of this unpleasant task, Hood determined to reverse Sherman's strategy and to move with his whole army around Atlanta to draw Sherman after him into Alabama or Tennessee. In late September the Confederates crossed the Chattahoochee and marched northward over many of the summer's battlefields. Sherman left a strong garrison in Atlanta and followed Hood northward for several weeks. Unable to bring his opponent to bay, Sherman detached a strong force to deal with the Confederates and returned to Atlanta. Hood's army was virtually destroyed in several battles fought in Tennessee in November and December. Sherman, meanwhile, reorganized his armies and on November 15 burned Atlanta and marched out of the city on his way to the sea.

The final importance of the Atlanta Campaign may lie more in its psychological impact than in any military results. Essentially, in early September, the Confederate military forces were in the same position relative to the Northern armies that they had held early in the spring. Psychologically, however, there had been a great shift. The news that Atlanta had fallen meant that the average Northerner had at last a tangible military victory that made it possible for him to see the end of the war in the future. There would be more months of marching, fighting, and dying, but Sherman's capture of Atlanta convinced many that the Confederacy was doomed.

SHERMAN IN ATLANTA: A Photographic Portfolio

On September 3, 1864, President Abraham Lincoln telegraphed the commanding officer of the Federal Military Division of the Mississippi: "The national thanks are rendered . . . to Major-General W. T. Sherman and the officers and soldiers of his command before Atlanta, for the distinguished ability and perserverence displayed in the campaign in Georgia which, under Divine favor, has resulted in the capture of Atlanta. The marches, battles, sieges and other military operations that have signalized the campaign, must render it famous in the annals of war, and have entitled those who have participated therein to the applause and thanks of the nation."

The Union soldiers had, in Sherman's words, "completed the grand task which has been assigned us by our Government." Atlanta, chief rail hub of the Confederacy and one of the South's principal distributing, industrial, commercial, and cultural centers, was in Federal hands at last. It was a choice prize.

The city was founded in 1837 as Terminus, so-named because a rail line ended there. It was incorporated as Marthasville in 1845; two years later it was renamed Atlanta. Only a few dozen people lived there in the 1840's, but by 1861, when the Civil War began, some 10,000 people called it home. By 1864, when Sherman's armies started south from Chattanooga, Atlanta's population was double that number. The city boasted factories, foundries, stores, arsenals, government offices, and hospitals, which, as the war progressed and drew closer, were hard pressed to handle the mounting number of casualties needing treatment. So strategic was Atlanta that Confederate President Jefferson Davis proclaimed that "Its fall would open the way for the Federal armies to the Gulf on one hand, and to Charleston on the other, and close up those granaries from which Gen. Robert E. Lee's armies are supplied. It would give them control of our network of railroads and thus paralyze our efforts." Now, with Federal soldiers in Atlanta, Davis' fears would be realized.

Sherman's troops occupied Atlanta for more than 2 months. The photographs and captions that follow highlight aspects of that occupation.

Library of Congress

Library of Congress

Above, top: *Atlanta, October 1864: "solid and business-like, wide streets and many fine houses."* Left: *Federal officers commandeered many of Atlanta's houses for staff headquarters. Col. Henry A. Barnum and his staff moved into General Hood's former headquarters, described as the "finest wooden building in the city."* Above: *After Sherman turned Atlanta into an armed camp, wagon trains, like this one on Whitehall Street, rumbled through the city day and night.*

Atlanta Historical Society

*The 2d Massachusetts Infantry, the "best officered regiment in the Army,"
set up camp in City Hall Square. When this photograph was taken, near*

the end of the occupation, the soldiers' tents had been replaced by more substantial wooden huts built from demolished houses.

Library of Congress

Library of Congress

Library of Congress

Left: *Atlanta residents, evicted from the city by General Sherman, await the departure of the baggage-laden train that will take them south beyond Union lines. Above, top: Federal soldiers pry up the city's railroad tracks before leaving on their march to the sea. Above: The railroad depot after it was blown up by Federal demolition squads.*

National Archives

This desolate scene marks the site where retreating Confederate soldiers blew up their ordnance train early on the morning of September 1, 1864.

Sherman's soldiers left similar scenes of destruction in their wake as they marched across Georgia in the closing months of the war.

SUGGESTED READING

Angle, Paul M., Editor, *The Lincoln Reader*. Rutgers University Press, New Brunswick, 1947

---- *Three Years in the Army of the Cumberland: The Letters and Diary of Major James A. Connolly*. Bloomington, 1959.

Appleman, Roy E., Editor, *Abraham Lincoln from His Own Words and Contemporary Accounts*. U.S. Government Printing Office, Washington, D.C. 1956.

Bradford, Ned, Editor, *Battles and Leaders of the Civil War*. Appleton-Century-Crofts, New York, 1956.

Catton, Bruce, *A Stillness at Appomattox*. New York, 1953

---- *The Coming Fury*. Doubleday & Co., Garden City, 1961.

---- *Glory Road*. Doubleday & Co., Garden City, NY 1952.

---- *Grant Takes Command*. Boston, 1969.

---- *Mr. Lincoln's Army*. Doubleday & Co., Garden City, 1951.

Chesnut, Mary B., *A Diary From Dixie*. Houghton Mifflin Co., Boston, 1941.

Commanger, Henry S., Editor, *The Blue and the Gray*. Bobbs-Merrill Company, Inc., NY 1950.

Dowdey, Clifford, *Death of a Nation*. Alfred A. Knopf, NY 1958.

Downey, Fairfax, *The Guns at Gettysburg*. David McKay Co., NY 1958.

Freeman, D.S., *Lees Lieutenants*, Three volumes. Charles Scribners Sons, NY 1944.

Kirwan, Albert D., Editor, *Johnny Green of the Orphan Brigade: The Journal of a Confederate Soldier.* Lexington, KY, 1956.

Longstreet, James, *From Manassas to Appomattox.* J.B. Lippincott and Co., Philadelphia, 1959.

Montgomery, James S., *The Shaping of a Battle: Gettysburg.* Chilton Co., Philadelphia, 1959.

Quaife, Milo M., Editor, *From the Cannon's Mouth: The Civil War Letters of General Alpheus S. Williams.* Detroit, 1959.

Randall, James G., *Civil War and Reconstruction.* D.C. Heath & Co., NY 1937.

---- *Lincoln, The President,* Volume II. Dodd, Mead & Co., NY 1945.

Schofield, John M., *Forty-Six Years in the Army.* NY, 1897

Sherman, William T., *Memoirs of General William T. Sherman, by Himself (2 vols.).* NY 1875, new, 1 vol. edition, Bloomington, 1957.

Stackpole Edward J., They Met at Gettysburg. Eagle Books, Harrisburg, PA, 1956.

Stampp, Kenneth M., *And The War Came.* Louisiana State University Press, Baton Rouge, 1950.

Stewert, George R., *Pickett's Charge.* Houghton, Mifflin Co., NY, 1959.

Swanberg, W.A., *First Blood.* Charles Scribners Sons, NY 1957.

Tucker, Glenn, *High Tide at Gettysburg.* The Bobbs-Merrill Co., Indianapolis, 1958.

U.S. War Department, comp., *War of the Rebellion: Official Records of the Union and Confederate Armies.* (128 vols.) Washington, D.C. 1880-91, Series 1, vol. 38.

Watkins, Sam R., *"Co. Aytch," Maury Grays, First Tennessee Regiment; or, A Side Show of the Big Show.* Chattanooga, 1900; new edition, Jackson, TN, 1952.

Wills, Charles W., *Army Life of an Illinois Soldier.* Washington, D.C. 1906.

---- *R.E. Lee.* Charles Scribners Sons, NY 1935.

Hassler, Warren W., Jr., *General George B. McClellan, Shield of the Union*. Louisiana State University Press, Baton Rouge, 1957.

Henderson, G.F.R., *Stonewall Jackson and the American Civil War*. Longmans, Green and Co., London, 1955 reprint.

Hood, John B., *Advance and Retreat: Personal Experiences in the United States Confederate Armies*. New Orleans, 1880, new edition, Bloomington, 1959.

Johnson, Robert U., & Clarence C. Buel, Editors, *Battles and Leaders of the Civil War*. Reprint edition by Thomas Yoseloff, Inc., NY, 1956 Vols. I and IV.

Johnston, Joseph E., *Narrative of Military Operations During the Late War Between the States*. New York, 1874, new edition, Bloomington, 1959.